Supercook's
Family Favorites Cookbook

Marshall Cavendish

Published by Marshall Cavendish Books Limited
58 Old Compton Street London W1V 5PA

© Marshall Cavendish Limited 1978, 1979, 1980, 1981, 1982, 1983, 1984

First printing 1978
This printing 1984

Printed and bound in Hong Kong
by Dai Nippon Printing Company

ISBN 0 85685 436 0

CONTENTS

INTRODUCTION

Cooking for a family every day is quite a challenge, especially when it has to be done on a strictly limited budget, and in order to do the job properly and provide the family with well-balanced and interesting meals without working yourself into the ground you need to be well organized.

SHOPPING

A blessing in many ways, supermarkets are a menace in another, tempting you into buying things you had no intention of getting when you left home; particularly if the children are with you. They don't put candies by the checkout just for fun!

The answer is to go with a list and don't buy anything not on it without a good reason, for instance if it is on special offer and it is also something you buy regularly. Don't include candies, ice creams and fizzy drinks for the children in your budget. Give them appropriate pocket money and make it clear that those are items they buy themselves if they want them, except on special occasions. Don't include a lot of frozen and convenience foods in your budget either. They are invariably more expensive than unprepared items, so use them as useful standbys rather than as a way of life.

Do make the best use of local street markets, if you are lucky enough to be near one, and buy fruit and vegetables when they are in season, which is when they are at the peak of quality and at the lowest price. Fresh meat and fish are nearly always better value than frozen, where available, and prices again vary with region and season.

Obviously you must tailor your shopping routine to fit in with your lifestyle, but in general it is best to shop every day or two for fresh produce if this is available locally, with a weekly session to stock up on all the staple food items. A monthly or quarterly trip to a supermarket or cash-and-carry store can save a lot on tinned goods and other non-perishables if you can raise the cash to buy and have enough storage space. But count the cost of getting there, always check that the mammoth-size can really is cheaper than a smaller one, and don't buy masses of unfamiliar brands; you might get stuck with them. Alternatively join a local bulk-buying group (members buy jointly and share items out so you have neither the cash-outlay nor storage problems of going it alone).

THE ECONOMICS OF A FREEZER

Having your own freezer means you can store perishable foods and buy in bulk. It can also save money, but not unless properly used.

As it costs a lot to buy it will take you up to two years to get this money back, and to make real savings you must be able to raise the lump sums required to stock it with bulk buys, particularly of meat where savings are highest. You must take into account the running costs: Electricity, packaging (all those plastic bags and boxes) and insurance against prolonged power failures. The convenience may in the end be more important than the economy, especially if you have an outside job, frequently have to entertain unexpected guests, or you live a long way from the stores. A freezer is also invaluable if you grow your own fruit and vegetables.

Use the freezer for storing bulk-bought frozen foods such as hamburgers, French fries, peas and meat; your own prepared dishes (stock up painlessly by cooking double quantities of all your family favorites for a week or two); fresh fruit and vegetables bought when prices are low (but quality must be good); basic recipe ingredients like baked pie shells, sauces or parsley; leftovers; and emergency rations such as a spare loaf. Whatever type and size of freezer you choose, remember that you must keep it stocked up all the time – it is a waste of electricity to keep a half-empty freezer running, and you will probably be actually losing money.

SAVING FUEL

Now that fuel prices, particularly electricity, have risen so much it is essential to be more conscious about the cost of cooking food as well as buying it.

On both gas and electric stoves it's the oven and broiler which use most fuel so these are the ones to watch.

Train yourself to switch off electric burners the second a dish is cooled, using the residual heat to keep it warm when necessary, and always double-check everything is off before leaving the kitchen.

Invest in a pressure cooker for making stews, casseroles, and anything that requires long, slow cooking. Cooking time is cut by about three-quarters. When cooking vegetables, use a double boiler. Potatoes or root vegetables go in the bottom half, and green vegetables such as cabbage or green beans are steamed in the top half. This is by far the best way to cook green vegetables because they do not break up or lose all their nutrients to the cooking water, and two vegetables get cooked at the same time on a single burner.

BALANCED EATING

Few family cooks are trained dieticians; most women plan their family's diet on the basis of what mother gave them, and what their likes and dislikes are. Generally speaking this works out fairly well, as the range of foods available to us is so wide and tempting that most people get more than enough vitamins, and are more likely to overeat than go hungry.

Here's where working to a strict budget is a positive bonus, because you will not be tempted to give the family bigger portions than they need, as opposed to what they can eat; and many of the cheaper foods, like herrings, liver and lentils, are highly nutritious. Nor will your menu be over-burdened with cholesterol-laden cream or fattening frosted cakes.

But to make sure you're getting it right it's as well to review what members of the family are actually eating now and then; and to keep a note in the back of your mind of the types and amounts of food people should have, on average, every day. (See table).

Also, ideas have changed a bit since mother's day in the light of discovering about the dangers of too much cholesterol (from meat and dairy products), too much starch and sugar leading to obesity and dental decay; and too little fiber (bran, cabbage stalks, oatmeal) leading to stomach complaints.

As most of these theories are not yet 100 per cent proved, the best thing you can do, unless you feel strongly that a particular thing is bad for you, is to work on the principle that most basic foods are good in moderation, and concentrate on providing a varied diet including cheese, milk, eggs, meat, fish, legumes, bread, potatoes, butter or margarine, plenty of fresh fruit and green vegetables and not too much sugar and starch.

Calories (kilojoules in metric) are units of energy produced by different foods, and unless you are trying to diet you don't need to bother about counting them. Just stick roughly to the portions and daily intake on the table, and remember that high-protein foods (fish, meat, cheese, etc), as well as sweet things and fatty foods, have a high number of calories; fruit and vegetables have fewer.

Three meals a day, perhaps with a sinful snack or two in between, is a generally-accepted Western meal pattern which provides more than adequate nutrition. Dieticians now say that it is better to eat small, frequent meals than starve for long periods. This leads to overeating; also when you are hungry your blood sugar is low and you may not function efficiently.

This means that one of the meals must be breakfast – research has shown that children who don't get breakfast can't concentrate on their work properly. This should include some protein (egg, bacon or the milk on the cornflakes; toast is not good enough unless you have cheese with it like the Dutch do). Then you will probably have one light meal and a main meal; when these are taken is a matter of fitting in with the family's needs. If your husband and children have substantial school or cafeteria lunches you are not doing them any good if you provide another big meal in the evening; save your skills for the weekend and give them soups and salads.

If you have your main meal in the evening, but people arrive at different times, plan either instant dishes like omelets which can be cooked for one or two as they arrive; or long slow oven dishes that can wait without harm. Sometimes it's convenient to feed the children early and then enjoy a quiet, late meal yourselves. Be flexible.

Feeding babies and small children. Diet for these age groups is a specialized subject, and you should get help from your pediatrician and, if necessary, your doctor. But a few general points:

Many babies are bottle-fed, and it is now thought that some unlucky ones who get overfed on sweetened products carry their sweet tooth and overweight with them all their lives, sometimes with pretty disastrous consequences. So keep a careful check on weight gain; if the formula recommended puts weight on your baby too fast, see about getting it changed.

Very small children vary enormously in what they need; some are greedy as puppies, others appear to take in virtually nothing. The great thing is not to succumb to irrational fears: So long as they are healthy and bouncing about the place they are obviously getting enough to eat. Never force children to eat; once you set up a "mealtimes are horrid" pattern the battle is virtually lost. Missing the occasional meal will do no harm, and they'll probably be ravenous a few hours later.

It's easy to overestimate portions for young children, whose stomachs are so much smaller than yours; much better to give them too little and fill them up with fruit and milk (swing milk on the milk-haters in the form of milk shakes, puddings, sauces and on breakfast cereal).

As young children's eating habits are infinitely adaptable, and you are setting the pattern, make it a good one. Don't offer candies and ice cream as treats, but apples and fresh carrots, oatmeal cookies and milk. Do yourself a favor and set a good example.

Feeding older children and teenagers. Growing children can eat what seems to be unhealthy quantities of stodgy food liked baked beans, French fries and bread and potatoes. But they need them. Your part is to see they also get things they're less keen on (like green vegetables – if they only like one, keep on serving it); fresh fruit and milk; and to curb their appetite for rubbish foods by the method mentioned under budgeting: They pay.

Overweight children (who may be undernourished at the same time, through eating too much of the wrong foods) are becoming a serious problem nowadays. It's up to you to keep an eye on their weights, and if they start to exceed the recommended averages for their age and height, to take some action, preferably with your doctor's advice. A fat child is never a happy child, and is storing up a lot of trouble for the future.

Feeding your partner. When cooking for your working partner, remember that they are just as likely to develop a weight problem as you are. The idea that all workers need big meals is inaccurate and can do a lot of harm: Unless the work is manual, they don't need much more to eat than you. So try not to get carried away, especially if you enjoy making rich custards and cakes, but have fruit or cheese for dessert after a heavy main course instead.

Workers who frequently eat short order food, sandwiches on-the-road and stodgy cafeteria lunches often find themselves putting on weight, especially when the meals are accompanied by horrendously fattening alcohol. Fortunately this is one problem that can easily be solved by making up brown-bag lunches. With just a little effort and imagination they can be tasty, nutritious and varied.

A lot of business is done over heavy restaurant lunches with clients, so get your partner to tell you about these occasions in advance, then produce something appetizing but very light in the evening, like a soufflé, omelet or salad.

Feeding yourself. As the family chef, you need looking after too, if you're not to become tired and irritable and see cooking as a chore rather than an interesting, ever-changing combination of job and hobby.

Don't neglect your breakfast because they are all in a hurry; have it later, or take something to work with you.

If you're at home all day, don't become a garbage pail and eat up their leftovers for lunch; this can get very depressing. Use the leftovers for chain cooking (today's leftover meat goes into tomorrow's casserole which starts off the following day's soup). Prepare something just for yourself, even if it's only bread and cheese. Or take turns having a lunch hour with a neighbor.

If you have an outside job never be tempted to skip lunch to do the shopping; you need the food, and even more the relaxation that goes with a leisurely lunch break. The busier you are, the more important it is to plan at least a week's menus in advance, so you know what you want when you go shopping, and can free your mind of nagging worries about what to prepare for the next meal.

A 14-day menu plan is even better, and surprisingly easy to work out. Just write down all the family's favorite main meals, then juggle them around so they're getting meat, fish, poultry, etc in rotation, and one light/one substantial meal each day if you cook twice. You don't have to stick to the plan rigidly; if you fancy cooking something different, or see a good bargain when you go shopping, alter it. The menu plan is for when you don't have the time or energy to think; to give you a framework to work to.

HERBS AND SPICES

Rosemary rubbed into a leg of lamb . . . fresh mint in the potatoes . . . basil sprinkled over tomato salad . . . cinnamon and cloves in the apple pie . . . herbs and spices add immensely to the flavor and aroma of our food and to the interest of meals produced on a tight budget. Their flavor should complement the food, not compete with it.

All herbs (except bay leaves) are better if fresh, but this is not usually practical and the dried variety are perfectly adequate. Exceptions are parsley and mint, which have little flavor when dried; these, together with chives, are well worth growing even if all you have is a window box. Nearly all spices are used dried, and can be bought whole or ground, as convenient. The one worth grinding yourself is the most often-used: Pepper. Only then will you get its full flavor. Buy all herbs and spices in the smallest quantities you can get, as most go stale in time and lose their flavor. Keep them in airtight jars, out of the sun.

Hot spices such as chili powder and curry vary considerably in strength, so go carefully.

A BALANCED DIET

Food	Daily Serving	Portion	Notes
Meat	One or more	100g (4oz); 225g (8oz) if on the bone	Serve liver, heart or kidney, rich in iron, every week
Fish	One or more	175-225g (6-8oz) depending on whether filleted	Oily fish (mackerel, herrings) are more nutritious than white
Cheese	One or more	50g (2oz)	
Eggs	Buy enough to give each person one, including those used in cooking	2 eggs = 100g (4oz) portion of meat	Brown eggs are no more nutritious than white; just prettier
Milk	Up to 600ml (1 pint) for adults, more for children	Allow 150ml (5fl oz) [$\frac{5}{8}$ cup] per person for custards and puddings	Unless they all love milk to drink this means making milk puddings, custard, sauces, etc.
Potatoes	Once or twice	100g (4oz)	Potatoes are not just fattening carbohydrate but also contain valuable minerals and vitamins
Pasta Rice	Serve as an alternative to potatoes, not as well as, and in puddings	100g (4oz) 50g (2oz) [$\frac{1}{3}$ cup]	Use different types of pasta. Use long-grain rice for savoury dishes
Vegetables	Once or twice, including at least one green one (not peas). Plenty of salads	100-225g (4-8oz) depending on type and amount lost in preparation	Always under rather than over cook vegetables, and try to avoid keeping hot for long
Fruit	Once or twice, in the form of fresh, bottled dried or juice	For cooking: 100-225g (4-8oz)	In winter serve plenty of citrus fruit to keep up Vitamin C levels
Bread, cakes and pastry; cereals	As required to fill up holes	Allow 50g (2oz) flour per person for desserts	These are the ones it's easy to eat too much of
Butter or margarine	For bread and cooking	Allow 1oz [2 tablespoons] per day per person	Margarine for low-cholesterol intake must be polyunsaturated. Or use safflower (not sunflower) oil
Pulses (mature dried peas and beans)	Fresh or dried, these contain cholesterol-free second-class protein, and can be used instead of, or to stretch, meat	50g (2oz); more if taken as a meat substitute	Bean cookery is well worth exploring; cheap and good for you. Soya beans are the most nutritious, but rather tasteless

The portions given are nutritionally correct for adults and older children. Many adults will eat larger helpings but this should only be necessary for those in heavy manual employment.

INDEX

Basic recipes

BASIC SPONGE CAKE MIX

This can be used for all sandwich cakes, or the mixture can be baked in a shallow tin, iced, cut into fancy shapes and decorated for a children's party.

Makes 2 x 15cm (6in) sandwich cakes

Metric/Imperial

100g (4oz) self-raising flour, or plain flour sifted with 1 teaspoon baking powder
100g (4oz) butter or margarine
100g (4oz) castor sugar
2 eggs, lightly beaten
¼ teaspoon vanilla essence

American

1 cup self-rising flour, or all-purpose flour sifted with 1 teaspoon baking powder
½ cup butter or margarine
½ cup fine sugar
2 eggs, lightly beaten
¼ teaspoon vanilla extract

Sift the flour. Cream the butter and sugar together until white, light and fluffy. Very gradually beat in the lightly beaten eggs and vanilla essence adding a tablespoon of the sieved flour with the last amount of egg. Carefully fold in the flour.

Turn the mixture into two 15cm (6 inch) prepared sandwich tins and bake in a moderate oven (180°C/ 350°F or Gas Mark 4) for 20-25 minutes or until the cakes spring back when lightly pressed with the tip of the finger.

Allow to cool in the tin for 5 minutes, then remove to a wire rack for final cooling.

BASIC SCONE DOUGH

These plain scones [biscuits] can be made in moments. The recipe is included here because it also makes an excellent quick base for pizzas when there is no time to make Pizza Dough.

8 scones [biscuits]

Metric/Imperial

50g (2oz) plus 1 teaspoon butter

250g (8oz) flour
2 teaspoons baking powder
½ teaspoon salt
150ml (5 fl oz) milk

American

4 tablespoons plus 1 teaspoon butter
2 cups flour
2 teaspoons baking powder
½ teaspoon salt
⅝ cup milk

Preheat the oven to very hot (230°C/ 450°F or Gas Mark 8). With the teaspoon of butter, grease a large baking sheet. Set aside.

Sift the flour, baking powder and salt into a large mixing bowl. Cut the butter into small pieces with a table knife. With your fingertips, rub the butter into the flour mixture until the mixture resembles coarse breadcrumbs. With the table knife, stir in the milk to form a soft dough.

To make 8 scones [biscuits] from the dough, form it into a ball with your hands and cut into 8 pieces. Pat each piece of dough into a ½-inch thick circle. Place the circles of dough, well spaced apart, on the baking sheet.

To make 2 pizza bases divide the dough into two and roll out into circles with a rolling pin.

Place the baking sheet in the oven and bake the scones [biscuits] for 15 minutes or until risen and golden.

YORKSHIRE PUDDING

Yorkshire Pudding, a savoury batter pudding which is traditionally eaten with roast beef, is one of the best-known of all British dishes. In Yorkshire, the pudding is cooked with the roast, so that the juices from the meat drip into the pudding. It is traditionally served before the meat.

More commonly, however, Yorkshire Pudding is cooked separately and served with the beef. It may be cooked in one large dish or in patty tins as small individual puddings. For extra flavour, sage, parsley and onion may be added.

Yorkshire Pudding may also be served with butter and sugar as a simple light dessert.

300ml (10 fl oz) [1¼ cups]

Metric/Imperial

100g (4oz) plain flour
½ teaspoon salt
1 large egg
300ml (10 fl oz) milk
1 tablespoon beef dripping or bacon fat

American

1 cup all-purpose flour
½ teaspoon salt
1 large egg
1¼ cups milk
1 tablespoon beef drippings or bacon fat

Sift the flour and salt into a large mixing bowl. Make a well in the centre, break in the egg and pour in half the milk. Using a wooden spoon, gradually draw the flour into the liquid a little at a time. When all the flour has been incorporated, beat the batter until it is smooth. Using a wire whisk or rotary beater, beat the batter for 5 minutes or until it is full of bubbles. Add the rest of the milk and stir well to blend. Cover and set the batter aside for 30 minutes.

Preheat the oven to hot (220°C/ 425°F or Gas Mark 7).

Heat the dripping or bacon fat in a flameproof baking tin or individual patty tins set over moderately high heat. When it is very hot, remove the tin or tins from the heat and quickly pour in the batter. Place the tin or tins in the upper part of the oven and bake for 30 minutes for small ones, or until the mixture has risen and is golden brown.

CHOUX PASTRY

Sweeten this light, quick pastry for cream puffs or use it as it is for hors d'oeuvres.

315g (10oz) [2½ cups]

Metric/Imperial

300ml (10 fl oz) water
75g (3oz) butter, cut into small pieces

Basic Sponge Cake Mix and Pancake Batter make delicious treats.

Yorkshire Pudding is a traditional British dish, served as an accompaniment to roast meat.

½ teaspoon salt
315g (10oz) flour
5 large eggs

American

1¼ cups water
⅓ cup butter, cut into small pieces
½ teaspoon salt
2½ cups flour
5 large eggs

Bring the water to the boil in a saucepan. Add the butter and salt and stir to melt the butter. Remove from the heat and sift in the flour. Beat well until the mixture pulls away from the sides of the pan.

Beat in the eggs, one at a time. When all the eggs have been absorbed, the dough should be thick and glossy. Use as required.

ROUGH PUFF PASTRY

A rich pastry which is easy and quick to make, Rough Puff Pastry does not rise high. It is used mainly, therefore, for pie crusts and turnovers.

250g (8oz) [2 cups]

Metric/Imperial

250g (8oz) plain flour
½ teaspoon salt
175g (6oz) butter
4-6 tablespoons ice-cold water

American

2 cups all-purpose flour
½ teaspoon salt
¾ cup butter
4-6 tablespoons ice-cold water

Sift the flour and salt into a mixing bowl. Add the butter and cut it into walnut-sized pieces with a tableknife. Pour in 4 tablespoons of the water and mix quickly with a knife to form a dough, which should be lumpy. Add a little more of the water if the dough looks too dry.

Shape the dough into a ball and place it on a lightly floured working surface. Using a floured rolling pin, roll out the dough again into an oblong.

Fold the dough in three, turning it so that one open end faces you. Roll out the dough again into an oblong shape and fold it in three. Repeat the rolling and folding process once more.

Wrap the dough in greaseproof or waxed paper and chill in the refrigerator for 30 minutes. Remove the dough from the refrigerator. If it looks streaky, roll it out and fold it once more before using.

SHORTCRUST PASTRY I

This is the basic two-crust pastry, used for making sweet or savoury pies and tarts.

250g (8oz) [2 cups]

Metric/Imperial

250g (8oz) flour
½ teaspoon salt
50g (2oz) butter
50g (2oz) vegetable fat
3-4 tablespoons ice-cold water

American

2 cups all-purpose flour
½ teaspoon salt
½ cup shortening (or half butter, half shortening)
3-4 tablespoons ice-cold water

Sift the flour and salt into a mixing bowl. Add the butter and vegetable fat and cut into small pieces with a table knife. With your fingertips rub the fat into the flour until the mixture resembles coarse breadcrumbs.

Add 3 tablespoons of the water and using the knife, mix it into the flour mixture. With your hands, mix and knead the dough until it is smooth. Add more water if it is too dry.

Form the dough into a ball, wrap in greaseproof or waxed paper and chill in the refrigerator for 30 minutes before using.

SHORTCRUST PASTRY II

This pastry can be used for making flan cases and pie shells to be filled with sweet or rich savoury fillings.

250g (8oz) [2 cups]

Metric/Imperial

250g (8oz) plain flour
¼ teaspoon salt
100g (4oz) butter, chilled
1 teaspoon sugar
1 egg, lightly beaten
2-3 tablespoons ice-cold water

American

2 cups all-purpose flour
¼ teaspoon salt
½ cup butter, chilled
1 teaspoon sugar
1 egg, lightly beaten
2-3 tablespoons ice-cold water

Sift the flour and salt into a mixing bowl. Add the butter and cut it into small pieces with a table knife. With your fingertips, rub the butter into the flour until the mixture resembles fine breadcrumbs. Stir in the sugar.

Add the beaten egg with a spoonful of the water and mix it into the flour mixture with a table knife. Add more water if the dough is too dry.

Turn the dough out on to a lightly floured board and knead it for 1 minute. Form into a ball, wrap in greaseproof or waxed paper and chill in the refrigerator for 30 minutes before using.

SUETCRUST PASTRY

A simple-to-make pastry, Suetcrust Pastry may be used in sweet or savoury steamed layer puddings, baked or steamed roly-poly puddings, or as a pastry container for steamed meat puddings. The dough may also be shaped into small balls and cooked in stock to make dumplings.

250g (8oz) [2 cups]

Metric/Imperial

250g (8oz) self-raising flour
¼ teaspoon salt
100g (4oz) shredded suet
150ml (5 fl oz) cold water

American

2 cups self-rising flour
¼ teaspoon salt
½ cup grated beef suet
⅔ cup cold water

Sift the flour and salt into a mixing bowl. Using a table knife, stir in the suet and water to make a firm dough. Form into a ball, wrap in greaseproof or waxed paper and chill for 10 minutes before using.

PIZZA DOUGH

For a quickly-made pizza, use the same pizza quantity of Scone Dough.

1 x 25cm (10in) pizza

Metric/Imperial

1 teaspoon sugar
4 tablespoons lukewarm water
2 teaspoons dried yeast
4 tablespoons lukewarm milk
250g (8oz) plain flour
1 teaspoon salt
40g (1½oz) butter

American

1 teaspoon sugar
4 tablespoons lukewarm water
2 teaspoons dried yeast
4 tablespoons lukewarm milk
2 cups all-purpose flour
1 teaspoon salt
3 tablespoons butter

Dissolve the sugar in the water and sprinkle the yeast on the top. Leave for 5 minutes until it begins to bubble, then add the milk to it.

Sift the flour and salt into a warmed bowl. Rub in the butter.

Add the yeast mixture to the flour and beat thoroughly. Cover and leave to rise in a warm place until double its bulk: this will take about 40 minutes.

Flour the dough and pat into shape on a large floured baking sheet, or it may be rolled into any shape with a rolling pin.

CHICKEN STOCK

A well-flavoured home-made chicken stock is invaluable. It forms the basis for so many sauces and soups and is used in a variety of dishes. The flavour can never be matched by a stock cube.

1¼ litres (2½ pints) [6¼ cups]

Metric/Imperial

1 carcass, bones and giblets (excluding the liver) of a cooked or raw chicken
1 carrot, scraped and sliced
4 celery stalks, sliced
1 onion stuck with 2 cloves
1 bouquet garni
grated rind of ½ lemon
1 teaspoon salt
10 peppercorns
1¾ litres (3 pints) water

American

1 chicken carcass and giblets (discard liver) raw or cooked
1 carrot, scraped and sliced
4 celery stalks, sliced
1 onion stuck with 2 cloves
1 bouquet garni
grated rind of ½ lemon
1 teaspoon salt
10 peppercorns
7½ cups water

Put the carcass, bones and giblets (if available) into a large saucepan with all the other ingredients.

Place the pan over high heat and bring the liquid to the boil. Remove any scum that rises to the surface. Half cover the pan with the lid, reduce the heat to low and simmer gently for about 2 hours.

Remove the pan from the heat and strain the liquid into a bowl. Discard the bones, vegetables and seasonings. Allow the stock to cool before covering the bowl with a large plate or piece of aluminium foil. If not using immediately, place in the refrigerator. Remove the fat from the surface before using.

BEEF STOCK

Another delicious and indispensable basic stock.

1½ litres (3 pints) [7½ cups]

Metric/Imperial

---

about 1kg (2lb) beef marrow or shin
   bones
1 onion, halved
1 large carrot, thickly sliced
1 bouquet garni
6 black peppercorns
1 teaspoon salt

American

---

about 2lb beef marrow or shin bones
1 onion, halved
1 large carrot, thickly sliced
1 bouquet garni
6 black peppercorns
1 teaspoon salt

Put the bones in a large saucepan and pour over water to cover. Bring to the boil, skimming off the scum that rises to the surface. Half cover and simmer for 2 hours.

Add the remaining ingredients and continue simmering for 2 hours. If necessary, add more boiling water so that the bones are covered.

Strain the stock and allow to cool. Skim off the layer of fat that will set on the surface before using. If not for immediate use, store in the refrigerator.

GRAVY

Traditionally gravy was made from the juices of a roast, simply by pouring off excess fat, adding flour if liked to thicken it, and seasoning to taste. Now

that the average family's joints of meat are smaller a few extras are required.

Makes about 300ml (10 fl oz) [1¼ cups]

Metric/Imperial

---

1 tablespoon flour
300ml (10 fl oz) beef or chicken stock,
   or vegetable water
1 tablespoon tomato purée (optional)
salt and pepper

American

---

1 tablespoon flour
1¼ cups beef or chicken stock, or
   vegetable water
1 tablespoon tomato paste (optional)
salt and pepper

Carefully pour off any excess fat from the baking tin, leaving about 1 tablespoon behind with the meat juices. Place on a low heat, sprinkle on the flour and stir it into the pan juices blending in all the crusty bits. Cook for 1 minute or until lightly coloured. Remove from the heat and gradually add the stock, stirring rapidly to avoid lumps. Return to the heat, add the tomato purée if using and cook briskly to reduce the liquid, stirring constantly. Season well and strain into a warmed gravy boat.

For thin gravy omit the flour and boil up the pan juices with the stock.

BASIC WHITE SAUCE

This extremely useful sauce is the beginning of many others.

300ml (½ pint) [1¼ cups]

Metric/Imperial

25g (1oz) butter or margarine
25g (1oz) flour
300ml (10 fl oz) milk, or milk and fish
   or meat stock combined
salt and pepper

American

---

2 tablespoons butter or margarine
4 tablespoons flour
1¼ cups milk, or milk and fish or meat
   stock combined
salt and pepper

Melt the butter or margarine in a saucepan. Stir in the flour and cook for about a minute over a low heat. This mixture is known as a roux.

Remove it from the heat and gradually stir in the milk, or the milk and fish or meat stock mixture. Return to the heat and bring to the boil, stirring all the time. Cook for about 3 minutes. Season to taste.

Note: This makes a sauce of coating consistency. For a thin pouring white sauce, halve the quantities of fat and flour. For a thick panada, used as a basis for soufflés and fish cakes, double them.

Variations:

Cheese Sauce: Add 25g (1 ounce) [4 tablespoons] grated Parmesan, or 50g (2 ounces) [½ cup] grated Cheddar, with a pinch of dry mustard.

Egg: Add 1–2 chopped hard-boiled eggs.

Parsley: Add 2 tablespoons of chopped parsley.

Shrimp: Add 75g (3 ounces) [⅜ cup] shrimps.

BREAD SAUCE

Traditionally served with roast turkey, chicken or pheasant, Bread Sauce should be neither too thin nor too thick, but the consistency is determined by individual taste. Coarse, crisply fried crumbs may be sprinkled on top of the sauce.

---

4 servings

Metric/Imperial

---

1 medium-sized onion, studded with
   2 cloves
1 bay leaf
300ml (10 fl oz) milk
50g (2oz) fresh white breadcrumbs
½ teaspoon salt
¼ teaspoon black pepper
1 tablespoon butter
1 tablespoon single cream

American

---

1 medium-sized onion, stuck with
   2 cloves
1 bay leaf
1¼ cups milk

1 cup fresh white breadcrumbs
½ teaspoon salt
¼ teaspoon black pepper
1 tablespoon butter
1 tablespoon light cream

Place the onion, bay leaf and milk in a medium-sized saucepan. Cover the pan and cook for 10 to 15 minutes over very low heat. In this time the milk will become infused with the flavour of the onion, cloves and bay leaf.

Remove the onion and bay leaf. Bring the milk to the boil and add the breadcrumbs. Reduce the heat to low and simmer for 3 to 4 minutes, or until the sauce is thick and creamy.

Remove the pan from the heat and stir in the salt, pepper, butter and cream. Gently reheat the sauce over very low heat, do not allow to boil.

BARBECUE SAUCE

This is a good piquant sauce to serve hot with grilled meat or chicken. It can also be used for basting.

225ml (8 fl oz) [1 cup]

Metric/Imperial

25g (1oz) butter
1 onion, chopped
1 garlic clove, crushed
½-in piece fresh ginger, peeled and finely chopped
150ml (5 fl oz) water
396g (14oz) can tomatoes
1 large celery stalk, chopped
2 tablespoons lemon juice
2 tablespoons vinegar
2 tablespoons tomato purée
1½ tablespoons Worcestershire sauce
2 teaspoons brown sugar
½ teaspoon dried oregano
1 large bay leaf
1 teaspoon salt
¼ teaspoon nutmeg

American

2 tablespoons butter
1 onion, chopped
1 garlic clove, crushed
½-in piece fresh ginger, peeled and finely chopped
⅔ cup water

14oz can tomatoes
1 large celery stalk, chopped
2 tablespoons lemon juice
2 tablespoons vinegar
2 tablespoons tomato paste
1½ tablespoons Worcestershire sauce
2 teaspoons brown sugar
½ teaspoon dried oregano
1 large bay leaf
1 teaspoon salt
¼ teaspoon nutmeg

Melt the butter in a small saucepan over moderate heat. Add the onion, garlic and ginger and fry until the onion is soft and translucent.

Add all the remaining ingredients, cover and cook over low heat for 40 minutes. Strain the sauce, taste, and add more salt and sugar if necessary.

ONION SAUCE

A traditional British sauce, Onion Sauce used to be served with roast or boiled mutton. However, it tastes equally good with roast lamb.

350ml (12 fl oz) [1½ cups]

Metric/Imperial

2 medium-sized onions, finely chopped
25g (1oz) butter
2 tablespoons flour
225ml (8 fl oz) milk
½ teaspoon salt
¼ teaspoon white pepper
⅛ teaspoon grated nutmeg
⅛ teaspoon ground cloves
100ml (4 fl oz) single cream

American

2 medium-sized onions, finely chopped
2 tablespoons butter
2 tablespoons flour
1 cup milk
½ teaspoon salt
¼ teaspoon white pepper
⅛ teaspoon grated nutmeg
⅛ teaspoon ground cloves
½ cup light cream

Fill a small saucepan 2.5cm (1 inch) full of water and add the onions. Bring to the boil, cover the pan, reduce heat to low and cook the onions for 10 to

15 minutes or until tender. Drain and keep warm.

In a small saucepan, melt the butter over moderate heat. Remove the pan from the heat and stir in the flour to make a smooth paste. Gradually add the milk, stirring constantly. Return the pan to moderate heat and cook, stirring constantly, for 2 to 3 minutes or until the sauce is thick and smooth. Stir in the salt, pepper, nutmeg, cloves, cream and onions. Cook the sauce for 3 minutes, stirring frequently, or until very hot but not boiling.

MUSTARD SAUCE

This delicious hot Mustard Sauce may be served with meat, game, poultry, fish or eggs.

300ml (10 fl oz) [1¼ cups]

Metric/Imperial

15g (½oz) butter
1 garlic clove, crushed
1½ tablespoons flour
½ teaspoon salt
¼ teaspoon black pepper
300ml (10 fl oz) single cream
1 tablespoon French mustard
1 teaspoon lemon juice

American

1 tablespoon butter
1 garlic clove, crushed
1½ tablespoons flour
½ teaspoon salt
¼ teaspoon black pepper
1¼ cups light cream
1 tablespoon French mustard
1 teaspoon lemon juice

In a medium-sized saucepan, melt the butter over moderate heat. When the foam subsides, add the garlic clove and cook, stirring occasionally, for 4 minutes.

Remove the pan from the heat. Stir in the flour, salt and pepper to make a smooth paste. Gradually stir in the cream, being careful to avoid lumps. Stir in the mustard and combine the mixture thoroughly.

Set the pan over moderately low heat and cook the sauce, stirring constantly and never letting it come to the boil, for 3 to 4 minutes, or until it is thick and smooth. Stir in the lemon juice.

THYME STUFFING

Thyme Stuffing is simple to make and economical. It tastes particularly good with fish, veal or poultry.

Stuffing for 1 x 2kg (4lb) chicken

Metric/Imperial

100g (4oz) fresh white breadcrumbs
2 dessert apples, peeled, cored and finely chopped
1 medium-sized onion, finely chopped
75g (3oz) sultanas or seedless raisins
2 teaspoons dried thyme
½ teaspoon salt
½ teaspoon black pepper
1 egg, lightly beaten

American

2 cups fresh white breadcrumbs
2 dessert apples, peeled, cored and finely chopped
1 medium-sized onion, finely diced
½ cup seedless raisins
2 teaspoons dried thyme
½ teaspoon salt
½ teaspoon black pepper
1 egg, lightly beaten

Place all the stuffing ingredients in a mixing bowl and stir them together until thoroughly combined. If the mixture is still slightly crumbly add a little water or lemon juice.

CHESTNUT AND SAUSAGE STUFFING

This is the traditional stuffing for turkey. It is simple to make and adds a delicious flavour to the bird.

Stuffing for 1 x 5-6kg (10-12lb) turkey

Metric/Imperial

575g (1¼lb) chestnuts, peeled
½ litre (1 pint) beef stock
1 celery stalk, chopped
½ teaspoon salt

¼ teaspoon pepper
2 tablespoons butter
1 large onion, finely chopped
250g (8oz) pork sausage meat
75g (3oz) fresh white breadcrumbs
2 eggs, lightly beaten

American

1¼lb chestnuts, peeled
2½ cups beef stock
1 celery stalk, chopped
½ teaspoon salt
¼ teaspoon pepper
2 tablespoons butter
1 large onion, finely chopped
½lb sausage meat
1½ cups fresh white breadcrumbs
2 eggs, lightly beaten

Put the chestnuts, stock, celery, salt and pepper in a medium-sized saucepan over moderate heat. Simmer for 1 hour, or until the chestnuts are tender and have absorbed all the stock. Transfer to a mixing bowl and allow to cool. Crumble the chestnuts into small pieces, or mash through a coarse strainer.

In a small saucepan melt the butter over moderate heat. Add the onion and sausage meat and cook for 8 minutes. Allow to cool. Add the breadcrumbs and eggs to the chestnuts along with the sausage mixture and mix well.

PARSLEY AND LEMON STUFFING

This is a light stuffing for a turkey.

Stuffing for 1 x 4kg (9lb) turkey

Metric/Imperial

175g (6oz) dry breadcrumbs
grated rind and juice of 2 lemons
4 tablespoons chopped fresh parsley
1 teaspoon grated orange rind
¼ teaspoon dried thyme
¼ teaspoon dried marjoram
175g (6oz) butter, softened
3 eggs

American

2 cups dry breadcrumbs
grated rind and juice of 2 lemons
4 tablespoons chopped fresh parsley

1 teaspoon grated orange rind
¼ teaspoon dried thyme
¼ teaspoon dried marjoram
¾ cup butter, softened
3 eggs

In a medium-sized mixing bowl combine the breadcrumbs, lemon rind, parsley, orange rind, thyme, marjoram and butter. Stir in the lemon juice and eggs and blend well.

Use the stuffing for the rib cavity and the neck end cavity of the turkey.

SAGE AND ONION STUFFING

A traditional British stuffing, Sage and Onion Stuffing is excellent with pork, goose, duck or chicken.

Stuffing for 1 x 2¼kg (5lb) bird

Metric/Imperial

2 large onions, finely chopped
1 tablespoon dried sage
100g (4oz) fresh white breadcrumbs
1 teaspoon salt
½ teaspoon black pepper
1 tablespoon melted butter
1 egg yolk

American

2 large onions, finely chopped
1 tablespoon dried sage
2 cups fresh white breadcrumbs
1 teaspoon salt
½ teaspoon black pepper
1 tablespoon melted butter
1 egg yolk

Half-fill a large saucepan with water and bring to the boil. Add the onions, reduce heat to low, cover the pan and simmer for 10 minutes or until the onions are tender.

Drain the onions and place in a small mixing bowl. Add the sage, breadcrumbs, salt and pepper and mix well. Stir in the melted butter and egg yolk until the mixture is combined.

DUMPLINGS (SAVOURY)

These light and puffy pastry balls are

quick to make and complement any boiled meat stew. Traditionally they are added to the cooking liquid from Boiled Beef and Carrots.

4 servings

Metric/Imperial

100g (4oz) self-raising flour
½ teaspoon salt
⅛ teaspoon black pepper
½ teaspoon dried thyme or sage
50g (2oz) shredded suet
4-5 tablespoons water

American

1 cup self-rising flour
½ teaspoon salt
⅛ teaspoon black pepper
½ teaspoon dried thyme or sage
¼ cup chopped beef suet
4-5 tablespoons water

Sift the flour, salt and pepper into a large bowl. Add the dried herbs and suet and mix well. Add 4 tablespoons of water and stir until the mixture forms large lumps. A little extra water may be needed to make a fairly stiff, non-sticky dough. Draw the mixture together with your hands and knead the dough lightly until smooth and elastic.

Cut the dough into eight pieces and shape into round balls.

Cook the dumplings for 15 to 20 minutes in boiling stock or water, or in the soup or stew they are to accompany. Do not lift the lid during cooking or they will be heavy.

PANCAKE BATTER

The batter should be as thin as cream for French crêpes.

About 12 pancakes

Metric/Imperial

100g (4oz) flour
½ teaspoon salt
2 eggs
300ml (10 fl oz) milk
1 tablespoon melted butter

American

1 cup all-purpose flour

½ teaspoon salt
2 eggs
1¼ cups milk
1 tablespoon melted butter

Sift the flour and salt into a large bowl. Make a well in the centre, and drop the eggs into it with a little of the milk and the butter. Mix this to a smooth batter, and when there are no lumps at all add a little more of the milk and mix again. When all of the milk has been added beat very well. Leave to one side for a few minutes before making pancakes.

AMERICAN PANCAKES

This is a basic recipe for American-style Pancakes, and sweet and savoury flavourings are usually added to or poured over them. These pancakes are traditionally served stacked up, with a pat of butter between each one.

36 pancakes

Metric/Imperial

350g (12oz) plain flour
½ teaspoon salt
3 teaspoons baking powder
1 tablespoon sugar
1 egg, lightly beaten
425ml (15 fl oz) milk
25g (1oz) butter, melted
4 tablespoons vegetable oil

American

3 cups all-purpose flour
½ teaspoon salt
3 teaspoons baking powder
1 tablespoon sugar
1 egg, lightly beaten
scant 2 cups milk
2 tablespoons butter, melted
4 tablespoons vegetable oil

Sift the flour, salt, baking powder and sugar into a large mixing bowl.

In a medium-sized mixing bowl, beat the egg, milk and melted butter together, using a wire whisk or rotary beater, until the mixture is light and frothy. With a wooden spoon, stir in the flour mixture and beat until the batter is smooth.

Lightly grease a large heavy-based

frying-pan or griddle with a little of the oil. Heat the pan or griddle over moderate heat. Depending on its size, drop in 4 or 5 spoonfuls of the batter, well spaced out.

Cook the pancakes for about 1 minute or until bubbles form and begin to break open on the surface, and the outer edges have browned. Turn the pancakes over and cook the other sides for 1 minute or until lightly browned.

Transfer the pancakes to a warmed serving plate and keep warm. Cook the remaining pancakes in the same way, greasing the pan or griddle with a little oil each time. Serve hot.

FRITTER BATTER I

This batter is suitable for coating fish, meat or fruits, such as apple, bananas and canned pineapple rings. A lighter coating can be made by beating the egg whites separately and folding them into the batter just before use.

300ml (10 fl oz) [1¼ cups]

Metric/Imperial

100g (4oz) self-raising flour
¼ teaspoon salt
2 eggs
75ml (3 fl oz) milk
1 teaspoon melted butter
¼ teaspoon lemon juice
2 teaspoons sugar (for a sweet batter)

American

1 cup self-rising flour
¼ teaspoon salt
2 eggs
⅜ cup milk
1 teaspoon melted butter
¼ teaspoon lemon juice
2 teaspoons sugar (optional)

Sift the flour and salt into a mixing bowl and place to one side.

In another mixing bowl, beat the eggs with a wire whisk until fluffy. Add the milk, butter, lemon juice and sugar, if you are making a sweet batter; stir well.

Add the sifted flour mixture to the egg mixture and beat until the batter is smooth.

FRITTER BATTER II

A very light batter with a slight yeasty flavour, this Fritter Batter goes very well with vegetables. The stronger flavour of this batter also makes it ideal for making fritters to be served with sweet fruit sauces.

$\frac{3}{4}$ litre (1$\frac{1}{4}$ pints) [3$\frac{1}{8}$ cups]

Metric/Imperial

15g ($\frac{1}{2}$oz) fresh yeast
$\frac{1}{4}$ teaspoon sugar
300ml (10 fl oz) lukewarm water
250g (8oz) plain flour
$\frac{1}{4}$ teaspoon salt
6 tablespoons milk
1 egg, lightly beaten

American

$\frac{1}{2}$oz compressed yeast cake
$\frac{1}{4}$ teaspoon sugar
1$\frac{1}{4}$ cups lukewarm water
2 cups all-purpose flour
$\frac{1}{4}$ teaspoon salt
6 tablespoons milk
1 egg, lightly beaten

Crumble the yeast into a small bowl and mash in the sugar with a fork. Add the water and cream together. Set the bowl aside in a warm, draught-free place for 15 to 20 minutes until the yeast mixture is frothy.

Sift the flour and salt into a large warmed mixing bowl. Make a well in the centre and pour in the yeast mixture, 4 tablespoons of the milk and the egg. Using a wooden spoon, gradually draw the flour mixture into the liquids. Continue mixing until all the flour is incorporated. Beat the batter until thick, add the remaining milk. Cover the bowl with a cloth and set in a warm, draught-free place. Leave for 45 minutes or until the batter has risen and almost doubled in bulk. Stir the batter gently.

FRENCH DRESSING

The ingredients for French Dressing and the proportion of vinegar to oil is very largely a matter of personal taste, but this is a good basic recipe.

4 servings

Metric/Imperial

pinch sugar
pinch salt
freshly milled black pepper
1 tablespoon vinegar, preferably wine
2 tablespoons olive oil

American

pinch sugar
pinch salt
freshly ground black pepper
1 tablespoon vinegar, preferably wine
2 tablespoons olive oil

Either mix together the sugar, salt, pepper and vinegar in a bowl, and then add in the oil, or put all the ingredients into a screw-topped jar and shake well. In either case, make sure all ingredients are thoroughly combined.

French dressing can be stored for months in a bottle in a cool place, and it is a good idea to make up a large quantity so that you always have some on hand.

Variations:
The above is a very simple dressing, and any of the following ingredients can also be added to make what should properly be called Vinaigrette Sauce:
$\frac{1}{4}$ teaspoon French mustard
Chopped chives, parsley or basil
A little very finely chopped onion
A crushed clove of garlic
A few very finely chopped capers

MAYONNAISE

Mayonnaise is a cold sauce made from egg yolks and oil which are beaten together to form an emulsion. The sauce is used to coat and combine cold vegetables, fish and eggs, and as a dressing with all types of salads. Once the making of the sauce is mastered, many flavourings and colourings may be added to increase its versatility.

If the oil is added to the egg yolks too quickly initially, and the mixture curdles, reconstitute the mixture by placing another egg yolk and the given seasonings in another bowl and beating well. Gradually add the curdled mixture to the fresh egg yolk, beating constantly, until the mixture thickens, then add the mixture a little more quickly until it is all absorbed.

When making mayonnaise it is important to use fresh eggs as they have a greater ability to hold the oil in a stable emulsion.

300ml (10 fl oz) [1$\frac{1}{4}$ cups]

Metric/Imperial

2 egg yolks at room temperature
$\frac{1}{2}$ teaspoon salt
$\frac{3}{4}$ teaspoon dry mustard
$\frac{1}{8}$ teaspoon white pepper
300ml (10 fl oz) olive oil, at room temperature
1 tablespoon white wine vinegar or lemon juice

American

2 egg yolks at room temperature
$\frac{1}{2}$ teaspoon salt
$\frac{3}{4}$ teaspoon dry mustard
$\frac{1}{8}$ teaspoon white pepper
1$\frac{1}{4}$ cups olive oil, at room temperature
1 tablespoon white wine vinegar or lemon juice

Place the egg yolks, salt, mustard and pepper in a mixing bowl. Using a wire whisk beat until thoroughly blended and thickened. Add the oil, a few drops at a time, whisking constantly. Do not add the oil too quickly or the mayonnaise will curdle.

After the mayonnaise has thickened the oil may be added a little more rapidly.

Beat in a few drops of vinegar or lemon juice from time to time to prevent the mayonnaise from becoming too thick. When all the oil has been added, stir in the remaining vinegar or lemon juice.

Taste and add more salt, mustard and vinegar if desired.

DEVIL SAUCE

This creamy Devil Sauce gives a delicious finishing touch to baked or poached eggs, fish or chicken. Spoon the sauce over the cooked dish and heat in the oven preheated to hot (220°C/ 425°F or Gas Mark 7) for 10 minutes.

TOMATO SAUCE

This home-made Tomato Sauce is the basic ingredient of many recipes.

About 300ml ($\frac{1}{2}$ pint) [$1\frac{1}{4}$ cups]

Metric/Imperial

25g (1oz) butter
1 small onion, peeled and chopped
2 tablespoons flour
225ml (8 fl oz) stock or water
a good pinch of mixed herbs
salt, pepper and a pinch of sugar
350ml (12 fl oz) canned tomatoes
1 teaspoon tomato purée

American

2 tablespoons butter
1 small onion, peeled and chopped
2 tablespoons flour
1 cup stock or water
1 bouquet garni
salt, pepper and a pinch of sugar
1$\frac{1}{2}$ cups canned tomatoes
1 teaspoon tomato paste

Melt the butter and gently sauté the chopped onion until transparent. Remove from the heat, sprinkle in the flour, blend in the stock or water, and add the herbs, seasonings, tomatoes and purée. Blend well together.

Return to the heat, bring to the boil, stirring constantly, and simmer for about 20 minutes. Strain. Adjust seasoning if necessary.

APPLE SAUCE

Tart Apple Sauce is a delicate accompaniment to goose, duck or pork dishes. Apple Sauce and horseradish is excellent served with pork dishes. Just blend horseradish into the Apple Sauce. A somewhat sweeter Apple Sauce, served with cream, is a tasty dessert.

4-6 servings

Metric/Imperial

750g (1$\frac{1}{2}$lb) cooking apples
finely grated rind of 1 lemon
1 tablespoon water
$\frac{1}{8}$ teaspoon salt
sugar to taste

Smooth and rich Mayonnaise is made with olive oil and egg yolks.

150ml (5 fl oz) [$\frac{5}{8}$ cup]

Metric/Imperial

150ml (5 fl oz) double cream
1 tablespoon chilli sauce
1 tablespoon Worcestershire sauce
$\frac{1}{4}$ teaspoon dried basil
$\frac{1}{4}$ teaspoon salt
$\frac{1}{4}$ teaspoon black pepper
$\frac{1}{4}$ teaspoon prepared mustard

American

$\frac{2}{3}$ cup heavy cream
1 tablespoon chili sauce
1 tablespoon Worcestershire sauce
$\frac{1}{4}$ teaspoon dried basil
$\frac{1}{4}$ teaspoon salt
$\frac{1}{4}$ teaspoon black pepper
$\frac{1}{4}$ teaspoon prepared mustard

In a medium-sized bowl, beat the cream until stiff. Whipping constantly, gradually add all the remaining ingredients.

40g (1½oz) butter

American

1½lb tart green apples
finely grated rind of 1 lemon
1 tablespoon water
⅛ teaspoon salt
sugar to taste
3 tablespoons butter

Peel, core and slice the apples. Place them in a bowl of water with a little salt as they are being prepared, to stop them going brown.

Drain the apples and rinse in fresh cold water. Put them into a large saucepan with the lemon rind, water and salt.

Cover the pan and simmer over low heat until the apples are soft. Add the sugar to taste, a little at a time, stirring constantly. Allow to cool.

Push the apples through a strainer to make a fine purée. Beat in the butter. If the sauce is to be served hot, simmer for 2 to 3 minutes in a clean saucepan.

FUDGE SAUCE

A rich and sweet fudge sauce to serve with ice cream, pancakes and sweet soufflés, Fudge Sauce should be served either hot or warm since it hardens as it cools.

400ml (14 fl oz) [1¾ cups]

Metric/Imperial

100g (4oz) butter
175g (6oz) sugar
50g (2oz) soft brown sugar
225ml (8 fl oz) evaporated milk
1 tablespoon dark rum (optional)

American

½ cup butter
¾ cup sugar
⅓ cup soft brown sugar
1 cup evaporated milk
1 tablespoon rum (optional)

In a medium-sized, heavy saucepan, combine the butter and sugars. Place the pan over moderate heat and cook, stirring constantly, until the butter has melted and the sugars have dissolved.

Stir in the evaporated milk. Increase the heat and boil the sauce for 5 minutes, stirring occasionally. Stir in the rum, if using.

CHOCOLATE SAUCE

This is a semi-sweet chocolate sauce, suitable for using on ice cream, sorbet, puddings, meringues and cakes.

500ml (1 pint) [2½ cups]

Metric/Imperial

175g (6oz) dark cooking chocolate, broken into pieces
400ml (14 fl oz) evaporated milk
1 teaspoon vanilla essence
¼ teaspoon almond essence

American

6 squares semi-sweet chocolate, broken into pieces
1¾ cups evaporated milk
1 teaspoon vanilla extract
¼ teaspoon almond extract

In a bowl placed over a pan of hot water or in a double saucepan, melt the chocolate with the milk, stirring occasionally. Remove from the heat and beat in the vanilla and almond essences. Continue beating until the sauce is smooth.

GLACE ICING

Glacé Icing is the simplest, quickest type of icing to make and ideal for topping a plain cake. If you like, flavour with ¼ teaspoon vanilla or coffee essence [extract]. The icing can also be tinted with a few drops of vegetable colouring.

To ice 1 x 20cm (8in) cake

Metric/Imperial

250g (8oz) icing sugar
2 tablespoons warm water or fruit juice
Flavouring/colouring to taste

American

2 cups confectioners' sugar
2 tablespoons warm water or fruit juice
Flavoring/coloring to taste

Sift the icing (confectioners') sugar; and mix with the warmed liquid; alternatively mix over hot water. Add just enough liquid to make the icing coat the back of a spoon without running off too quickly. It should look smooth and glossy.

Use immediately.

To ice a cake, stand it on a wire rack and pour the icing over; if the consistency is right it should not need smoothing with a palette knife.

BUTTERCREAM ICING

Versatile and easy-to-make Buttercream Icing may be used to fill and cover any plain cake. You can flavour it, colour it, and it is ideal for freezing.

To fill and ice 1 x 23cm (9in) cake

Metric/Imperial

75g (3oz) unsalted butter at room temperature
350g (12oz) icing sugar, sifted
⅛ teaspoon salt
1½ teaspoons vanilla essence
2 tablespoons double cream

American

⅓ cup sweet butter, at room temperature
3 cups confectioners' sugar, sifted
⅛ teaspoon salt
1½ teaspoons vanilla extract
2 tablespoons heavy cream

Place the butter in a mixing bowl and cream it with the back of a wooden spoon. When it is smooth gradually add half of the sugar and the salt. Cream the butter and sugar together until the mixture is pale and fluffy. Mix in the vanilla essence and cream and beat in the remaining sugar.

Variations:

Chocolate Buttercream Icing
Add 50g (2oz) of melted dark cooking (semi-sweet) chocolate with the cream and vanilla essence.

Orange or Lemon Buttercream Icing
Substitute the grated rind of ½ orange or lemon and 3 tablespoons of orange or lemon juice for the cream.

Soups and starters

It is a pity that the custom of serving a first course or appetizer seems to have disappeared in so many households today. The full three-course meal often seems to be a luxury reserved for dinner parties or for dining out in a restaurant where someone else has to clear away and do the washing-up. It cannot be denied that serving a starter for a family meal means more work; but on the other hand a first course can range from something extremely simple like chilled melon, grapefruit or egg mayonnaise to something more ambitious for a special occasion. Small amounts of leftover meat and poultry which will not stretch to another main course can be combined with other ingredients to make many delicious appetizers (try serving in a savoury sauce as a hot filling for vol-au-vents [pastry shells]; or toss with mayonnaise and salad vegetables and serve cold). A substantial first course also makes up for a skimpy main course and no other branch of cuisine gives the cook quite so much scope for improvisation and invention.

Home-made soups have also declined in popularity now that so many canned and packet soups are available. Wise cooks will profit from this state of affairs because nothing impresses people so much or earns quite so many compliments from friends and family as a really delicious soup made from fresh ingredients. The soups in this section have been chosen because they are generally easy to make and they include all the popular favourites like tomato, chicken and mushroom.

Later in the section are the more substantial soups, which can feature in your family's menu in many ways. These soups are ideal for serving before a cold main course such as a salad, but they are probably even more useful when they are served as a lunch or supper dish in their own right, accompanied by crusty bread. So ring the changes on your family's eating habits by making use of this versatile collection of recipes. Serve a home-made chicken liver pâté with crusty bread and tomatoes as a quick Saturday lunch when you are too busy to cook; or when you have a houseful of people for dinner let them help themselves to pâté and toast and other cold hors d'oeuvre while you are busy putting the finishing touches to the main course.

Remember too that the finishing touches make all the difference. Even a packet soup can be given a personal touch if it is served with a dash of cream or a sprinkling of fresh parsley, or any of the suggested accompaniments in this chapter (Croûtons and Garlic Bread) or Melba Toast (see page 252).

AVOCADO PATE

Avocados can be simply served with a vinaigrette dressing. But here is a delicious and simple alternative which is particularly useful if you have small or less-than-perfect avocados, providing they are sound and fully ripe.

4 servings

Metric/Imperial

2 shallots or 1 small onion
1 large or 2 small avocados
2 tablespoons sour cream
1 tablespoon lemon juice
salt and pepper

American

2 shallots or 1 small onion
1 large or 2 small avocados
2 tablespoons sour cream
1 tablespoon lemon juice
salt and pepper

Peel the onion or shallots and grate finely into a bowl. Press with the back of a spoon to extract as much juice as possible. Reserve the juice and discard the grated shallots/onion.

Peel the avocado, discard the stone [pit] and pound the flesh in a mortar with a pestle, or blend in a blender until reduced to a pulp. Add the onion juice, sour cream, lemon juice, salt and pepper and beat until well-blended. Chill well.

Serve in small amounts on individual plates, with brown bread and butter.

QUICK LIVER PATE

Many people are put off making their own pâté by the tedious and time-consuming effort that is usually involved. Here are two recipes which by-pass this process. Quick liver pâté may seem like cheating, but it's delicious all the same!

4 servings

Metric/Imperial

175g (6oz) good quality liver sausage
1 small onion, finely chopped
4 tablespoons single cream
1 small garlic clove, crushed
   (optional)
1 tablespoon dry sherry or brandy
   (optional)
salt and black pepper
chopped parsley

American

6oz liverwurst
1 small onion, finely chopped
4 tablespoons light cream
1 small garlic clove, crushed
   (optional)
1 tablespoon dry sherry or brandy
   (optional)
salt and black pepper
chopped parsley

Remove the skin and fat from the liver sausage [liverwurst] and mash with a fork. Add the onion and cream, and the garlic and sherry or brandy if these are being used, and mix well. Season to taste. Pile up in a small bowl and sprinkle with chopped parsley.

Serve with hot toast and butter.

QUICK CHICKEN LIVER PATE

Chicken livers are usually cheap if you can obtain them, and they make a delicious smooth pâté. Serve with triangles of toast as a starter to a light meal, or with plenty of crusty bread and a bowl of salad for a sustaining summer lunch.

4 servings

Metric/Imperial

75g (3oz) butter
1 medium-sized onion, finely chopped
1 garlic clove, crushed
250g (8oz) chicken livers
1 bay leaf
sprig of parsley
sprig of thyme
salt and pepper
2 teaspoons brandy

American

$\frac{3}{8}$ cup butter
1 medium-sized onion, finely chopped
1 garlic clove, crushed
½lb chicken livers
1 bay leaf
sprig of parsley
sprig of thyme
salt and pepper
2 teaspoons brandy

Melt about one-third of the butter in a frying-pan, and sauté the onion and garlic until they are softened but not browned.

Meanwhile wash the chicken livers and dry them on paper towels. Add these with the bay leaf to the onions, and sauté for 2 or 3 minutes. Chop the parsley and thyme, and add them with seasoning to the frying-pan. Cook for about another minute. Cool the mixture, chop it, then pound it well with a pestle and mortar (or if you like a very fine pâté, purée in a blender).

Melt the remaining butter in the frying-pan, and stir into the pâté with the brandy. Turn the pâté into a small mould, pot or tin and chill. It may then be turned out or served from the pot.

GRILLED [BROILED] GRAPEFRUIT

This easy-to-prepare starter makes a refreshing beginning to any meal.

4 servings

Metric/Imperial

2 large grapefruit
2 tablespoons soft brown sugar

American

2 large grapefruit
2 tablespoons soft brown sugar

Preheat the grill [broiler] to moderate.

Halve the grapefruit and loosen the segments. Remove any seeds. Arrange the grapefruit halves, cut sides up, in the grill [broiler] pan. Sprinkle the tops with brown sugar.

Grill [broil] for 4 minutes or until the sugar has melted and the tops are lightly browned. Serve hot.

PRAWN OR SHRIMP COCKTAIL

This is one of the all-time favourites on any restaurant menu and very easy to prepare yourself. Here is a version to serve the family as a starter to a special meal.

4 servings

Metric/Imperial

4 large lettuce leaves, washed, shaken dry and very finely shredded
150ml (5 fl oz) mayonnaise
4 tablespoons double cream
2 teaspoons Worcestershire sauce
2 teaspoons lemon juice
2 teaspoons tomato ketchup
¼ teaspoon cayenne pepper
½ teaspoon salt
½ teaspoon black pepper
400g (14oz) prawns or shrimps, shelled
1 teaspoon paprika
4 thin cucumber slices

1 lemon, quartered

American

4 large iceberg lettuce leaves, washed, shaken dry and very finely shredded
⅔ cup mayonnaise
4 tablespoons heavy cream
2 teaspoons Worcestershire sauce
2 teaspoons lemon juice
2 teaspoons tomato ketchup
¼ teaspoon cayenne pepper or a few drops Tabasco sauce
½ teaspoon salt
½ teaspoon black pepper
1lb clean cooked or 3 x 5¾oz cans shrimp
1 teaspoon paprika
4 thin cucumber slices
1 lemon, quartered

This Chicken Liver Pate is decorative enough for a dinner party. Serve with a green salad and chilled white wine.

Stand 4 individual serving glasses on 4 small plates. Divide the shredded lettuce equally among the glasses and set aside.

In a medium-sized mixing bowl, combine the mayonnaise, cream, Worcestershire sauce, lemon juice, tomato ketchup, cayenne, salt and pepper, beating with a wooden spoon until the mixture is smooth and evenly coloured. Stir in the prawns or shrimps.

Spoon the mixture equally over the lettuce in the glasses and sprinkle over the paprika.

Garnish with the cucumber and lemon quarters and serve immediately.

CREAMY KIPPER PATE

This delicious pâté is best made a day or two beforehand, then covered and refrigerated. It can also be deep frozen. Serve with thinly cut brown bread and butter.

4-6 servings

Metric/Imperial

500g (1lb) kipper fillets
1 small garlic clove, crushed
6 tablespoons olive oil
3 tablespoons single cream
salt and pepper
lemon slices to garnish

American

1lb kippered herring
1 small garlic clove, crushed
6 tablespoons olive oil
3 tablespoons light cream
salt and pepper
lemon slices to garnish

Poach the kippers in water for 10 minutes until they are just cooked. Drain and remove the skins, then put the cooked flesh into a saucepan and beat with a wooden spoon to break it up. Beat in the garlic and heat gently, stirring to prevent it from sticking. Add

A classic cold Spanish tomato soup, Gazpacho makes a refreshing summer lunch.

the olive oil gradually, beating well between each addition. Beat in the cream. Remove from the heat and season. Turn into a serving dish, cover and refrigerate for up to 2 to 3 days. Garnish the pâté with lemon slices before serving.

GAZPACHO

This Spanish soup is a perfect beginning to a summer meal.

4 servings

Metric/Imperial

3 slices of brown bread, cut into
    small cubes
300ml (10 fl oz) tomato juice
2 garlic cloves, very finely chopped
$\frac{1}{2}$ cucumber, peeled and finely chopped
1 green pepper, white pith removed,
    seeded and finely chopped
1 red pepper, white pith removed,
    seeded and finely chopped
1 large onion, finely chopped
675g (1$\frac{1}{2}$lb) tomatoes, peeled, seeded

and chopped
75ml (3 fl oz) olive oil
2 tablespoons red wine vinegar
½ teaspoon salt
¼ teaspoon black pepper
¼ teaspoon dried marjoram
¼ teaspoon dried basil

American

3 slices of brown bread, cut into
  small cubes
1¼ cups tomato juice
2 garlic cloves, very finely chopped
½ cucumber, peeled and finely chopped
1 green pepper, membrane and seeds
  removed, finely chopped
1 red pepper, membrane and seeds
  removed, finely chopped
1 large onion, finely chopped
3 cups tomatoes, peeled, seeded and
  chopped
⅜ cup olive oil
2 tablespoons red wine vinegar
½ teaspoon salt
¼ teaspoon black pepper
¼ teaspoon dried marjoram
¼ teaspoon dried basil

Put the bread cubes in a mixing bowl
and pour over the tomato juice. Leave
to soak for 5 minutes, then squeeze the
bread cubes to be sure they are completely softened.

Pour the bread and tomato juice
mixture into a blender and add as many
of the vegetables as will fit. Blend to a
smooth purée. When all the vegetables
and the tomato juice mixture have been
blended, stir in the remaining ingredients. Chill for at least 1 hour.

Just before serving, stir the soup well
and add a few ice cubes. Serve with
finely chopped hard-boiled egg, cucumber, onion and croûtons.

VICHYSSOISE

A classic soup, Vichyssoise, in spite of
its French name, is supposed to have
been invented in the United States.

6 servings

Metric/Imperial

100g (4oz) butter
1kg (2lb) leeks, trimmed and chopped

500g (1lb) potatoes, peeled and
  chopped
2 celery stalks, chopped
500ml (1 pint) milk
1 teaspoon salt
½ teaspoon white pepper
½ teaspoon sugar
¼ teaspoon grated nutmeg
300ml (10 fl oz) double cream
chopped chives to garnish

American

½ cup butter
4 cups leeks, trimmed and chopped
1lb potatoes, peeled and chopped
2 celery stalks, chopped
2½ cups milk
1 teaspoon salt
½ teaspoon white pepper
½ teaspoon sugar
¼ teaspoon grated nutmeg
1¼ cups heavy cream
chopped chives to garnish

Melt the butter in a saucepan. Add the
leeks, potatoes and celery and cook until
the vegetables are soft but not brown.
Stir in the milk and bring to the boil.

Add the salt, pepper, sugar and
nutmeg. Cover and simmer for 35
minutes.

Purée the soup in a blender or by
pushing through a strainer until smooth.
Allow to cool, then stir in half the
cream. Chill for at least 4 hours.

To serve, ladle into individual bowls
and swirl in the remaining cream.
Sprinkle with chopped chives.

ICED CARROT AND ORANGE SOUP

This unusual soup looks very decorative
garnished with thin orange slices.

6 servings

Metric/Imperial

25g (1oz) butter
1 large onion, thinly sliced
3 tablespoons flour

Vichyssoise is one of the most
famous cold soups.

¾ litre (1½ pints) chicken stock
500ml (1 pint) orange juice
2 tablespoons finely chopped chives
1 teaspoon salt
½ teaspoon black pepper
⅛ teaspoon grated nutmeg
⅛ teaspoon ground allspice
500g (1lb) carrots, chopped

American

2 tablespoons butter
1 large onion, thinly sliced
3 tablespoons flour
3¾ cups chicken stock
2½ cups orange juice
2 tablespoons finely chopped chives
1 teaspoon salt
½ teaspoon black pepper
⅛ teaspoon grated nutmeg
⅛ teaspoon ground allspice
1lb carrots, chopped

Melt the butter in a saucepan. Add the onion and fry until it is soft but not brown. Stir in the flour and cook, stirring, for 1 minute. Remove from the heat and gradually stir in the stock and orange juices. Return to the heat and bring to the boil, stirring. Simmer until thickened and smooth.

Add the chives, salt, pepper, nutmeg, allspice and carrots. Cover and simmer for 1 hour.

Purée the soup in an electric blender or by pushing through a strainer until smooth. Allow to cool, then chill for at least 2 hours before serving.

COLD PUMPKIN SOUP

This pumpkin soup originated in the West Indies. Serve garnished with thin slices of peeled, chilled orange and chopped chives.

4-6 servings

Metric/Imperial

25g (1oz) butter
1 medium onion, chopped
2 tablespoons flour

1 litre (2 pints) chicken stock
500g (1lb) pumpkin flesh, chopped
¼ teaspoon grated nutmeg
⅛ teaspoon ground cloves
1 teaspoon salt
½ teaspoon black pepper
250g (8oz) tomatoes, peeled, seeded and chopped
300ml (10 fl oz) milk

American

2 tablespoons butter
1 medium onion, chopped
2 tablespoons flour
5 cups chicken stock
2 cups pumpkin flesh, chopped
¼ teaspoon grated nutmeg
⅛ teaspoon ground cloves
1 teaspoon salt
½ teaspoon black pepper
1 cup tomatoes, peeled, seeded and chopped
1¼ cups milk

Melt the butter in a saucepan. Add the onion and fry until it is soft but not

brown. Stir in the flour and cook, stirring, for 1 minute. Gradually stir in the stock and bring to the boil, stirring. Add the pumpkin, nutmeg, cloves, salt, pepper, tomatoes and milk.

Cover and simmer for 30 minutes. Purée the soup in a blender or by pushing through a strainer until smooth. Allow to chill before serving.

CREAM OF WATERCRESS SOUP

When watercress comes into season in the spring, why not make this green, fresh-tasting soup to serve as an appetizer?

4 servings

Metric/Imperial

2 bunches watercress
25g (1oz) butter
1 small leek, finely chopped
¾ litre (1½ pints) chicken stock
1½ teaspoons salt
½ teaspoon white pepper
150ml (5 fl oz) single cream

American

2 bunches watercress
2 tablespoons butter
1 small leek, finely chopped
3¾ cups chicken stock or broth
½ teaspoons salt
½ teaspoon white pepper
⅔ cup light cream

Clean the watercress thoroughly in cold running water and reserve 2 or 3 sprigs to garnish. Chop the leaves finely.

In a medium-sized saucepan melt the butter over moderate heat. When the foam subsides add the watercress and leek and cook for 5 minutes. Pour in the stock, add the salt and pepper and bring to the boil. Reduce the heat, cover and simmer for 20 minutes. Strain the mixture into a large saucepan, using a wooden spoon to push the vegetables through.

Add the cream to the pan, mixing

Watercress and cream are combined in Watercress Soup.

to blend well. Place over low heat and heat very gently until hot but not boiling. Taste and add more salt and pepper if desired.

Pour the soup into a warmed tureen and scatter over reserved watercress.

CUCUMBER SOUP

This hot soup, subtly flavoured with cinnamon and garlic, is an excellent starter for a chilly summer evening meal.

4 servings

Metric/Imperial

1 litre (2 pints) chicken stock
2 cucumbers, peeled and minced and the juice reserved
25g (1oz) butter
1 onion, finely diced
300ml (10 fl oz) single cream
100g (4oz) mushrooms, wiped and thinly sliced
1 teaspoon ground cinnamon
1 garlic clove, crushed
½ teaspoon white pepper
½ cucumber, peeled and diced
½ teaspoon salt

American

5 cups chicken stock
2 cucumbers, peeled and minced and the juice reserved
2 tablespoons butter
1 onion, finely diced
1¼ cups light cream
¼lb mushrooms, wiped and thinly sliced
1 teaspoon ground cinnamon
1 garlic clove, crushed
½ teaspoon white pepper
½ cucumber, peeled and diced
½ teaspoon salt

Place the stock and the minced cucumbers and their juice in a large, heavy saucepan and bring to the boil. Cover, reduce the heat and simmer for 10 minutes.

In a frying-pan melt half the butter over moderate heat. When the foam subsides add the onion and cook for 5 to 8 minutes, or until pale golden. Transfer to the saucepan.

Stir the cream into the stock mixture.

Melt the rest of the butter in the frying-pan over moderate heat. When the foam subsides add the mushrooms and cook for 2 minutes or until just soft. Stir the mushrooms and their cooking liquid into the stock mixture.

Add the cinnamon, garlic and pepper and mix thoroughly. Taste and add more pepper if necessary.

Place the diced cucumber in a small saucepan and cover with water. Add the ½ teaspoon of salt and bring the water to the boil. Cook for 5 minutes then drain thoroughly and set aside.

Heat the stock mixture over moderate heat until it is very hot but not boiling. Stir in the diced cucumber.

BORSCHT

Borscht outside Eastern Europe is usually known as a thin soup, served hot or cold as a starter. In fact it has many variations, and like Scotch Broth it can be made with a variety of meat and vegetables as a substantial meal in its own right. For this version you can make a good stock from beef bones. The soup is a distinctive bright red, and the addition of sour cream is the perfect complement to the sweetness of the beetroot [beets].

4 servings

Metric/Imperial

675g (1½lb) uncooked beetroot
1 large onion
2 teaspoons salt
¼ teaspoon black pepper
1 tablespoon lemon juice
1¾ litres (3 pints) beef stock or water
350g (12oz) carrots, peeled and chopped
500g (1lb) potatoes, peeled and halved
500g (1lb) stewing beef, cut into small chunks
350g (12oz) white cabbage, shredded
150ml (5 fl oz) sour cream

American

6 cups raw beets, grated or chopped
1 large onion
2 teaspoons salt
¼ teaspoon black pepper
1 tablespoon lemon juice

2 quarts beef stock or water
1½ cups carrots, peeled and chopped
1lb potatoes, peeled and halved
1lb boneless beef chuck, etc., cubed
1½ cups white cabbage, shredded
⅔ cup sour cream

First make the beetroot [beet] stock. This can be done the day before if more convenient. Peel about two-thirds of the beetroot [beets] and chop or grate coarsely into a large saucepan. Chop the onion and add to the pan with the salt, pepper and lemon juice. Pour over the stock or water. Cover and bring to the boil, then simmer for one hour.

Remove the pan from the heat. Strain the beetroot [beet] stock through a strainer, pressing down to extract all the juice. Discard the vegetables.

Return the stock to the pan and add the carrots, potatoes, meat and shredded cabbage. Grate the remaining beetroot [beets] and add to the pan. Bring back to the boil, skim if necessary, and simmer for a further hour, or until the vegetables are tender. Stir occasionally and top up with a little water if the soup becomes too thick.

Taste the soup and add more seasoning if necessary. Spoon into warmed serving dishes, topping each helping with a lightly swirled spoonful of sour cream.

QUICK TOMATO SOUP

This quick soup takes just 10 minutes to prepare.

4 servings

Metric/Imperial

25g (1oz) butter
1 medium-sized onion, finely diced
4 tablespoons flour
300ml (10 fl oz) milk
300ml (10 fl oz) water
4 tablespoons tomato purée
1 teaspoon sugar
pinch of dried mixed herbs
salt and pepper

American

1 tablespoon butter
1 medium-sized onion, finely diced
4 tablespoons flour
1¼ cups milk
1¼ cups water
4 tablespoons tomato paste
1 teaspoon sugar
bouquet garni, removed before
    serving
salt and pepper

Melt the butter in a medium-sized saucepan and fry the onion in it until soft but not brown. Remove from heat and gradually stir in the milk and water, beating until smooth. Stir in the tomato purée [paste], sugar and herbs. Season with salt and pepper to taste, and simmer for about 6 to 7 minutes or until the onion is cooked. Serve with chopped parsley or fried croûtons.

TOMATO SOUP

This Tomato Soup allows the fresh taste of the tomatoes to predominate. For the family serve the soup with fresh bread.

4 servings

Metric/Imperial

25g (1oz) butter
675g (1½lb) tomatoes, quartered
¾ litre (1½ pints) chicken stock
1 medium-sized onion, finely chopped
1 bay leaf
½ teaspoon black pepper
¼ teaspoon salt
thinly pared rind of ¼ orange
2 teaspoons lemon juice
1 teaspoon sugar

American

2 tablespoons butter
3 cups tomatoes, quartered
3¾ cups chicken stock or broth
1 medium-sized onion, finely chopped
1 bay leaf
½ teaspoon black pepper
¼ teaspoon salt
thinly pared rind of ¼ orange
2 teaspoons lemon juice
1 teaspoon sugar

In a medium-sized saucepan, melt the butter over low heat. When the foam subsides add the tomatoes and cook for 10 minutes, stirring frequently. Increase the heat to moderate and add the stock, onion, bay leaf, pepper, salt and orange rind. Bring to the boil, reduce the heat, cover and simmer for 45 minutes.

Remove the pan from the heat and pour the contents through a strainer into another saucepan. Using the back of a wooden spoon rub the tomato mixture through the strainer into the pan until only a dry pulp is left behind.

Add the lemon juice and sugar and place over low heat. Bring the soup to the boil, stirring frequently.

CREAM OF CHICKEN SOUP

This easy to make but tasty soup is an excellent way of using leftover chicken. The chicken carcass can be used to make the stock.

4-6 servings

Metric/Imperial

40g (1½oz) butter
3 tablespoons flour
½ litre (1 pint) chicken stock
½ litre (1 pint) milk
250g (8oz) cooked chicken, finely
    chopped
1 teaspoon salt
¼ teaspoon white pepper
1 teaspoon dried basil
2 egg yolks
100ml (4 fl oz) single cream
1 tablespoon chopped parsley

American

3 tablespoons butter
3 tablespoons flour
2½ cups chicken stock or broth
2½ cups milk
1 cup cooked chicken, finely diced
1 teaspoon salt
¼ teaspoon white pepper
1 teaspoon dried basil
2 egg yolks
½ cup light cream
1 tablespoon chopped parsley

In a large saucepan, melt the butter over moderate heat. Remove the pan from the heat and stir in the flour, mixing to a smooth paste.

Return the pan to moderate heat and gradually stir in the chicken stock and milk. Bring to the boil, stirring constantly. Add the chicken, salt and pepper and basil. Reduce the heat, cover and simmer for 15 minutes. Remove the pan from the heat.

Mix the egg yolks and cream together in a small bowl. Mix in 3 tablespoons of the soup liquid, then stir the egg-and-cream mixture into the soup. Return the pan to the heat and heat the soup gently until hot but not boiling.

Sprinkle with the parsley just before serving.

MUSHROOM SOUP

No canned mushroom soup can compare with the real thing. This version will earn you plenty of compliments.

---

4 servings

Metric/Imperial

50g (2oz) butter
1 medium-sized onion, finely diced
250g (8oz) mushrooms, washed and sliced
4 tablespoons flour
425ml (15 fl oz) chicken stock
150ml (5 fl oz) milk
1 tablespoon chopped parsley
60ml (2½ fl oz) single cream
salt and pepper

American

---

4 tablespoons butter
1 medium-sized onion, finely diced
½lb fresh mushrooms, washed and sliced
4 tablespoons flour
2 cups chicken stock
⅔ cup milk
1 tablespoon chopped parsley
5 tablespoons light cream
salt and pepper

Melt the butter in a saucepan and fry the onion until soft but not brown. Add the mushrooms and flour and fry for 5 minutes. Remove from the heat and add the stock, slowly at first, stirring all the time. Return to the heat and bring to boiling point, stirring until it

has thickened. Blend in the milk and add most of the parsley, saving a little to garnish. Purée in a blender until smooth. Return to the saucepan, reheat, and season with salt and pepper to taste.

Just before serving remove from the heat and stir in the cream. Sprinkle each bowl with chopped parsley.

CREAM OF CELERY SOUP

Serve this distinctively flavoured soup with well-buttered French bread or hot toast. It makes a delicious supper dish.

---

4 servings

Metric/Imperial

50g (2oz) butter
1 large head of celery, washed and finely sliced
1 large onion, finely sliced
¾ litre (1½ pints) milk
1 teaspoon dried mixed herbs
3 bay leaves
8 peppercorns
2 tablespoons flour
1½ teaspoons salt
½ teaspoon white pepper
2 egg yolks
75ml (3 fl oz) single cream
1 tablespoon chopped parsley

American

¼ cup butter
1 large head of celery, washed and finely sliced
1 large onion, finely sliced
3¾ cups milk
1 bouquet garni plus 2 bay leaves
8 peppercorns
2 tablespoons flour
1½ teaspoons salt
½ teaspoon white pepper
2 egg yolks
⅓ cup light cream
1 tablespoon chopped parsley

In a medium-sized saucepan melt half the butter over low heat. When the foam subsides add the celery and onion. Cover the pan and simmer very gently for 30 minutes, or until they are soft.

Meanwhile in a small saucepan bring the milk, mixed herbs, bay leaves and

peppercorns to the boil over low heat. Cover and simmer for 5 minutes. Taste the milk and when it is quite strongly flavoured strain it into a small bowl and allow it to cool.

In a large saucepan melt the remaining butter over moderate heat. Remove the pan from the heat and stir in the flour, mixing to a smooth paste. Return the pan to the heat and gradually stir in the milk. Bring to the boil, stirring constantly. Reduce the heat and simmer for 5 minutes. Add the salt and pepper.

Strain the celery and onion into a bowl using the back of a wooden spoon to push the vegetables through. Remove the milk mixture from the heat and gradually whisk in the celery and onion purée.

Beat the egg yolks and cream together. Mix in 3 tablespoons of the soup liquid, then stir the egg-and-cream mixture back into the soup. Return the pan to the heat and heat the soup gently until hot but not boiling.

Pour the soup into a warmed tureen and sprinkle with the parsley.

EGG AND CHEESE SOUP

Egg and Cheese Soup is one of the easiest and quickest of all soups to prepare.

---

4 servings

Metric/Imperial

---

2 eggs
½ teaspoon salt
¼ teaspoon black pepper
1 litre (2 pints) cold chicken stock
50g (2oz) noodles, cooked
3 tablespoons Parmesan cheese, grated

American

---

2 eggs
½ teaspoon salt
¼ teaspoon black pepper
5 cups cold chicken stock
½ cup noodles, cooked
3 tablespoons Parmesan cheese, grated

Whisk the eggs, salt, pepper and a little of the chicken stock together with a wire whisk.

Pour the remaining stock into a saucepan and add the noodles and cheese. Bring to the boil, reduce the heat to low and whisk in the egg mixture.

Cook the soup for 2 minutes, beating constantly; do not allow to boil.

LEEK SOUP

This rich, warming soup is best served with croûtons of fried bread as their crunchiness is a nice contrast to the creaminess of the soup.

4 servings

Metric/Imperial

25g (1oz) butter
2 small onions, thinly sliced and pushed out into rings
2 tablespoons flour
1 litre (2 pints) chicken stock
⅛ teaspoon celery salt
1 teaspoon salt
½ teaspoon black pepper
1 teaspoon paprika
¼ teaspoon grated nutmeg
675g (1½lb) leeks, trimmed, washed and sliced
2 egg yolks
150ml (5 fl oz) double cream

American

2 tablespoons butter
2 small onions, thinly sliced and separated into rings
2 tablespoons flour
5 cups chicken stock
⅛ teaspoon celery salt
1 teaspoon salt
½ teaspoon black pepper
1 teaspoon paprika
¼ teaspoon grated nutmeg
3 cups leeks, trimmed, washed and sliced
2 egg yolks
⅔ cup heavy cream

In a large heavy saucepan, melt the butter over moderate heat. When the foam subsides add the onions and cook, stirring occasionally, for 5 to 7 minutes or until soft and translucent but not brown.

Remove the pan from the heat. Stir in the flour to make a smooth paste. Gradually add the chicken stock, stirring to avoid lumps. Stir in the celery salt, salt, pepper, paprika, nutmeg and leeks.

Return the pan to the heat and bring to the boil, stirring constantly. Reduce the heat, cover and simmer for 30 to 35 minutes.

Beat the egg yolks and the cream together with a fork until thoroughly combined. Stir into the soup and cook, stirring constantly, for 4 to 5 minutes, or until the soup is thick and smooth. Do not let the soup boil or it will curdle.

SUBSTANTIAL SOUPS

The soup recipes in the remainder of this chapter are really substantial meals in themselves. Serve them as a starter when the main course is a very light one such as a salad. Or serve them with French bread or hot rolls for supper.

GEORGIAN SOUP

An inexpensive and easy-to-make vegetable soup, Georgian Soup makes a light and warming winter lunch or dinner.

4-6 servings

Metric/Imperial

25g (1oz) butter
1 large onion, thinly sliced and pushed out into rings
2 tablespoons flour
1 litre (2 pints) chicken stock
396g (14oz) can tomatoes
500g (1lb) leeks, washed, trimmed and sliced
1 teaspoon salt
½ teaspoon black pepper

Cock-a-Leekie is ideal for a cold winter's day.

Below:
Georgian Soup is almost a meal in itself.

½ teaspoon dried oregano
1 bay leaf
1 tablespoon finely chopped chives

American

2 tablespoons butter
1 large onion, thinly sliced and separated into rings
2 tablespoons flour
5 cups chicken stock
14oz can tomatoes
2 cups leeks, washed, trimmed and sliced
1 teaspoon salt
½ teaspoon black pepper
½ teaspoon dried oregano
1 bay leaf
1 tablespoon finely chopped chives

In a large saucepan, melt the butter over moderate heat. When the foam subsides, add the onion and cook, stirring occasionally, for 5 to 7 minutes, or until soft and translucent but not brown. Remove the pan from the heat and stir in the flour to make a smooth paste.

Gradually stir in the chicken stock, then add the tomatoes, leeks, salt, pepper, oregano and the bay leaf.

Return the pan to high heat and bring the soup to the boil, stirring constantly. Reduce the heat, cover and simmer for 20 minutes or until the leeks are soft. Sprinkle with chives.

COCK-A-LEEKIE

A warming, traditional Scots soup of chicken and leeks, Cock-a-Leekie is served with hot crusty bread.

6 servings

Metric/Imperial

1 x 2kg (1 x 4lb) chicken
7 leeks, including part of the green stems, washed and sliced
2 celery stalks, chopped
50g (2oz) pearl barley
1 bouquet garni
1 teaspoon salt
1 tablespoon chopped parsley

American

1 x 4lb chicken
7 leeks, including part of the green
   stems, washed and sliced
2 celery stalks, chopped
¼ cup pearl barley
1 bouquet garni
1 teaspoon salt
1 tablespoon chopped parsley

Place the chicken in a large saucepan and pour over enough water to cover it. Bring to the boil; skim off any scum that rises to the surface. Add the leeks, celery, barley, bouquet garni and salt and reduce the heat to low. Partly cover the pan and simmer for 1½ to 2 hours, or until the meat is almost falling off the bones.

Transfer the chicken to a wooden board or platter. Leave it to cool slightly. Remove the bouquet garni. Skim the fat off the surface of the cooking liquid.

Detach the chicken meat from the skin and bones, shred and return it to the cooking liquid in the pan.

Place the pan over moderate heat and simmer the soup for 5 minutes to reheat. Sprinkle with parsley.

CABBAGE AND POTATO SOUP WITH SAUSAGE

This filling and pungent soup is a national dish of Portugal.

4 servings

Metric/Imperial

100g (4oz) smoked garlic pork sausage
500g (1lb) potatoes, peeled and thinly
   sliced
1 litre (2 pints) water
1 teaspoon salt
2 tablespoons vegetable oil
1 teaspoon freshly ground black
   pepper
1 medium-sized green cabbage,
   washed and finely shredded

American

¼lb smoked garlic sausages
1lb potatoes, peeled and thinly sliced
5 cups water

1 teaspoon salt
2 tablespoons vegetable oil
1 teaspoon freshly ground black
   pepper
1 medium-sized green cabbage,
   washed and finely shredded

Prick the sausage in two or three places with a fork. Place it in a saucepan and add enough water to cover. Bring to the boil, then reduce the heat to very low. Cover and simmer for 15 minutes. Drain the sausage, allow to cool and then remove the skin. Slice thinly and set aside.

Meanwhile, boil the potatoes. Transfer to a mixing bowl, reserving the cooking liquid. Mash the potatoes to a purée and return to the saucepan containing the cooking liquid. Stir in the oil, pepper and cabbage and bring to the boil, stirring to blend together. Cook the mixture, uncovered, over moderate heat for 5 to 6 minutes. Add the sausage slices to the saucepan and continue cooking for 4 minutes.

FARM SOUP

This economical and hearty soup is ideal to serve on cold wintry evenings.

4 servings

Metric/Imperial

500g (1lb) stewing steak, cut into cubes
1 litre (2 pints) water
100g (4oz) lentils, soaked overnight
   and drained
1 large onion, sliced
1 large carrot, scraped and sliced
2 celery stalks, chopped
1 leek, washed, trimmed and finely
   chopped
2 medium-sized potatoes, peeled and
   diced
1 bay leaf
2 teaspoons salt
1 teaspoon black pepper

American

1lb chuck or round steak, cut into
   cubes
5 cups water
½ cup lentils, soaked overnight and
   drained

1 large onion, sliced
1 large carrot, scraped and sliced
2 celery stalks, chopped
1 leek, washed, trimmed and finely
   chopped
2 medium-sized potatoes, peeled and
   diced
1 bay leaf
2 teaspoons salt
1 teaspoon black pepper

Put all the ingredients into a large saucepan. Place the pan over moderately high heat and bring the liquid to the boil.

Reduce the heat to low, cover the pan and simmer gently for 2 hours.

FRENCH ONION SOUP

A classic thick onion soup with toasted French bread and cheese, French Onion Soup is a complete light winter meal or first course.

4 servings

Metric/Imperial

75g (3oz) butter
4 large onions, thinly sliced and
   pushed out into rings
2 tablespoons flour
½ teaspoon salt
¼ teaspoon black pepper
¾ litre (1½ pints) beef stock
6 small slices of French bread, toasted
3 garlic cloves, halved
75g (3oz) Parmesan cheese, grated

American

⅓ cup butter
4 large onions, thinly sliced and
   separated into rings
2 tablespoons flour
½ teaspoon salt
¼ teaspoon black pepper
3¾ cups beef stock
6 small slices of French bread, toasted
3 garlic cloves, halved
¾ cup Parmesan cheese, grated

In a medium-sized heavy flameproof casserole, melt the butter over moderate heat. When the foam subsides, reduce the heat to low and add the onions. Cook, stirring occasionally, for 25 to

30 minutes, or until golden brown. Remove the pan from the heat.

Stir in the flour, salt and pepper. Gradually add the stock, stirring constantly. Return the pan to high heat and bring the soup to the boil. Reduce the heat, cover and simmer for 20 minutes.

Preheat the grill [broiler] to high.

Rub each bread slice on each side with a garlic half. Discard the garlic. Float the slices on the surface of the soup. Sprinkle the cheese generously over the top and place the casserole under the grill [broiler]. Cook for 5 minutes, or until the cheese is golden and bubbling.

SWEETCORN AND CHICKEN SOUP

This wholesome and satisfying dish originated with the Pennsylvania Dutch, who are famous for their delicious soups. It makes a nourishing lunch.

4-6 servings

Metric/Imperial

225g (8oz) cooked chicken, coarsely chopped
½ teaspoon salt
½ teaspoon white pepper
⅛ teaspoon ground saffron
1 litre (2 pints) strong chicken stock
50g (2oz) noodles
225g (8oz) fresh or canned and drained sweetcorn
1 hard-boiled egg, coarsely chopped
1 tablespoon chopped fresh parsley

American

1 cup cooked chicken, coarsely chopped
½ teaspoon salt
½ teaspoon white pepper
⅛ teaspoon ground saffron
5 cups strong chicken stock or broth
½ cup noodles
1 cup fresh or canned and drained corn
1 hard-boiled egg, coarsely chopped
1 tablespoon chopped fresh parsley

Arrange the chicken over the bottom of a very large saucepan. Sprinkle with the salt, pepper and saffron and cover with the chicken stock. Place over moderate heat and bring the mixture to the boil,

stirring occasionally.

Add the noodles and sweetcorn, cover and cook for 15 to 20 minutes or until the noodles are tender. Add the chopped egg, stirring to blend well.

Pour the soup into a warmed tureen, and sprinkle over the parsley.

BARLEY COUNTRY SOUP

This delicious soup with vegetables and barley is nourishing and filling. Serve it with crisp bread or toast. Other vegetables may be used if preferred and, if chicken livers are not available, the soup is equally good if minced [ground] beef is added instead. The sour cream stirred into the soup before serving gives it an extra special flavour.

6-8 servings

Metric/Imperial

100g (4oz) chicken livers, chopped
50g (2oz) mushrooms, chopped
2 large carrots, scraped and thinly sliced
2 parsnips, peeled and diced
1 small cauliflower, separated into flowerets and washed
1 large celery stalk, chopped
1 teaspoon oregano
1 bay leaf
¼ teaspoon nutmeg
1 teaspoon salt
¼ teaspoon black pepper
1¼ litres (2½ pints) cold water
500ml (1 pint) chicken stock
40g (1½oz) butter
50g (2oz) pearl barley
2 large potatoes, peeled and cubed
150ml (5 fl oz) sour cream
1 tablespoon chopped parsley

American

¼lb chicken livers, chopped
¼ cup mushrooms, chopped
2 large carrots, scraped and thinly sliced
2 parsnips, peeled and diced
1 small cauliflower, separated into florets and washed
1 large celery stalk, chopped
1 teaspoon oregano
1 bay leaf
¼ teaspoon nutmeg

1 teaspoon salt
¼ teaspoon black pepper
6¼ cups cold water
2½ cups chicken stock
3 tablespoons butter
¼ cup pearl barley
2 large potatoes, peeled and cubed
⅔ cup sour cream
1 tablespoon chopped parsley

Put the chicken livers, vegetables, herbs, nutmeg, salt and pepper in a large heavy saucepan. Pour in the water and chicken stock and bring to the boil, reduce the heat, cover and simmer for 30 minutes, or until the vegetables are cooked.

Remove the pan from the heat and strain the vegetables and livers into a bowl. Return the liquid to the saucepan.

Melt the butter over moderate heat. Remove the pan from the heat, add the barley and stir well. Add the barley to the stock in the saucepan and stir well. Place over high heat and bring to the boil. Reduce the heat, cover the pan and simmer for 15 minutes, stirring occasionally.

Add the potatoes to the pan and simmer, covered, for a further 15 minutes, or until the potatoes are tender.

Return the livers and vegetables to the pan and stir well to combine with the barley. Simmer for 10 minutes. Mix the sour cream into the soup and sprinkle with the parsley.

FISH SOUP

This is a standard fish soup recipe which can be adapted to use almost any strongly flavoured fish, for example herring or monkfish.

4 servings

Metric/Imperial

500g (1lb) mackerel, filleted, heads and bones reserved
¾ litre (1½ pints) water
parsley stalks
peppercorns
25g (1oz) butter
2 leeks, washed and sliced
3 carrots, scraped and sliced

1 turnip, peeled and sliced
2 stalks celery, washed and sliced
1 bay leaf
salt, pepper and dried thyme
chopped parsley or croûtons

American

1lb mackerel, skinned and filleted,
   head and bones reserved

3¾ cups water
parsley stalks
peppercorns
2 tablespoons butter
2 leeks, washed and sliced
3 carrots, scraped and sliced
1 turnip, peeled and sliced
2 stalks celery, washed and sliced
1 bay leaf

salt, pepper and dried thyme
chopped parsley or croûtons

Place the fish trimmings in a large saucepan with the water, a few parsley stalks and peppercorns. Simmer gently for a few minutes, to make stock.

Melt the butter and gently cook the vegetables in it until they are glossy but

Fish Soup served with fresh crusty French bread and butter is a truly filling meal in itself.

still firm. Pour the strained stock over them; cut the mackerel into large chunks and add.

Add the bay leaf and season with salt, pepper and thyme. Simmer only until the mackerel is cooked; no longer or the ingredients will break up and make the soup look unattractive.

Sprinkle with chopped parsley or croûtons and serve.

ITALIAN MEAT AND VEGETABLE SOUP

This is a filling and warming soup for a family lunch or supper. Serve with hot, crusty bread.

4 servings

Metric/Imperial

50g (2oz) butter
2 tablespoons vegetable oil
1 large onion, finely chopped
1 garlic clove, chopped
500g (1lb) minced beef
1¾ litres (3 pints) beef stock
2 teaspoons salt
½ teaspoon black pepper
1 teaspoon dried oregano

½ teaspoon dried basil
3 courgettes, trimmed, washed and thinly sliced
100g (4oz) peas
100g (4oz) canned peeled tomatoes, drained and coarsely chopped
50g (2oz) Parmesan cheese, grated

American

¼ cup butter
2 tablespoons vegetable oil
1 large onion, finely chopped
1 garlic clove, chopped
1lb ground beef
7½ cups beef stock
2 teaspoons salt
½ teaspoon black pepper
1 teaspoon dried oregano
½ teaspoon dried basil
3 zucchini, trimmed, washed and thinly sliced
½ cup peas
½ cup canned peeled tomatoes, drained and coarsely chopped
½ cup Parmesan cheese, grated

In a large saucepan, melt the butter and oil over moderate heat. When the foam subsides add the onion and garlic and fry, stirring occasionally for 6 to 8 minutes or until golden brown.

Tasty Italian Meat and Vegetable Soup is made with minced [ground] beef, garlic and herbs.

Add the beef and fry, stirring occasionally, for 8 minutes, or until the meat is broken up and browned.

Pour in the stock and add the salt, pepper, herbs, courgettes [zucchini] and peas and bring to the boil. Reduce the heat to low and simmer for 15 minutes. Add the tomatoes and simmer for a further 5 minutes. Sprinkle with cheese just before serving.

SCOTCH BROTH

A filling, meaty soup, Scotch Broth is thickened with pearl barley and dried peas. Serve with bread for a hearty lunch. If you wish to remove all the fat from the broth, allow to cool for at least 8 hours or overnight. Remove and discard the fat that rises to the surface.

4-6 servings

Metric/Imperial

1.25kg (3lb) neck of lamb, chined and trimmed of excess fat
1¾ litres (3 pints) water
1 teaspoon salt
1 teaspoon black pepper
50g (2oz) pearl barley
50g (2oz) split peas, soaked overnight and drained
1 large carrot, scraped and chopped
1 large onion, chopped
2 leeks, trimmed, washed and chopped
2 celery stalks, trimmed and chopped
1 large turnip, peeled and coarsely chopped
2 tablespoons chopped fresh parsley

American

3lb neck of lamb, chined and trimmed of excess fat
7½ cups of water
1 teaspoon salt
1 teaspoon black pepper
¼ cup pearl barley
¼ cup split peas, soaked overnight and drained
1 large carrot, scraped and chopped
1 large onion, chopped
2 leeks, trimmed, washed and chopped
2 celery stalks, trimmed and chopped
1 large turnip, peeled and coarsely chopped
2 tablespoons chopped fresh parsley

Cut the meat into large chunks, place in a large saucepan and pour over the water. Bring to the boil; skim off and discard any scum which rises to the surface. Add the salt, pepper, barley and peas. Reduce the heat, cover and simmer for 1½ hours.

Add the vegetables, cover the pan and continue cooking for 1 hour or until they are very tender.

Transfer the meat to a chopping board, slice from the bone and return to the pan. Cook for a further 5 minutes. Taste and add more salt and pepper if necessary; sprinkle with the parsley.

SPLIT PEA SOUP

Flavoured with herbs and enriched with pork, Split Pea Soup is filling and may be served as a light lunch sprinkled with grated cheese.

6 servings

Metric/Imperial

1 tablespoon butter
225g (8oz) lean belly of pork, chopped
2 garlic cloves, crushed
500g (1lb) split peas, soaked overnight and drained
1¼ litres (2½ pints) chicken stock
2 tablespoons lemon juice
225ml (8 fl oz) water
1 teaspoon salt
½ teaspoon black pepper
½ teaspoon dried marjoram
½ teaspoon dried oregano
¼ teaspoon dried thyme
100ml (4 fl oz) single cream

American

1 tablespoon butter
½lb lean pork flank, chopped
2 garlic cloves, crushed
2 cups split peas, soaked overnight and drained
6¼ cups chicken stock
2 tablespoons lemon juice
1 cup water
1 teaspoon salt
½ teaspoon black pepper
½ teaspoon dried marjoram
½ teaspoon dried oregano
¼ teaspoon dried thyme
½ cup light cream

In a large saucepan, melt the butter over moderate heat. When the foam subsides add the pork and cook, stirring frequently, for 8 to 10 minutes or until the meat is golden brown all over. Add the garlic and cook for 1 minute, stirring frequently. Add the split peas and stir until they are coated with the fat.

Pour in the chicken stock, lemon juice and water and stir in the seasoning and herbs. Bring the soup to the boil, stirring constantly. Cover, reduce the heat and simmer for 1½ hours or until the peas are very soft and the soup is fairly smooth.

Stir the cream into the soup and reheat for 5 minutes before serving.

IRISH LEEK AND OATMEAL BROTH

For centuries, oatmeal, milk and leeks were the staple diet of the Irish. In this recipe, all three are combined to make a tasty and substantial soup.

4 servings

Metric/Imperial

6 large leeks, washed and trimmed
1 litre (2 pints) milk
50g (2oz) butter
2 tablespoons medium oatmeal
1 teaspoon salt
½ teaspoon white pepper
1 tablespoon chopped fresh parsley

American

6 large leeks, washed and trimmed
5 cups milk
¼ cup butter
2 tablespoons oatmeal
1 teaspoon salt
½ teaspoon white pepper
1 tablespoon chopped fresh parsley

Cut the leeks into thick slices and set them aside.

In a large saucepan, bring the milk and butter to the boil. When the butter has melted stir in the oatmeal and cook the mixture, stirring constantly, for 1 minute.

Stir in the leeks, salt and pepper and cover the pan. Reduce the heat to low

and simmer for 45 minutes, stirring occasionally.

Add the parsley and increase the heat to moderate. Bring the soup to the boil and cook for a further 3 minutes.

ACCOMPANIMENTS

Crusty bread is often the best accompaniment for a home-made soup, but here are a few other ideas.

CROUTONS

Croûtons (kroo-tohn) are garnishes made of stale white bread, diced or cut into decorative shapes and fried, grilled [broiled] or dried in the oven.

Quick croûtons for garnishing soups are best made by frying the bread cubes fast in hot oil. Sprinkle a few on each helping and serve the soup quickly while the croûtons are still sizzling hot.

GARLIC BREAD

Metric/Imperial

225g (8oz) butter, softened
2 tablespoons finely chopped fresh parsley
2 garlic cloves, very finely chopped
2 long loaves of French bread

American

1 cup butter, softened
2 tablespoons finely chopped fresh parsley or 1 tablespoon dried parsley flakes
2 garlic cloves, very finely chopped
2 long loaves of French bread

Preheat the oven to fairly hot (200°C/400°F or Gas Mark 6).

Cream the butter, parsley and garlic together with a wooden spoon. Thickly slice the loaves crosswise to within about 6mm (¼ in) of the bottom.

Spread the butter mixture generously on one side of each of the slices. Wrap the loaves in aluminium foil and place them on a baking sheet in the centre of the oven. Bake for 15 to 20 minutes, or until the bread is very crusty and the butter has melted. Serve immediately, in the foil.

Stews and casseroles

Everyone who cooks regularly soon comes to realize that the most labour-saving meals are not necessarily those which can be cooked quickly. Often they are those recipes which require long, slow cooking, the stews and casseroles covered in this section. The advantages of this type of cooking are immense. First of all, the preparations (often minimal) are done well beforehand, and you can clear away, wash up and attend to other matters knowing that the dinner is cooking away and needs no further attention until it is time to eat. Second, you can vary the cooking time to suit your schedule for the day, turning the oven down really low if you know you will be out of the house for a long time. If you go out to work and you have an automatic timer you can prepare a casserole the night before - or even in the morning before going to work - and set the oven to switch on at the right time. So instead of rushing home from work to prepare the evening meal you can be greeted by the delicious smell of cooking as you walk through the front door. The third advantage, and probably the most important one for most of us, is that stews and casseroles generally use cheap cuts of meat. Long, slow cooking has a tenderizing effect and is therefore used for cuts such as stewing beef, neck of lamb, oxtail and so forth. These cuts are not only economical but also extremely nutritious and with a flavour often superior to the more expensive cuts sold for roasting, frying and grilling (broiling).

Many of the recipes here are old favourites – Hot Pot, Irish Stew and Oxtail Casserole for example. These are great standbys, and many people have their own version. Others may not be so familiar, but hopefully there are many dishes here which will become established favourites in your family.

RED CABBAGE AND BACON CASEROLE

This hearty winter dish from Czechoslovakia, makes an economical and filling meal with a distinctive flavour.

4 servings

Metric/Imperial

1½ tablespoons vegetable oil
1 large onion, finely sliced
6 streaky bacon slices, chopped
1 large cooking apple, peeled, cored and sliced
2 large potatoes, sliced
1 medium-sized red cabbage, washed and shredded
1½ teaspoons caraway seeds (optional)
2 tablespoons lemon juice
1 tablespoon vinegar
1 teaspoon salt
½ teaspoon black pepper
300ml (10 fl oz) chicken stock
1 tablespoon brown sugar

American

1½ tablespoons vegetable oil
1 large onion, finely sliced
6 slices bacon, chopped
1 large tart apple, peeled, cored and sliced
2 large potatoes, sliced
1 medium-sized red cabbage, washed and shredded
1½ teaspoons caraway seeds (optional)
2 tablespoons lemon juice
1 tablespoon vinegar
1 teaspoon salt
½ teaspoon black pepper
1¼ cups chicken stock
1 tablespoon brown sugar

In a large flameproof casserole, heat the oil over moderate heat. Add the onion and cook, stirring occasionally, for 8 minutes, or until lightly browned. Add the bacon to the pan and, stirring occasionally, cook until the pieces brown.

Preheat the oven to moderate (180°C/350°F or Gas Mark 4).

Stir the remaining ingredients into the pan and bring the liquid to the boil, stirring occasionally. Cover and transfer to the oven.

Cook for 2 hours, or until the cabbage is very tender.

Just the dish for a family meal, Red Cabbage and Bacon Casserole is an economical and delicious casserole from Czechoslovakia.

BACON AND POTATO HOTPOT

Here is an invaluable recipe for the end of the week when time and money are both in short supply! It is a filling dish for a cold day and needs to be accompanied only by a green vegetable such as braised celery or cabbage.

4 servings

Metric/Imperial

50g (2oz) plus 1 teaspoon butter
3 tablespoons flour
450ml (16 fl oz) milk
50g (2oz) grated cheese
grated nutmeg (optional)
½ teaspoon salt
¼ teaspoon white pepper
4 large onions, thinly sliced in rings
4 large potatoes, thinly sliced
250g (8oz) bacon rashers, chopped, or scraps of cooked bacon from a joint

American

¼ cup plus 1 teaspoon butter
3 tablespoons flour
2 cups milk
½ cup grated cheese
grated nutmeg (optional)
½ teaspoon salt
¼ teaspoon white pepper
4 large onions, thinly sliced in rings
4 large potatoes, thinly sliced
8oz bacon, chopped, or scraps of cooked ham from a joint

Grease a casserole with the teaspoon of butter and set aside. Preheat the oven to hot (200°C/400°F or Gas Mark 6).

In a medium-sized saucepan, melt the remaining butter over low heat. Remove the pan from the heat and stir in the flour. Return to low heat, cook for one minute, then gradually add the milk, stirring continuously until the sauce thickens. Sprinkle in half the cheese, the salt and pepper and the nutmeg, if used, to taste. Stir until blended. Keep warm.

Fill the greased casserole with alternate layers of sliced onion, bacon and potato, beginning with a layer of onions and finishing with a layer of potato. Pour over the sauce, shaking the casserole gently to distribute evenly. Sprinkle over the remaining cheese, cover and cook in the preheated oven for 1 hour. Uncover and cook for a further hour at 170°C/325°F or Gas Mark 3 or until the top is golden brown and the potatoes feel well cooked when a knife is inserted into the centre of the casserole.

APPLE AND PORK CASSEROLE

A simple pork dish, served in the casserole in which it is cooked, this is a good family lunch which can be made with inexpensive cuts of pork.

4 servings

Metric/Imperial

1kg (2lb) lean pork
2 medium-sized onions, chopped
½ teaspoon dried sage
½ teaspoon salt
¼ teaspoon black pepper
2 medium-sized cooking apples, peeled, cored and thinly sliced
3 tablespoons water
675g (1½lb) potatoes, peeled
2 tablespoons hot milk
40g (1½oz) butter

American

2lb lean pork
2 medium-sized onions, chopped
½ teaspoon dried sage
½ teaspoon salt
¼ teaspoon black pepper
2 medium-sized tart green apples, peeled, cored and thinly sliced
3 tablespoons water
1½lb potatoes, peeled
2 tablespoons hot milk
1 tablespoon butter, cut into pieces

Preheat the oven to warm (170°C/325°F or Gas Mark 3).

Remove any excess fat from the pork, then cut it into cubes. Grease a large ovenproof casserole.

Put the onions, sage, salt and pepper in a mixing bowl and stir to mix.

Into the casserole place about one-third of the pork cubes. Cover them with one-half of the onion mixture and then with half of the sliced apples. Continue to fill the casserole with the remaining pork, onions and apples finishing with a layer of pork. Add the water.

A popular Hungarian dish, Goulash is delicious topped with sour cream.

Cover the casserole and cook for 2 to 2½ hours or until the pork is tender.

About 30 minutes before the pork is cooked, boil the potatoes, drain and mash with the milk and most of the butter.

When the pork is cooked, spread the potato over it, roughening the surface into small peaks. Dot with small pieces of butter and return the casserole to the oven for 15 minutes, or until the potato topping is golden brown.

BEEF CASSEROLE

A simple but satisfying dish to serve at lunch or dinner, Beef Casserole may be accompanied by lightly buttered rice or creamed potatoes and a root vegetable.

4 servings

Metric/Imperial

4 tablespoons cooking oil
1kg (2lb) stewing beef cut into cubes
16 small onions, peeled
8 small carrots, scraped
8 small white turnips, peeled
6 celery stalks, roughly chopped
100g (4oz) mushrooms, washed
1 teaspoon paprika
1 tablespoon tomato purée
2 tablespoons flour

$\frac{3}{4}$ litre (1$\frac{1}{4}$ pints) beef stock
1 bay leaf
1 teaspoon salt
$\frac{1}{2}$ teaspoon black pepper

American

4 tablespoons cooking oil
2lb rump or boneless chuck of beef, cubed
16 small onions, peeled
8 small carrots, scraped
8 small white turnips, peeled
6 celery stalks, roughly chopped
$\frac{1}{4}$lb mushrooms, washed
1 teaspoon paprika
1 tablespoon tomato paste
2 tablespoons flour

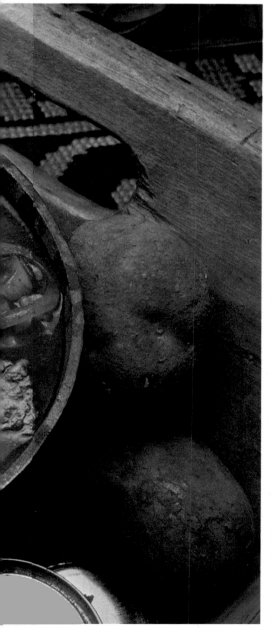

3 cups beef stock
1 bay leaf
1 teaspoon salt
$\frac{1}{2}$ teaspoon black pepper

Put 2 tablespoons oil in a large, flameproof casserole over moderate heat. Add the beef cubes a few at a time and brown them well on all sides, set aside on a plate.

Heat the rest of the oil in the casserole, put in the onions, carrots, turnips and celery, and sauté stirring occasionally, until they are brown. Add the mushrooms and cook for 2 minutes.

Remove the casserole from the heat and stir in the paprika, purée and flour. Stirring continuously, add the stock, and bay leaf. Return the pan to the heat and bring to the boil. Add the salt and pepper.

Return the meat to the casserole, cover and simmer over low heat for 1$\frac{1}{2}$ to 2 hours, or until the meat is tender.

GOULASH

A simple, easy-to-make stew, Goulash is flavoured with paprika and sour cream. Serve with noodles.

4 servings

Metric/Imperial

40g (1$\frac{1}{2}$oz) butter
2 tablespoons vegetable oil
1kg (2lb) stewing steak, cut into cubes
500g (1lb) onions, sliced
1 garlic clove, crushed
2 tablespoons paprika
1 teaspoon salt
$\frac{1}{2}$ teaspoon black pepper
150ml (5 fl oz) water
1 bay leaf
500g (1lb) potatoes, peeled and sliced
150ml (5 fl oz) sour cream

American

3 tablespoons butter
2 tablespoons vegetable oil
2lb beef shinbone or round steak, cubed
1lb onions, sliced
1 garlic clove, crushed
2 tablespoons paprika

1 teaspon salt
$\frac{1}{2}$ teaspoon black pepper
$\frac{5}{8}$ cup water
1 bay leaf
1lb potatoes, peeled and sliced
$\frac{5}{8}$ cup sour cream

In a large saucepan, melt the butter with the oil over moderately high heat. When the foam subsides, reduce the heat to moderate. Add the beef cubes, a few at a time, and fry them quickly, stirring frequently, for 3 to 4 minutes, or until brown on all sides. Set aside.

Add the onions to the pan and fry, stirring occasionally, for 8 to 10 minutes, or until golden brown.

Stir in the garlic, paprika, salt and pepper. Add the beef, the water and the bay leaf and stir to mix. When the stew comes to the boil, cover the pan, reduce the heat and simmer for 1 hour.

Add the potatoes and simmer for another hour.

Taste and add more salt and pepper if necessary. Remove the bay leaf and spoon over the sour cream.

FLEMISH BEEF STEW

For a special occasion why not try this beef stew made with beer? It is one of Belgium's classic dishes.

4 servings

Metric/Imperial

50g (2oz) flour
1 teaspoon salt
$\frac{1}{4}$ teaspoon black pepper
1kg (2lb) chuck steak, cut into cubes
4 tablespoons vegetable oil
6 medium-sized onions, thinly sliced
2 garlic cloves, chopped
500ml (18 fl oz) beer
1 tablespoon brown sugar
1 bouquet garni

American

$\frac{1}{2}$ cup flour
1 teaspoon salt
$\frac{1}{4}$ teaspoon black pepper
2lb beef shoulder or chuck, cubed
4 tablespoons vegetable oil
6 medium-sized onions, thinly sliced
2 garlic cloves, chopped

2¼ cups beer
1 tablespoon brown sugar
1 bouquet garni

Sift the flour, salt and pepper into a mixing bowl. Roll the cubes in the seasoned flour until well coated.

In a flameproof casserole heat the oil over moderate heat. Add the meat cubes a few at a time and brown on all sides. Set aside on a plate.

Add the onions and garlic to the pan and fry for 8 to 10 minutes or until soft and translucent but not brown. Add more oil if necessary. Return the meat to the casserole and add the beer, sugar and bouquet garni.

Cover the casserole, reduce the heat and simmer gently for about 2 hours, or until the meat is tender. (After 1½ hours cooking, remove the lid and simmer the stew uncovered for the remaining 30 minutes. This will reduce the liquid slightly.)

HOT POT

A traditional English dish, Hot Pot makes a simple but warming and satisfying meal, especially on a cold day. Serve with buttered green beans or peas.

4 servings

Metric/Imperial

1kg (2lb) topside of beef, trimmed and cut into large cubes
1 teaspoon salt
¼ teaspoon black pepper
350g (12oz) carrots, scraped and thickly sliced
2 large onions, thickly sliced
750g (1½lb) potatoes, peeled and thickly sliced
600ml (1 pint) beef stock

American

2lb top round of beef, trimmed and cut into large cubes
1 teaspoon salt
¼ teaspoon black pepper
¾lb carrots, scraped and thickly sliced
2 large onions, thickly sliced
1½lb potatoes, peeled and thickly sliced
2½ cups beef stock

Preheat the oven to warm (170°C/325°F or Gas Mark 3).

Arrange a layer of beef in an overproof casserole. Sprinkle over a little of the salt and pepper and top with a layer of carrots, onions and potatoes. Continue making layers until all the ingredients have been used, ending with a layer of potatoes, arranged in overlapping slices.

Pour in the stock. Cover and bake for 2 to 2½ hours, or until the meat is tender.

Increase the oven temperature to fairly hot (200°C/400°F or Gas Mark 6). Remove the lid and cook for a further 30 minutes or until the top layer of potatoes is browned.

SWISS STEAK

An inexpensive and tasty dish of succulent steak served in a simple sauce, Swiss Steak tastes excellent with creamed potatoes and a crisp green salad.

4 servings

Metric/Imperial

50g (2oz) flour seasoned with
 1 teaspoon salt, ½ teaspoon black pepper and ¼ teaspoon celery salt
1kg (2lb) chuck steak, cut into pieces
25g (1oz) butter
2 tablespoons vegetable oil
2 medium-sized onions, finely chopped
4 spring onions, trimmed and finely chopped
4 carrots, scraped and finely chopped
4 celery stalks, trimmed and finely chopped
4 medium-sized tomatoes, peeled and finely chopped
225ml (8 fl oz) tomato juice
225ml (8 fl oz) beef stock

American

½ cup flour seasoned with 1 teaspoon salt, ½ teaspoon black pepper and ¼ teaspoon celery salt
2lb chuck or round steak, cut into pieces
2 tablespoons butter
2 tablespoons vegetable oil
2 medium-sized onions, finely chopped

4 scallions, trimmed and finely chopped
4 carrots, scraped and finely chopped
4 celery stalks, trimmed and finely chopped
4 medium-sized tomatoes, peeled and finely chopped
1 cup tomato juice
1 cup beef stock

Preheat the oven to cool (150°C/300°F or Gas Mark 2).

Place the seasoned flour on a plate and press the steak cubes, a few at a time, in it to coat them thoroughly. Shake off any excess.

In a medium-sized flameproof casserole, melt the butter with the oil over moderate heat. When the foam subsides, add the meat and fry for 5 minutes, stirring frequently. Add the vegetables and fry for 2 minutes, stirring frequently. Pour over the tomato juice and beef stock and bring to the boil. Cover the casserole, and place it in the centre of the oven.

Cook for 1½ to 2 hours or until the meat is tender. Transfer the meat and vegetables to a warmed serving dish and keep hot while you prepare the sauce.

Strain the cooking juices in the casserole into a saucepan. Place over high heat and bring the sauce to the boil. Boil for 5 to 8 minutes or until the sauce has reduced by about one-third and thickened slightly. Pour over the steak and vegetables.

WELSH STEW

Wholesome and thoroughly delicious, Welsh Stew contains beef, bacon and a host of vegetables. It needs no accompaniment.

4-6 servings

Metric/Imperial

25g (1oz) butter

Filling and warming Hot Pot is a favourite English stew with layers of beef, carrots, onions and potatoes—perfect on a cold day.

250g (8oz) lean bacon, rinds removed and chopped
675g (1½lb) stewing steak, cut into chunks
2 large carrots, scraped and sliced
1 parsnip, peeled and chopped
1 large swede, peeled and chopped
3 large potatoes, peeled and sliced
1 medium-sized cabbage, washed and shredded
1 teaspoon salt
1 teaspoon freshly ground black pepper
6 bay leaves
2 teaspoons dried thyme
600ml (1 pint) beef stock
50g (2oz) fine oatmeal
3 leeks, white part only, trimmed and finely chopped

American

2 tablespoons butter
½lb bacon, chopped
1½lb boneless round steak, cut into chunks
2 large carrots, scraped and sliced
1 parsnip, peeled and chopped
1 large rutabaga, peeled and chopped
3 large potatoes, peeled and sliced
1 medium-sized cabbage, washed and shredded
1 teaspoon salt
1 teaspoon freshly ground black pepper
6 bay leaves
2 teaspoons dried thyme
2½ cups beef stock
½ cup fine oatmeal
3 leeks, white part only, trimmed and finely chopped

In a large flameproof casserole, melt the butter over moderate heat. When the foam subsides add the bacon and steak and cook, stirring frequently, for 6 to 8 minutes or until the meat is slightly browned all over. Add all the vegetables except the leeks. Season with the salt and pepper and all the bay leaves and thyme.

Pour over the beef stock and bring to

A warming, meaty dish, Jamaican Casserole is very easy to make. Serve with garlic bread and a crisp green salad for an informal meal.

the boil. Reduce the heat and simmer for 2 hours.

Stir in the oatmeal and leeks, cover and continue cooking for 30 minutes.

JAMAICAN CASSEROLE

Here is a nice spicy casserole guaranteed to appeal to healthy appetites.

6 servings

Metric/Imperial

50g (2oz) flour seasoned with 1 teaspoon salt and ½ teaspoon black pepper
1.25g (3lb) stewing steak, cut into cubes
50g (2oz) butter
4 tablespoons vegetable oil
2 onions, thinly sliced
1 green chilli, seeded and finely chopped
1 garlic clove, chopped
1 teaspoon ground ginger
396g (14oz) can tomatoes, coarsely chopped
½ teaspoon dried thyme

American

½ cup flour seasoned with 1 teaspoon salt and ½ teaspoon black pepper
3lb chuck steak, cubed
¼ cup butter
4 tablespoons vegetable oil
2 onions, thinly sliced
1 green chili pepper, seeded and finely chopped
1 garlic clove, chopped
1 teaspoon ground ginger
1 x 14 oz can tomatoes, coarsely chopped
½ teaspoon dried thyme

Put the seasoned flour on a plate and roll the meat cubes in it to coat them thoroughly on all sides.

In a medium-sized flameproof casserole, melt the butter with the oil over moderate heat. When the foam subsides, add the meat and cook, turning occasionally, for 5 minutes, or until lightly browned on all sides. Set aside.

Add the onions, chilli, garlic and ginger to the pan. Stir well and fry, stirring occasionally, for 5 to 7 minutes or until the onions are soft.

Return the meat to the casserole and add the tomatoes and the thyme. Cover and simmer gently for 3 hours, or until the meat is tender.

OVEN BEEF CASSEROLE

A marvellously sustaining dish, Oven Beef Casserole makes an excellent family dinner. Serve with a green salad.

4 servings

Metric/Imperial

1kg (2lb) stewing beef, cut into large cubes
50g (2oz) flour seasoned with 1 teaspoon salt and ½ teaspoon black pepper
50g (2oz) butter
2 tablespoons vegetable oil
2 medium-sized onions, sliced
1 garlic clove, crushed
3 medium-sized carrots, scraped and chopped
3 celery stalks, trimmed and chopped
300ml (10 fl oz) beef stock
3 medium-sized potatoes, peeled and quartered
1 tablespoon lemon juice
1 teaspoon salt
½ teaspoon black pepper
1 teaspoon dried thyme

American

2lb beef, shoulder or chuck cut into large cubes
½ cup flour seasoned with 1 teaspoon salt and ½ teaspoon black pepper
¼ cup butter
2 tablespoons vegetable oil
2 medium-sized onions, sliced
1 garlic clove, crushed
3 medium-sized carrots, scraped and chopped
3 celery stalks, trimmed and chopped
1¼ cups beef stock
3 medium-sized potatoes, peeled and quartered
1 tablespoon lemon juice
1 teaspoon salt
½ teaspoon black pepper
1 teaspoon dried thyme

Roll the beef cubes in the seasoned flour and set aside.

In a large flameproof casserole, melt the butter with the oil over moderate heat. When the foam subsides add the beef cubes and fry, turning occasionally, for 5 to 8 minutes or until lightly and evenly browned. Transfer to a plate and set aside.

Preheat the oven to moderate (180°C/350°F or Gas Mark 4).

Add the onions and garlic to the casserole and cook, stirring occasionally, for 5 to 7 minutes or until soft and translucent but not brown. Add the carrots and celery and cook, stirring occasionally, for a further 3 minutes or until slightly browned.

Return the meat to the casserole. Pour in the stock and bring to the boil stirring occasionally. Add the potatoes and stir in the lemon juice, salt, pepper and thyme. Cover and cook for 1½ to 2 hours or until the beef is tender.

OXTAIL CASSEROLE

A rich dish, Oxtail Casserole is full of vegetables and may be served as a lunch dish or for a family meal. Serve with rice or mashed potatoes.

---

4 servings

Metric/Imperial

---

2 tablespoons vegetable oil
1 oxtail, skinned and cut into pieces
2 medium-sized onions, sliced
2 large carrots, scraped and sliced
4 medium-sized potatoes, peeled and thinly sliced
1 leek, trimmed and sliced
100g (4oz) mushrooms, wiped clean and sliced
2 bouquet garni
1 teaspoon salt
½ teaspoon black pepper
¼ teaspoon celery salt
½ teaspoon dried thyme
½ teaspoon dried marjoram
½ teaspoon Worcestershire sauce
1 tablespoon lemon juice
2 tablespoons tomato purée
1¾ litres (3 pints) beef stock or water

American

---

2 tablespoons vegetable oil
1 oxtail, skinned and joints separated
2 medium-sized onions, sliced
2 large carrots, scraped and sliced
4 medium-sized potatoes, peeled and thinly sliced
1 leek, trimmed and sliced
¼lb raw mushrooms, wiped clean and sliced
2 bouquet garni
1 teaspoon salt
½ teaspoon black pepper
¼ teaspoon celery salt
½ teaspoon dried thyme
½ teaspoon dried marjoram
½ teaspoon Worcestershire sauce
1 tablespoon lemon juice
2 tablespoons tomato paste
7½ cups beef stock or water

Preheat the oven to cool (150°C/300°F or Gas Mark 2).

In a large frying-pan, heat the oil over moderate heat. Add the oxtail pieces and cook, turning occasionally, for 5 minutes or until evenly browned. Transfer to a large ovenproof casserole.

Add the onions and carrots to the pan and cook, stirring occasionally, for 8 to 10 minutes or until the onions are golden brown. Remove the pan from the heat and, using a slotted spoon, transfer the onions and carrots to the casserole.

Add the remaining ingredients and stir well to mix. Bake for 4 hours or until the meat is very tender and comes away from the bones.

Let the casserole cool completely, then place in the refrigerator to chill for at least 8 hours or overnight.

Remove and discard the fat that has risen to the surface. Reheat in a moderate oven (180°C/350°F or Gas Mark 4) for 30 minutes.

SEAMEN'S STEW

Seamen's Stew is a delicious and filling stew for hearty male appetites. It may be accompanied by a mixed or green salad and lots of chilled lager or beer for the adults.

---

4 servings

Metric/Imperial

75g (3oz) butter

A substantial dish for a winter dinner, Oxtail Casserole is cooked in rich beef stock with onions, carrots, turnips and celery.

1kg (2lb) rump steak, cut into large chunks
1½ teaspoons salt
1 teaspoon black pepper
2 large onions, sliced
2 garlic cloves, crushed
1kg (2lb) potatoes, peeled and thinly sliced
300ml (10 fl oz) pale beer
2 bay leaves

American

¼ cup butter

2lb rump steak, cut into large chunks

1½ teaspoons salt

1 teaspoon black pepper

2 large onions, sliced

2 garlic cloves, crushed

2lb potatoes, peeled and thinly sliced

1¼ cups beer

2 bay leaves

Preheat the oven to moderate (180°C/350°F or Gas Mark 4).

In a large frying-pan, melt one-third of the butter over moderate heat. When the foam subsides add half the steak pieces and a ½ teaspoon of salt and pepper. Cook for 2 to 3 minutes on each side or until lightly browned all over. Remove from the pan and keep warm while you brown the remaining pieces in the same way, using another one-third of the butter, ½ teaspoon of salt and pepper. Remove from the pan.

Melt the remaining butter in the frying-pan. When the foam subsides add the onions and garlic and fry, stirring occasionally for 5 to 6 minutes or until soft and translucent but not brown. Remove the pan from the heat.

Arrange one-third of the potatoes on the bottom of a large, heatproof casserole and sprinkle over one-third of the remaining salt. Place half the steak on top. Lift half the onions and garlic out of the frying-pan and arrange over the meat. Repeat the process until all the ingredients are used up, ending with a layer of potatoes.

Add the beer to the frying-pan and place the pan over high heat. Bring the liquid to the boil, scraping with a wooden spoon to dislodge any sediment sticking to the bottom of the pan. Pour the liquid into the casserole. Add the bay leaves, cover and cook for 1 to 1¼ hours or until the meat is tender.

CABBAGE AND SAUSAGE CASSEROLE

A satisfying main dish which is bound to be popular with children. Cabbage and Sausage Casserole is economical and easy to prepare.

4 servings

Metric/Imperial

250g (8oz) lean bacon, sliced
1 medium-sized green cabbage, washed, quartered and cored
1 onion, sliced
1 small turnip, chopped
½ teaspoon salt
½ teaspoon black pepper
225ml (8 fl oz) beef stock
¼ teaspoon caraway seeds (optional)
500g (1lb) pork sausages

American

½lb bacon
1 medium-sized green cabbage, washed, quartered and cored
1 onion, sliced
1 small turnip, sliced
½ teaspoon salt
½ teaspoon black pepper
1 cup beef stock
¼ teaspoon caraway seeds (optional)
1lb sausages

Preheat the oven to moderate (180°C/350°F or Gas Mark 4).

Line a large, ovenproof casserole with the bacon slices. Put in the cabbage quarters, onion, turnip, salt, pepper, stock and caraway seeds if used. Place the sausages on top.

Bake the casserole in the oven for 1 hour, or until the cabbage is tender.

CODDLE

A traditional Saturday night Irish supper dish, Coddle is tasty sausage, ham, onion and potato casserole. It may be served with cabbage or Brussels sprouts.

4 servings

Metric/Imperial

1 litre (2 pints) beef stock

8 pork sausages
8 thick slices of ham, diced
3 large onions, thinly sliced
2 tomatoes, sliced
1kg (2lb) potatoes, peeled and sliced
½ teaspoon salt
¼ teaspoon black pepper

American

5 cups beef stock
8 sausages
8 thick slices of ham, diced
3 large onions, thinly sliced
2 tomatoes, sliced
2lb potatoes, peeled and sliced
½ teaspoon salt
¼ teaspoon black pepper

Preheat the oven to warm (170°C/325°F or Gas Mark 3).

In a large saucepan, bring the stock to the boil over high heat. Add the sausages and ham and cook for 5 minutes.

Remove the pan from the heat, drain off the stock.

In a medium-sized casserole, arrange the meats in a layer with the onions. Top with a layer of the tomatoes. Spread the potato slices over the mixture. Sprinkle with the salt and pepper and pour in enough of the reserved stock to almost cover the potatoes.

Place a sheet of greaseproof or waxed paper over the top of the casserole and cover with the lid. Bake for 1½ hours, or until the liquid has reduced by half and the vegetables are tender.

FRANKFURTER STEW

This attractive dish tastes just as good as it looks. Ideal for a family supper, it may be accompanied by buttered noodles or mashed potatoes.

4 servings

Metric/Imperial

4 tablespoons vegetable oil
3 medium-sized onions, chopped
1 garlic clove, chopped
2 medium-sized green peppers, white pith removed, seeded and sliced
1 medium-sized red pepper, white pith removed, seeded and sliced
396g (14oz) can tomatoes
1 teaspoon salt
½ teaspoon black pepper
½ teaspoon chilli powder
1½ tablespoons paprika
500g (1lb) frankfurters, cooked and thickly sliced

American

4 tablespoons vegetable oil
3 medium-sized onions, chopped
1 garlic clove, chopped
2 medium-sized green peppers, membrane and seeds removed, sliced
1 medium-sized red pepper, membrane and seeds removed, sliced

1 x 14oz can tomatoes
1 teaspoon salt
½ teaspoon black pepper
½ teaspoon chili powder
1½ tablespoons paprika
1lb frankfurters, cooked and thickly
   sliced

In a large, deep frying-pan, heat the oil over moderate heat. Add the onions and garlic and fry, stirring occasionally, for 8 to 10 minutes, or until golden brown.

Add the green and red peppers and fry for a further 5 minutes, stirring frequently.

Add the tomatoes, salt, pepper, chilli powder and paprika. Cover the pan, reduce the heat and simmer for 25 minutes, stirring occasionally. Add the frankfurters and simmer for a further 10 minutes.

SAUSAGE AND LEEK CASSEROLE

This delicious, economical dish is an adaptation of a traditional Swiss recipe. Served as a warming family supper it needs no accompaniment apart from crusty bread and butter.

6-8 servings

Metric/Imperial

100g (4oz) butter or margarine
5 large leeks, trimmed, cleaned and
   cut into short lengths
750g (1½lb) sausages, halved
1 teaspoon salt
1½ teaspoons black pepper
1 teaspoon dried thyme
6 tablespoons flour
600ml (1 pint) milk

Frankfurter Stew is an exotic-looking dish made from sausages, peppers and tomatoes. Serve with buttered noodles or potatoes.

175g (6oz) Cheddar cheese, grated
2 teaspoons Worcestershire sauce
1 teaspoon dry mustard
125g (5oz) tomato purée
500g (1lb) small macaroni, cooked and drained

American

½ cup butter or margarine
5 large leeks, trimmed, cleaned and cut into short lengths
1¼ lb sausages, halved
1 teaspoon salt
1½ teaspoons black pepper
1 teaspoon dried thyme
6 tablespoons flour
2½ cups milk
1½ cups Cheddar cheese, grated
2 teaspoons Worcestershire sauce
1 teaspoon dry mustard

Paprika, Vegetable and Sausage Stew is an especially tasty and decorative lunch dish.

⅝ cup tomato paste
4 cups small macaroni, cooked and drained

Preheat the oven to moderate (180°C/350°F or Gas Mark 4).

In a large frying-pan, melt half the butter or margarine over moderate heat. When the foam subsides add the leeks and sausages and fry, stirring and turning occasionally, for 8 to 10 minutes or until the leeks are golden brown. Remove the pan from the heat and stir in the salt, pepper and thyme.

In a medium-sized saucepan, melt the remaining butter or margarine over moderate heat. Remove the pan from the heat and, using a wooden spoon, stir in the flour to form a smooth paste. Gradually add the milk, stirring constantly and being careful to avoid lumps. Return the pan to the heat and cook, stirring constantly, for 2 to 3 minutes or until the sauce is thick and smooth. Add two-thirds of the grated cheese and

cook, stirring constantly, until it has dissolved into the sauce. Remove the pan from the heat and stir in the Worcestershire sauce, mustard and tomato purée.

Put half of the cooked macaroni into a large, ovenproof baking dish. Cover with the sausage and leek mixture and top with the remaining macaroni. Pour over the cheese sauce and sprinkle with the remaining grated cheese. Bake for 20 to 30 minutes or until the top is brown and bubbling.

PAPRIKA, VEGETABLE AND SAUSAGE STEW

A tasty adaptation of a traditional Hungarian dish, Paprika, Vegetable and Sausage Stew is a quick and simple casserole to prepare. Serve it with lots of crusty bread.

4 servings

Metric/Imperial

3 tablespoons vegetable oil
2 medium-sized onions, finely
    chopped
2 garlic cloves, crushed
1 medium-sized green pepper, white
    pith removed, seeded and coarsely
    chopped
1 medium-sized red pepper, white
    pith removed, seeded and coarsely
    chopped
1 tablespoon paprika
½ teaspoon salt
¼ teaspoon black pepper
½ teaspoon dried dill
396g (14oz) can tomatoes
500g (1lb) potatoes, cooked and sliced
250g (8oz) garlic sausage, chopped
150ml (5 fl oz) sour cream

American

¼ cup vegetable oil
2 medium-sized onions, finely chopped
2 garlic cloves, crushed
1 medium-sized green pepper,
    membrane and seeds removed,
    coarsely chopped
1 medium-sized red pepper,
    membrane and seeds removed,
    coarsely chopped
1 tablespoon paprika
½ teaspoon salt
¼ teaspoon black pepper
½ teaspoon dried dill leaf or ¼ teaspoon
    dill seeds
1 x 14oz can tomatoes
2 cups potatoes, cooked and sliced
½lb garlic sausage, diced
⅝ cup sour cream

In a medium-sized flameproof casserole, heat the oil over moderate heat. Add the onions and garlic and cook, stirring occasionally, for 5 to 7 minutes or until soft and translucent but not brown. Add the green and red peppers and cook, stirring occasionally, for a further 5 minutes.

Lower the heat and stir in the paprika, salt, pepper, dill and tomatoes mixing well to blend. Simmer for 25 to 30 minutes or until the vegetables are tender. Stir in the potatoes, sausage and sour cream and simmer for a further 5 minutes or until the potatoes and sausage are heated through.

IRISH STEW

Irish Stew is a traditional dish eaten all over Great Britain. It may be served alone or accompanied by pickled cabbage.

4-6 servings

Metric/Imperial

12 lamb cutlets, from the scrag or
    middle neck
1.25g (3lb) potatoes, peeled and sliced
500g (1lb) onions, thickly sliced
1 teaspoon salt
½ teaspoon black pepper
1 teaspoon dried thyme
450ml (16 fl oz) cold water

American

6 lamb neck slices or 1½lb stewing
    lamb
3lb potatoes, peeled and sliced
1lb onions, thickly sliced
1 teaspoon salt
½ teaspoon black pepper
1 teaspoon dried thyme
2 cups cold water

Trim as much fat as possible from the cutlets.

Arrange a layer of potato slices on the bottom of a large heavy-bottomed saucepan. Cover with a layer of onions and then meat.

Sprinkle with a little of the salt, pepper and thyme.

Continue making layers until all the ingredients are used up, ending with a layer of potatoes.

Pour in the water and place the pan over moderately high heat. Bring to the boil. Reduce the heat and tightly cover the pan. Simmer gently for 2 to 2½ hours or until the lamb cutlets are tender. (Shake the pan occasionally to ensure that the potatoes do not stick to the bottom.)

HOTCH-POTCH

An economical and filling dish, Hotch Potch is an ideal dinner dish to feed a hungry family.

4 servings

Metric/Imperial

1kg (2lb) lean shoulder of lamb, cut
    into large cubes
1¾ litres (3 pints) water
1 teaspoon salt
½ teaspoon black pepper
1 bouquet garni
2 medium-sized onions, finely chopped
4 large carrots, scraped and chopped
2 large potatoes, peeled and diced
1 turnip, peeled and diced
250g (8oz) runner beans, roughly
    trimmed and chopped
250g (8oz) fresh peas, shelled

American

2lb lean shoulder of lamb, cut into
    large cubes
7½ cups water
1 teaspoon salt
½ teaspoon black pepper
1 bouquet garni
2 medium-sized onions, finely chopped
4 large carrots, scraped and chopped
2 large potatoes, peeled and diced
1 turnip, peeled and diced
1 cup string beans, trimmed and
    roughly chopped
1 cup fresh peas, shelled

Place the meat in a large saucepan and pour over the water. Add the salt and pepper. Bring the water to the boil, reduce the heat, add the bouquet garni and simmer for 30 minutes.

Add the onions, carrots, potatoes and turnip and simmer the mixture for 1 hour.

Add the beans and peas and continue to cook for a further 30 minutes.

LAMB WITH APPLES

The addition of tart apples to lamb gives this dish a piquant flavour.

3-4 servings

Metric/Imperial

1kg (2lb) middle neck of lamb
25g (1oz) butter
2 medium-sized onions, thinly sliced
2 large cooking apples, peeled, cored
    and chopped
1 tablespoon brown sugar

½ teaspoon salt
¼ teaspoon black pepper
2 teaspoons lemon juice
1 tablespoon raisins

American

2lb lamb neck slices
2 tablespoons butter
2 medium-sized onions, thinly sliced
2 large tart apples, peeled, cored and
   chopped
1 tablespoon brown sugar
½ teaspoon salt
¼ teaspoon black pepper
2 teaspoons lemon juice
1 tablespoon raisins

Preheat the oven to warm (170°C/
325°F or Gas Mark 3).

Remove all excess fat from the lamb
and cut the meat and bones into neat
pieces.

In a small frying-pan melt the butter
over moderate heat. When the foam
subsides, add the onions and cook,
stirring occasionally, for 5 to 7 minutes,
or until soft and translucent but not
brown. Place half of them in an ovenproof casserole. Add the meat and
cover with the remainder. Add the
apples and sprinkle the sugar, salt,
pepper, lemon juice and raisins over
the top.

A warming, winter dish, Lamb Hot
Pot is tasty, economical and ideal
for a family lunch or supper.

Cover and cook for 1½ hours or until
the meat is very tender.

LAMB HOT POT

This tasty, easy-to-make Lamb Hot
Pot is a satisfying dish to serve for a
family lunch or supper.

4 servings

50

Metric/Imperial

1 tablespoon vegetable oil

4 large lamb chops

1 medium-sized green cabbage, coarsely shredded

1 teaspoon salt

¼ teaspoon black pepper

½ teaspoon dried rosemary

125g (5oz) tomato purée

3 tablespoons water

American

1 tablespoon vegetable oil

4 rib or shoulder lamb chops

1 medium-sized green cabbage, coarsely shredded

1 teaspoon salt

¼ teaspoon black pepper

½ teaspoon dried rosemary

⅝ cup tomato purée or paste

¼ cup water

In a large saucepan, heat the oil over moderate heat and brown the chops for 3 minutes on both sides. Add the remaining ingredients and stir well.

Reduce the heat to low and cook for 45 minutes, or until the meat is tender when pierced with a fork.

LANCASHIRE HOT POT

Lancashire Hot Pot is one of the great British dishes. Traditionally it was cooked in a tall earthenware hot-pot. It is equally delicious cooked in an ovenproof casserole.

4 servings

Metric/Imperial

675g (1½lb) potatoes, peeled and thickly sliced

1½ teaspoons salt

675g (1½lb) middle neck of lamb

100g (4oz) mushrooms, wiped clean and sliced

4 lamb's kidneys, prepared and sliced

1 large onion, sliced

½ teaspoon black pepper

1 teaspoon dried thyme

300ml (10 fl oz) beef stock

American

1½lb potatoes, peeled and thickly sliced

1½ teaspoons salt

8 small lamb chops, trimmed of excess fat

¼lb mushrooms, wiped clean and sliced

4 lamb kidneys, skinned and sliced, membrane removed

1 large onion, sliced

½ teaspoon black pepper

1 teaspoon dried thyme

1¼ cups beef stock

Preheat the oven to moderate (180°C/350°F or Gas Mark 4).

Cover the bottom of a deep ovenproof casserole with a layer of half the potatoes. Sprinkle over ¼ teaspoon of salt. Arrange the meat on top and cover with the mushrooms, kidneys and onion.

Sprinkle over 1 teaspoon of the salt, the pepper and thyme. Cover with the remaining potatoes. Pour in the stock and sprinkle the remaining salt on top.

Cover the casserole and cook for 2 hours. Remove the lid and increase the heat to fairly hot (200°C/400°F or Gas Mark 6). Cook for a further 30 minutes, or until the potatoes are golden brown.

Tasty and substantial Lancashire Hot Pot is made with lamb, kidneys and vegetables.

LAMB AND VEGETABLE CASSEROLE

This is a Jewish dish known as Tzimmis (sim-miss), traditionally prepared by Orthodox Jews during the day before Sabbath when, by rabbinical law, they are not allowed to cook. It can be left to simmer in a very slow oven for up to 24 hours, although we have, for convenience, speeded up the cooking process. Working wives might find it convenient to leave the casserole in a low oven to cook while they are at work.

6 servings

Metric/Imperial

1 whole breast of lamb, trimmed of excess fat and cut into 6 pieces
1kg (2lb) carrots, scraped and sliced
500g (1lb) white turnips, peeled and cubed
500g (1lb) potatoes, peeled and cubed
500g (1lb) butter beans, soaked overnight in cold water and drained
1 teaspoon sugar
300ml (10 fl oz) golden syrup
175ml (6 fl oz) water

American

1 whole breast of lamb, trimmed of excess fat and cut into 6 pieces
2lb carrots, scraped and sliced
1lb white turnips, peeled and cubed
1lb potatoes, peeled and diced
$2\frac{1}{3}$ cups dry lima beans, soaked overnight in cold water and drained
1 teaspoon sugar
$1\frac{1}{4}$ cups light corn syrup
$\frac{3}{4}$ cup water

In a very large flameproof casserole, combine the lamb and vegetables. Add the sugar and pour over the golden [light corn] syrup. Pour in the water and stir well to mix.

Place the casserole over moderate heat and bring the mixture to the boil. Reduce the heat, cover and simmer for 1 hour.

Preheat the oven to warm (170°C/ 325°F or Gas Mark 3).

Transfer the casserole to the centre of the oven. Cook for 3 hours or until the meat falls away from the bones and the vegetables are very tender.

LOIN OF LAMB WITH TOMATOES AND POTATOES

This easy-to-make casserole may be served with a green vegetable or salad.

4-6 servings

Metric/Imperial

1 tablespoon vegetable oil
25g (1oz) butter
1 x 2kg (1 x 4lb) loin of lamb, chined and trimmed of excess fat
1 large onion, thinly sliced and pushed out into rings
4 large potatoes, peeled and thickly sliced
396g (14oz) can tomatoes
1 teaspoon salt
$\frac{1}{2}$ teaspoon black pepper
1 teaspoon dried thyme

American

1 tablespoon vegetable oil
2 tablespoons butter
4lb boneless loin of lamb, trimmed of excess fat
1 large onion, thinly sliced and separated into rings
4 large potatoes, peeled and thickly sliced
1 x 14oz can tomatoes
1 teaspoon salt
$\frac{1}{2}$ teaspoon black pepper
1 teaspoon dried thyme

In a large heavy flameproof casserole, heat the oil and butter over moderate heat. When the foam subsides, add the lamb and cook, turning occasionally for 8 to 10 minutes, or until it is lightly browned on all sides. Lift out and set aside.

Add the onion to the casserole and fry, stirring occasionally, for 5 minutes. Add the potatoes and fry, stirring occasionally for 5 to 6 minutes, or until lightly browned.

Stir in the tomatoes, salt, pepper and thyme. Cook the mixture, stirring constantly, for 2 to 3 minutes, or until it is hot but not boiling. Reduce the heat, add the lamb and cover the casserole. Simmer for 1 hour or until the meat is tender.

Lift the meat out of the casserole and transfer it to a carving board. Separate

Colourful Lamb and Vegetable Casserole is a rich stew.

into chops and place in a warmed serving dish, together with the potato slices. Keep hot.

Boil the sauce, stirring constantly, for 3 to 4 minutes or until it has reduced slightly. Spoon it over the chops and potatoes.

LAMB AND MUSHROOMS

A simple and nourishing dish, Lamb and Mushrooms makes a delicious family supper. Serve on a bed of rice.

4 servings

Metric/Imperial

50g (2oz) flour seasoned with
  2 teaspoons dried rosemary,
1 teaspoon salt and ½ teaspoon black
  pepper
1kg (2lb) best end of neck of lamb,
  trimmed and cubed
50g (2oz) butter
3 medium-sized onions, thinly sliced
250g (8oz) mushrooms, wiped clean
  and sliced
⅜ teaspoon salt
¼ teaspoon black pepper
150ml (5 fl oz) chicken stock

300ml (10 fl oz) sour cream

American

½ cup flour seasoned with 2 teaspoons
  dried rosemary, 1 teaspoon salt and
  ½ teaspoon black pepper
2lb boned leg of lamb, cubed
¼ cup butter
3 medium-sized onions, thinly sliced
½lb mushrooms, wiped clean and
  sliced

½ teaspoon salt
¼ teaspoon black pepper
½ cup chicken stock
1½ cups sour cream

Place the seasoned flour on a plate. Roll the meat cubes in it, shaking off any excess.

In a large, deep frying-pan, melt the butter over moderate heat. When the foam subsides add the onions and cook, stirring occasionally, for 5 to 7 minutes, or until soft and translucent but not brown.

Add the lamb cubes and cook, stirring and turning occasionally, for 5 minuted, or until lightly and evenly browned.

Add the mushrooms, salt, pepper and chicken stock to the pan, mix well and bring to the boil.

Reduce the heat, cover and cook for 1 to 1½ hours, or until the meat is very tender.

Stir in the sour cream, mix well, and reheat gently.

VEAL STEW

A warming, sustaining dish, veal stew makes a marvellous winter dinner, served with Brussels sprouts and creamy mashed potatoes.

4 servings

Metric/Imperial

1kg (2lb) pie veal cut into large cubes
4 medium-sized potatoes, peeled and sliced
2 medium-sized onions, thinly sliced
2 garlic cloves, crushed
1 teaspoon salt
1 teaspoon black pepper
1 bouquet garni
600ml (1 pint) chicken stock
150 g (5oz) tomato purée
2 teaspoons paprika

One of the great classics of Italian cuisine, Osso Buco is a superb stew of veal knuckle or shank with the meat so tender that it falls off the bones!

American

2lb shoulder or breast of veal, cubed
4 medium-sized potatoes, peeled and sliced
2 medium-sized onions, thinly sliced
2 garlic cloves, crushed
1 teaspoon salt
1 teaspoon black pepper
1 bouquet garni
2½ cups chicken stock
5 tablespoons tomato paste
2 teaspoons paprika

Place about one-third of the veal cubes on the bottom of a flameproof casserole. Cover with a layer of about half of the potato slices, then half of the onions and garlic. Sprinkle over one-third of the salt and pepper and add the bouquet garni. Continue making layers in the same way, ending with a layer of veal cubes sprinkled with the remaining salt and pepper.

In a large jug, combine the chicken stock, tomato purée and paprika, beating with a fork to mix well. Pour into the casserole and bring to the boil. Reduce the heat, cover and simmer for 1½ to 2 hours or until the veal is very tender.

Transfer the veal cubes and vegetables to a large serving dish and pour over some of the cooking liquid.

OSSO BUCO
(Stewed veal knuckle or shank)

One of the internationally recognized classics of Italian cuisine, Osso Buco (awh-soh boo-koh) is made from veal knuckle or shank with a sauce of tomatoes and wine.

The addition of wine may seem extravagant for a family meal but it can make all the difference to dishes made with the cheaper cuts of meat.

6 servings

Metric/Imperial

75g (3oz) flour seasoned with 1 teaspoon salt and ½ teaspoon black pepper
1.25kg (3lb) veal knuckle or shank, sawn into 7cm (3in) pieces

100g (4oz) butter
1 large onion, thinly sliced
396g (14oz) can tomatoes
2 tablespoons tomato purée
175ml (6 fl oz) dry white wine
1 teaspoon salt
½ teaspoon black pepper
1 teaspoon sugar
1 tablespoon finely grated lemon rind
2 garlic cloves, crushed
1½ tablespoons finely chopped fresh parsley

American

¾ cup flour seasoned with 1 teaspoon salt and ½ teaspoon black pepper
3lb fore or hind shank of veal, sawn into 3in pieces
½ cup butter
1 large onion, thinly sliced
1 x 14oz can tomatoes
2 tablespoons tomato paste
¾ cup dry white wine
1 teaspoon salt
½ teaspoon black pepper
1 teaspoon sugar
1 tablespoon finely grated lemon rind
2 garlic cloves, crushed
1½ tablespoons minced fresh parsley

Place the seasoned flour on a large plate and dip in the veal pieces, one by one, to coat them on all sides. Shake off any excess. Set aside.

In a very large flameproof casserole melt the butter over moderate heat. When the foam subsides, add the veal pieces and cook, turning occasionally, for 5 to 8 minutes or until lightly and evenly browned. Transfer to a plate.

Add the onion to the casserole and cook, stirring occasionally, for 5 to 7 minutes or until soft and translucent but not brown. Add the tomatoes and tomato purée and cook, stirring occasionally, for a further 3 minutes. Add the wine and sprinkle over the salt, pepper and sugar. Bring the mixture to the boil.

Return the veal pieces to the casserole and stir well. Reduce the heat, cover and simmer for 1½ to 2 hours or until the veal is so tender it is almost dropping off the bone.

Combine the lemon rind, garlic and parsley and stir into the veal mixture. Cook for a further 1 minute.

CZECHOSLOVAKIAN VEAL RAGOUT

This simple meat casserole is a warming and nourishing dish for a family meal.

4 servings

Metric/Imperial

4 tablespoons flour seasoned with 1 teaspoon salt and ½ teaspoon black pepper
1kg (2lb) boned veal shoulder, cut into large cubes
50g (2oz) butter

2 medium-sized onions, finely chopped
2 teaspoons caraway seeds
225ml (8 fl oz) chicken stock
2 teaspoons paprika
⅛ teaspoon cayenne pepper
175g (6oz) mushrooms, wiped and sliced
150ml (5 fl oz) sour cream

American

4 tablespoons flour seasoned with 1 teaspoon salt and ½ teaspoon black pepper
2lb boned shoulder of veal, cut into large cubes

Czechoslovakian Veal Ragoût makes a tasty family dish.

¼ cup butter
2 medium-sized onions, finely chopped
2 teaspoons caraway seeds
1 cup chicken stock
2 teaspoons paprika
⅛ teaspoon cayenne pepper
2 cups raw mushrooms, wiped and sliced
⅝ cup sour cream

Sprinkle the seasoned flour on to a plate

56

and roll the cubes of meat in it until well coated.

In a large frying-pan, melt the butter over moderate heat. When the foam subsides, add the onions and cook them for 6 minutes or until soft but not brown. Add the meat cubes and the caraway seeds. Cook, stirring occasionally, for 5 minutes. Gradually add the stock to the pan, stirring constantly, and bring to the boil. Reduce the heat and mix in the paprika, cayenne and sliced mushrooms. Cover the pan and simmer for 1 hour, or until the meat is tender.

Just before serving, stir in the sour cream. Taste and add more salt and pepper if necessary.

A delicious mixture of veal and mushrooms, White Meat Casserole may be served with salad.

WHITE MEAT CASSEROLE

A super way to prepare veal, White Meat Casserole is easy to make and tastes simply delicious served with rice and a crisp green salad.

---

6 servings

Metric/Imperial

75g (3oz) butter
1 medium-sized onion, finely chopped
1.25kg (3lb) lean veal, cut into cubes
792g (28 fl oz) canned cream of mushroom soup
1 teaspoon paprika
¼ teaspoon grated nutmeg
1 teaspoon salt
½ teaspoon white pepper
250g (8oz) button mushrooms, wiped clean and halved

American

¼ cup plus 2 tablespoons butter
1 medium-sized onion, finely chopped
3lb lean veal, cubed
3½ cups canned cream of mushroom soup
1 teaspoon paprika
¼ teaspoon grated nutmeg
1 teaspoon salt
½ teaspoon white pepper
½lb small mushrooms, wiped clean and halved

Preheat the oven to moderate (180°C/350°F or Gas Mark 4).

In a large flameproof casserole, melt two-thirds of the butter over moderate heat. When the foam subsides add the onion and fry, stirring occasionally, for 5 to 7 minutes or until soft and translucent but not brown. Add the veal cubes and fry, stirring occasionally, for 6 to 8 minutes or until lightly browned all over. Pour over the soup.

Season the mixture with the paprika, nutmeg, salt and pepper. Cover the casserole, transfer to the oven and cook for 2 hours.

Meanwhile, in a small frying-pan, melt the remaining butter over moderate heat. When the foam subsides add the mushrooms and fry, stirring constantly, for 3 minutes.

Add the mushrooms to the casserole and cook, covered, for a further 30 minutes or until the veal is tender.

KIDNEY CASSEROLE

Kidneys combine with bacon and onions to make a light and tasty main dish. Serve with peas and baked potatoes.

3-4 servings

Metric/Imperial

4 tablespoons flour seasoned with
    1 teaspoon salt and 1 teaspoon black
    pepper
12 lambs' kidneys, cleaned, prepared
    and sliced
8 streaky bacon slices, chopped
25g (1oz) butter
2 onions, sliced
1 garlic clove, crushed
1 green pepper, white pith removed,
    seeded and sliced
1 tablespoon soy sauce
250ml (8 fl oz) beef stock

American

4 tablespoons flour seasoned with
    1 teaspoon salt and 1 teaspoon
    black pepper
12 lamb kidneys, cleaned, skinned
    and sliced
8 slices bacon, chopped
2 tablespoons butter
2 onions, sliced
1 garlic clove, crushed
1 green pepper, membrane and seeds
    removed, sliced
1 tablespoon soy sauce
1 cup beef stock

Preheat the oven to moderate (180°C/ 350°F or Gas Mark 4).

Sprinkle the seasoned flour on a plate and roll the kidney slices in it to coat them all over. Shake off any excess flour and set aside.

Boil the bacon pieces for 5 minutes, drain and dry.

In a large frying-pan, melt the butter over moderate heat. When the foam subsides, add the bacon and fry it, stirring occasionally, for 5 minutes or until lightly browned. Remove to an ovenproof casserole.

Add the onions, garlic and green pepper to the fat remaining in the frying-pan. Fry, stirring occasionally, for 5 to 7 minutes or until the onions are soft and translucent but not brown. Transfer to the casserole.

Add the sliced kidneys to the frying-pan and cook, turning occasionally, for 3 minutes. Transfer to the casserole. Pour the soy sauce and beef stock over, cover and bake for 20 to 25 minutes, or until the kidneys are cooked.

HOT POT OF LIVER, BACON AND APPLE

This simple Hot Pot of Liver, Bacon and Apple makes a satisfying and nourishing family meal. Serve it with mashed potatoes.

4 servings

Metric/Imperial

675g (1½lb) cooking apples, peeled,
    cored and thinly sliced
2 medium-sized onions, thinly sliced
675g (1½lb) lamb's liver, thinly sliced
500g (1lb) tomatoes, blanched, peeled
    and sliced
¼ teaspoon salt
¼ teaspoon black pepper
300ml (10 fl oz) beef stock
4 lean bacon slices, rinds removed

American

1½lb tart apples, peeled, cored and
    thinly sliced
2 medium-sized onions, thinly sliced
1½lb lamb liver, thinly sliced
2 cups tomatoes, blanched, peeled
    and sliced
¼ teaspoon salt
¼ teaspoon black pepper
1¼ cups beef stock
4 slices of bacon

Preheat the oven to moderate (180°C/ 350°F or Gas Mark 4).

Line the bottom of an ovenproof casserole with about one-third of the apple and onion slices. Top with half of the liver slices, then half of the tomato slices and season with half of the salt and pepper. Continue to make layers until all the ingredients have been used up, finishing with a layer of apple and onion slices.

Pour the beef stock over the mixture and lay the bacon slices on top. Bake for 1½ hours or until the liver is tender.

LIVER WITH OLIVES AND MUSHROOMS

Liver casseroled with olives and mushrooms is a delicious and original way to serve liver.

4 servings

Metric/Imperial

1 tablespoon vegetable oil
4 streaky bacon slices, chopped
4 medium-sized onions, finely
    chopped
100g (4oz) mushrooms, wiped clean
    and sliced
40g (1½oz) butter
500g (1lb) pig's liver, trimmed and
    thinly sliced
350ml (12 fl oz) beef stock
1 teaspoon salt
½ teaspoon black pepper
½ teaspoon dried thyme
1 tablespoon cornflour dissolved in
    1 tablespoon water
12 green olives, halved and stoned
juice of ½ lemon

American

1 tablespoon vegetable oil
4 slices bacon, chopped
4 medium-sized onions, finely
    chopped
¼lb mushrooms, wiped clean and
    sliced
3 tablespoons butter
1lb lamb's liver, thinly sliced
1½ cups beef stock
1 teaspoon salt
½ teaspoon black pepper
½ teaspoon dried thyme

1 tablespoon cornstarch dissolved
   in 1 tablespoon water
12 olives, halved and pitted
juice of ½ lemon

Preheat the oven to moderate (180°C/
350°F or Gas Mark 4).

In a medium-sized frying-pan, heat
the vegetable oil over moderate heat.
Add the bacon and cook, stirring and
turning occasionally, for 3 minutes.
Add the onions and cook, stirring
occasionally, for 5 to 7 minutes or until
soft and translucent but not brown.
Stir in the mushrooms and cook,
stirring occasionally for 3 minutes.
Transfer to an ovenproof casserole.

Add the butter to the oil remaining
in the frying-pan and melt it over
moderate heat. When the foam subsides, add the liver and cook, turning

occasionally, for 5 to 6 minutes, or
until the meat is lightly and evenly
browned. Transfer to the casserole.

Pour the stock into the frying-pan
and add the salt, pepper and thyme.
Bring to the boil, stirring and scraping
in any brown bits sticking to the
bottom. Stir in the cornflour [corn-
starch] mixture and cook, stirring
constantly, for 1 minute or until the
liquid has thickened and is smooth.
Pour into the casserole.

Stir in the olives and lemon juice
and bake for 1 to 1¼ hours, or until the
meat is tender.

LIVER CASSEROLE

Liver Casserole is a nourishing dish
suitable for a family supper. It can be

Liver with Olives and Mushrooms
may be served with potatoes.

served on its own or with new potatoes.

4-6 servings

Metric/Imperial

3 tablespoons vegetable oil
500g (1lb) lamb's liver, thinly sliced
2 medium-sized onions, chopped
8 lean bacon slices, diced
250g (8oz) mushrooms, wiped clean
   and sliced
2 celery stalks, trimmed and chopped
1 tablespoon butter
2 tablespoons flour
396g (14oz) can tomatoes
1 teaspoon salt
½ teaspoon black pepper

Liver Italian Style is a tasty combination of lamb's liver, vegetables and herbs.

¼ teaspoon dried rosemary
225ml (8 fl oz) beef stock

American

3 tablespoons vegetable oil
1lb lamb liver, thinly sliced
2 medium-sized onions, chopped
8 slices bacon, diced
½lb mushrooms, wiped clean and sliced
2 celery stalks, trimmed and chopped
1 tablespoon butter
2 tablespoons flour
1 x 14oz can tomatoes
1 teaspoon salt
½ teaspoon black pepper
¼ teaspoon dried rosemary
1 cup beef stock

Preheat the oven to moderate (180°C/350°F or Gas Mark 4).

In a large heavy frying-pan, heat 2 tablespoons of the oil over moderate heat. Add the liver slices and cook for 1 to 2 minutes on each side or until lightly browned. Transfer to an oven-proof casserole.

Add the remaining oil to the pan. When it is hot, add the onions and bacon and fry, stirring frequently, for 5 to 7 minutes or until the onions are soft and translucent but not brown. Add the mushrooms and celery and fry, stirring occasionally, for 3 minutes. Transfer to the casserole.

In the same frying-pan, melt the butter over moderate heat. When the foam subsides, stir in the flour. Cook, stirring, for 1 minute. Add the tomatoes, salt, pepper and rosemary. Pour in the stock. Increase the heat and, stirring constantly, bring to the boil. Pour into the casserole and bake for 30 minutes.

LIVER ITALIAN STYLE

A tasty and nutritious dish, Liver Italian Style is easy to prepare. Serve with boiled rice and a green salad.

4 servings

Metric/Imperial

100g (4oz) butter
2 shallots, finely chopped
2 garlic cloves, crushed
6 spring onions, finely chopped
100g (4oz) mushrooms, wiped clean and sliced
675g (1½lb) lamb's liver, thickly sliced and cut into large pieces
396g (14oz) can peeled tomatoes
2 tablespoons tomato purée
150ml (4 fl oz) beef stock
½ tablespoon vinegar
½ teaspoon salt
¼ teaspoon black pepper
½ teaspoon dried thyme
½ teaspoon dried basil
1 bay leaf

American

½ cup butter
2 shallots, finely chopped
2 garlic cloves, crushed
6 scallions, finely chopped
¼lb mushrooms, wiped clean and sliced
1½lb lamb liver, thickly sliced and cut into large pieces
1 x 14oz can peeled tomatoes
2 tablespoons tomato paste
½ cup beef stock
½ tablespoon vinegar
½ teaspoon salt
¼ teaspoon black pepper
½ teaspoon dried thyme
½ teaspoon dried basil
1 bay leaf

Preheat the oven to moderate (180°C/350°F or Gas Mark 4).

In a large frying-pan, melt half the butter over moderate heat. When the foam subsides, add the shallots, garlic and spring onions [scallions] to the pan and cook, stirring occasionally for 3 to 5 minutes, or until soft and translucent but not brown.

Add the mushrooms and cook stirring occasionally for 4 minutes, or until lightly browned. Transfer to an oven-proof casserole.

Add the remaining butter to the pan and melt it over moderate heat. When the foam subsides add the liver pieces a few at a time, and cook them, stirring and turning occasionally, for 3 to 5 minutes or until lightly and evenly browned. Transfer to the casserole and cook the remaining liver pieces in the same way; transfer.

Add the tomatoes, tomato purée, stock and vinegar to the pan and bring the liquid to the boil, stirring occasionally. Stir in the seasoning and herbs and cook, stirring, for 1 minute.

Pour the mixture over the liver in the casserole and stir well to mix. Bake for 30 to 45 minutes, or until the liver is very tender.

OX TONGUE BRAISED WITH BACON

This is a rich dish, with the taste of the meat so transformed that it will please even those who profess to dislike offal [variety meats]. Serve Ox Tongue Braised with Bacon with a green vegetable and buttered noodles. This dish must be prepared in advance to allow for the soaking of the tongue.

8-10 servings

Metric/Imperial

1 salted ox tongue, soaked for 36 hours, drained, cooked, drained and skinned
6 streaky bacon slices
1 tablespoon butter
1 large onion, chopped
1 garlic clove, crushed
$\frac{1}{4}$ teaspoon salt
$\frac{1}{2}$ teaspoon black pepper
2 tablespoons flour
1 bouquet garni
175ml (6 fl oz) red wine
225ml (8 fl oz) beef stock
8 lean bacon slices, rinds removed
250g (8oz) button mushrooms, wiped clean and sliced

American

1 pickled ox or beef tongue, soaked for 36 hours, drained, cooked, drained and skinned
6 slices bacon
1 tablespoon butter
1 large onion, chopped
1 garlic clove, crushed
$\frac{1}{4}$ teaspoon salt
$\frac{1}{2}$ teaspoon black pepper
2 tablespoons flour
1 bouquet garni
$\frac{3}{4}$ cup red wine
1 cup beef stock
8 slices bacon
$\frac{1}{2}$lb small raw mushrooms, wiped clean and sliced

Place the tongue on a board and cut it into cubes. Discard bones and gristle.

In a large frying-pan, fry the bacon over moderate heat, stirring frequently, for 5 minutes or until it has rendered all of its fat. Remove and discard.

Add the butter, onion and garlic to the pan and cook, stirring occasionally, for 5 to 7 minutes or until soft and translucent but not brown. Using a

A delicious dish for family meals, Ox Tongue Braised with Bacon may be served with buttered noodles and vegetables.

wooden spoon, stir in the salt, pepper and flour to form a smooth paste. Add the bouquet garni. Gradually stir in the stock, being careful to avoid lumps.

Increase the heat and, stirring constantly, bring the sauce to the boil. Add the tongue cubes and stir well. Cover the pan, reduce the heat and simmer for 30 minutes, stirring occasionally.

Preheat the grill [broiler] to high. Cook the bacon until very crisp, drain and keep warm.

Add the mushrooms to the ox tongue mixture and continue cooking, uncovered, for a further 10 minutes. Pour into a warmed serving dish and crumble over the bacon.

TRIPE AND ONIONS

This traditional warming dish is best served in a tureen accompanied by a dish of boiled potatoes.

---
4 servings

Metric/Imperial

675g (1½lb) prepared tripe, cut into small pieces
4 medium-sized onions, sliced
¾ litre (1½ pints) milk
1 teaspoon salt
40g (1½oz) butter
3 tablespoons flour
1 teaspoon black pepper
½ teaspoon grated nutmeg
1 tablespoon finely chopped fresh parsley

American

1½lb prepared honeycomb tripe, cut into small pieces
4 medium-sized onions, sliced
3¾ cups milk
1 teaspoon salt
3 tablespoons butter
3 tablespoons flour
1 teaspoon black pepper
½ teaspoon grated nutmeg
1 tablespoon finely chopped fresh parsley

Place the tripe, onions, milk and salt in a large saucepan and bring to the boil, stirring frequently. Cover, reduce

the heat and simmer, stirring occasionally, for 1 hour or until the tripe is tender.

Remove the pan from the heat and strain the mixture into a bowl. Transfer the tripe and onions to another bowl.

In a large saucepan, melt the butter over moderate heat. When the foam subsides remove the pan from the heat and stir in the flour to make a smooth paste. Gradually add the reserved cooking liquid, stirring constantly and being careful to avoid lumps. Return the pan to the heat and cook, stirring, for 3 minutes or until the liquid thickens slightly. Stir in the pepper and nutmeg.

Return the tripe and onions to the liquid and cook for a further 5 minutes until heated through. Pour into a warmed soup tureen and sprinkle with parsley.

TRIPE AND TOMATO CASSEROLE

An economical supper dish for the family, Tripe and Tomato Casserole may be served with a green salad.

---
4 servings

Metric/Imperial

675g (1½lb) prepared tripe, cut into 5cm (2in) strips
2 tablespoons vegetable oil
2 tablespoons vinegar
2 tablespoons lemon juice
50g (2oz) plus 1 teaspoon butter
2 medium-sized onions, sliced and pushed out into rings
1 garlic clove, crushed
100g (4oz) button mushrooms, wiped clean and coarsely chopped
100g (4oz) cooked French beans, halved
25g (1oz) flour
396g (14oz) can tomatoes
1 tablespoon tomato purée
1 teaspoon dried basil
1 teaspoon salt
1 teaspoon black pepper
75g (3oz) fresh white breadcrumbs

American

1½lb prepared honeycomb tripe, cut into 2in strips

2 tablespoons vegetable oil
2 tablespoons vinegar
2 tablespoons lemon juice
¼ cup plus 1 teaspoon butter
2 medium-sized onions, sliced and separated into rings
1 garlic clove, crushed
¼lb small mushrooms, wiped clean and coarsely chopped
½ cup cooked green beans, halved
¼ cup flour
1 x 14oz can tomatoes
1 tablespoon tomato paste
1 teaspoon dried basil
1 teaspoon salt
1 teaspoon black pepper
1½ cups fresh white breadcrumbs

Place the tripe in a large shallow dish. Mix together the oil, vinegar and lemon juice and pour over the tripe. Toss well and marinate for 1 hour.

Preheat the oven to fairly hot (190°C/375°F or Gas Mark 5). With the teaspoon of butter, grease a large shallow baking dish.

In a small frying-pan, melt half the remaining butter over moderate heat. When the foam subsides, add the onions and garlic and fry, stirring, for 3 minutes. Add the mushrooms and beans and continue cooking, stirring constantly, for 2 to 4 minutes or until the onions are soft and translucent but not brown. Transfer to a plate.

Remove the pan from the heat and stir the flour into the juices to make a smooth paste. Gradually add the tomato can juice, stirring constantly to avoid lumps. Return to the heat and bring to the boil, stirring.

Stir in the tomatoes, tomato purée, basil, salt and pepper and cook for a further 2 minutes, stirring, until the sauce thickens. Remove the pan from the heat and keep hot.

Arrange half the mushrooms and bean mixture in the prepared baking dish and sprinkle over half the breadcrumbs. Transfer the tripe to the baking dish, discarding the marinade.

Pour over the tomato sauce. Arrange the remaining vegetables in the dish and sprinkle over the remaining breadcrumbs. Dot with the remaining butter.

Bake in the centre of the oven for 1 hour or until the tripe is tender.

Meat meals for the family

This recipe section ranges over a vast spectrum of cheap and cheerful cooking. Expensive cuts of meat such as escalopes and steaks are special occasion foods for most of us, and often the best way to cook them is by simple grilling [broiling] or frying. It is when it comes to cooking cheaper cuts that the cook's real flair and ingenuity comes into play. There are many ways of cooking cheaper cuts (apart from cutting up and stewing, see pages 35–62). Roasting is best with first class meat, but you can successfully roast tougher pieces of meat by cooking at a reduced temperature for longer than the normal cooking period. (Meat for roasting should be at room temperature so remove it from the refrigerator at least 30 minutes before cooking.)

But a cheap cut of meat is better pot roasted. The meat is browned, then cooked in a heavy pot or casserole with onion, herbs and a little stock.

Braised meat is cooked in a heavy pot on top of a bed of vegetables with liquid coming a quarter of the way up the meat. Cooking can be in the oven or on top of the stove.

Some cheaper cuts can be boiled - cooked, covered with water, at boiling point - or steamed, cooked in steam rising from boiling water. Very tough meat is often steamed first before roasting.

Much of the secret of good budget cooking lies in attractive presentation. Take a little extra time to serve a meal attractively garnished, make it colourful, and you will be rewarded (hopefully) with clean plates. Don't be afraid, either, of trying out unfamiliar cuts of meat, if necessary adapting a recipe. They may not be available in your supermarket, but a good butcher respects a customer who knows how to cook belly pork, tripe, spareribs or oxtail. There are many other ways in which you can economize in your everyday cooking for example, serving a sauce, or a portion of stuffing, or crispy fried onion with each helping makes skimpy meat portions look bigger. Finally, make use of all those cheap continental sausages as well as sausage meat, frankfurters and all kinds of processed meat products, which all help to stretch the budget and add variety and interest to your diet.

CORNISH PASTIES

These savoury pasties were traditionally eaten by the Cornish tin miners for their lunch. The pasty is semi-circular in shape and in the old days the pasty was marked at the lower end with the initials of the miner, so that if part of the pasty was left it could be claimed by its owner!

12 pasties

Metric/Imperial

350g (12oz) Shortcrust Pastry I
1 small turnip, peeled and coarsely chopped
350g (12oz) lean beef, finely chopped
1 small kidney, skinned and chopped
1 large onion, finely chopped
4 medium-sized potatoes, peeled and finely diced
1 teaspoon salt
½ teaspoon black pepper
a little milk

American

1 recipe Shortcrust Pastry I
1 small turnip, peeled and coarsely chopped
¾lb lean beef steak, finely chopped
1 small kidney, skinned and chopped
1 large onion, finely chopped
4 medium-sized potatoes, peeled and finely diced
1 teaspoon salt
½ teaspoon black pepper
a little milk

Preheat the oven to fairly hot (200°C/400°F or Gas Mark 6).

Roll out the pastry and, using a large pastry cutter or small plate, cut into rounds. The scraps can be worked together and rolled out again until too little is left for another round. Twelve should be obtained from this amount of dough.

In a large bowl, combine the filling ingredients and seasonings, blend thoroughly.

Place a small heap of filling in the centre of each round of dough. Coat the edges of the pastry with water and join them to form a semi-circle. Press the edges together firmly to seal. Place on a large baking sheet.

Cut slits across the top of each pasty and brush with milk.

Bake in the middle of the oven for 15 minutes. Reduce the heat to moderate (180°C/350°F or Gas Mark 4) and bake for 40 minutes longer, or until deep golden.

BEEFSTEAK AND KIDNEY PUDDING

A traditional English meat pudding, Beefsteak and Kidney Pudding is a perfect main dish for a winter's meal. It should be brought to the table steaming hot with the basin wrapped in a white napkin.

6 servings

Metric/Imperial

350g (12oz) Suetcrust Pastry
500g (1lb) leg or shin beef, cubed
250g (8oz) ox kidney, cut into small pieces
2 tablespoons flour
¼ teaspoon salt
⅛ teaspoon black pepper
1 teaspoon dried mixed herbs

American

2 recipes Suetcrust Pastry
1lb chuck steak, cubed
½lb kidney, cut into small pieces
2 tablespoons flour
¼ teaspoon salt
⅛ teaspoon black pepper
¼ teaspoon each of basil, marjoram, oregano and thyme

With a floured rolling pin roll out the dough to a large circle about 1cm (½ inch) thick. Cut a triangle (about one-third of the diameter) out of the circle and reserve it. Line a 1½-litre (2½-pint) pudding basin with the large piece of dough, dampen the edges from where the triangle was cut and bring them together. Press the dough to the shape of the basin and trim the top edges.

Half fill a large saucepan with water and bring slowly to the boil.

Roll the beef and kidney pieces in a mixture of the flour, salt, pepper and mixed herbs. Coat on all sides.

Put the meat into the lined basin and half fill with cold water. Lightly knead the reserved piece and the trimmings of dough together and roll out to a circle large enough to cover the basin. Dampen the edges of the dough and place on top of the meat. Press the edges of the dough together to seal. Cover with aluminium foil, large enough to contain a pleat across the centre. Tie a piece of string under the rim of the basin.

Put the basin into, or in a steamer over, the boiling water, cover with a lid and steam for 3 hours or longer. Add more boiling water when necessary.

BRAISED STEAK

This is a tempting and easy-to-prepare main dish. Serve it with buttered noodles, and sautéed courgettes [zucchini] or peas. If you prefer, you may cook this dish in a casserole in the oven preheated to warm (170°C/325°F or Gas Mark 3). The meat will require the same cooking time.

6 servings

Metric/Imperial

4 tablespoons flour
1 teaspoon salt
½ teaspoon black pepper
1kg (2lb) braising steak, 2.5cm (1in) thick
50g (2oz) butter
1 onion, thinly sliced
2 carrots, scraped and sliced
1 green pepper, white pith removed, seeded and diced
396g (14oz) can tomatoes
1 bay leaf

American

4 tablespoons flour
1 teaspoon salt
½ teaspoon black pepper
2lb round steak
¼ cup butter
1 onion, thinly sliced
2 carrots, scraped and sliced
1 green pepper, membrane and seeds removed, diced
1 x 14oz can tomatoes
1 bay leaf

Mix the flour, salt and pepper in a bowl. Coat the steak with the mixture.

Heat the butter in a large, heavy frying-pan over moderate heat. When the foam has subsided, add the meat and brown for 5 minutes on each side. Add the remaining ingredients to the pan and stir well. Cover and simmer gently for 2 to 2½ hours, or until the meat is tender.

MIXED GRILL

This popular meal needs accurate timing to ensure that all the ingredients are perfectly cooked and ready to serve piping hot at the same time.

4 servings

Metric/Imperial

4 lamb chops
4 pork sausages
4 slices lamb's liver
4 slices bacon, rinds removed
4 tomatoes, halved
8 mushrooms, wiped clean
2 tablespoons butter
salt and pepper

American

4 lamb chops
4 sausages
4 slices lamb's liver
4 slices bacon
4 tomatoes, halved
8 large mushrooms, wiped clean
2 tablespoons butter
salt and pepper

Heat the grill [broiler] on a high setting.

Wipe and trim the chops and place on the tray with the sausages, remembering to turn the sausages gradually as they brown, and to lower the heat when the chops are browned on both sides.

Meanwhile wash and trim the liver, and pat it dry with absorbent paper. Sprinkle each piece with salt and pepper, and add small knobs of butter.

After about 8 minutes add the liver to the tray, each piece with a slice of bacon on top. Grill for about 2 minutes, then turn the bacon and grill the other

Always serve Beefsteak and Kidney Pudding steaming hot at the table.

side. Remove the bacon and keep hot on a serving dish. Turn the liver and cook for a further few minutes.

When the chops and sausages are cooked remove these too to keep hot.

Place the tomatoes in the tray with the mushrooms, dotted with butter and sprinkled with salt and pepper. Grill these for about 2-3 minutes, then add to the serving dish.

CORNED BEEF HASH

Corned Beef Hash is an easy, tasty and popular dish to serve at a family lunch. It may be served by itself, topped with fried eggs or with a green vegetable.

4 servings

Metric/Imperial

350g (12oz) canned corned beef, diced
350g (12oz) cold, cooked potatoes, diced
½ teaspoon salt
1 teaspoon black pepper
1 teaspoon prepared mustard
2 tablespoons butter
1 medium-sized onion, sliced
4 tablespoons milk
1 teaspoon Worcestershire sauce

American

¾lb canned corned beef, diced
1½ cups cold, cooked potatoes, diced
½ teaspoon salt
1 teaspoon black pepper
1 teaspoon prepared mustard
2 tablespoons butter
1 medium-sized onion, sliced
4 tablespoons milk
1 teaspoon Worcestershire sauce

In a large mixing bowl, mix the corned beef, potatoes, salt, pepper and mustard together until well blended.

In a medium-sized saucepan, melt the butter over moderate heat. When the foam subsides, add the onion and cook until lightly browned.

Add the beef-and-potato mixture to the pan. Stir in the milk and Worcestershire sauce and mix the ingredients together thoroughly. Reduce the heat to low and cook for 15 minutes.

SWEDISH HASH

A sustaining potato and meat hash from Sweden, Pytt i Panna (pewt ee pahn-nah) or Swedish Hash is traditionally served with a raw egg yolk stirred into each portion, but you may prefer to top each portion with a fried egg as described here.

4 servings

Metric/Imperial

25g (1oz) butter
4 tablespoons vegetable oil
6 medium-sized potatoes, peeled and
    finely diced
2 medium-sized onions, chopped
350g (12oz) cooked beef, finely diced
100g (4oz) cooked lamb, finely diced
1 teaspoon salt

A hash of potatoes, beef and lamb, Swedish Hash (Pytt i Panna) is topped with a fried egg to make a tasty supper dish.

½ teaspoon black pepper
4 eggs

American

2 tablespoons butter
4 tablespoons vegetable oil
6 medium-sized potatoes, peeled and
    finely diced
2 medium-sized onions, chopped
2 cups cooked beef, finely diced
⅔ cup cooked lamb, finely diced
1 teaspoon salt
½ teaspoon black pepper
4 eggs

In a large frying-pan, melt the butter with 2 tablespoons of the oil over moderate heat. When the foam subsides, add the potatoes and fry, stirring and turning frequently, for 20 to 25 minutes or until they are cooked and evenly browned. Remove and set aside.

Add the remaining oil to the pan. When hot add the onions and fry, stirring occasionally, for 5 to 7 minutes or until soft and translucent but not brown. Add the beef and lamb and

increase the heat to moderately high. Fry, stirring frequently, for 5 minutes or until the meat is evenly browned.

Return the potatoes to the pan and cook for a further 5 minutes or until heated through. Season with the salt and pepper. Keep hot while you fry the eggs.

Spoon the hash on to 4 plates and top each serving with a fried egg.

SEA PIE

A traditional English pie made in a pot or casserole with a suetcrust topping, Sea Pie, contrary to its name, is made with stewing steak. It is a tasty dish to serve to the family.

6-8 servings

Metric/Imperial

50g (2oz) flour seasoned with
    1 teaspoon black pepper and
    1 teaspoon dried mixed herbs
1kg (2lb) stewing beef, cubed

8 streaky bacon slices, rind removed and chopped

2 tablespoons dripping

1 large onion, chopped

1 medium-sized carrot, scraped and thickly sliced

2 celery stalks, trimmed and chopped

1 parsnip, peeled and chopped

600ml (1 pint) beef stock

250g (8oz) Suetcrust Pastry

American

½ cup flour seasoned with 1 teaspoon black pepper and 1 teaspoon mixed herbs (basil, oregano, marjoram and rosemary)

2lb boneless chuck steak, cubed

8 bacon slices, chopped

2 tablespoons drippings

1 large onion, chopped

1 medium-sized carrot, scraped and thickly sliced

2 celery stalks, trimmed and chopped

1 parsnip, peeled and chopped

2½ cups beef stock

1 recipe Suetcrust Pastry

Place the seasoned flour on a plate and thoroughly coat the beef cubes in it, shaking off any excess.

Place the bacon in a large flameproof casserole and, stirring frequently, cook over moderate heat for 6 to 8 minutes or until it is crisp and has rendered most of its fat. Add 1 tablespoon of the dripping and, when melted, the beef cubes. Cook, stirring frequently for 6 to 8 minutes or until the meat is lightly browned all over. Transfer to a plate and keep warm.

Melt the remaining dripping in the casserole. Add the onion, carrot, celery and parsnip and cook, stirring occasionally, for 5 to 7 minutes or until the onion is soft and translucent but not brown. Return the meat and bacon to the casserole and pour in the beef stock.

Bring to the boil, stirring frequently, then cover the casserole, reduce the heat and simmer for 30 minutes. Preheat the oven to moderate (180°C/350°F or Gas Mark 4).

On a lightly floured working surface, roll out the dough to just fit inside the casserole. Lay it on top of the stew, cover and place the casserole in the oven for a further 1½ hours. Uncover

the casserole and cook for a further 20 minutes, or until the crust is well risen and the meat tender.

GLAZED BACON (HAM)

A tasty and economical supper for the family, Glazed Bacon is delicious with mashed potatoes and French beans.

4-6 servings

Metric/Imperial

2 x 750g (2 x 1½lb) bacon (ham) joints, ready to cook

1 tablespoon treacle

3 tablespoons brown sugar

1 tablespoon French mustard

4 tablespoons orange juice

American

3lb processed ham

1 tablespoon molasses

3 tablespoons brown sugar

1 tablespoon French mustard

4 tablespoons orange juice

Place the joints in a large saucepan, cover with cold water and bring to the boil. Reduce the heat, cover the pan and simmer for 1 hour, adding more water from time to time if necessary.

Preheat the oven to fairly hot (200°C/400°F or Gas Mark 6).

Lift the bacon out of the pan. If it has not been skinned, remove the skin at this stage. Place on a rack in a roasting tin.

Combine the treacle [molasses], brown sugar, mustard and orange juice. Pour the mixture over the fat on the bacon. Bake for 15 to 20 minutes, basting frequently.

DEVILLED PORK

A warming dish, Devilled Pork can be served with mashed potatoes or Bubble and Squeak. The sauce can also be used for other cheap pork cuts.

4 servings

Metric/Imperial

75g (3oz) butter

1 tablespoon Worcestershire sauce

1 tablespoon tomato purée

2 shallots, finely chopped

1 teaspoon dry mustard

1 teaspoon curry powder

1 teaspoon black pepper

1 teaspoon paprika

1 teaspoon salt

1.25kg (3lb) lean spareribs of pork, cut into serving pieces

50g (2oz) flour

American

⅜ cup butter

1 tablespoon Worcestershire sauce

1 tablespoon tomato paste

2 shallots, finely chopped

1 teaspoon dry mustard

1 teaspoon curry powder

1 teaspoon black pepper

1 teaspoon paprika

1 teaspoon salt

3lb lean spareribs of pork, cut into serving pieces

½ cup flour

Preheat the oven to fairly hot (200°C/400°F or Gas Mark 6).

With one-third of the butter, generously grease a shallow ovenproof casserole large enough to hold all the ribs in one layer.

Place the rest of the butter in a small bowl and mash it with the Worcestershire sauce, tomato purée, shallots, mustard, curry powder, black pepper, paprika and half the salt.

With a sharp knife, score the ribs on their meaty side in a criss-cross pattern. Place the flour on a plate. Roll the ribs in it to coat them evenly, shaking off any excess. Sprinkle them with the rest of the salt.

Place the ribs, meaty side up, in the casserole and coat with the butter mixture.

Roast for 1 hour. Reduce the oven temperature to moderate (180°C/350°F or Gas Mark 4), and roast for a further hour, or until the meat is tender.

PORK CHOPS WITH ROSEMARY

Pork chops flavoured with rosemary, basil and marjoram and cooked in cider,

Pork Chops with Rosemary may be served with a green vegetable and sautéed potatoes.

6 servings

Metric/Imperial

25g (1oz) flour seasoned with ¼ teaspoon salt and ⅛ teaspoon black pepper
6 large loin or sparerib pork chops
40g (1½oz) butter
1 tablespoon vegetable oil
1 large onion, finely chopped
1 teaspoon dried rosemary
½ teaspoon dried basil
½ teaspoon dried marjoram
¼ teaspoon salt
⅛ teaspoon black pepper
300ml (10 fl oz) dry cider

American

¼ cup flour seasoned with ¼ teaspoon salt and ⅛ teaspoon black pepper
6 loin or rib pork chops
3 tablespoons butter
1 tablespoon vegetable oil
1 large onion, finely chopped
1 teaspoon dried rosemary
½ teaspoon dried basil
½ teaspoon dried marjoram
¼ teaspoon salt
⅛ teaspoon black pepper
1¼ cups hard cider

Preheat the oven to moderate (180°C/350°F or Gas Mark 4).

Place the seasoned flour on a plate and dip each chop into it, coating thoroughly on both sides. Shake off any excess.

In a large flameproof casserole, melt the butter with the oil over moderate heat. When the foam subsides, add the chops and fry for 5 minutes on each side or until well browned all over. Transfer to a plate.

Add the onion to the casserole and fry, stirring occasionally, for 5 to 7 minutes or until soft and translucent but not brown.

Return the chops to the casserole and sprinkle with the herbs, salt and pepper. Pour over the cider.

Cover the casserole and bake for 1 to 1½ hours or until the chops are thoroughly cooked.

PORK CHOPS WITH MUSHROOMS AND TOMATOES

A succulent and simple dish to prepare, Pork Chops with Mushrooms and Tomatoes is attractive enough for a really special meal.

4 servings

Metric/Imperial

4 sparerib pork chops
2 tablespoons vegetable oil
1 teaspoon dried thyme
1 teaspoon salt
½ teaspoon black pepper
1 tablespoon butter
100g (4oz) mushrooms, wiped clean and sliced
396g (14oz) can tomatoes
1 teaspoon dried sage

American

4 boned pork loin chops
2 tablespoons vegetable oil
1 teaspoon dried thyme
1 teaspoon salt
½ teaspoon black pepper
1 tablespoon butter
¼lb mushrooms, wiped clean and sliced
1 x 14oz can tomatoes
1 teaspoon dried sage

Preheat the grill [broiler] to high. Brush the pork chops with the oil and sprinkle with the thyme, half the salt and half the pepper. Lay the chops on the rack in the pan and place under the heat. Cook for 5 minutes on each side. Reduce the heat to moderately low and cook for a further 15 to 20 minutes on each side, depending on the thickness of the chops, until they are well done.

Meanwhile, make the sauce. In a large frying-pan, melt the butter over moderate heat. When the foam subsides, add the mushrooms and fry, stirring occasionally, for 3 minutes. Add the tomatoes, sage, and the remaining salt and pepper. Cover the pan, reduce the heat and cook, stirring occasionally, for 25 minutes.

Arrange the meat in a warmed serving dish and spoon the sauce over and around it.

PORK CHOPS WITH APPLES

This is probably the simplest, certainly the most traditional and, to many people, the best way of serving pork chops. They are seasoned, fried in a little butter and cooked with apples. Roast potatoes are the traditional accompaniment to this dish.

4 servings

Metric/Imperial

4 large pork chops
½ teaspoon salt
¼ teaspoon black pepper
1 teaspoon dried rosemary
25g (1oz) butter
3 cooking apples, peeled, cored and thinly sliced
1 tablespoon soft brown sugar

American

4 large pork chops
½ teaspoon salt
¼ teaspoon black pepper
1 teaspoon dried rosemary
2 tablespoons butter
3 tart apples, peeled, cored and thinly sliced
1 tablespoon soft brown sugar

Place the pork chops on a board and rub them all over with the salt, pepper and rosemary.

In a large frying-pan, melt the butter over moderate heat. When the foam subsides, add the chops and cook them for 10 minutes on each side.

Add the sliced apples to the pan and sprinkle over the sugar. Cover the pan and cook for 20 to 30 minutes or until both pork chops and apples are thoroughly cooked.

Arrange the chops attractively on the serving plates and spoon over the apples and the pan juices.

ZURICH ROAST PORK

Zurich Roast Pork is the ideal dish to serve for a family Sunday luncheon. Serve with roast potatoes and a green vegetable.

6-8 servings

Metric/Imperial

1 x 2kg (1 x 4lb) knuckle end half leg
   of pork, scored
1 garlic clove, crushed
1 teaspoon salt
1 teaspoon black pepper
½ teaspoon ground cinnamon
½ teaspoon ground nutmeg
1kg (2lb) canned pineapple rings,
   juice reserved
1 teaspoon vegetable oil
2 tablespoons sugar

American

4lb fresh picnic shoulder of pork,
   scored
1 garlic clove, crushed
1 teaspoon salt
1 teaspoon black pepper
½ teaspoon ground cinnamon
½ teaspoon ground nutmeg
2 x 16oz cans pineapple rings, juice
   reserved
1 teaspoon vegetable oil
2 tablespoons sugar

Preheat the oven to fairly hot (190°C/
375°F or Gas Mark 5).

Place the pork on a working surface
and rub it all over with the garlic, salt
and pepper, cinnamon and nutmeg.
Carefully slide a long sharp knife
between the fat and the flesh of the
pork, without breaking the skin.

Stuff the pineapple rings into this
cavity. Secure the skin with wooden
cocktail sticks. Transfer the meat to a
large roasting tin and pour over the oil.
Pour over the reserved pineapple juice.

Place the tin in the centre of the oven
and roast for 3 hours, basting occasionally. Sprinkle over the sugar and
increase the temperature to hot (220°C/
425°F or Gas Mark 7). Roast for a
further 20 minutes or until the juice
that runs out is clear when the meat is
pierced.

PORK CHILLI

A simple, easy-to-prepare supper dish,
Pork Chilli makes good use of convenience foods.

4 servings

Metric/Imperial

1 tablespoon butter
1 tablespoon vegetable oil
2 medium-sized onions, thinly sliced
1 green pepper, white pith removed,
   seeded and finely chopped
675g (1½lb) streaky pork, rind removed,
   trimmed of excess fat and cubed
396g (14oz) can condensed tomato soup
1 large celery stalk, trimmed and
   finely chopped
¼ teaspoon chilli powder
396g (14oz) can red kidney beans
1 teaspoon salt
½ teaspoon black pepper

American

1 tablespoon butter
1 tablespoon vegetable oil
2 medium-sized onions, thinly sliced
1 green pepper, membrane and seeds
   removed, finely chopped
1½lb boned pork, cubed
1 x 14oz can condensed tomato soup
1 large celery stalk, trimmed and
   finely chopped
¼ teaspoon chili powder
1 x 14oz can kidney beans
1 teaspoon salt
½ teaspoon black pepper

In a large saucepan, melt the butter
with the oil over moderate heat. When
the foam subsides, add the onions. Fry,
stirring occasionally, for 8 to 10
minutes or until golden brown.

Add the green pepper and pork
cubes and cook, stirring frequently, for
6 to 8 minutes or until the pork cubes
are lightly and evenly browned. Reduce
the heat, cover the pan and cook for
35 minutes.

Add the soup, celery and chilli powder and stir well. Continue to cook,
covered, for 15 minutes, or until the
pork is tender.

Stir in drained kidney beans, salt
and pepper and increase the heat to
moderate. Cook, uncovered and stirring
occasionally, for 5 minutes.

STUFFED LOIN OF LAMB

This recipe makes a tasty and inexpensive family Sunday lunch.

6-8 servings

Metric/Imperial

100g (4oz) sausage meat
75g (3oz) fresh breadcrumbs
½ teaspoon salt
¼ teaspoon black pepper
1 tablespoon chopped fresh parsley
1 teaspoon dried dill
1 teaspoon dried tarragon
1 garlic clove, crushed
1 egg yolk, lightly beaten
1 tablespoon butter
1 medium-sized onion, chopped
1 x 1.25kg (1 x 3lb) boned loin of lamb,
   trimmed of excess fat
2 tablespoons vegetable oil
3 carrots, scraped and halved
   lengthways
10 pickling onions
600ml (1 pint) chicken stock

American

¼lb sausage meat
1½ cups fresh breadcrumbs
½ teaspoon salt
¼ teaspoon black pepper
1 tablespoon chopped fresh parsley
1 teaspoon dried dill
1 teaspoon dried tarragon
1 garlic clove, crushed
1 egg yolk, lightly beaten
1 tablespoon butter
1 medium-sized onion, diced
3lb boned loin of lamb, trimmed of
   excess fat
2 tablespoons vegetable oil
3 carrots, scraped and halved
   lengthwise
10 pearl onions
2 cups chicken stock

Preheat the oven to warm (170°C/
325°F or Gas Mark 3).

In a large mixing bowl, combine the
sausage meat, breadcrumbs, salt,
pepper, parsley, dill, tarragon, garlic
and egg yolk. Mix well to combine
thoroughly.

In a small frying-pan, melt the butter
over moderate heat. When the foam
subsides, add the onion and fry, stirring
occasionally, for 5 to 7 minutes, or until
soft and translucent but not brown.
Add to the sausage meat mixture.

Lay the meat out on a flat surface
and spread the stuffing evenly over it.

Carefully roll up, Swiss [jelly] roll style, and tie with string at 2.5cm (1 inch) intervals.

In a large flameproof casserole, heat the oil over moderate heat. Place the rolled lamb in it and cook, turning occasionally, for 10 to 15 minutes or until evenly browned all over.

Add the carrots and pickling [pearl] onions, shaking the casserole gently to coat them with oil. Cook for a further 3 minutes. Pour off and discard the pan liquid; pour in the chicken stock and bring to the boil.

Cover the casserole and place in the bottom of the oven. Cook for 2 to 2½ hours or until the meat is tender.

Transfer the meat roll to a warmed serving dish and arrange the vegetables decoratively around it. Skim off any fat from the cooking juices and strain into a warmed sauceboat.

SAUSAGE AND APPLE CAKE

A savoury apple mixture sets off sausages to perfection.

___

4 servings

___

Metric/Imperial

___

8 pork sausages

40g (1½oz) butter

4 large cooking apples, peeled, cored and sliced

1 teaspoon sugar

½ teaspoon salt

¼ teaspoon black pepper

½ teaspoon ground coriander

2 teaspoons vinegar

1 medium-sized onion, thinly sliced and pushed out into rings

2 tablespoons melted butter

___

American

___

8 sausages

3 tablespoons butter

4 large tart apples, peeled, cored and sliced

1 teaspoon sugar

½ teaspoon salt

¼ teaspoon black pepper

½ teaspoon ground coriander

2 teaspoons vinegar

1 medium-sized onion, thinly sliced and separated into rings

2 tablespoons melted butter

___

Place the sausages in a large saucepan

A delicious and substantial dish, Stuffed Loin of Lamb garnished with onions and carrots is the perfect dish for a family meal.

and pour over enough water to cover. Bring to the boil, cover and simmer for 5 minutes.

Place 4 sausages on a wooden board and slice them thinly crosswise.

Preheat the oven to fairly hot (190°C/375°F or Gas Mark 5).

In a large frying-pan, melt two-thirds of the butter. When the foam subsides, add the apple slices and cook, stirring frequently, for 5 minutes or until tender.

Arrange one-half of the apples on the bottom of a round ovenproof dish. Top with the sliced sausages. Sprinkle over the sugar, salt, pepper, coriander and vinegar. Top with the remaining apples.

In the same frying-pan, melt the remaining butter over moderate heat. When the foam subsides add the onion and cook, stirring occasionally, for 5 to 7 minutes or until soft and translucent but ot brown. Arrange the onion rings on top of the apple mixture.

Slice the remaining sausages lengthways and place them, skin sides uppermost, like the spokes of a wheel on top of the apple and onion mixture. Pour over the melted butter from the frying-pan.

Bake for 30 minutes or until the sausages are crisp and deep golden brown.

MEAT FLAN

This is a French meat flan containing beef, sausage meat and onion. Serve it hot or cold for a light luncheon.

4-6 servings

Metric/Imperial

250g (8oz) Shortcrust Pastry I
50g (2oz) butter
2 medium-sized onions, chopped
300g (10oz) sausage meat
300g (10oz) cooked beef, finely diced
1 tablespoon tomato purée
½ teaspoon salt
½ teaspoon black pepper
½ teaspoon dried sage
a little milk

American

1 recipe Shortcrust Pastry I
¼ cup butter
2 medium-sized onions, chopped
1¼ cups sausage meat
1¼ cups cooked beef, finely diced
1 tablespoon tomato paste
½ teaspoon salt
½ teaspoon black pepper
½ teaspoon dried sage
a little milk

Preheat the oven to moderate (180°C/ 350°F or Gas Mark 4).

On a lightly floured surface, roll out three-quarters of the dough into a circle 6mm (¼-inch) thick. Lift the dough on the rolling pin and lay it over a 23cm (9-inch) flan tin. Ease into the tin and trim the edges.

In a large frying-pan, melt the butter over moderate heat. When the foam subsides, add the onions and fry, stirring occasionally, for 5 to 7 minutes or until soft and translucent but not brown.

Add the sausage meat to the pan and cook, stirring frequently, for 3 to 4 minutes or until it has lost its pinkness. Stir in the beef, tomato purée, salt, pepper and sage and fry for a further 2 minutes. Remove the pan from the heat and set aside to cool for 10 minutes. Spoon the filling into the flan case.

Roll out the remaining dough to a rectangle 6mm (¼in) thick and 25cm (10in) long. Cut the dough into narrow strips and lay them over the filling to form a lattice.

Brush the dough with milk. Bake for 40 minutes or until the pastry is golden brown.

HEARTS WITH APRICOT STUFFING

This well-flavoured stuffing of fruit, nuts and wholemeal [wholewheat] crumbs turns an inexpensive meat into a very good supper dish. Serve with boiled rice and a crisp green salad.

4 servings

Metric/Imperial

8 dried apricots
25g (1oz) chopped almonds
1 egg
2 tablespoons butter
25g (1oz) wholemeal breadcrumbs
1 teaspoon salt
½ teaspoon black pepper
1 orange
4 lambs' hearts, trimmed and cleaned
40ml (2 fl oz) chicken stock
1 tablespoon sherry
watercress to garnish (optional)

American

8 dried apricots
1 tablespoon slivered almonds
1 egg
2 tablespoons butter
½ cup wholewheat breadcrumbs
1 teaspoon salt
½ teaspoon black pepper
1 orange
4 lamb hearts, trimmed and cleaned
¼ cup chicken stock
1 tablespoon sherry
watercress to garnish (optional)

Heat the oven to moderate (180°C/ 350°F or Gas Mark 4).

Pour boiling water over the apricots and leave them to soak for 10 minutes. Beat the egg. Melt the butter in a small saucepan. Combine the almonds, butter and breadcrumbs and season with salt and pepper. Drain the apricots, snip them into small pieces and add them to the mixture. Grate in 2 teaspoons of orange zest.

Pack the stuffing into hearts, secure with skewers or cocktail sticks and place in an ovenproof dish. Pour the stock over, cover and bake in the oven for 1½ hours or until hearts are tender.

Pour the juices from the dish into a small pan and boil briskly, to reduce. Squeeze the orange, add the orange juice and sherry to the pan and simmer for 5 minutes. Pour over the hearts and serve garnished with watercress.

BRAISED NECK OF VEAL

A very simple dish to make, Braised Neck of Veal makes a delicious Sunday lunch, served with a green vegetable and boiled new potatoes. Ask your butcher to chine the veal as this makes it easier to carve.

4 servings

Metric/Imperial

1 x 2kg (1 x 4lb) best end of neck of
   veal, chine bone removed
1 teaspoon salt
½ teaspoon black pepper
¼ teaspoon ground cloves
¼ teaspoon ground mace
4 streaky bacon slices, rinds removed
1 medium-sized onion, finely chopped
1 large carrot, scraped and sliced
2 celery stalks, trimmed and cut into
   2-inch pieces
1 bouquet garni
6 black peppercorns
1 bay leaf
350ml (12 fl oz) chicken stock
1 tablespoon lemon juice

American

4lb boneless rolled shoulder of veal
1 teaspoon salt
½ teaspoon black pepper

¼ teaspoon ground cloves
¼ teaspoon ground mace
4 slices bacon
1 medium-sized onion, finely chopped
1 large carrot, scraped and sliced
2 celery stalks, trimmed and cut into
  2-inch pieces
1 bouquet garni
6 black peppercorns
1 bay leaf
1½ cups chicken stock
1 tablespoon lemon juice

Using a sharp knife, cut off the short pieces of rib bone from the flap on the veal. Rub the meat all over with the salt, pepper, cloves and mace and set aside.

In a large flameproof casserole, fry the bacon over moderate heat, stirring occasionally, for 5 to 6 minutes or until it is crisp and has rendered most of its fat. Remove and discard.

Add the onion to the casserole and fry, stirring occasionally, for 5 to 7

Serve these delicious little Veal and Tongue Pies hot or cold.

minutes, or until soft and translucent but not brown. Add the carrot and celery and stirring occasionally, cook for 2 minutes. Stir in the bouquet garni, peppercorns and bay leaf and pour the stock on to the vegetables. Bring the stock to the boil. Put in the veal, cover, reduce the heat and simmer for 2 hours, basting occasionally, or until the veal is very tender.

Preheat the oven to moderate (180°C/350°F or Gas Mark 4).

Remove the lid and place the casserole in the oven. Braise, uncovered, for 20 minutes.

Transfer the veal to a warmed serving dish. Skim off any fat from the cooking liquid and strain into a warmed sauceboat.

Using a sharp-bladed knife, cut between the rib bones of the veal. Sprinkle with the lemon juice.

VEAL AND TONGUE PIES

These tasty little pies are ideal to take on a picnic. Alternatively, they are delicious served hot with a salad.

12 pies

Metric/Imperial

350g (12oz) Shortcrust Pastry I
250g (8oz) cooked pie veal, finely
  chopped
125g (4oz) cooked tongue, finely chopped
½ teaspoon dried sage
½ teaspoon dried rosemary
¼ teaspoon ground mace
juice of ½ lemon
1 teaspoon salt
¼ teaspoon black pepper
3 tablespoons veal stock
a little milk

American

1½ recipes Shortcrust Pastry I
1 cup cooked veal, finely chopped
½ cup cooked tongue, finely chopped
½ teaspoon dried sage
½ teaspoon dried rosemary
¼ teaspoon ground mace
juice of ½ lemon
1 teaspoon salt
¼ teaspoon black pepper
¼ cup veal stock
a little milk

Preheat the oven to very hot (230°C/450°F or Gas Mark 8).

Place three-quarters of the dough on a lightly floured working surface and roll out to a circle. Cut out 12 circles large enough to line 12 patty tins.

Chill the tins and the remaining dough in the refrigerator.

Combine the meats, herbs, lemon juice, salt and pepper. Pour in the stock and mix thoroughly.

Remove the tins and the dough from the refrigerator. Spoon a little of the filling into each tin and dampen the edges of the dough with a little water.

Roll out the remaining dough to a circle and cut out 12 circles large enough to fit over the patty tins. Crimp the dough edges together to seal them. Cut a small cross in the centre of each pie. Brush the dough with milk.

Bake the pies in the centre of the oven for 5 minutes. Reduce the heat to moderate (180°C/350°F or Gas Mark 4), and continue baking for a further 15 to 20 minutes or until golden brown.

Allow the pies to cool in their tins for 10 minutes before removing.

Meals with mince (ground meat)

Mince, or ground meat as it is known in the United States, is any raw meat (most commonly beef) which has been passed through a mincer [grinder]. The best is undoubtedly that which you prepare yourself at home, as mince [ground meat] does not keep very well.

A whole section of recipes has been devoted to this versatile ingredient in so many economical and delicious family dishes. It turns up regularly in every household in meat loaf, meatballs and hamburgers. You will find here traditional dishes, and plenty of new ideas too.

It is best to buy good quality mince [ground meat], as the cheaper kinds tend to be fatty. Nevertheless, there is much that you can do to disguise the shortcomings of the cheaper variety by the addition of suitable seasoning and other ingredients such as onion, tomatoes and mushrooms, which will also help to expand a small quantity of meat. A tablespoon of porridge oats added to 500g (1lb) of cheap minced [ground] beef will help to pad it out.

Mention should also be made here of textured vegetable protein which is now marketed to be used as a substitute for all or part of the meat in any mince [ground meat] recipe. If used in the proportion of one part of T.V.P. to three parts of meat it will be virtually undetectable. There is no doubt that T.V.P., which is made largely from soya beans and therefore high in second grade protein, is here to stay and will feature increasingly in our diets. At present it is used mainly as a 'bulking' agent in various processed foods, and those products which are made exclusively with soya protein, though textured and flavoured to resemble minced [ground] meat or chunks of meat are not really an acceptable substitute to most people. But if you have never experimented with textured vegetable protein, try using it to replace part of the meat in a meat pie or savoury meat loaf. You will save money and you will also have the assurance that the nutritional quality of the meal you are serving is as high or higher than that of an all-meat dish.

OHIO MEAT PIE

An economical, unusual and tasty pie, Ohio Meat Pie may be made with almost any combination of vegetables.

6 servings

Metric/Imperial

3 tablespoons vegetable oil
2 medium-sized onions, sliced
2 garlic cloves, crushed
1kg (2lb) lean minced beef
350g (12oz) carrots, scraped and thinly sliced
1 large green pepper, white pith removed, seeded and finely sliced
500g (1lb) courgettes, thinly sliced
50g (2oz) raisins
1½ teaspoons salt
½ teaspoon pepper
428g (15oz) can baked beans
340g (12oz) can sweetcorn, drained
75g (3oz) butter
75g (3oz) flour
¾ litre (1½ pints) milk
100g (4oz) Cheddar cheese, grated
4 egg yolks

American

3 tablespoons vegetable oil
2 medium-sized onions, sliced
2 garlic cloves, crushed
2lb lean ground beef (chuck or round steak)
¾lb carrots, scraped and thinly sliced
1 large green pepper, membrane and seeds removed, thinly sliced
1lb zucchini, thinly sliced
⅓ cup raisins
1½ teaspoons salt
½ teaspoon pepper
1¾ cups baked beans
1½ cups canned corn, drained
6 tablespoons butter
¾ cup flour
3¾ cups milk
1 cup Cheddar or American cheese, grated
4 egg yolks

In a large, deep frying-pan, heat the oil over moderate heat. Add the onions and garlic and fry, stirring occasionally, for 8 to 10 minutes or until golden brown.

Add the meat and fry, stirring frequently, for 10 minutes or until well browned. Add the carrots, green pepper, courgettes [zucchini], raisins, 1 teaspoon of the salt and the pepper. Cover the pan, reduce the heat and simmer for 20 to 25 minutes or until the vegetables are tender.

Stir in the beans and corn and simmer, uncovered, for a further 2 minutes.

Remove the pan from the heat and spoon the mixture into a large baking dish. Set aside and keep warm.

Preheat the oven to moderate (180°C/ 350°F or Gas Mark 4).

In a medium-sized saucepan, melt the butter over moderate heat. Remove the pan from the heat and stir in the flour to make a smooth paste. Gradually add the milk, stirring constantly. When all the milk has been added, return the pan to the heat. Cook the sauce for 3 to 4 minutes, stirring constantly, until it comes to the boil and is thick and smooth. Stir in the cheese and the remaining salt. Remove from the heat.

In a small mixing bowl, beat the egg yolks until well mixed. Add 4 or 5 tablespoons of the hot sauce. Stir the egg yolk mixture into the sauce.

Pour the sauce over the meat mixture in the baking dish. Place the dish in the top of the oven and bake for 25 to 30 minutes, or until the top is lightly browned.

A tasty and economical dish, Ohio Meat Pie is an unusual combination of vegetables and beef with a cheese and egg topping.

BEEF AND TOMATO PIE

This savoury pie may be served as a

main dish, accompanied by a green salad and a vegetable.

4 servings

Metric/Imperial

175g (6oz) Shortcrust Pastry I
25g (1oz) butter
12 spring onions, chopped
500g (1lb) minced beef
2 large tomatoes, peeled and chopped
1 teaspoon dried basil
1 teaspoon salt
½ teaspoon ground black pepper
350ml (12 fl oz) single cream
4 eggs

American

1 recipe Shortcrust Pastry
2 tablespoons butter
12 scallions, chopped
1lb ground beef
2 large tomatoes, peeled and chopped
1 teaspoon dried basil
1 teaspoon salt
½ teaspoon ground black pepper
1½ cups light cream
4 eggs

Preheat the oven to moderate (180°C/350°F or Gas Mark 4). Lightly grease a 23cm (9in) pie dish and dust it lightly with flour.

Prepare the pastry, wrap in grease-proof or waxed paper and refrigerate for 20 minutes.

To prepare the filling melt the butter in a medium-sized frying-pan over moderate heat. Sauté the spring onions [scallions] for 3 minutes. Add the beef and continue cooking, stirring occasionally, until the meat is brown.

Stir in the tomatoes, basil, salt and pepper and continue cooking for 10 more minutes. Take the pan from the heat and set aside.

Remove the pastry from the refrigerator. On a floured surface, roll into a shape 5cm (2in) larger than the pie dish. Line the pie dish with the pastry and prick it all over with a fork. Bake blind for 10 minutes.

Meanwhile heat the cream until it is hot but not boiling. Break the eggs into a mixing bowl and beat them lightly. Beating continuously, gradually pour in the hot cream. Add to the meat mixture. Mix well and pour into the pastry shell. Bake in the oven for 30 minutes. Serve hot.

SHEPHERD'S PIE

A favourite with children and adults alike, Shepherd's Pie is surely one of the best ways to use up leftover lamb.

4 servings

Metric/Imperial

75g (3oz) butter
2 medium-sized onions, finely chopped
1kg (2lb) cooked lamb, minced
2 teaspoons salt
1 teaspoon black pepper
1 teaspoon dried mixed herbs
2 teaspoons Worcestershire sauce
50ml (2 fl oz) beef stock or gravy
1.25kg (3lb) potatoes, cooked, mashed and kept warm
50ml (2 fl oz) milk

American

6 tablespoons butter
2 medium-sized onions, diced
2lb ground leftover lamb roast
2 teaspoons salt
1 teaspoon black pepper
¼ teaspoon each dried basil, oregano, marjoram and thyme
2 teaspoons Worcestershire sauce
¼ cup beef stock or gravy
3lb potatoes, cooked, mashed and kept warm
¼ cup milk

Preheat the oven to fairly hot (200°C/400°F or Gas Mark 6).

In a large saucepan, melt one-third of the butter over moderate heat. When

Serve Shepherd's Pie with buttered Brussels sprouts for a delicious and sustaining family meal.

the foam subsides, add the onions and cook, stirring occasionally, for 5 to 7 minutes or until soft and translucent but not brown. Stir in the meat, half the salt and pepper, the herbs and Worcestershire sauce and cook for 5 minutes, stirring frequently. Stir in the stock and transfer to a shallow ovenproof dish.

Place the potatoes in a large mixing bowl and stir in half the remaining butter, the milk and the remaining salt and pepper. Beat until the ingredients are thoroughly combined and spoon over the meat in an even layer. Using a fork, draw decorative lines on top. Dot with the remaining butter.

Place the dish in the centre of the oven and bake for 25 to 35 minutes.

QUICK ITALIAN-STYLE BEEF

A simple and economical dish, Quick

Italian-Style Beef is a meal in itself and need only be accompanied by some crusty bread for a quick lunch or supper.

4 servings

Metric/Imperial

1 tablespoon vegetable oil
2 medium-sized onions, thinly sliced and pushed out into rings
1 garlic clove, crushed
500g (1lb) minced beef
½ teaspoon dried oregano
½ teaspoon dried basil
175g (6oz) macaroni, cooked and drained
396g (14oz) can tomatoes
2 tablespoons tomato purée
2 teaspoons paprika
75g (3oz) Cheddar cheese, thinly sliced

American

1 tablespoon vegetable oil
2 medium-sized onions, thinly sliced

Quick Italian-style Beef is a delicious dish of beef mixed with vegetables, herbs and macaroni, covered with a cheese topping.

and separated into rings
1 garlic clove, crushed
1lb ground beef
½ teaspoon dried oregano
½ teaspoon dried basil
3 cups cooked macaroni
1 x 14oz can tomatoes
2 tablespoons tomato paste
2 teaspoons paprika
¾ cup Cheddar cheese, thinly sliced

Preheat the oven to moderate (180°C/350°F or Gas Mark 4).

In a medium-sized flameproof casserole, heat the oil gently. Add the onions and garlic and cook, stirring occasionally, for 5 to 7 minutes or until soft and translucent but not brown.

Add the beef to the pan and fry, stirring occasionally, for 5 minutes or until it loses its pinkness.

Stir in the oregano, basil, cooked macaroni, tomatoes with the can juice, tomato purée and paprika. Increase the heat and bring the liquid to the boil, stirring constantly. Remove the casserole from the heat and lay the sliced cheese over the beef mixture.

Bake for 20 minutes or until the cheese has melted and become browned.

MINCE [HAMBURGER] CASSEROLE

This is a quickly made and economical dish from Scotland. Use good quality minced [ground] meat or the dish will be very fatty. Serve the casserole with creamed potatoes and triangles of fried bread.

4 servings

Metric/Imperial

1 tablespoon butter
1 tablespoon vegetable oil
1kg (2lb) minced beef
1 large carrot, scraped and finely chopped
1 medium-sized onion, finely chopped
1 teaspoon salt
½ teaspoon black pepper
½ teaspoon dried thyme
½ teaspoon dried sage
225ml (8 fl oz) beef stock
2 tablespoons rolled porridge oats

American

1 tablespoon butter
1 tablespoon vegetable oil
2lb ground beef

1 large carrot, scraped and finely
  chopped
1 medium-sized onion, finely chopped
1 teaspoon salt
½ teaspoon black pepper
½ teaspoon dried thyme
½ teaspoon dried sage
1 cup beef stock
2 tablespoons rolled oats

In a large frying-pan, melt the butter
with the oil over moderate heat. When
the foam subsides add the meat and
cook, stirring constantly, for 8 minutes
or until well browned. Add the carrot,
onion, salt, pepper, thyme and sage and
stir to mix.

Cover, reduce the heat and cook for
10 minutes or until the carrot is almost
tender.

Pour in the stock and add the oats.
Increase the heat until the mixture
begins to bubble; reduce and simmer
for another 20 minutes or until the
mixture is thick and the vegetables are
tender.

SAVOURY MINCE [GROUND BEEF]

This delicious and quick method of
preparing minced [ground] beef is a
particular favourite with children,
served with creamy mashed potatoes and
a green vegetable.

4 servings

Metric/Imperial

1 medium-sized onion, chopped
1 garlic clove, crushed
2 tablespoons butter
500g (1lb) minced beef
395g (14oz) can tomatoes
2 tablespoons tomato purée
1 teaspoon sugar
salt and pepper
½ teaspoon dried oregano

American

1 medium-sized onion, chopped
1 garlic clove, crushed
2 tablespoons butter
1lb ground beef
1 x 14oz can tomatoes
2 tablespoons tomato paste

1 teaspoon sugar
salt and pepper
½ teaspoon dried oregano

Fry the onion and garlic in the butter
until translucent, then add the beef and
continue to cook, stirring occasionally,
until the beef has browned and is
crumbly.

Add the tomatoes, breaking them up
with a fork, the purée, sugar, salt,
pepper, and oregano and bring to the
boil, stirring.

Reduce the heat, cover and simmer
for about 30 minutes or until the mixture has thickened and the flavours
have combined.

BEEF COBBLER

This simple variation on the previous
recipe needs only to be accompanied by
a green vegetable for a sustaining
family meal.

4 servings

Metric/Imperial

500g (1lb) prepared Savoury Mince
400g (14oz) self-raising flour
½ teaspoon salt
4 tablespoons butter
2 tablespoons milk and a little water
beaten egg to glaze

American

1 recipe prepared Savoury Mince
  [Ground Beef]
3½ cups self-raising flour
½ teaspoon salt
4 tablespoons butter
2 tablespoons milk and a little water
beaten egg to glaze

Preheat the oven to hot (230°C/450°F
or Gas Mark 8). Put the prepared
savoury mince into a heat-proof dish.

To prepare the topping, sift the flour
and salt into a bowl and rub in the
butter until the mixture resembles
breadcrumbs. Add sufficient milk and
water to make a scone-like dough (just
enough liquid to make the mixture form
a ball, and leave the sides of the bowl
clean). Roll out the dough and cut into
5cm (2in) diameter circles. Arrange the

circles around the edge of the dish,
overlapping them slightly.

Brush the tops with beaten egg and
put into the oven for about 20 minutes
or until golden brown.

BOBOTIE

A South African dish, Bobotie (boh-
boo-tee) is baked minced [ground] meat,
with herbs and curry powder. It is quick
and easy to make and very tasty. It may
be served with rice and a mixed salad.

4-6 servings

Metric/Imperial

2½ tablespoons butter
1 tablespoon vegetable oil
2 medium-sized onions, coarsely
  chopped
1 garlic clove, finely chopped
1½ tablespoons curry powder
50g (2oz) shredded almonds
100g (4oz) sultanas or raisins
1 teaspoon mixed herbs
juice of ½ lemon
1 teaspoon salt
1 tablespoon sugar
1 tablespoon vinegar
⅛ teaspoon black pepper
1kg (2lb) minced beef
3 thick slices white bread
300ml (10 fl oz) milk
2 eggs, lightly beaten

American

2½ tablespoons butter
1 tablespoon vegetable oil
2 medium-sized onions, coarsely
  chopped
1 garlic clove, finely chopped
1½ tablespoons curry powder
½ cup slivered almonds
⅔ cup golden or dark raisins
¼ teaspoon each basil, oregano,
  marjoram, thyme
juice of ½ lemon
1 teaspoon salt
1 tablespoon sugar
1 tablespoon vinegar
⅛ teaspoon black pepper
2lb ground beef
3 thick slices white bread
1¼ cups milk
2 eggs, lightly beaten

Preheat the oven to moderate (180°C/ 350°F or Gas Mark 4). Grease a large, deep pie dish with ½ tablespoon butter.

In a small frying-pan, melt the remaining butter and oil. When the foam subsides, add the onions and garlic and fry over moderate heat for about 10 minutes or until lightly browned.

Remove the onions and garlic from the pan and place them in a large mixing bowl. Sprinkle over the curry powder and add the almonds, raisins, mixed herbs, lemon juice, salt, sugar, vinegar, pepper and meat. Mix well.

Soak the bread in the milk. Squeeze out the milk and mash the bread into the meat mixture together with 1 beaten egg. Turn the mixture into the buttered pie dish and press it down.

If necessary add a little extra milk to the milk squeezed from the bread to make up to just over half the original quantity.

Beat the remaining egg into the milk and pour the mixture over the meat in the pie dish. Stand the dish in a pan of water and bake for about 1 hour, or until the top is light golden brown and firm.

CHILI CON CARNE

A dish originating in the southwestern United States which enjoys immense popularity all over the North American continent, Chili con Carne (kon-kahr-nee) is economical and simple to make.

6 servings

Metric/Imperial

2 tablespoons olive oil
2 medium-sized onions, finely sliced
2 garlic cloves, chopped
675g (1½lb) minced beef
226g (8oz) can tomatoes
75g (3oz) tomato purée

Baked minced [ground] beef with herbs and curry powder, Bobotie is an easy to make and economical supper dish from South Africa.

1 bay leaf
1 teaspoon dried oregano
1 teaspoon ground cumin
1 teaspoon cayenne pepper
2 teaspoons chilli seasoning
2 teaspoons salt
350ml (12 fl oz) beef stock
396g (14oz) can red kidney beans

American

2 tablespoons olive oil
2 medium-sized onions, finely sliced
2 garlic cloves, chopped
1½lb ground beef
1 x 8oz can tomatoes
6 tablespoons tomato purée or paste
1 bay leaf
1 teaspoon dried oregano
1 teaspoon ground cumin
1 teaspoon cayenne pepper
2 teaspoons chili powder
2 teaspoons salt
1½ cups beef stock
1 x 14oz can red kidney beans

In a large fying-pan, heat the oil over moderate heat. Add the onions and garlic and fry for 5 to 6 minutes, stirring constantly. Add the meat and brown it, stirring from time to time to make sure it breaks up properly and does not stick.

Put the mixture into a large heavy saucepan and, mixing well, add the tomatoes, tomato purée, herbs and spices, salt and stock. Cover the pan and bring to the boil over moderate heat. Reduce the heat and simmer the mixture, stirring occasionally, for 1 hour.

Add the kidney beans, cover the pan again and continue simmering for 30 minutes.

MARROW [SUMMER SQUASH] WITH SAVOURY STUFFING

An inexpensive dish, Marrow [Summer Squash] with Savoury Stuffing makes an ideal family meal. Serve with mashed potatoes and hot Tomato Sauce.

6 servings

Metric/Imperial

50g (2oz) plus 1 tablespoon butter

1 x 1.25kg (1 x 3lb) vegetable marrow

2 medium-sized onions, coarsely
  chopped

1 large green pepper, white pith
  removed, seeded and coarsely
  chopped

500g (1lb) minced beef

4 medium-sized tomatoes, peeled and
  coarsely chopped

2 small carrots, scraped and finely
  diced

1½ teaspoons salt

½ teaspoon black pepper

1 teaspoon paprika

50g (2oz) fresh white breadcrumbs

2 egg yolks, well beaten with 3
  tablespoons milk

100g (4oz) Parmesan cheese, finely
  grated

American

5 tablespoons butter

1 x 3lb summer squash

2 medium-sized onions, coarsely
  chopped

1 large green pepper, membrane and
  seeds removed, coarsely chopped

1lb ground beef

4 medium-sized tomatoes, peeled and
  coarsely chopped

2 small carrots, scraped and finely
  diced

1½ teaspoons salt

½ teaspoon black pepper

1 teaspoon paprika

1 cup fresh white breadcrumbs

2 egg yolks, well beaten with 3
  tablespoons milk

1 cup Parmesan cheese, finely grated

Preheat the oven to moderate (180°C/
350°F or Gas Mark 4).

With a tablespoon of butter, gener-ously grease a large, oblong baking dish.

Cut the marrow [squash] in half lengthways, scoop out and discard the seeds. Place the halves, side by side, cut sides up, in the prepared baking dish.

In a medium-sized saucepan, melt half the remaining butter over moderate heat. When the foam subsides, add the onions and green pepper and fry, stirring occasionally, for 6 to 8 minutes, or until the onions are golden brown.

Add the beef and tomatoes to the pan and cook, stirring to break up the meat, for 6 to 8 minutes, or until the meat loses its pinkness.

Remove the pan from the heat. Stir in the carrots, salt, pepper and paprika.

In a small mixing bowl, combine the breadcrumbs with the egg yolks and milk. Stir into the meat mixture in the pan and combine thoroughly.

Pile this stuffing into the marrow [squash] halves and lightly pat down.

Sprinkle the Parmesan cheese over the stuffing, and dot with the remaining butter. Place the dish in the centre of the oven and bake for 1 hour, or until the marrow [squash] is very tender.

BEEF STUFFED CABBAGE ROLLS

A tasty, inexpensive dinner dish, Beef Stuffed Cabbage Rolls must be made with good quality beef. Serve it hot as a main dish or cold as a first course.

4 servings

Metric/Imperial

1 cabbage

500g (1lb) minced beef

2 tomatoes, peeled and finely chopped

2 tablespoons uncooked rice

juice and grated rind of ½ lemon

½ teaspoon dried mixed herbs

½ teaspoon salt

½ teaspoon black pepper

5 tablespoons cooking oil

SAUCE

1 onion, finely chopped

1 garlic clove, crushed

¼ teaspoon dried basil

396g (14oz) can tomatoes, drained and
  chopped

½ teaspoon salt

¼ teaspoon black pepper

1 teaspoon sugar

American

1 cabbage

1lb ground beef

2 tomatoes, peeled and finely chopped

2 tablespoons uncooked rice

juice and grated rind of ½ lemon

½ teaspoon dried mixed herbs (basil,
  oregano, marjoram and thyme)

½ teaspoon salt

½ teaspoon black pepper

5 tablespoons vegetable oil

SAUCE

1 onion, finely chopped

1 garlic clove, crushed

¼ teaspoon dried basil

1 x 14oz can tomatoes, drained and
  chopped

½ teaspoon salt

¼ teaspoon black pepper

1 teaspoon sugar

Trim the outer leaves from the cabbage. Boil the cabbage in unsalted water for 4 minutes only; drain well.

When cool enough to handle carefully detach the leaves and set them aside on a plate.

Put the minced beef in a bowl with the tomatoes, rice, lemon juice and grated rind, the mixed herbs, salt and pepper. Mix well with your hands and shape into small sausages.

Wrap each meat sausage in a cabbage leaf. Make a neat parcel and tie with thread. Cover and set aside.

To make the sauce, heat 2 tablespoons of oil in a small saucepan over moderate heat. Put in the onion and fry gently until soft and turning brown. Add the crushed garlic and basil and cook for 1 minute. Put in the tomatoes, salt, pepper and sugar. Stir, cover, lower the heat and simmer for 35 to 40 minutes.

In a large, heavy pot, heat the re-maining 3 tablespoons of oil over moderate heat. Add the cabbage; when slightly brown, turn them over and brown on the other side. Pour the tomato sauce over, cover, lower the heat and simmer for 1 hour.

Remove the thread from the cabbage rolls, put them on a warmed serving dish and pour over the sauce.

MINCED [GROUND] BEEF AND AUBERGINE [EGGPLANT] CASSEROLE

This dish is a delicious combination of flavours and makes a popular family dinner. Serve the casserole with boiled rice.

4-6 servings

Minced [Ground] Beef and Aubergine [Eggplant] Casserole is superb.

Metric/Imperial

3 small aubergines
1 tablespoon plus 1 teaspoon salt
6 tablespoons vegetable oil
1kg (2lb) minced beef
4 spring onions, chopped
6 tomatoes, peeled and chopped
1 large green pepper, white pith
   removed, seeded and sliced
2 slices pineapple, chopped
¼ teaspoon black pepper
½ teaspoon dried marjoram
175g (6oz) Cheddar cheese, grated

American

3 small eggplants
1 tablespoon plus 1 teaspoon salt
6 tablespoons vegetable oil
2lb ground beef
4 scallions, chopped
6 tomatoes, peeled and chopped
1 large green pepper, membrane and
   seeds removed, sliced
2 slices pineapple, chopped
¼ teaspoon black pepper
½ teaspoon dried marjoram
1½ cups Cheddar cheese, grated

Cut the aubergines [eggplants] into thin slices. Place them in a colander and sprinkle over the 1 tablespoon of salt. Set aside for 30 minutes.

Meanwhile, in a large frying-pan, heat 2 tablespoons of the oil, over moderate heat. Add the beef and fry, stirring constantly, for 6 minutes or until the meat is lightly browned. Add the spring onions [scallions], tomatoes, green pepper and pineapple to the pan and cook for 4 minutes, stirring occasionally.

Stir in the remaining salt, the pepper and marjoram. Reduce the heat to low and simmer, stirring occasionally, for 15 minutes. Remove the pan from the heat and set aside.

Preheat the oven to moderate (180°C/ 350°F or Gas Mark 4).

Dry the aubergine [eggplant] slices on kitchen paper.

In a medium-sized frying-pan, heat the remaining oil over moderate heat. Add half of the aubergine [eggplant] slices. Fry them for 2 to 3 minutes on each side or until soft. Remove from the pan and drain on kitchen paper. Set aside while you fry the remaining slices in the same way, adding more oil to the pan if necessary.

Place one-third of the aubergine [eggplant] slices in a medium-sized ovenproof dish. Cover with half of the meat mixture then with another one-third of aubergine [eggplant] slices. Top with the remaining meat mixture and aubergine [eggplant] slices. Sprinkle over the cheese.

Bake for 30 minutes or until the top is golden.

MOUSSAKA

A basic version of the more traditional Moussaka (moo-sah-kah) made with mutton, or lamb, tomatoes and aubergines [eggplants] and topped with a creamy sauce, this dish makes a filling lunch or dinner.

4 servings

Metric/Imperial

500g (1lb) aubergines, sliced
1 tablespoon plus 1 teaspoon salt
25g (1oz) butter
1 medium-sized onion, finely chopped
1 large garlic clove, crushed
500g (1lb) lean lamb, minced
4 medium-sized tomatoes, coarsely
    chopped
2 tablespoons tomato purée
¾ teaspoon dried thyme
½ teaspoon black pepper
3 tablespoons flour
100ml (4 fl oz) vegetable oil
300ml (10 fl oz) White Sauce
2 egg yolks
25g (1oz) Parmesan cheese, finely
    grated

American

1lb eggplants, sliced
1 tablespoon plus 1 teaspoon salt

Probably the best known and liked
Greek dish, Moussaka is delicious
served with a tossed salad.

2 tablespoons butter
1 medium-sized onion, finely chopped
1 large garlic clove, crushed
1lb lean ground lamb
4 medium-sized tomatoes, coarsely
    chopped
2 tablespoons tomato paste
¾ teaspoon dried thyme
½ teaspoon black pepper
3 tablespoons flour
½ cup vegetable oil
1¼ cups White Sauce
2 egg yolks
2 tablespoons Parmesan cheese, finely
    grated

Preheat the oven to fairly hot (190°C/
375°F or Gas Mark 5).

Place the aubergine [eggplant] slices
in a colander and sprinkle over the
tablespoon of salt. Set aside for 30
minutes.

Meanwhile, in a medium-sized
frying-pan, melt the butter over moderate heat. When the foam subsides, add
the onion and garlic and fry, stirring
occasionally, for 5 to 7 minutes, or until
soft and translucent but not brown.

Add the meat, and fry, stirring

frequently, for 8 minutes or until
thoroughly browned.

Add the tomatoes, tomato purée,
thyme, pepper and the remaining salt
and cook, stirring occasionally, for 4
minutes. Remove the pan from the heat.

Dry the aubergine [eggplant] slices
on kitchen paper. Place the flour on a
plate and dip the aubergine [eggplant]
slices in it, coating them thoroughly.

In a medium-sized frying-pan, heat
half the oil over moderate heat. Add
about half the aubergine [eggplant]
slices and fry them for 3 to 4 minutes on
each side, or until lightly and evenly
browned. Remove from the pan and
drain on kitchen paper. Fry the remaining slices in the same way, adding
more oil as necessary.

Arrange half the aubergine [eggplant]
slices in a deep-sided large baking dish.
Spoon over the lamb mixture and cover
with the remaining slices.

In a small mixing bowl, beat together
the White Sauce and egg yolks. Pour
the mixture into the dish and sprinkle
with Parmesan cheese.

Bake in the centre of the oven for 35
to 40 minutes, or until the top is lightly

browned.

PASTITSIO

Here is a warming herb-scented Greek favourite. The flavour is improved if it is prepared in advance, kept in the refrigerator overnight, and cooked the following day.

4 servings

Metric/Imperial

2 tablespoons oil or dripping
2 onions, finely chopped
500g (1lb) minced beef or lamb
40g (1½oz) tomato purée
freshly ground black pepper
1 garlic clove, crushed
a pinch of cinnamon
a pinch of dried thyme
350g (12oz) macaroni
25g (1oz) butter or margarine
25g (1oz) flour
425ml (15 fl oz) milk
salt and pepper
grated nutmeg
75g (3oz) grated cheese
150ml (5 fl oz) plain yogurt

American

Pastitso is a delicious warming and original Greek dish of herbs, meat and pasta.

2 tablespoons oil or drippings
2 onions, finely chopped
1lb ground beef or lamb
1½ tablespoons tomato paste
freshly ground black pepper
1 garlic clove, crushed
a pinch of cinnamon
a pinch of dried thyme
¾lb macaroni
2 tablespoons butter or margarine
¼ cup flour

2 cups milk
salt and pepper
grated nutmeg
¾ cup grated cheese
1 carton plain yogurt

Heat the oven to fairly hot 190°C/375° F or Gas Mark 5.

Warm the oil or dripping in a large frying-pan and fry the onions until they start to brown.

Add the meat and tomato purée [paste] and stir well with a fork to prevent lumps from forming. Sprinkle on the seasonings and cook for a few minutes, adding a little beef stock if the mixture is too dry.

Cook the pasta in plenty of salted boiling water in an uncovered pan for 10-15 minutes or until just tender. Drain thoroughly.

Meanwhile prepare a white sauce with the margarine, flour and milk. Season generously with salt, pepper, nutmeg and half the grated cheese. Remove from the heat and stir in the yogurt.

Line a large greased fireproof dish with the pasta, spoon half of the sauce

Vary the ingredients for cold meat loaf according to what you have available. For an interesting serving alternative garnish the top with sliced tomatoes and halved olives.

over the top and cover with the meat mixture. Pour on the remaining sauce and sprinkle the rest of the cheese on top.

Bake in the oven for 45 minutes.

MEAT LOAF

An economical cold meat loaf for the family, this may be served with salad for supper or at a picnic.

---
4 servings

Metric/Imperial

500g (1lb) lean minced beef
75g (3oz) fresh breadcrumbs
1 medium-sized onion, finely chopped
100g (4oz) mushrooms, wiped clean and chopped
2 eggs, lightly beaten

2 teaspoons French mustard
1 teaspoon celery salt
1 teaspoon Worcestershire sauce
½ teaspoon black pepper
½ teaspoon dried marjoram
½ teaspoon dried parsley
¼ teaspoon dried thyme
3 streaky bacon slices

American

1lb ground round steak
1½ cups fresh breadcrumbs
1 medium-sized onion, finely chopped
¼lb mushrooms, wiped clean and chopped
2 eggs, lightly beaten
2 teaspoons French mustard
1 teaspoon celery salt
1 teaspoon Worcestershire sauce
½ teaspoon black pepper
½ teaspoon dried marjoram
½ teaspoon parsley flakes
¼ teaspoon dried thyme
3 slices bacon

Preheat the oven to warm (170°C/325°F or Gas Mark 3).

In a large mixing bowl, combine all the ingredients except the bacon. Using your hands, mix and knead well.

Press the meat mixture into a 675g (1½lb) loaf tin and smooth top. Lay the bacon slices over the top.

Put the loaf tin into a large baking tin half-filled with boiling water. Place in the centre of the oven and bake for 1½ hours.

Remove from the oven, pour off any fat and leave to cool for 1 hour. Turn out, wrap in aluminium foil and chill in the refrigerator for at least 4 hours before serving.

POLISH MEAT LOAF

This is a very tasty and easy-to-make meat loaf, combining the flavours of pork and veal with aromatic herbs. Polish Meat Loaf is an adaptation of a Polish recipe and may be served hot with fried onions, potatoes, and a green vegetable or cold with a crunchy garden salad.

4-6 servings

Metric/Imperial

½ teaspoon butter
675g (1½lb) lean pork, coarsely minced
250g (8oz) pie veal, coarsely minced
1 teaspoon dried marjoram
½ teaspoon dried thyme
1 garlic clove, finely chopped
2 teaspoons salt
½ teaspoon black pepper

American

½ teaspoon butter
1½lb lean ground pork
½lb coarsely ground veal
1 teaspoon dried marjoram
½ teaspoon dried thyme
1 garlic clove, finely chopped
2 teaspoons salt
½ teaspoon black pepper

Preheat the oven to moderate (180°C/350°F or Gas Mark 4). Lightly grease a 1kg (2lb) loaf tin with the butter. Set aside.

Put all the ingredients in a large mixing bowl and stir to blend them thoroughly.

Spoon the mixture into the loaf tin. Place the tin in a large baking tin, half filled with cold water. Place the tin in the centre of the oven and bake for 1¼ to 1½ hours, or until the meat loaf has shrunk slightly away from the sides of the tin.

After removing from the oven, leave the meat loaf in the tin for 10 to 15 minutes, or until it has cooled slightly. Pour off any fat.

MEAT LOAF WITH EGG

This traditional Israeli dish is usually served cold, accompanied by a well flavoured tomato sauce.

6 servings

Metric/Imperial

1 teaspoon vegetable oil
1kg (2lb) minced beef
50g (2oz) fresh white breadcrumbs
2 celery stalks, trimmed and finely chopped
1 carrot, scraped and grated
2 medium-sized onions, finely grated
1 garlic clove, crushed
1 tablespoon chopped fresh parsley
1 teaspoon salt
1 teaspoon sugar
½ teaspoon black pepper
1 teaspoon grated nutmeg
2 eggs, lightly beaten
5 hard-boiled eggs

American

1 teaspoon vegetable oil

Delicious Polish Meat Loaf combines the flavours of pork and veal with aromatic herbs. Serve hot, or cold with a crisp salad.

2lb ground beef
1 cup fresh white breadcrumbs
2 celery stalks, trimmed and finely
    chopped
1 carrot, scraped and grated
2 medium-sized onions, finely grated
1 garlic clove, crushed
1 tablespoon chopped fresh parsley
1 teaspoon salt
1 teaspoon sugar
½ teaspoon black pepper
1 teaspoon grated nutmeg
2 eggs, lightly beaten
5 hard-boiled eggs

Preheat the oven to very hot (240°C/ 475°F or Gas Mark 9). Lightly grease a 1kg (2lb) loaf tin with the oil.

In a large mixing bowl, combine the beef, breadcrumbs, celery, carrot, onions, garlic, parsley, salt, sugar, pepper and nutmeg and mix well to blend.

Stir in the eggs, beating constantly until the mixture is smooth and pliable but not runny.

Spoon half the mixture into the prepared loaf tin. Top with the hard-boiled eggs, placed side by side along the length of the tin. Spoon the remaining meat mixture over the top, pressing down firmly.

Bake for 20 minutes, reduce the oven temperature to moderate (180°C/350°F or Gas Mark 4) and bake for 1 hour.

Remove the tin from the oven and set aside for 1 hour in a cool place, or until the loaf has cooled completely. Turn out.

LAMB PATTIES, GREEK-STYLE

Lamb Patties, Greek-style is one of the simplest dishes for a 'spur-of-the-

Flavoured with nuts and spices, Lamb Patties, Greek-Style makes a marvellously different snack meal.

moment' meal. Serve with Melba Toast.

4 servings

Metric/Imperial

1kg (2lb) minced lamb
1 small onion, grated
1 teaspoon salt
½ teaspoon black pepper
½ teaspoon grated nutmeg
125g (5oz) pine nuts or blanched
   almonds, roughly chopped

American

2lb ground lamb
1 small onion, grated
1 teaspoon salt
½ teaspoon black pepper
½ teaspoon grated nutmeg
1 cup blanched almonds, roughly

chopped (pine or Indian nuts can
be substituted)

Preheat the grill [broiler] to high.

In a large bowl, combine all the ingredients and mix until well blended.
Form into 12 small patties.

Place the patties on a rack in the grill
[broiler] pan and cook for 8 minutes on
each side or until cooked through. If
they brown too quickly, reduce the heat
to moderate after the first 2 minutes.

WESTERN BURGERS

A spicy variation on traditional
American hamburgers, Western
Burgers make the perfect snack meal
served with mixed salad and crusty

Western Burgers, a spicy variation
on traditional hamburgers.

bread. Or serve them on their own,
between toasted hamburger buns.

4 servings

Metric/Imperial

1kg (2lb) minced beef
1 small onion, very finely chopped
25g (1oz) fine dry breadcrumbs
1 teaspoon salt
½ teaspoon black pepper
1 tablespoon chilli seasoning or
   1 teaspoon pure chilli powder
½ teaspoon dried mixed herbs
½ teaspoon grated orange rind
2 tablespoons orange juice

1 large egg
4 fried eggs, kept hot

American

2lb ground beef
1 small onion, very finely chopped
⅓ cup fine dry breadcrumbs
1 teaspoon salt
½ teaspoon black pepper
1 teaspoon chili powder
⅛ teaspoon each dried basil, oregano,
   marjoram and thyme
½ teaspoon grated orange rind
2 tablespoons orange juice
1 large egg
4 fried eggs, kept hot

Preheat the grill [broiler] to high.

In a medium-sized mixing bowl, combine the beef, onion, breadcrumbs, salt, pepper, chilli powder, mixed herbs, orange rind and orange juice and mix well. Stir in the egg and, using your hands, mix the ingredients together thoroughly.

Form the mixture into 4 balls and flatten into patty shapes.

Place the patties on the grill [broiler] rack and cook for 2 to 3 minutes on each side or until well browned. Reduce the temperature to moderate and cook for a further 5 to 7 minutes on each side or until the burgers are well cooked. Serve topped with the fried eggs.

MEATBALLS IN PIQUANT SAUCE

These beef meatballs in a tangy sauce are sure to be popular. Serve with rice.

4 servings

Metric/Imperial

1 small onion, cut into wedges
500g (1lb) lean minced beef
1 teaspoon chopped fresh mint
1 tablespoon chopped parsley
1 tablespoon fresh breadcrumbs
salt and pepper
425ml (15 fl oz) beef stock
300ml (10 fl oz) water
2 egg yolks
juice of 1 lemon

American

1 small onion, cut into wedges
1lb lean ground round steak
1 teaspoon chopped fresh mint or
   ¼ teaspoon dried mint flakes
1 tablespoon chopped parsley
1 tablespoon fresh breadcrumbs
salt and pepper
2 cups beef stock
1¼ cups water
2 egg yolks
juice of 1 lemon

Mince [grind] the beef one extra time with the onion, if possible. If you do not have a mincer [meat grinder], chop the onion finely and mix it thoroughly with the beef.

Mix the beef and onion with the mint, parsley, breadcrumbs, salt and pepper to taste and about 3 tablespoons of the beef stock. Put the remaining stock and the water to boil in a large saucepan.

Meanwhile, with wet hands, form the meat mixture into small balls about the size of a walnut. Drop these into the stock and boil for about 20 minutes. Drain, reserving the stock, and keep hot on a serving dish.

Beat the egg yolks with the lemon juice. Slowly add some of the hot stock, beating constantly. Stir the egg yolk mixture into the remaining stock. Cover and let stand for 5 minutes off the heat. Serve the meat balls with the sauce poured over them.

MEATBALLS IN TOMATO SAUCE

A tasty and economical dish, Meatballs in Tomato Sauce may be served with spaghetti or with potatoes and a green vegetable. Hand round a bowl of grated Parmesan cheese and one of finely chopped fresh parsley.

4 servings

Metric/Imperial

SAUCE
1 tablespoon butter
2 tablespoons vegetable oil
1 onion, finely chopped
2 garlic cloves, finely chopped
½ teaspoon dried basil
½ teaspoon dried oregano
792g (28oz) can tomatoes
4 tablespoons tomato purée
½ teaspoon salt
¼ teaspoon black pepper
1 teaspoon sugar
MEATBALLS
500g (1lb) minced beef
500g (1lb) minced veal
25g (1oz) fresh breadcrumbs
1 garlic clove, crushed
2 tablespoons finely chopped fresh
   parsley
2 tablespoons grated Parmesan cheese
1 egg, lightly beaten
1 teaspoon salt
½ teaspoon black pepper
4 tablespoons vegetable oil

American

SAUCE
1 tablespoon butter
2 tablespoons vegetable oil
1 onion, finely chopped
2 garlic cloves, finely chopped
½ teaspoon dried basil
½ teaspoon dried oregano
3½ cups Italian plum tomatoes
4 tablespoons tomato paste
½ teaspoon salt
¼ teaspoon black pepper
1 teaspoon sugar
MEATBALLS
1lb ground beef
1lb ground veal
½ cup fresh breadcrumbs
1 garlic clove, crushed
2 tablespoons finely chopped fresh
   parsley
2 tablespoons grated Parmesan cheese
1 egg, lightly beaten
1 teaspoon salt
½ teaspoon black pepper
4 tablespoons vegetable oil

First make the sauce. In a medium-sized saucepan, melt the butter with the oil over moderate heat. When the foam subsides, add the onion and garlic and fry, stirring occasionally, for 8 to 10 minutes or until golden brown.

Add the basil, oregano, the tomatoes with the can juices, the tomato purée, salt, pepper and sugar. Stir to mix. When the sauce comes to the boil, cover the pan, reduce the heat to low and simmer for 45 minutes, stirring occasionally.

Small meatballs flavoured with all-spice, nutmeg, cloves and ginger, Swedish Meatballs are served in a deliciously creamy sauce. Serve them with a crisp green salad.

Meanwhile make the meatballs. In a large mixing bowl, combine all the ingredients for the meatballs except the oil. Using floured hands, mix and knead the ingredients well. Shape the mixture into about 36 walnut-sized balls.

In a large frying-pan, heat the oil over high heat. Reduce the heat to moderate and add as many meatballs as can be contained easily in the pan. Fry, turning occasionally, for 6 to 8 minutes or until well browned. Transfer the meatballs as they brown to the pan in which the sauce is cooking.

Simmer the meatballs in the tomato sauce for 10 minutes.

SWEDISH MEATBALLS

Köttbullar (shut-bohl-ler), small, spicy meatballs in a deliciously creamy sauce, is the Swedish national dish. Serve with boiled rice, a tossed green salad and crusty white bread for a perfectly delightful meal.

4 servings

Metric/Imperial

25g (1oz) fresh white breadcrumbs
500g (1lb) minced beef
250g (8oz) minced pork
2 medium-sized potatoes, cooked and mashed
1 egg, lightly beaten
1 teaspoon salt
½ teaspoon soft brown sugar
½ teaspoon black pepper
¼ teaspoon ground allspice
¼ teaspoon grated nutmeg
40g (1½oz) fine dry breadcrumbs
75g (3oz) butter
SAUCE
2 tablespoons flour
¼ teaspoon salt
⅛ teaspoon black pepper
225ml (8 fl oz) beef stock
225ml (8 fl oz) double cream

American

½ cup fresh white breadcrumbs
1lb ground beef
½lb ground pork
2 medium-sized potatoes, cooked and mashed
1 egg, lightly beaten
1 teaspoon salt
½ teaspoon soft brown sugar
½ teaspoon black pepper
¼ teaspoon ground allspice
¼ teaspoon grated nutmeg
½ cup fine dry breadcrumbs
⅜ cup butter
SAUCE
2 tablespoons flour
¼ teaspoon salt
⅛ teaspoon black pepper
1 cup beef stock
1 cup heavy cream

First, make the meatballs. In a large mixing bowl, combine all the meatball ingredients, except the dry bread-crumbs and the butter, beating with a wooden spoon until they are well blended.

With your hands, shape spoonfuls of the mixture into small, walnut-sized balls.

Place the dry breadcrumbs on a large plate. Roll the meatballs in the breadcrumbs to coat them all over, shaking off any excess.

In a large frying-pan, melt the butter over moderate heat. When the foam subsides, add the meatballs, a few at a time, and cook them, stirring and turning occasionally, for 10 to 12 minutes, or until they are cooked through and brown all over. Keep warm while you cook the remaining meatballs in the same way.

To prepare the sauce, stir the flour, salt and pepper into the juices in the frying-pan to make a smooth paste. Gradually add the beef stock and cream, stirring constantly. Place the pan over low heat and cook, stirring constantly, until the sauce has thickened.

Return the meatballs to the frying-pan, baste them with the sauce and simmer for 12 to 15 minutes.

YORKSHIRE SAVOURY MEATBALLS

A marvellously sustaining yet economical dish, Yorkshire Savoury Meatballs may be served with salad, crusty bread and beer for a hearty meal.

4 servings

Metric/Imperial

75ml (3 fl oz) vegetable oil
1 large onion, finely chopped
3 carrots, scraped and sliced
175ml (6 fl oz) beef stock
175ml (6 fl oz) beer
1 tablespoon Worcestershire sauce
3 tablespoons tomato ketchup
1 teaspoon dried thyme
½ teaspoon salt
1 teaspoon black pepper
2 tablespoons cornflour mixed to a paste with 3 tablespoons beer
MEATBALLS
500g (1lb) minced beef
500g (1lb) sausage meat
75g (3oz) fine dry breadcrumbs
grated rind of 1 lemon

1 egg, lightly beaten
2 tablespoons milk
1 tablespoon Worcestershire sauce
½ teaspoon salt
1 teaspoon black pepper
1 teaspoon dried thyme
1 garlic clove, crushed

American

⅜ cup vegetable oil
1 large onion, finely chopped
3 carrots, scraped and sliced
¾ cup beef stock
¾ cup beer
1 tablespoon Worcestershire sauce
3 tablespoons tomato ketchup
1 teaspoon dried thyme
½ teaspoon salt
1 teaspoon black pepper
2 tablespoons cornstarch mixed to a paste with 3 tablespoons beer
MEATBALLS
1lb ground beef
1lb sausage meat
1 cup fine dry breadcrumbs
grated rind of 1 lemon
1 egg, lightly beaten
2 tablespoons milk
1 tablespoon Worcestershire sauce
½ teaspoon salt
1 teaspoon black pepper
1 teaspoon dried thyme
1 garlic clove, crushed

Preheat the oven to moderate (180°C/350°F or Gas Mark 4).

First make the meatballs. In a large mixing bowl, combine all the meatball ingredients, beating with a wooden spoon until well mixed. Using your hands, shape the mixture into small, walnut-sized balls.

In a large, flame-proof casserole, heat the oil over moderate heat. Add the meatballs, a few at a time, and fry, turning them frequently, for 6 to 8 minutes or until lightly browned all over. Transfer to a plate as they brown. Add the onion and carrots to the casserole and fry, stirring occasionally, for 5 to 7 minutes or until the onion is soft and translucent but not brown. Pour in the beef stock, beer, Worcestershire sauce and ketchup. Add the thyme, salt, pepper and cornflour [cornstarch] mixture; stir well to mix. Bring the liquid to the boil.

Add the meatballs and cook in the oven for 1 hour or until they are cooked through and the vegetables are tender but still firm.

YORKSHIRE PANCAKES

These delicious, crunchy pancakes make a pleasant lunch or supper dish served with French-fried potatoes and fresh green peas.

4-6 servings

Metric/Imperial

4 eggs, separated
250g (8oz) minced beef
½ teaspoon salt
½ teaspoon black pepper
½ teaspoon baking powder
1 small onion, very finely chopped
1 tablespoon Worcestershire sauce
2 tablespoons chopped fresh parsley
½ teaspoon dried basil
3 tablespoons vegetable oil

American

4 eggs, separated
½lb ground beef
½ teaspoon salt
½ teaspoon black pepper
½ teaspoon baking powder
1 small onion, very finely chopped
1 tablespoon Worcestershire sauce
2 tablespoons chopped fresh parsley
½ teaspoon dried basil
3 tablespoons vegetable oil

In a large mixing bowl, beat the egg yolks until pale and thick. Fold in the beef, salt, pepper, baking powder, onion, Worcestershire sauce, parsley and basil and stir until the ingredients are thoroughly combined.

Beat the egg whites until they form stiff peaks. Using a metal spoon, gently fold them into the beef mixture.

In a large frying-pan, heat the oil over moderate heat. Drop tablespoons of the beef mixture into the hot oil and fry for 3 minutes or until the pancakes are puffed up and brown at the edges. Turn and fry for a further 2 to 3 minutes. Drain on kitchen paper and keep warm while you fry the remaining beef mixture in the same way.

Poultry and game

Chicken for a family meal is unbeatable value, not only because it is an economical buy but also because it is popular with everyone and lends itself to a host of very different recipes, from the simple to the exotic. A large chicken will supply a family with meat for two good meals, and the giblets and bones can be used to produce tasty gravy or soup stock, so nothing is wasted.

Most of the recipes in this section are for chicken or rabbit, both of which can be considered as staple buys for everyday cooking, whereas turkey, goose and game birds are still for most of us a special occasion luxury. However, if you have meat left over from the Christmas or Thanksgiving turkey, try Turkey Coronation or Turkey Meat Mould (see Leftovers).

Traditional accompaniments for turkey include Chestnut and Sausage Stuffing or Parsley and Lemon Stuffing, cranberry sauce or redcurrant jelly and sausagemeat. Goose and duck need the contrast of pungent Sage and Onion Stuffing or a sweet stuffing containing fruit, and the rather strong flavour of the meat is often offset by serving with a sweet sauce such as orange sauce. This applies to game birds and game animals, all of which have strongly flavoured flesh. Chicken, on the other hand, is not strongly-flavoured (unfortunately modern oven-ready frozen birds frequently have very little flavour at all). Traditional accompaniments are a lighter herb stuffing and bread sauce, though you can also serve a spring chicken in the classic French manner, which brings out its full delicate flavour. This means cooking it in butter, with butter also rubbed inside the body cavity. Fresh herbs and half an onion are often placed in the cavity during cooking. Baste frequently so that the cooked bird is a beautiful golden-brown in colour, and serve cut into portions with sautéed potatoes and a green salad.

An older, tougher chicken should be boiled, and this may take from one hour to three hours or longer, depending on size and age. Try Chicken, English-Style for a really delicious way of serving an older fowl. For young birds there is a wide range of delicious recipes to choose from here.

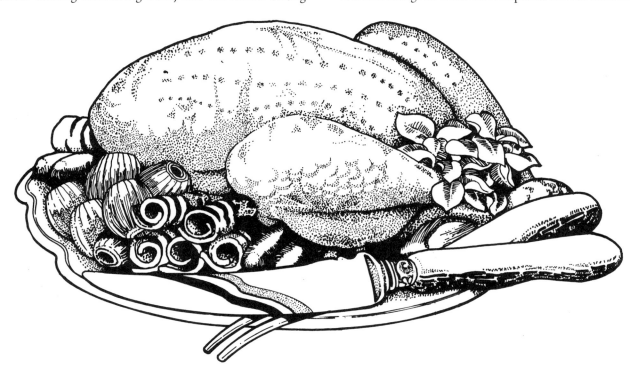

Chicken and Leek Pie, topped with crisp, golden pastry, makes a tasty dish for the family

CHICKEN AND LEEK PIE

This crisp golden pastry-topped pie with a filling of chicken and leeks makes a tasty lunch or supper dish. When cold, a piece of it is ideal for a packed lunch.

6 servings

Metric/Imperial

175g (6oz) Rough Puff Pastry
1 x 2.75kg (1 x 5lb) chicken
2 medium-sized onions, halved
2 celery stalks, quartered
1 bouquet garni
2½ teaspoons salt
1¼kg (2½lb) leeks, including 5cm (2in) of the green stems, thoroughly washed and sliced

1 teaspoon sugar
100g (4oz) ham, thinly sliced
1 tablespoon chopped parsley
a little milk

American

1 recipe Rough Puff Pastry
5lb stewing chicken
2 medium-sized onions, halved
2 celery stalks, quartered
1 bouquet garni
2½ teaspoons salt
2½lb leeks, including 2in of the green stems, washed and sliced
1 teaspoon sugar
¼lb ham, thinly sliced
1 tablespoon chopped parsley
a little milk

Place the chicken, onions, celery, bouquet garni and 2 teaspoons of salt in a large saucepan. Cover with water. Bring to the boil and skim off any scum that rises to the surface. Reduce the heat, partly cover the pan and simmer for 1 to 1½ hours or until the chicken is tender.

Transfer the chicken to a wooden board or platter. Strain the stock into a measuring jug. Return 450ml (16 fl oz) [2 cups] of the stock to the saucepan and add the leeks. Cook until just tender.

Preheat the oven to fairly hot (200°C/400°F or Gas Mark 6).

Detach the chicken meat from the skin and bones, cut into bite-sized pieces and put in a deep pie dish. Pour in the leeks and stock and sprinkle over the sugar and remaining salt.

Arrange the slices of ham in a layer over the leeks and sprinkle with the parsley.

Roll out the dough to 2.5cm (1in) larger than the top of the pie dish. With a knife cut a strip around the pastry. Dampen the rim of the dish and press the pastry strip on top. Lightly moisten the strip.

Lift the dough on to the dish, trim and crimp the edges to seal.

Cut a cross in the middle of the pastry and brush with milk. Roll out the trimmings and decorate the pie. Brush with milk.

Place the pie in the oven and bake for 1 hour, or until the top is golden brown.

CHICKEN TAMALE PIE

This unusual American chicken pie has subtle spicy flavourings. If the pie has to be kept waiting, just turn off the oven and leave the pie inside with the door closed.

6 servings

Metric/Imperial

1 x 2½kg (1 x 5lb) chicken
3½ teaspoons salt
10 peppercorns
1 bay leaf
50g (2oz) cornmeal
1 teaspoon chilli powder
2 tablespoons butter
1 green pepper, white pith removed, seeded and sliced
1 large onion, chopped
1 garlic clove, finely chopped
3 large tomatoes, peeled and chopped
¼ teaspoon Tabasco sauce
pinch each dried oregano, thyme and tarragon
275g (10oz) sweetcorn kernels
50g (2oz) Parmesan cheese, grated

American

5lb stewing chicken
3½ teaspoons salt
10 peppercorns
1 bay leaf
⅓ cup cornmeal
1 teaspoon chili powder
2 tablespoons butter
1 green pepper, membrane and seeds removed, sliced
1 large onion, chopped
1 garlic clove, finely chopped
3 large tomatoes, peeled and chopped
¼ teaspoon Tabasco sauce
⅛ teaspoon each dried oregano, thyme and tarragon
1 cup whole kernel corn
½ cup Parmesan cheese, grated

Place the chicken in a large saucepan and cover with water. Add 2 teaspoons of salt, the peppercorns and bay leaf.

Bring to the boil, reduce the heat,

This unusual Chicken Tamale Pie is subtly flavoured with garlic, chilli powder and herbs.

cover and simmer for 1 to 1½ hours, or until the chicken is tender, occasionally skimming any fat off the surface.

Allow to cool in the liquid, then detach the meat from the skin and bones.

Skim any fat off the surface of the stock in the pan and put it through a strainer into a measuring jug. Reserve 450ml (16 fl oz) [2 cups].

In a medium-sized saucepan, bring 350ml (12 fl oz) [1½ cups] of the strained stock to the boil over high heat.

Mix the cornmeal with the remaining reserved stock. Pour into the boiling stock in the pan and stir to combine. Add 1 teaspoon of salt and ½ teaspoon chilli powder. Cook for 15 minutes, or until the mixture is very thick.

Preheat the oven to moderate (180°C/ 350°F or Gas Mark 4).

Line the sides and bottom of a 3 litre (5 pint) [3 quart] casserole with the cornmeal mixture.

In a small frying-pan, melt the butter over a moderate heat. When the foam subsides add the green pepper, onion and garlic and fry for 8 to 10 minutes or until the onion is soft and translucent but not brown.

Add the tomatoes, Tabasco sauce, herbs and remaining chilli powder to the pan, reduce the heat and simmer gently for 2 to 3 minutes. Add the corn kernels and remaining salt.

Place the chicken in the bottom of the lined casserole and cover it with the tomato and corn mixture.

Sprinkle the top of the dish with the Parmesan cheese and bake for 30 minutes.

CHICKEN A LA KING

This is an excellent recipe for using cooked chicken. It is good enough for a dinner party, yet very simple to prepare. Plain boiled rice makes a good accompaniment.

4 servings

Metric/Imperial

25g (1oz) butter
1 green pepper, white pith removed, seeded and finely chopped

175g (6oz) button mushrooms, finely sliced
1 tablespoon flour
1 teaspoon salt
300ml (10 fl oz) single cream
300ml (10 fl oz) milk
750g (1¾lb) cooked chicken, diced
3 egg yolks
2 teaspoons lemon juice
1 tablespoon paprika
2 teaspoons chopped parsley
2 tablespoons sweet sherry (optional)

American

2 tablespoons butter
1 green pepper, membrane and seeds removed, finely chopped
6oz small mushrooms, finely sliced
1 tablespoon flour
1 teaspoon salt
1¼ cups light cream
1¼ cups milk
3 cups cooked chicken, diced
3 egg yolks
2 teaspoons lemon juice
1 tablespoon paprika
2 teaspoons chopped parsley
2 tablespoons sweet sherry (optional)

In a medium-sized saucepan, melt the butter over moderate heat. When the foam subsides add the green pepper and, stirring occasionally, cook gently for 6 minutes. Add the mushrooms and cook for a further 4 minutes. Stir in the flour and salt and cook for 2 minutes longer. Gradually add the cream and milk, stirring continuously. Bring the mixture to the boil, reduce the heat to low and cook for 3 minutes. Stir in the chicken and reduce the heat to very low.

In a small bowl, beat the egg yolks, lemon juice, paprika and parsley together. Add 4 tablespoons of the hot sauce, a spoonful at a time, and stir well. Pour this mixture into the pan, stir and cook gently for 4 minutes; do not boil. Mix in the sherry if used and serve.

CHICKEN, ENGLISH-STYLE

This is one of the best ways to cook an older, tougher chicken. The addition of vegetables, as well as the long, slow cooking makes the chicken tender and flavourful.

6 servings

Metric/Imperial

1 x 2½kg (1 x 5lb) boiling chicken
2 large leeks, sliced
2 carrots, scraped and sliced
1 small turnip, peeled and quartered
8 peppercorns
1 bouquet garni
2 tablespoons butter
2 tablespoons flour
4 tablespoons fresh parsley, finely chopped

American

5lb stewing chicken
2 large leeks, sliced
2 carrots, scraped and sliced
1 small turnip, peeled and quartered
8 peppercorns
1 bouquet garni
2 tablespoons butter
2 tablespoons flour
4 tablespoons fresh parsley, finely chopped

Put the chicken in a large saucepan and pour over enough water to cover. Add the vegetables, peppercorns and bouquet garni. Bring to the boil, cover and simmer for about 2½ hours or until tender.

Strain off ¾ litre (1¼ pints) [3 cups] of the stock into a small saucepan. Leave the chicken in the remaining stock and keep warm.

Place the small saucepan over moderate heat and boil the stock until it has reduced by about one-third. Remove from the heat and allow to cool. Skim off the fat from the surface.

In another pan, melt the butter over low heat. Remove from the heat and stir in the flour. Gradually add the cooled and skimmed stock, stirring constantly. Return the pan to moderate heat and bring the sauce to the boil. Boil for 1 minute, stirring constantly. Remove from the heat and stir in the parsley.

Beat the sauce for 2 minutes, then cover and return to very low heat to keep warm.

Carve the chicken and arrange on a warmed serving platter. Spoon over a little of the parsley sauce and serve the rest in a sauceboat.

CHICKEN PAPRIKASH

A richly coloured Hungarian dish, Chicken Paprikash may be served with a cucumber salad and boiled rice, or with creamy mashed potatoes.

6 servings

Metric/Imperial

6 chicken pieces
1 teaspoon salt
½ teaspoon black pepper
2 tablespoons butter
2 large onions, chopped
1 large garlic clove, crushed
1½ tablespoons paprika
300ml (10 fl oz) chicken stock
2 green peppers, white pith removed, seeded and sliced
4 tomatoes, peeled and chopped
1½ tablespoons flour
150ml (5 fl oz) sour cream

American

6 chicken quarters
1 teaspoon salt
½ teaspoon black pepper

Chicken Paprikash is a colourful dish of chicken, tomatoes and peppers.

2 tablespoons butter
2 large onions, chopped
1 large clove garlic, crushed
1½ tablespoons paprika
1¼ cups chicken stock
2 green peppers, membrane and seeds removed, sliced
4 tomatoes, peeled and chopped
1½ tablespoons flour
⅝ cup sour cream

Danish Chicken Casserole with capsicum and tomatoes and topped with cheese is a nourishing and tempting dish for the family.

Rub the chicken pieces with the salt and pepper.

In a large saucepan, melt the butter over moderate heat. When the foam subsides add the onions and garlic and fry for 8 to 10 minutes or until lightly coloured.

Stir in the paprika and cook for a further 2 to 3 minutes.

Pour in the stock and add the chicken pieces, peppers and tomatoes to the pan. Cover, reduce the heat and cook for 1 hour or until the chicken is tender.

Blend the flour with 2 tablespoons of the sour cream until smooth.

Pour this mixture into the saucepan and stir. Increase the heat to moderate, bring to the boil and cook for 2 minutes. Pour in the rest of the cream, stir and serve.

DANISH CHICKEN CASSEROLE

A tempting and easy-to-make dish, Danish Chicken Casserole is ideal to serve for a family lunch or supper with rice and a tossed salad.

4-6 servings

Metric/Imperial

50g (2oz) flour

1 teaspoon salt

½ teaspoon black pepper

2 teaspoons dried dill

1 x 2.5kg (1 x 5lb) chicken, skinned and cut into 8 serving pieces

2 eggs, lightly beaten

50g (2oz) butter

2 tablespoons vegetable oil

300ml (10 fl oz) chicken stock

1 green pepper, white pith removed, seeded and cut into thin rings

2 tomatoes, peeled and sliced

100ml (4 fl oz) double cream

50g (2oz) Cheddar cheese, grated

American

½ cup flour

1 teaspoon salt

½ teaspoon black pepper

2 teaspoons dried dill

5lb roasting chicken, skinned and cut into 8 serving pieces
2 eggs, lightly beaten
¼ cup butter
2 tablespoons vegetable oil
1¼ cups chicken stock
1 green pepper, membrane and seeds removed, cut into thin rings
2 tomatoes, peeled and sliced
½ cup heavy cream
½ cup Cheddar cheese, grated

Combine the flour, salt, pepper and dill. Dip the chicken pieces first in the beaten eggs and then coat them thoroughly in the flour mixture.

In a large flameproof casserole, melt the butter and oil over moderate heat. When the foam subsides add the chicken pieces to the pan and fry for about 8 minutes or until lightly browned on all sides, turning frequently.

Add the chicken stock and bring to the boil. Reduce the heat, cover the pan and simmer gently for 40 minutes or until the chicken is tender.

Arrange the chicken pieces in the centre of a large, warmed flameproof serving dish. Keep warm.

Preheat the grill [broiler] to moderate. Add the green pepper to the liquid in the casserole and simmer for 4 minutes. Add the tomatoes and cook for a further 2 minutes. Arrange around the chicken pieces. Remove the pan from the heat and stir in the cream. Return to the heat and cook gently for 2 to 3 minutes.

Pour the sauce over the chicken. Sprinkle the cheese on top and place under the grill [broiler] for 5 minutes or until the cheese is bubbling.

MARYLAND CHICKEN

This famous American dish, for which there are almost as many 'correct' versions as there are states in the United States, is a quickly prepared dinner dish. Accompaniments can vary considerably, but traditionally corn fritters are served, as are fried bananas and bacon rolls. Other accompaniments may include potato pancakes, boiled rice, mashed potatoes and horseradish sauce – so it's up to you to choose.

4 servings

Metric/Imperial

350ml (12 fl oz) milk
25g (1oz) flour, seasoned with ¼ teaspoon salt and ¼ teaspoon black pepper
4 chicken breasts
1 egg, lightly beaten with 1 teaspoon water
75g (3oz) fresh breadcrumbs
100g (4oz) butter
3 tablespoons vegetable oil
½ teaspoon sugar
1 tablespoon flour

Maryland Chicken is delicious served with fried bananas, bacon rolls, potato pancakes and horseradish sauce. But vary the accompaniments to suit your taste.

American

1½ cups milk
¼ cup flour, seasoned with ¼ teaspoon
    salt and ¼ teaspoon black pepper
4 chicken breasts
1 egg, lightly beaten with 1 teaspoon
    water
1½ cups fresh breadcrumbs
½ cup butter
3 tablespoons vegetable oil
½ teaspoon sugar
1 tablespoon flour

Place 3 tablespoons of the milk in a saucer and the seasoned flour in another. Dip the chicken breasts, one by one, in the milk, then in the flour to coat them on all sides, shaking off any excess. Set aside for 10 minutes to allow the coating to dry slightly.

Pour the egg mixture on to a large plate and place the breadcrumbs on another. Dip the breasts, one by one, in the egg mixture, then in the breadcrumbs, shaking off any excess.

In a large frying-pan, melt three-quarters of the butter with the oil over moderate heat. When the foam subsides reduce the heat, add the chicken breasts and cook, turning occasionally, for 20 minutes or until tender. Remove and keep warm.

In a medium-sized saucepan, melt the remaining butter over moderate heat. When the foam subsides stir in the sugar, mixing and stirring until it becomes dark brown and caramelizes.

Stir in the flour and cook for 1 minute, stirring constantly. Remove the pan from the heat. Gradually add the remaining milk, stirring constantly to avoid lumps. Return the pan to the heat and cook, stirring, for 2 to 3 minutes or until the sauce is thick and smooth. Serve in a sauceboat.

CHICKEN IN CHERRY SAUCE

A sweet and succulent sauce accompanies this unusual and delicious dish. Serve it with small roast potatoes, new peas and carrots.

4 servings

Metric/Imperial

1 x 2kg (1 x 4lb) chicken
1 teaspoon salt
½ teaspoon black pepper
1 teaspoon dried rosemary
50g (2oz) butter
225ml (8 fl oz) chicken stock
396g (14oz) can stoned Morello
    cherries, drained and with 175ml
    (6 fl oz) of the juice reserved
2 teaspoons lemon juice
2 teaspoons cornflour dissolved in
    2 tablespoons water

American

4lb roasting chicken
1 teaspoon salt
½ teaspoon black pepper
1 teaspoon dried rosemary
¼ cup butter
1 cup chicken stock
1 x 14oz can Morello cherries, pitted,
    drained and ½ cup of the juice
    reserved
2 teaspoons lemon juice
2 teaspoons cornstarch dissolved in
    2 tablespoons water

Preheat the oven to moderate (180°C/350°F or Gas Mark 4).

Rub the chicken, inside and out, with the salt, pepper and rosemary.

In a large flameproof casserole, melt the butter over moderate heat. When the foam subsides add the chicken and cook, turning frequently, for 8 to 10 minutes or until evenly browned. Pour over the stock and bring to the boil. Cover the casserole, place in the centre of the oven and cook for 45 minutes to 1 hour or until the chicken is tender. Transfer to a warmed serving dish.

Skim off any fat from the surface of the juices in the casserole. Strain the liquid into a small saucepan. Place over moderate heat and add the reserved cherry juice and the lemon juice. Bring to the boil, stirring constantly. Stir in the dissolved cornflour [cornstarch], reduce the heat to low and simmer the sauce, stirring constantly, for 5 minutes or until thickened.

Add the drained cherries to the sauce and continue cooking for 2 minutes or until they are heated through.

Pour half the sauce over the chicken and half into a warmed sauceboat.

CHICKEN FRICASSEE

This creamy-flavoured chicken casserole may be served with peas and croquette potatoes.

6 servings

Metric/Imperial

50g (2oz) flour, seasoned with ½ tea-
    spoon dried thyme, 1 teaspoon salt
    and ½ teaspoon black pepper
1 x 2½kg (1 x 5lb) chicken, skinned and
    cut into 8 serving pieces
4 tablespoons vegetable oil
425ml (15 fl oz) chicken stock
1 heaped teaspoon cornflour dissolved
    in 1 tablespoon water
1 bay leaf
1 garlic clove, crushed
6 medium-sized tomatoes, peeled and
    chopped
250g (8oz) small button mushrooms,
    wiped clean and halved
2 egg yolks
150ml (5 fl oz) double cream
¼ teaspoon paprika

American

½ cup flour seasoned with ½ teaspoon
    dried thyme, 1 teaspoon salt and ½
    teaspoon black pepper
5lb roasting chicken, skinned and cut
    into 8 serving pieces
4 tablespoons vegetable oil
2 cups chicken stock
1 heaped teaspoon cornstarch
    dissolved in 1 tablespoon water
1 bay leaf
1 garlic clove, crushed
6 medium-sized tomatoes, peeled and
    chopped
½lb small mushrooms, wiped clean
    and halved
2 egg yolks
⅝ cup heavy cream
¼ teaspoon paprika

Sprinkle the seasoned flour on to a plate. Dip the chicken pieces in it, coating them on all sides. Shake off any excess.

In a large, flameproof casserole, heat the oil over moderate heat. Add the chicken pieces and cook for 8 to 10 minutes or until golden brown on all sides.

Stir in the chicken stock, dissolved cornflour [cornstarch], bay leaf and garlic. Bring to the boil, reduce heat, cover and simmer for 35 minutes. Add the tomatoes and mushrooms, stir well and cook for a further 20 minutes.

Remove the chicken pieces to a deep, warmed serving dish.

Beat the egg yolks and cream together and stir into the liquid in the casserole. Cook, stirring constantly, for 5 minutes or until the sauce thickens. Pour the sauce over the chicken and sprinkle on the paprika.

FRENCH CHICKEN CASSEROLE

This is a classic French dish of chicken cooked with bacon, potatoes, onions and herbs.

4 servings

Metric/Imperial

1 x 2kg (1 x 4lb) chicken
1 teaspoon salt
½ teaspoon black pepper
50g (2oz) butter
675g (1½lb) small onions, peeled
675g (1½lb) small new potatoes, scrubbed
6 slices streaky bacon, rinds removed and diced
1 bouquet garni

American

4lb roasting chicken
1 teaspoon salt
½ teaspoon black pepper
¼ cup butter
1½lb small onions, peeled
1½lb small new potatoes, scrubbed
6 slices bacon, diced
1 bouquet garni

Preheat the oven to moderate (180°C/350°F or Gas Mark 4).

Rub the chicken inside and out with the salt and pepper.

In a large flameproof casserole, melt the butter over moderate heat. When the foam subsides add the chicken and

A delicious combination of fresh oranges and rosemary makes Orange Chicken with Rosemary a special dish for a dinner party.

cook, turning frequently for 8 to 10 minutes or until evenly browned. Remove and keep warm.

Add the onion, potatoes and bacon to the casserole and cook for 10 minutes, shaking frequently.

Return the chicken to the casserole and add the bouquet garni. Cover, place in the oven and cook for 45 minutes to 1 hour or until the chicken is tender.

ORANGE CHICKEN WITH ROSEMARY

An easy-to-make dish, Orange Chicken with Rosemary is a fragrant and

delicious light dinner dish. Serve with rice and green beans.

4 servings

Metric/Imperial

4 chicken quarters
1 teaspoon salt
½ teaspoon black pepper
75g (3oz) butter
2 large onions, thinly sliced
450ml (16 fl oz) orange juice
1½ teaspoons dried rosemary
1 tablespoon grated orange rind
1½ tablespoons cornflour dissolved in 1 tablespoon water

American

4 chicken quarters
1 teaspoon salt
½ teaspoon black pepper
6 tablespoons butter
2 large onions, thinly sliced
2 cups orange juice

1½ teaspoons dried rosemary
1 tablespoon grated orange rind
1½ tablespoons cornstarch dissolved
   in 1 tablespoon water

Rub the chicken pieces all over with the salt and pepper.

In a large flameproof casserole, melt two-thirds of the butter over moderate heat. When the foam subsides add the chicken pieces and cook, turning occasionally, for 8 to 10 minutes or until lightly and evenly browned. Remove.

Add the remaining butter to the casserole. When the foam subsides add the onions and cook, stirring occasionally for 5 to 7 minutes or until soft and translucent but not brown. Pour over the orange juice and bring to the boil, stirring occasionally. Stir in the rosemary and orange rind.

Reduce the heat and return the chicken pieces to the casserole. Cover and simmer for 30 to 40 minutes or until the chicken is tender. Transfer to a warmed serving dish and keep warm.

Increase the heat to high and bring the casserole liquid to the boil. Boil for 3 minutes or until slightly reduced. Lower the heat and stir in the cornflour [cornstarch] mixture. Cook, stirring constantly, for 2 minutes or until the sauce is hot and thick.

SPICED CHICKEN WITH HONEY

A deliciously different way to cook chicken, Spiced Chicken with Honey makes an excellent lunch or supper dish. Serve with boiled new potatoes and a green vegetable.

4 servings

Metric/Imperial

50g (2oz) butter
100ml (4 fl oz) clear honey
4 tablespoons German mustard
1 teaspoon salt
1 teaspoon mild curry powder
1.25kg (1 x 3lb) chicken, cut into 8 pieces

American

¼ cup butter
½ cup clear honey

Spiced Chicken with Honey is very simple to prepare but tastes magnificent – a superb dinner dish.

4 tablespoons spiced mustard
1 teaspoon salt
1 teaspoon mild curry powder
3lb roasting chicken, cut into 8 pieces

Preheat the oven to fairly hot (190°C/375°F or Gas Mark 5).

In a roasting tin, melt the butter over moderate heat. When the foam subsides add the honey, mustard, salt and curry powder, stirring to mix well. Remove from the heat.

Add the chicken pieces and roll in the mixture to coat thoroughly. Arrange in one layer over the bottom of the tin. Bake for 1 hour, or until tender, basting frequently with the honey mixture. Serve with the cooking liquid poured over.

CHICKEN LIVERS WITH SWEET AND SOUR SAUCE

An unusual combination of chicken livers, pineapple, soy sauce and vinegar gives this dish a delicious sweet and sour taste.

4 servings

Metric/Imperial

3 tablespoons soy sauce
500g (1lb) chicken livers, cut in halves
50g (2 fl oz) vegetable oil
368g (13oz) can pineapple chunks
100g (4oz) blanched almonds
3 tablespoons vinegar
¼ teaspoon salt
1 teaspoon sugar
2 tablespoons cornflour

American

3 tablespoons soy sauce
1lb chicken livers, halved
¼ cup vegetable oil
1½ cups canned pineapple chunks
⅔ cup blanched almonds
¼ cup vinegar
¼ teaspoon salt
1 teaspoon sugar
2 tablespoons cornstarch

Put 2 tablespoons of the soy sauce in a small bowl. Dip the chicken liver halves in it, adding more sauce if necessary.

In a large frying-pan, heat the oil over moderate heat. Add the chicken livers and cook for 10 minutes, stirring occasionally. Drain the pineapple and reserve the syrup. Add the pineapple

chunks and almonds to the pan, stir to mix and cook for 1 minute. Remove.

Add cold water to the reserved pineapple syrup to make 300ml (10 fl oz) [1¼ cups]. Put the pineapple syrup, vinegar, remaining soy sauce, salt and sugar into the pan. Cook over low heat, stirring constantly, for 10 minutes or until the sauce is thick and smooth. Taste and add more salt, if necessary.

Put the liver and pineapple mixture into a warmed serving dish and pour on the sauce.

CHICKEN FLAN

Chicken Flan, full of mushrooms, ham and chicken and topped with grated cheese, makes a delicious supper dish. Garnish with parsley sprigs and serve with mashed potatoes and a green salad.

4 servings

Metric/Imperial

1 x 23cm (1 x 9in) flan case made with
   Shortcrust Pastry
1 tablespoon butter
6 large button mushrooms, wiped
   clean and chopped
50g (2oz) ham, chopped
½ teaspoon salt

¼ teaspoon white pepper
¼ teaspoon cayenne pepper
2 tablespoons creamy milk
350g (12oz) cooked chicken, cut into
   large pieces
75g (3oz) Cheddar cheese, grated

American

1 x 9in pie shell made with Shortcrust
   Pastry
1 tablespoon butter
6 large mushrooms, wiped clean and
   chopped
¼ cup ham, chopped
½ teaspoon salt
¼ teaspoon white pepper
¼ teaspoon cayenne pepper
2 tablespoons creamy milk
1½ cups cooked chicken, cut into large
   pieces
¾ cup Cheddar cheese, grated

Preheat the oven to fairly hot (200°C/ 400°F or Gas Mark 6). Place the flan case on a baking sheet.

In a small frying-pan, melt the butter over moderate heat. When the foam subsides add the mushrooms and cook, stirring occasionally, for 3 minutes. Stir in the ham, salt, pepper and cayenne. Remove from the heat and stir in the milk.

Spoon the mixture over the bottom of the flan case, then lay the chicken pieces on top. Sprinkle over the grated cheese.

Bake the flan for 20 to 30 minutes or until the top is brown and bubbling and the pastry cooked and lightly browned.

RABBIT HOT POT

A simple casserole Rabbit Hot Pot makes a warming meal for a winter day.

6 servings

Metric/Imperial

3 tablespoons flour seasoned with 1
   teaspoon salt and ½ teaspoon black
   pepper
1 rabbit, cleaned and cut into 6
   serving pieces
2 large onions, thinly sliced
3 carrots, scraped and sliced
2 tablespoons finely chopped fresh
   parsley
½ teaspoon dried thyme
500g (1lb) potatoes, peeled and thickly
   sliced
450ml (16 fl oz) chicken stock

American

3 tablespoons flour seasoned with 1
   teaspoon salt and ½ teaspoon black
   pepper
1 rabbit, cleaned and cut into 6
   serving pieces
2 large onions, thinly sliced
3 carrots, scraped and sliced
2 tablespoons finely chopped fresh
   parsley
½ teaspoon dried thyme
1lb potatoes, peeled and thickly sliced
2 cups chicken stock

Preheat the oven to warm (170°C/ 325°F or Gas Mark 3).

Place the seasoned flour on a plate and coat the rabbit pieces in it, shaking off any excess.

Place half the sliced onion on the bottom of a large ovenproof casserole. Top with half the carrots, then with all the rabbit pieces. Sprinkle the rabbit with parsley and thyme and cover with the rest of the onion and carrot. Top with potatoes in overlapping slices.

Pour in the stock, cover and bake for 2 hours or until the rabbit is just tender.

Increase the oven temperature to moderate (180°C/350°F or Gas Mark 4). Uncover the casserole and continue to bake for a further 30 minutes or until the potatoes are lightly browned.

RABBIT AND LEEK CASSEROLE

This simple-to-make and economical dish makes an ideal family meal.

6 servings

Metric/Imperial

50g (2oz) butter
1 rabbit, cleaned and cut into serving
   pieces
1 large onion, thinly sliced and pushed
   out into rings
675g (1½lb) leeks, washed, trimmed
   and cut into lengths

300ml (10 fl oz) chicken stock
¼ teaspoon grated nutmeg
1 teaspoon salt
½ teaspoon black pepper
150ml (5 fl oz) creamy milk
1 teaspoon cornflour dissolved in
  1 tablespoon chicken stock

American

¼ cup butter
1 rabbit, cleaned and cut into serving
  pieces
1 large onion, thinly sliced and
  separated into rings
1½lb leeks, washed, trimmed and
  sliced
1¼ cups chicken stock
¼ teaspoon grated nutmeg
1 teaspoon salt
½ teaspoon black pepper
⅝ cup creamy milk
1 teaspoon cornstarch dissolved in
  1 tablespoon chicken stock

In a medium-sized flameproof casserole, melt the butter over moderate heat. When the foam subsides add the rabbit pieces and cook, turning occasionally, for 8 to 10 minutes, or until lightly and evenly browned. Remove and set aside.

Add the onion and leeks to the pan

Rabbit Stew is a rich and warming French stew of rabbit and bacon, flavoured with white wine and garlic.

and cook, stirring occasionally, for 5 minutes. Stir in the chicken stock, nutmeg, salt and pepper and bring to the boil.

Return the rabbit pieces to the pan. Reduce the heat, cover and simmer for 1 to 1¼ hours, or until the rabbit pieces are tender. Remove the rabbit pieces and vegetables from the pan, arrange on a warmed serving dish and keep warm.

Pour the pan liquid into a small saucepan. Blend in the dissolved cornflour [cornstarch]. Place over moderate heat and bring to the boil. Reduce the heat to low and add the milk, a little at a time, stirring constantly, for 3 minutes or until it is hot but not boiling and has thickened. Pour over the rabbit pieces.

RABBIT STEW

This is a popular and economical version of the classic French beef daubes. Served with mashed potatoes and green vegetables it makes a richly sustaining winter meal.

6 servings

Metric/Imperial

1¼kg (3lb) rabbit, cut into serving
  pieces
250g (8oz) streaky bacon slices, cut
  into strips

2 medium-sized onions, thinly sliced
1 garlic clove, finely chopped
3 large carrots, scraped and thinly
  sliced
MARINADE
450ml (16 fl oz) dry white wine
1 tablespoon vegetable oil
1 teaspoon salt
6 black peppercorns
2 parsley sprigs
1 bay leaf
2 garlic cloves, crushed
½ teaspoon dried thyme

American

3lb rabbit, cut into serving pieces
½lb bacon cut into strips
2 medium-sized onions, thinly sliced
1 garlic clove, finely chopped
3 large carrots, scraped and thinly
  sliced
MARINADE
2 cups dry white wine
1 tablespoon vegetable oil
1 teaspoon salt
6 black peppercorns
2 parsley sprigs
1 bay leaf
2 garlic cloves, crushed
½ teaspoon dried thyme

In a large shallow bowl, combine all the marinade ingredients and stir well to mix. Add the rabbit pieces and baste them thoroughly. Cover the dish and leave the rabbit to marinate overnight, or for at least 12 hours.

Remove the rabbit from the marinade and dry on kitchen paper. Strain the marinade into a jug and reserve it.

Preheat the oven to moderate (180°C/350°F or Gas Mark 4).

In a large flameproof casserole, fry the bacon strips over moderate heat until they are quite crisp. Set aside.

Add the onions, garlic and carrots to the fat in the casserole and cook them for 5 to 6 minutes, or until lightly coloured. Add the rabbit pieces and turn frequently to brown them evenly and quickly.

Add the reserved marinade to the casserole and bring to the boil.

Remove the casserole from the heat, add the bacon pieces and place in the oven. Cook for 1 hour, or until the rabbit is tender.

Fish dishes

Fish is a delicious and protein-rich supplement to our diets which is also low in calories and cholesterol. Unfortunately, it suffers from unimaginative cooking. Half the time white fish simply gets coated in batter and deep-fried and, in many households, it only appears in the form of fish fingers [fish sticks] and other processed frozen fish dishes.

Those people who live inland and have no local fresh fish merchant are less to blame for this state of affairs, but there are many recipes in this section which are equally suitable for frozen fish steaks or fillets, and some great serving ideas for kippers [kippered herring] and other forms of smoked fish.

The price of fish varies so much with region, season and weather conditions which affect catches from day to day, that it is very hard to say anything about the economy of buying particular kinds of fish. Cod and plaice [flounder] seem to be the staples of our Western fish diet, but alternative species of white fish are rapidly increasing in popularity, and we are very slowly becoming more adventurous both in our choice of fish and our cooking methods.

There is much snobbery attached to the upper price bracket (salmon, trout, and other fish which are generally beyond the budget for family cooking): it has been truly pointed out that mackerel, herring, smelts, sardines and other oily fish would be gourmet foods were it not for the fact they are cheap and plentiful.

When buying fresh fish, look for fish that has obviously been packed in ice. The eyes should be clear and bulging, the gills pinkish-red to red, the flesh firm to the touch, and there should be no unpleasant smell. Good quality fish steaks or fillets are often at their best either steamed, sautéed in butter or grilled [broiled] and served plain or with a sauce. The important thing is never to overcook: ten minutes is usually the maximum for an average-sized fish fillet when steaming or pan-frying. Test by pricking with a fork – the flesh should flake but still feel firm.

This kind of simple cooking brings out the delicate flavour of white fish; but it can be rather bland for some tastes, and young children, particularly, like their food to look colourful and interesting. You may even need to 'disguise' fish before they will eat it willingly, so try serving White Fish Pie, Fish Cakes or Fish Kebabs. There are plenty of well-known recipes and new ideas here which will help to make fish a favourite dish in every family.

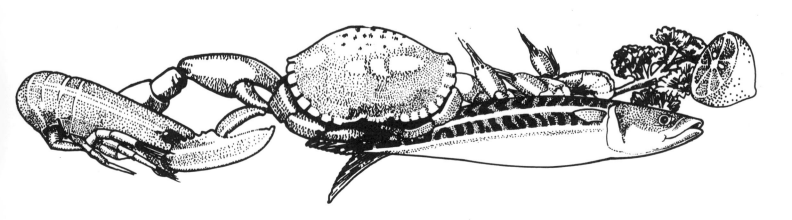

Barbecued Fish is a tempting dish of grilled fish steaks, served with a piquant caper sauce.

BARBECUED FISH

Grilled fish steaks served with a piquant sauce are a lunch or dinner dish which is very quick to make. Serve the fish with peas and creamed potatoes.

4 servings

Metric/Imperial

4 cod or haddock steaks, up to 250g (8oz) each
1 teaspoon salt
50g (2oz) butter
SAUCE
225ml (8 fl oz) red wine
$\frac{1}{8}$ teaspoon cayenne pepper
1 teaspoon prepared mustard
2 teaspoons chilli sauce
2 tablespoons lemon juice
1 teaspoon brown sugar
1 tablespoon capers
$\frac{1}{2}$ tablespoon salt

American

4 fish steaks, halibut, fresh cod or fresh haddock
1 teaspoon salt
$\frac{1}{4}$ cup butter
SAUCE
1 cup red wine
$\frac{1}{8}$ teaspoon cayenne pepper
1 teaspoon prepared mustard
2 teaspoons chili sauce
2 tablespoons lemon juice
1 teaspoon brown sugar
1 tablespoon capers
$\frac{1}{2}$ tablespoon salt

Preheat the grill [broiler] to moderate. Sprinkle the fish steaks with salt and dot them with half the butter. Place on the rack and cook for about 4 minutes on each side, or until the flakes separate easily. Remove to a serving dish and keep hot.

Pour any juice from the grilling pan into a small saucepan. Add the remaining butter and melt it over moderate heat. Add all the ingredients for the sauce, stir and bring to the boil. Reduce the heat and simmer for 10 minutes.

FISH IN WHITE SAUCE

Poached fish, coated with a white sauce and topped with cheese and breadcrumbs, is a marvellously simple and tasty supper dish. Broccoli or spinach go particularly well with this dish.

4 servings

Metric/Imperial

$\frac{3}{4}$ litre (1$\frac{1}{2}$ pints) water
2 tablespoons vinegar
2 carrots, scraped and sliced
1 onion, sliced
2 celery stalks, chopped
$\frac{1}{2}$ teaspoon salt
1 bouquet garni
675g (1$\frac{1}{2}$lb) white fish fillets
SAUCE
2 tablespoons butter
1$\frac{1}{2}$ tablespoons flour
150ml (5 fl oz) milk, warmed
$\frac{1}{2}$ teaspoon salt
$\frac{1}{4}$ teaspoon white pepper
50g (2oz) Parmesan cheese, grated
50g (2oz) dry white breadcrumbs

American

3$\frac{1}{2}$ cups water
2 tablespoons vinegar
2 carrots, scraped and sliced
1 onion, sliced
2 celery stalks, chopped

½ teaspoon salt
1 bouquet garni
1½lb white fish fillets
SAUCE
2 tablespoons butter
1½ tablespoons flour
⅝ cup milk, warmed
½ teaspoon salt
¼ teaspoon white pepper
½ cup Parmesan cheese, grated
⅔ cup dry white breadcrumbs

Put the water, vinegar, carrots, onion, celery, salt and bouquet garni in a large saucepan. Bring to the boil, reduce the heat and simmer gently for 30 minutes.

Allow to cool to lukewarm, then add the fish and return the pan to low heat. Cook gently for 10 to 12 minutes or until the fish flakes easily.

Allow the fish to cool slightly, then remove the skin. Place the fish in a warmed flameproof serving dish, cover with aluminium foil to keep it hot. Strain the fish stock into a measuring jug, discarding the vegetables and flavourings. Reserve 150ml (5 fluid ounces) [⅔ cup].

In a small pan melt the butter over moderate heat. Remove the pan from the heat and stir in the flour. Stirring constantly, gradually add the reserved fish stock, then slowly stir in the milk.

Return the pan to moderate heat and cook, stirring, until the sauce boils. Reduce the heat to low and continue cooking for 3 minutes, stirring. Add the salt and pepper. Remove the pan from the heat and pour the sauce over the fish.

Preheat the grill [broiler] to high.

Combine the grated cheese with the breadcrumbs. Sprinkle the sauce-covered fish with this mixture and place under the grill [broiler]. Cook for 3 to 5 minutes, or until the top is browned and bubbling.

FISH GRILLED [BROILED] WITH CHEESE

Marvellously quick and easy to prepare, Fish Grilled [Broiled] with Cheese is the ideal dish for a tasty but economical family supper. Serve with a tomato salad and mashed potatoes.

4 servings

Metric/Imperial

4 white fish fillets
25g (1oz) butter
1 small onion, grated
100g (4oz) Cheddar cheese, grated
1 teaspoon prepared mustard
2 teaspoons tomato ketchup
½ teaspoon salt
¼ teaspoon black pepper
⅛ teaspoon cayenne pepper

American

4 white fish fillets
2 tablespoons butter
1 small onion, grated
1 cup Cheddar cheese, grated
1 teaspoon prepared mustard
2 teaspoons tomato ketchup
½ teaspoon salt
¼ teaspoon black pepper
⅛ teaspoon cayenne pepper

Preheat the grill [broiler] to high.

Place the fish in the pan and dot with butter. Reduce the heat to moderate and grill [broil] for 5 to 6 minutes on each side, or until the fish flakes easily

Meanwhile, combine the remaining ingredients and mash well with a wooden spoon.

Remove the fish from the heat and spread some of the mixture on top of each one. Return to the heat and cook for a further 3 to 5 minutes or until the cheese mixture is bubbling and beginning to brown.

WILDSPITZER FISH CASSEROLE

An unusual method of cooking whiting or any white fish, Wildspitzer Fish Casserole, from Austria, may be served with Basil Baked Tomatoes.

4 servings

Metric/Imperial

50g (2oz) butter
2 medium-sized onions, finely chopped
1 garlic clove, crushed
1 tablespoon paprika
675g (1½lb) white fish fillets, skinned and cut into chunks

50ml (2 fl oz) White Sauce
4 tablespoons tomato purée
½ teaspoon salt
¼ teaspoon black pepper
1 teaspoon lemon juice
225ml (8 fl oz) sour cream
½ teaspoon dried dill

American

¼ cup butter
2 medium-sized onions, finely chopped
1 garlic clove, crushed
1 tablespoon paprika
1½lb white fish fillets, skinned and cut into chunks
¼ cup White Sauce
4 tablespoons tomato paste
½ teaspoon salt
¼ teaspoon black pepper
1 teaspoon lemon juice
1 cup sour cream
½ teaspoon dried dill

In a medium-sized flameproof casserole, melt the butter over moderate heat. When the foam subsides add the onions and garlic and fry, stirring occasionally, for 5 to 7 minutes or until soft and translucent but not brown. Stir in the paprika and fry the mixture, stirring constantly, for 1 minute.

Add the fish pieces to the casserole and cook, turning occasionally, for 5 minutes. Transfer to a plate.

Add the White Sauce, tomato purée, salt, pepper and lemon juice to the casserole, stirring to mix well. Bring the mixture to the boil stirring constantly.

Return the fish pieces to the casserole and reduce the heat to low. Simmer for 5 minutes or until the fish flakes easily.

Stir in the sour cream, transfer the mixture to a warmed serving dish and sprinkle over the dill.

FISH KEBABS

Fish Kebabs are delicious served piping hot on a bed of rice.

4 servings

Metric/Imperial

675g (1½lb) fresh tuna fish, bones and skin removed, cut into cubes

105

2 medium-sized onions, quartered

4 tomatoes, quartered

250g (8oz) mushrooms, wiped clean

1 green pepper, white pith removed,
   cut into small squares

100ml (4 fl oz) dry white wine

3 tablespoons vegetable oil

½ teaspoon salt

½ teaspoon paprika

4 bay leaves

1 lemon, quartered

American

1½lb tuna fish, bones and skin
   removed, cut into chunks

2 medium-sized onions, quartered

4 tomatoes, quartered

½lb mushrooms, wiped clean

1 green pepper, membrane and seeds
   removed, diced

½ cup dry white wine

3 tablespoons vegetable oil

½ teaspoon salt

½ teaspoon paprika

4 bay leaves

1 lemon, quartered

Thread the fish cubes on to 4 skewers,
alternating them with the onions,
tomatoes, mushrooms and green pepper
squares.

In a large shallow dish, combine the
wine, oil, salt and paprika. Lay the
skewers in the dish and leave to marinate
at room temperature for 2 hours, turning occasionally.

Preheat the grill [broiler] to high.

Remove the kebabs from the marinade. Place them in the pan and cook
for 5 to 7 minutes, turning the skewers
frequently, or until the fish flakes easily.

Add a bay leaf and a lemon quarter to
the end of each skewer.

HADDOCK WITH PARSLEY SAUCE

Haddock with Parsley Sauce is one of
those most delicious of dishes, which,
because it is so easy to make, is often
sadly neglected. Serve it with plenty of
creamy mashed potatoes.

4 servings

Metric/Imperial

675g (1½lb) fresh haddock, skinned and
   filleted

2 medium-sized onions, sliced and
   pushed out into rings

450ml (16 fl oz) milk

¼ teaspoon salt

25g (1oz) butter

2 tablespoons flour

¼ teaspoon white pepper

4 tablespoons chopped fresh parsley

American

1½lb fresh haddock, skinned and
   filleted

Fish Kebabs are excellent and taste
even better than they look!

Haddock with Parsley Sauce is a simple but delicious dish.

2 medium-sized onions, sliced and separated into rings
2 cups milk
¼ teaspoon salt
2 tablespoons butter
2 tablespoons flour
¼ teaspoon white pepper
4 tablespoons chopped fresh parsley

Cut the fish fillets into 8 pieces, place the fish on the bottom of a heavy saucepan and top with the onion rings. Pour over the milk and sprinkle with the salt. Place the saucepan over moderate heat and bring to just below boiling point. Reduce the heat and simmer for 15 minutes.

Remove the fish and onions and place in a warmed serving dish; keep warm. Set the cooking liquid aside.

In a small saucepan, melt the butter over moderate heat. Remove the pan from the heat and stir in the flour to make a smooth paste. Gradually add the reserved cooking liquid, stirring constantly. Return to the heat and cook, stirring for 2 to 3 minutes or until the sauce is thick and smooth.

Stir in the pepper and parsley, reduce the heat and cook for a further 1 minute. Pour the sauce over the fish.

HERRINGS IN BUTTER

A simple yet delicious lunch or supper dish, Herrings in Butter is very good served with boiled new potatoes and French beans.

4 servings

Metric/Imperial

6 herrings, filleted
6 tablespoons flour, seasoned with 1 teaspoon salt and ½ teaspoon black pepper
75g (3oz) butter
2 teaspoons lemon juice
1 tablespoon chopped fresh parsley

American

6 herrings, filleted
6 tablespoons flour, seasoned with 1 teaspoon salt and ½ teaspoon black pepper
6 tablespoons butter
2 teaspoons lemon juice
1 tablespoon chopped fresh parsley

Wash the herring fillets under cold running water and pat dry with kitchen paper.

Place the seasoned flour on a plate and, one by one, dip the herring fillets into it, shaking off any excess flour.

In a large frying-pan, melt the butter over moderate heat. When the foam subsides add the herring fillets and cook for 3 minutes on each side or until they are lightly browned and the flesh flakes easily.

Transfer the herrings to a warmed serving dish. Spoon over the lemon juice, then the pan juices, and sprinkle with the parsley.

SOUSED [ROLL MOP] HERRING

A delicious way to cook herring, Soused Herring is inexpensive and is well worth making in large quantities since it will keep for several days. The marinade offsets any oiliness of the fish and the slow cooking makes even the bones of the fish as soft as butter.

5 servings

Metric/Imperial

10 herring fillets, rolled up with the skin on the outside
300ml (10 fl oz) vinegar
juice of 1 lemon
5 bay leaves
1 teaspoon pickling spice
8 black peppercorns
1 teaspoon salt
2 mace blades
1 green chilli, seeded and coarsely chopped

2 medium-sized onions, thinly sliced and pushed out into rings

American

10 herring fillets, rolled up with the skin on the outside

$\frac{5}{8}$ cup vinegar

juice of 1 lemon

5 bay leaves

1 teaspoon mixed pickling spices

8 black peppercorns

1 teaspoon salt

2 mace blades

1 green chili pepper, seeded and coarsely chopped

2 medium-sized onions, thinly sliced and separated into rings

Preheat the oven to cool (150°C/300°F or Gas Mark 2).

Pack the herring rolls, seam sides down, in one layer in a shallow oven-proof dish.

Combine the vinegar and lemon juice and pour over the herrings. Sprinkle over the remaining ingredients.

Cover the dish with aluminium foil and place in the centre of the oven and bake for 1½ to 2 hours or until the fish flakes easily.

Transfer the fish to a large serving dish and strain the cooking juices over. Allow to cool completely before serving.

SUMMER CASSEROLE

A tasty and economical Swedish dish suitable for lunch or supper, Summer Casserole may be served with peas.

8 servings

Metric/Imperial

1½kg (3lb) haddock fillets, skinned

1 teaspoon salt

1 tablespoon finely chopped fresh parsley

2 tablespoons finely chopped fresh chives

1 tablespoon butter

2 tablespoons flour

juice of 1 lemon

4 tomatoes, thickly sliced

American

3lb fresh haddock fillets, skinned

1 teaspoon salt

1 tablespoon finely chopped fresh parsley

2 tablespoons finely chopped fresh chives

1 tablespoon butter

2 tablespoons flour

juice of 1 lemon

4 tomatoes, thickly sliced

Sprinkle the fillets with the salt and place in a flameproof casserole. Sprinkle over the parsley and chives. Blend the butter and flour together in a saucer. Form into small balls and dot them over the fish. Add the lemon juice and enough water to come halfway up the sides of the fish.

Place the casserole over moderate heat, and bring the liquid to the boil. Reduce the heat, cover and simmer for 10 minutes. Place the sliced tomatoes over the fish and simmer for a further 5 minutes or until the fish flakes easily.

MACKEREL FILLETS WITH MUSTARD SAUCE

Mackerel, a tasty fish at all times, is especially good when accompanied by this piquant sauce. Serve with new potatoes or a green vegetable for lunch.

2 servings

Metric/Imperial

1 tablespoon vegetable oil

2 mackerel, cleaned

1 tablespoon lemon juice

75g (3oz) butter

1½ tablespoons French mustard

2 egg yolks

1 tablespoon cider vinegar

½ teaspoon salt

½ teaspoon black pepper

1 tablespoon dried mixed herbs

American

1 tablespoon vegetable oil

2 fresh mackerel, cleaned

1 tablespoon lemon juice

6 tablespoons butter

1½ tablespoons French mustard

2 egg yolks

1 tablespoon cider vinegar

½ teaspoon salt

½ teaspoon black pepper

1 tablespoon dried mixed herbs (basil, oregano, marjoram and thyme)

Preheat the oven to moderate (180°C/350°F or Gas Mark 4).

Grease two large pieces of aluminium foil with the oil. Lay one mackerel on each piece and sprinkle over the lemon juice. Wrap the fish loosely in the foil, envelope-fashion, so that it is completely enclosed, but allowing it some room to 'breathe'. Place the fish parcels in the oven and bake for 20 minutes, or until the mackerel is tender.

Meanwhile, prepare the sauce. In a large mixing bowl, cream the butter with a wooden spoon until soft.

Beat the mustard, egg yolks, vinegar, salt and pepper together until well blended. Gradually add to the butter, beating well with the wooden spoon until all the ingredients have been combined and the sauce is thick and smooth. Stir in the herbs and mix well. Taste and add more seasoning if necessary. Spoon the sauce into a sauceboat and put it in the refrigerator to chill.

Remove the mackerel parcels from the oven, pour the cooking juices into a bowl and reserve. Remove the skin from the mackerel by gently scraping it off with the point of a sharp knife, being careful not to break the flesh. Cut each fish into four fillets and gently remove the bones. Arrange on a large serving dish. Strain the reserved cooking juices over and allow the fish to cool to room temperature. Place in the refrigerator to chill for at least 2 hours.

SOUSED MACKEREL

Soused Mackerel is an economical dish, ideal for a family supper. Serve with a mixed salad and brown bread.

8 servings

Metric/Imperial

8 mackerel, cleaned

425ml (15 fl oz) vinegar

425ml (15 fl oz) water

2 carrots, scraped and thinly sliced

2 medium-sized onions, thinly sliced

2 teaspoons dried marjoram
2 whole cloves
4 bay leaves
1 teaspoon black peppercorns
1 teaspoon allspice berries
1 teaspoon salt

American

8 x 1lb mackerel, cleaned
2 cups vinegar
2 cups water
2 carrots, scraped and thinly sliced
2 medium-sized onions, thinly sliced
2 teaspoons dried marjoram
2 whole cloves
4 bay leaves
1 teaspoon black peppercorns
1 teaspoon whole allspice
1 teaspoon salt

Preheat the oven to cool (150°C/300°F or Gas Mark 2).

Remove the heads and tails from the mackerel; leave any roes inside. Pack into an ovenproof dish.

Bring the vinegar, water, carrots and onions to the boil over moderate heat. Reduce the heat and simmer for 10 minutes. Pour the liquid through a strainer on to the fish. Sprinkle over the marjoram, cloves, bay leaves, peppercorns, allspice and salt.

Place the dish in the centre of the oven and bake for 1½ to 2 hours or until the fish flakes easily when tested with a fork.

Set aside to cool completely before serving.

Summer Casserole is a light and sustaining dish for a summer meal.

FISH AND LEEK FLAN

This delicately flavoured flan is filled with leeks and fish in a thick white sauce.

4 servings

Metric/Imperial

175g (6oz) Shortcrust Pastry I
25g (1oz) butter
500g (1lb) leeks, washed and sliced
500g (1lb) white fish, cooked, skinned, boned and flaked
1 teaspoon salt
½ teaspoon black pepper
⅛ teaspoon cayenne pepper
¼ teaspoon grated nutmeg
1 tablespoon finely chopped fresh parsley
300ml (10 fl oz) thick White Sauce, hot

American

1 recipe Shortcrust Pastry I
2 tablespoons butter
1lb leeks, washed and sliced
1lb cod or other white fish, cooked, skinned, boned and flaked
1 teaspoon salt
½ teaspoon black pepper
⅛ teaspoon cayenne pepper
¼ teaspoon grated nutmeg
1 tablespoon finely chopped fresh parsley
1¼ cups thick White Sauce, hot

Preheat the oven to fairly hot (200°C/400°F or Gas Mark 6).

On a lightly floured board, roll out the dough into a circle and lay it over a 23cm (9-inch) pie dish. Gently ease into the dish and trim the edges. Place in the refrigerator to chill for 10 minutes, then bake blind for 15 minutes.

Reduce the oven temperature to moderate (180°C/350°F or Gas Mark 4).

To make the filling, in a medium-sized saucepan, melt the butter over moderate heat. When the foam subsides, add the leeks and cook, stirring occasionally, for 5 minutes. Remove the pan from the heat.

Stir in the fish, seasonings, parsley and White Sauce. Taste and add more salt and pepper if necessary. Pour into the baked pastry case.

Return the pie to the oven and bake for 30 minutes.

FISH AND POTATO PIE

Quick and easy to prepare, Fish and Potato Pie is a marvellously economical dish for a family supper.

6 servings

Metric/Imperial

1kg (2lb) white fish fillets, skinned and cut into small chunks
4 potatoes, cooked and sliced
100ml (4 fl oz) milk
2 eggs
1 teaspoon salt
¼ teaspoon white pepper
3 tomatoes, sliced
50g (2oz) fine, dry breadcrumbs
50g (2oz) Cheddar cheese, grated
25g (1oz) butter

American

2lb white fish fillets, skinned and cut into small chunks
4 potatoes, cooked and sliced
½ cup milk
2 eggs
1 teaspoon salt
¼ teaspoon white pepper
3 tomatoes, sliced
⅔ cup fine, dry breadcrumbs
½ cup Cheddar or American cheese, grated
2 tablespoons butter

Preheat the oven to moderate (180°C/350°F or Gas Mark 4).

Arrange the fish and potato in layers in a medium-sized baking dish, finishing with potato.

Beat the milk and eggs together, add the salt and pepper and pour over the fish and potatoes. Arrange the tomato slices on top.

Combine the breadcrumbs and cheese and sprinkle this over the tomato slices. Dot with the butter.

Bake for 50 to 60 minutes or until the top is brown and crisp.

WHITE FISH PIE

White Fish Pie makes an ideal family supper dish. Serve with minted peas.

6 servings

Metric/Imperial

75g (3oz) butter
1 small onion, finely chopped
1kg (2lb) white fish fillets, cut into chunks
2 hard-boiled eggs, sliced
½ teaspoon salt
½ teaspoon black pepper
4 tablespoons chopped fresh parsley
1kg (2lb) cooked potatoes, mashed
25g (1oz) flour
350ml (12 fl oz) milk
175g (6oz) Cheddar cheese, grated

American

6 tablespoons plus 1 teaspoon butter
1 small onion, finely chopped
2lb white fish fillets, cut into chunks
2 hard-boiled eggs, sliced
½ teaspoon salt
½ teaspoon black pepper
4 tablespoons chopped fresh parsley
2lb cooked potatoes, mashed
¼ cup flour
1½ cups milk
1½ cups Cheddar or American cheese, grated

Preheat the oven to fairly hot (190°C/375°F or Gas Mark 5). Grease a 25cm (10in) deep-sided ovenproof pie dish.

In a large frying-pan, melt two-thirds of the remaining butter over moderate heat. When the foam subsides add the onion and fry, stirring occasionally, for 5 to 7 minutes or until soft and translucent but not brown. Add the fish and fry for a further 6 minutes, stirring frequently. Transfer to the pie dish.

Lay the sliced eggs over the fish. Sprinkle with the salt, pepper and 3 tablespoons of the parsley. Spoon the mashed potatoes over the top.

In a small saucepan, melt the remaining butter over moderate heat. Remove the pan from the heat and stir in the flour to make a smooth paste. Gradually add the milk, stirring constantly to avoid lumps. Stir in the cheese. Return the pan to the heat and cook, stirring, for 2 to 3 minutes or until the cheese has melted and the sauce is smooth and thick. Pour over the potatoes.

Bake for 20 to 25 minutes or until the pie is golden brown on top. Sprinkle over the remaining parsley.

FISH CAKES

Wholesome and simple to make, Fish Cakes are ideal for family meals. A larger quantity may be made and kept in the refrigerator. Serve with green peas and grilled [broiled] tomatoes.

2 servings

Metric/Imperial

300g (10oz) white fish fillets, cooked, skinned and flaked
300g (10oz) potatoes, cooked and mashed
1 tablespoon melted butter
1 egg
1 tablespoon flour
½ teaspoon salt
¼ teaspoon cayenne pepper
2 tablespoons chopped fresh parsley
1 egg, lightly beaten
100g (4oz) fine dry breadcrumbs
4 tablespoons vegetable oil

American

10oz white fish fillets, cooked, skinned and flaked
½ lb potatoes, cooked and mashed
1 tablespoon melted butter
1 egg
1 tablespoon flour
½ teaspoon salt
¼ teaspoon cayenne pepper
2 tablespoons chopped fresh parsley
1 egg, lightly beaten
1⅓ cups fine dry breadcrumbs
4 tablespoons vegetable oil

In a large mixing bowl, combine the fish, potatoes, butter, egg, flour, salt, cayenne and parsley and mix well with a wooden spoon. Place in the refrigerator to chill for 1 hour.

With floured hands, shape the mixture into about 6 balls. On a lightly floured board flatten the balls into patties.

Dip the patties in the beaten egg and then roll them in the breadcrumbs to coat them thoroughly.

In a large heavy frying-pan, heat the vegetable oil over high heat. Add the fish cakes and fry for 5 to 8 minutes, turning frequently until golden brown on all sides.

Serve Onion and Mackerel Salad as a tasty snack meal.

ONION AND MACKEREL SALAD

Serve this tasty salad with chunks of freshly baked crusty bread.

4 servings

Metric/Imperial

396g (14oz) can mackerel, drained and flaked
1 large onion, coarsely chopped
½ teaspoon salt
¼ teaspoon black pepper
2 tablespoons tomato purée
2 tablespoons lemon juice
1 crisp lettuce, washed
2 large tomatoes, thinly sliced
½ cucumber, thinly sliced
2 tablespoons chopped fresh parsley

American

1 x 14oz can mackerel, drained and flaked

1 large onion, coarsely chopped
½ teaspoon salt
¼ teaspoon black pepper
2 tablespoons tomato paste
2 tablespoons lemon juice
1 crisp head of lettuce, washed
2 large tomatoes, thinly sliced
½ cucumber, thinly sliced
2 tablespoons chopped fresh parsley

Place the mackerel, onion, salt, pepper, tomato purée and lemon juice in a mixing bowl. Mash all the ingredients together until well blended.

Line a large salad bowl with the lettuce leaves. Spoon the mackerel mixture on to the lettuce base. Arrange the tomato and cucumber slices alternately in circles around the edge. Sprinkle with the parsley.

Cover and place in the refrigerator to chill for 30 minutes before serving.

SARDINE SALAD

A marvellous combination of salad ingredients, served on lettuce, Sardine Salad makes an appetizing meal.

4 servings

Metric/Imperial

250g (8oz) can sardines, drained and chopped
3 small beetroots, finely chopped
4 streaky bacon slices, rinds removed, fried until crisp and chopped
2 medium-sized potatoes, cooked, peeled and chopped
2 hard-boiled eggs, chopped
1 shallot, finely chopped
1 tablespoon chopped fresh chives
1 bunch mustard and cress, washed, shaken dry and chopped
1 teaspoon salt
½ teaspoon freshly ground black pepper
1 tablespoon paprika
150ml (4 fl oz) sour cream, mixed with 3 tablespoons mayonnaise
2 teaspoons lemon juice
1 large lettuce, washed and shaken dry

American

1 x 8oz can sardines, drained and chopped

3 small beets, finely chopped
4 slices bacon, fried until crisp and crumbled
2 medium-sized potatoes, cooked, peeled and diced
2 hard-boiled eggs, chopped
1 shallot, finely chopped
1 tablespoon chopped fresh chives
1 bunch watercress, washed, shaken dry and chopped
1 teaspoon salt
½ teaspoon freshly ground black pepper
1 tablespoon paprika
½ cup sour cream, mixed with ¼ cup mayonnaise
2 teaspoons lemon juice
1 large head of lettuce, washed and shaken dry

In a medium-sized mixing bowl, combine the sardines, beetroots [beets], bacon, potatoes, eggs, shallot, chives and mustard and cress. Season with the salt, pepper and paprika and stir well.

Pour over the sour cream and mayonnaise mixture and the lemon juice. Toss the salad ingredients until well coated with the dressing.

Arrange the lettuce on a serving dish and spoon the sardine mixture into the centre. Place in the refrigerator to chill for 15 minutes before serving.

ROES ON TOAST

Roes on Toast makes a nourishing light supper or luncheon snack.

4 servings

Metric/Imperial

500g (1lb) soft herring roes
2 tablespoons flour, seasoned with ¼ teaspoon salt, ¼ teaspoon black pepper and ½ teaspoon dry mustard
25g (1oz) butter
4 slices hot buttered toast
1 tablespoon chopped fresh parsley

American

1lb herring milt (soft roe)
2 tablespoons flour, seasoned with ¼ teaspoon salt, ¼ teaspoon black pepper and ½ teaspoon dry mustard
2 tablespoons butter

4 slices hot buttered toast
1 tablespoon chopped fresh parsley

Dip each roe in the seasoned flour, to coat it completely. Shake off any excess.

In a large frying-pan, melt the butter over moderate heat. When the foam subsides add the roes and cook for 8 to 10 minutes, turning once, or until lightly browned and tender. Remove from the heat.

Place the toast on 4 warmed plates and arrange the roes on top. Sprinkle with the parsley.

EGGS BAKED WITH HADDOCK

An appetizing and nourishing lunch or dinner dish, Eggs Baked with Haddock is easy and quick to make.

4 servings

Metric/Imperial

4 large potatoes, cut into quarters
4 tablespoons creamy milk
25g (1oz) butter
⅛ teaspoon grated nutmeg
¼ teaspoon black pepper
⅛ teaspoon cayenne pepper
500g (1lb) smoked haddock fillets, cooked, skinned and flaked
8 eggs
75g (3oz) Cheddar cheese, grated

American

4 large potatoes, cut into quarters
4 tablespoons creamy milk
2 tablespoons butter
⅛ teaspoon grated nutmeg
¼ teaspoon black pepper
⅛ teaspoon cayenne pepper
1lb finnan haddie (smoked haddock) fillets, cooked, skinned and flaked
8 eggs
¾ cup Cheddar cheese, grated

Preheat the oven to moderate (180°C/350°F or Gas Mark 4). Lightly grease a medium-sized baking dish.

Boil the potatoes and mash with the milk, butter, nutmeg, pepper, cayenne and extra salt if needed. Stir in the flaked haddock.

Line the bottom of the baking dish with the potato-and-fish mixture.

Using the back of a spoon, make 8 depressions in the mixture. Break an egg into each one. Sprinkle the cheese on top, allowing an extra sprinkling for each egg. Bake in the centre of the oven for 30 minutes, or until the eggs are set.

SMOKED HADDOCK BAKED WITH MUSHROOMS

A delightful way to cook haddock, Smoked Haddock Baked with Mushrooms makes a tasty meal.

4 servings

Metric/Imperial

500g (1lb) smoked haddock fillets, poached, skinned and boned
40g (1½oz) butter
175g (6oz) mushrooms, wiped clean and sliced
350g (12 fl oz) White Sauce, hot
5 tablespoons creamy milk
100g (4oz) Cheddar cheese, grated
½ teaspoon grated nutmeg
½ teaspoon cayenne pepper

American

1lb finnan haddie (smoked haddock) fillets, poached, skinned and boned
3 tablespoons butter
6oz mushrooms, wiped clean and sliced
1½ cups White Sauce, hot
5 tablespoons creamy milk
1 cup Cheddar cheese, grated
½ teaspoon grated nutmeg
½ teaspoon cayenne pepper

Preheat the oven to hot (220°C/425°F or Gas Mark 7).

Cut the haddock into cubes and transfer to a medium-sized baking dish.

In a medium-sized saucepan, melt the butter over moderate heat. When the foam subsides add the mushrooms and cook, stirring frequently, for 3 minutes. Transfer to the baking dish.

In another saucepan, combine the White Sauce, milk, cheese, nutmeg and cayenne. Cook, stirring constantly, for 3 to 5 minutes or until the cheese has melted and the mixture is smooth.

Pour over the fish and mushrooms. Bake for 15 to 20 minutes or until the top is lightly browned.

CULLEN SKINK

This is an old Scottish recipe which is a mixture of a soup and a stew.

4 servings

Metric/Imperial

500g (1lb) smoked haddock
300ml (10 fl oz) water
2 onions, finely chopped
3 large potatoes, peeled and sliced
½ teaspoon white pepper
425ml (15 fl oz) milk
1 tablespoon butter
¼ teaspoon salt

American

1lb finnan haddie (smoked haddock)
1¼ cups water
2 onions, finely chopped
3 large potatoes, peeled and sliced
½ teaspoon white pepper
2 cups milk
1 tablespoon butter
¼ teaspoon salt

Place the haddock in a large frying-pan with the water. Cook over low heat for 15 minutes, lift out and set aside.

Strain the cooking liquid into a saucepan and add the onions, potatoes and pepper. Cover the pan and cook over moderate heat for 20 minutes.

Meanwhile remove the skin and bones from the haddock and flake flesh into large pieces.

Mash the potatoes with the onions and cooking liquid. Gradually add the milk, stirring constantly, until it is blended with the potatoes. Return the pan to low heat. Add the flaked fish and butter, stir and cook until hot.

DEEP-FRIED SPRATS

Fried sprats make a tasty supper dish. Serve with quartered lemons.

4 servings

Metric/Imperial

50g (2oz) flour
1 teaspoon salt
1 teaspoon white pepper
grated rind of 1 lemon
500g (1lb) sprats, rinsed and drained
vegetable oil for deep frying
1 tablespoon chopped fresh parsley

American

½ cup flour
1 teaspoon salt
1 teaspoon white pepper
grated rind of 1 lemon
1lb smelt or sprats, rinsed and drained
vegetable oil for deep frying
1 tablespoon chopped fresh parsley

Mix the flour, salt, pepper and lemon rind together on a plate. Roll the sprats in the seasoned flour to coat.

Heat the oil in a large heavy saucepan until a cube of stale bread dropped in turns golden in 50 seconds. Fry the sprats in small batches for 2 to 3 minutes, or until light brown. Drain thoroughly on kitchen paper.

Place on a warmed serving dish and sprinkle with the parsley.

KIPPER PIE

Covered with a golden pastry crust, this tasty pie is delicious hot or cold.

4 servings

Metric/Imperial

25g (1oz) butter
2 tablespoons flour
225ml (8 fl oz) single cream or creamy milk
350g (12oz) kipper fillets, poached, skinned and flaked
¼ teaspoon cayenne pepper
¼ teaspoon salt
½ teaspoon grated lemon rind
2 hard-boiled eggs, sliced
175g (6oz) Rough Puff Pastry
a little milk

American

2 tablespoons butter
2 tablespoons flour
1 cup light cream or creamy milk

¾lb kipper or bloater fillets, poached, skinned and flaked
¼ teaspoon cayenne pepper
¼ teaspoon salt
½ teaspoon grated lemon rind
2 hard-boiled eggs, sliced
1 recipe Rough Puff Pastry
a little milk

In a medium-sized saucepan, melt the butter over moderate heat. Remove from the heat and stir in the flour to make a smooth paste. Gradually add the cream, stirring constantly. Return the pan to the heat and add the flaked kipper, cayenne, salt and lemon rind. Cook, stirring for 3 minutes or until the mixture begins to boil.

Turn into a medium-sized pie dish and place the egg slices on top. Set aside while you prepare the pastry.

Preheat the oven to fairly hot (200°C/400°F or Gas Mark 6).

On a floured surface, roll out the dough to a circle 2.5cm (1in) larger than the top of the pie dish. Cut a narrow strip around the dough. Dampen the rim of the dish and press on the dough strip. Dampen lightly.

Lift the dough circle on to the dish, trim and crimp the edges to seal. Cut a slit in the centre of the dough and brush with milk.

Bake for 1 hour or until the pastry is golden brown.

BAKED HERRINGS

A delicious dish of herrings baked with herbs, lemon juice, potatoes and onions, Baked Herrings makes a quick and inexpensive light lunch or dinner meal.

4-6 servings

Metric/Imperial

4 medium-sized potatoes, peeled, washed, parboiled and thinly sliced
6 herrings, filleted, washed and dried
½ teaspoon dried marjoram
½ teaspoon dried thyme
1 teaspoon salt
½ teaspoon black pepper
1 tablespoon lemon juice
2 medium-sized onions, thinly sliced and pushed out into rings

150ml (4 fl oz) water
25g (1oz) butter

American

4 medium-sized potatoes, peeled, washed, parboiled and thinly sliced
6 herrings, filleted, washed and dried
½ teaspoon dried marjoram
½ teaspoon dried thyme
1 teaspoon salt
½ teaspoon black pepper
1 tablespoon lemon juice
2 medium-sized onions, thinly sliced and separated into rings
½ cup water
2 tablespoons butter

Preheat the oven to fairly hot (190°C/375°F or Gas Mark 5).

Grease a large baking dish. Line the bottom with half the potato slices. Lay the herring fillets on top and sprinkle over the marjoram, thyme, ½ teaspoon of the salt and ¼ teaspoon of the pepper.

Pour over the lemon juice. Cover the fish with the onion slices. Lay the remaining potato slices on top. Pour over the water, dot with the butter and sprinkle over the remaining salt and pepper.

Cover the dish with a lid or aluminium foil. Bake in the centre of the oven for 40 minutes or until the potatoes are tender and the fish flakes easily.

SOLOMON GRUNDY

A northern English dish traditionally eaten during Lent, Solomon Grundy originally required that the fish mixture be placed back on the skeleton of the fish before serving. This, however, is extremely difficult to do and we have therefore adapted the recipe.

4 servings

Metric/Imperial

4 herrings, cleaned, poached, boned and flaked
1 medium-size cooking apple, cored, peeled and finely chopped
8 anchovy fillets, chopped
8 spring onions, chopped
grated rind of 1 lemon
3 tablespoons milk

Eggs, tomatoes, gherkins and parsley add colour and flavour to this rich and creamy Salmon Loaf.

4 lettuce leaves, washed
1 lemon, quartered

American

4 herrings, cleaned, poached, boned and flaked
1 medium-sized green apple, cored, peeled and finely chopped
8 anchovy fillets, chopped
8 scallions, chopped
grated rind of 1 lemon
3 tablespoons milk

4 lettuce leaves, washed
1 lemon, quartered

In a large mixing bowl, mix together the herrings, apple, anchovy fillets, spring onions [scallions] and lemon rind. Pour in the milk and mix until the ingredients are thoroughly combined.

Arrange the lettuce leaves on 4 plates and spoon equal quantities of the fish on to each leaf. Garnish with the lemon.

SALMON LOAF

Salmon Loaf is an excellent means of using fresh or frozen salmon. It stretches a small amount of this expensive fish and brings it within the family budget for a special treat.

6 servings

Metric/Imperial

1 tablespoon vegetable oil
500g (1lb) cooked fresh salmon, skinned and flaked
5 hard-boiled eggs, coarsely chopped
500g (1lb) tomatoes, peeled and chopped
8 pickled gherkins, thinly sliced
3 tablespoons chopped fresh parsley
1 teaspoon salt
½ teaspoon black pepper

300ml (10 fl oz) mayonnaise
3 tablespoons creamy milk
1 tablespoon lemon juice
15g (½oz) gelatine dissolved in 4 tablespoons hot water

American

1 tablespoon vegetable oil
1lb cooked fresh salmon, skinned and flaked
5 hard-boiled eggs, coarsely chopped
1lb tomatoes, peeled and chopped
8 sweet gherkins, thinly sliced
3 tablespoons chopped fresh parsley
1 teaspoon salt
½ teaspoon black pepper
1¼ cups mayonnaise

3 tablespoons creamy milk
1 tablespoon lemon juice
2 x ¼oz envelopes gelatin, dissolved in
   4 tablespoons hot water

Grease a 1kg (2-pound) loaf tin with the oil.

In a large mixing bowl, combine the fish, eggs, tomatoes, gherkins, parsley, salt and pepper. Combine the mayonnaise, milk, lemon juice and the dissolved gelatine. Stir into the salmon mixture and mix thoroughly.

Spoon the mixture into the loaf tin and smooth it down. Place in the refrigerator and chill for 2 hours or until the loaf is firm and set.

Run a knife around the edge of the loaf tin and quickly dip the base in hot water. Place a large serving dish, inverted, over the tin and reverse the two, giving a sharp shake. The loaf should slide out easily.

HERRINGS IN ROLLED OATS

A different and very easy way of cooking herrings, Herrings in Rolled Oats makes a tasty light lunch or dinner.

4 servings

Metric/Imperial

100g (4oz) rolled (porridge) oats
1 teaspoon salt
½ teaspoon black pepper
1 egg, lightly beaten
4 herrings, cleaned and prepared
100g (4oz) butter or margarine

American

1 cup rolled oats
1 teaspoon salt
½ teaspoon black pepper
1 egg, lightly beaten
4 herrings, cleaned and prepared
½ cup butter or margarine

On a large plate, mix together the rolled oats, salt and pepper. Place the egg on another plate.

Dip the herrings first in the egg and then in the oat mixture, coating them thoroughly and shaking off any excess.

In a large, heavy frying-pan, melt the butter over moderate heat. When the foam subsides add the herrings and cook for 5 to 6 minutes on each side, or until the flesh flakes easily.

KEDGEREE

If you don't relish the thought of eating any remaining cold kedgeree, use it as a filling for pancakes and serve with cheese sauce, or toss with mayonnaise and serve as a cold salad dish.

4 servings

Metric/Imperial

350g (12oz) smoked haddock
½ teaspoon salt
½ teaspoon hot curry powder
250g (8oz) long-grain rice
50g (2oz) butter or margarine
1 onion, diced
2 hard-boiled eggs
50g (2oz) raisins (optional)

American

¾ lb finnan haddie (smoked haddock)
½ teaspoon salt
½ teaspoon hot curry powder
1⅓ cups long-grain rice
¼ cup butter or margarine
1 onion, diced
2 hard-boiled eggs
⅓ cup raisins (optional)

Place the haddock in a saucepan and pour over enough boiling water to cover. Put the lid on the saucepan and leave to stand for 5 to 10 minutes. Drain the fish, reserving the liquid. Measure 600ml (1 pint) [2½ cups] of the fish liquid and bring to the boil with the salt and the curry powder.

Sprinkle the rice into the boiling liquid, then cover the saucepan with a well-fitting lid and cook over very low heat for about 25 minutes, when the rice should have absorbed the liquid.

Meanwhile, heat the butter or margarine in a small saucepan and fry the onion until golden and soft. Flake the fish, discarding skin and bones.

Chop the whites of the hard-boiled eggs and rub the yolks through a sieve on to a plate. Plump the raisins in a bowl of hot water for 10 minutes, then drain.

When the rice is cooked, stir in the fried onion and all the melted butter or margarine, plus the chopped egg whites, fish and the plumped, drained raisins. Heat through, then pile on to a warmed serving dish. Scatter the surface with the sieved egg yolks.

HADDOCK WITH POACHED EGGS

This is one of the simplest of light supper dishes. Serve it with creamy mashed potatoes, or with thin slices of buttered toast.

4 servings

Metric/Imperial

50g (2oz) butter
600ml (1 pint) milk
675g (1½lb) smoked haddock, cut into
   4 equal pieces
2 tablespoons cornflour
½ teaspoon black pepper
4 hot poached eggs

American

¼ cup butter
2½ cups milk
1½lb finnan haddie (smoked haddock),
   cut into 4 equal portions
2 tablespoons cornstarch
½ teaspoon black pepper
4 hot poached eggs

In a medium-sized saucepan, melt the butter over moderate heat. When the foam subsides add the milk and the haddock pieces. Bring to the boil. Reduce the heat to low, cover the pan and poach the haddock for 6 minutes. Remove and keep warm on a warmed serving dish.

Transfer 3 tablespoons of the milk to a small mixing bowl. Add the cornflour [cornstarch] and pepper and beat the mixture until it forms a smooth paste. Add this to the milk in the saucepan. Bring to the boil, stirring constantly with a wooden spoon. Reduce the heat and simmer, stirring frequently, for 2 minutes or until the sauce is thick and smooth. Remove the pan from the heat.

Place a poached egg on each haddock slice and surround with the sauce.

Cheese and eggs

Cheese and eggs feature prominently in the menus of the average household today. At least one meal in the week will probably be a meatless one for the sake of economy and variety; and of course, cheese and eggs are rich in protein and especially good for growing children.

Eggs particularly have the virtue of being quick to cook and versatile. You will find no omelettes in this section because they all come under 'Meals in a Hurry', the omelette being one of the best lightning meals for busy people. Cheese and eggs are the basis for many favourite snacks too: toasted cheese sandwiches, Welsh rarebit, scrambled eggs and fried eggs on toast to name but a few. This section contains many favourite recipes for main courses with cheese and eggs, and others which you may never have tried.

A few words on the vast range of cheeses available today may be helpful here. All cheeses are suitable for eating on their own, but some are more useful for cooking than others. Hard cheeses such as Cheddar, Edam, Gruyère, and Emmenthal are ideal for cooking. Very hard cheeses such as Parmesan are always grated before use, and so are the hard cheeses like Cheddar, but a soft cheese should be shredded or thinly sliced. Mozzarella cheese, for example, is used in slices for pizza.

The United States is the world's largest producer of cheese, although there are only two well-known American cheeses, Liederkranz and Brick, all the rest being either processed cheeses (commonly used for cooking) or imitations of foreign varieties, many of which are considered to be as good as or even better than the real thing. Britain produces many fine cheeses, including the famous Cheddar which is now duplicated all over the world and is probably the most versatile all-purpose cheese there is. France produces the widest range of cheeses, and only a few of the 400 to 500 varieties are generally known and available elsewhere. Bread and cheese is still an unbeatable balanced lunchtime snack and if you can offer a selection of cheeses so much the better.

Make sure that cheese and eggs are two of the items always available in your storecupboard or refrigerator. Then you will never be short of the basic ingredients for a suppertime snack or a complete meal.

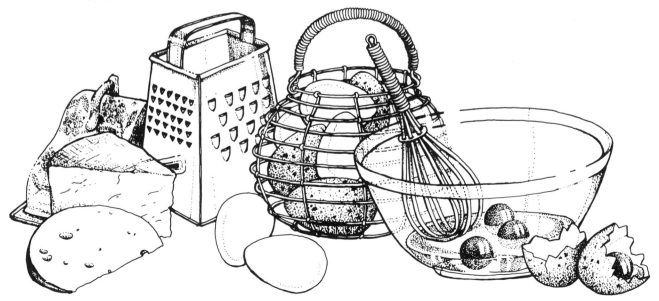

Eggs in Baked Potatoes makes a superb dish for an informal meal.

EGGS IN BAKED POTATOES

A delicious and filling dish suitable for a light informal lunch, these baked potatoes are stuffed with a mixture of eggs, butter, cream and chives.

4 servings

Metric/Imperial

4 large potatoes, scrubbed and dried
1 tablespoon butter
1 tablespoon chopped chives
1 teaspoon salt
¼ teaspoon black pepper
⅛ teaspoon grated nutmeg
4 tablespoons creamy milk
4 eggs

American

4 large potatoes, scrubbed and dried
1 tablespoon butter
1 tablespoon chopped chives
1 teaspoon salt
¼ teaspoon black pepper
⅛ teaspoon grated nutmeg
4 tablespoons creamy milk
4 eggs

Preheat the oven to fairly hot (190°C/375°F or Gas Mark 5).

Prick the potatoes lightly with a fork. Place on the centre shelf in the oven and bake for 1½ hours.

Cut off the top of each potato and, using a teaspoon, scoop out the inside, taking care not to break the skin.

Mash the potato flesh and butter together. Add the chives, salt, pepper and nutmeg. Stir in the milk and beat until thoroughly combined. Gradually beat in the eggs.

Stuff equal amounts of the filling into each potato. Place in a baking dish, return to the oven and bake for 10 to 12 minutes, or until the top of the filling is lightly browned.

EGGBURGERS

Eggburgers are especially popular with children. They make a delicious snack, but can also be served as a light meal if you allow 2 burgers per person.

4 servings

Metric/Imperial

4 soft round rolls, halved
50g (2oz) butter

2 slices ham, halved and roughly cut to fit the rolls
2 teaspoons prepared mustard
4 slices of Cheddar cheese, roughly cut to fit the rolls
4 eggs
2 tablespoons vegetable oil

American

4 soft round rolls, halved
¼ cup butter
2 slices ham, halved and trimmed to fit the rolls
2 teaspoons prepared mustard
4 slices of Cheddar cheese, trimmed to fit the rolls
4 eggs
2 tablespoons vegetable oil

Preheat the grill [broiler] to high. When hot, lightly toast the cut sides of the rolls until golden brown.

Spread each roll half with butter and top with a slice of ham. Spread a little of the mustard over and cover with a slice of cheese.

Place the roll halves under the hot grill [broiler] and cook for 5 minutes, or until the cheese has melted and turned golden brown. Meanwhile fry the eggs in the oil.

Place a fried egg on each roll half, put the tops on and serve.

OEUFS FLORENTINE

Oeufs Florentine is a light and nourishing supper dish. The bechamel sauce is made like White Sauce, but creamier milk is used. This is warmed with a bay leaf, salt, peppercorns and a little nutmeg and left to infuse before it is strained and used to make the sauce.

4 servings

Metric/Imperial

675g (1½lb) spinach
¼ teaspoon grated nutmeg
350ml (12 fl oz) béchamel sauce, hot
8 eggs
50g (2oz) Parmesan cheese, grated

American

1½lb spinach

½ teaspoon grated nutmeg
1½ cups béchamel sauce hot
8 eggs
½ cup Parmesan cheese, grated

Put the spinach in a saucepan and cook for about 7 minutes or until it is tender. (Do not add any water: there should be enough left on leaves after washing.) Drain the spinach, pressing out any excess moisture. Chop finely.

Put the spinach in the goblet of an electric blender and add the nutmeg and one-quarter of the sauce. Blend to a smooth purée. Pour the purée into a warmed shallow flameproof serving dish and keep hot.

Preheat the grill [broiler] to high. Poach the eggs in boiling water (or using an egg poacher) until they are just set. Drain well and arrange on the spinach purée. Pour over the remaining hot béchamel sauce and sprinkle the top with the Parmesan cheese.

Place the dish under the grill [broiler] and cook for 3 to 4 minutes or until the top is lightly browned and bubbling. Serve hot, in the dish.

EGGS BAKED WITH ONIONS

A delicious light dish, Eggs Baked with Onions may be accompanied by hot crusty bread and a crisp green salad.

4 servings

Metric/Imperial

25g (1oz) plus 1 teaspoon butter
2 tablespoons vegetable oil
3 medium-sized onions, thinly sliced and pushed out into rings
6 hard-boiled eggs, sliced
1 teaspoon salt
⅛ teaspoon cayenne pepper
1 tablespoon flour
150ml (5 fl oz) single cream
150ml (5 fl oz) milk
1 teaspoon prepared mustard
3 tablespoons grated Cheddar cheese

American

2 rounded tablespoons butter
2 tablespoons vegetable oil
3 medium-sized onions, thinly sliced and separated into rings
6 hard-boiled eggs, sliced
1 teaspoon salt
⅛ teaspoon cayenne pepper
1 tablespoon flour
⅝ cup light cream
⅝ cup milk
1 teaspoon prepared mustard
3 tablespoons grated Cheddar cheese

With 1 teaspoon of butter, lightly grease a shallow flameproof dish.

In a medium-sized frying-pan, heat the oil over moderate heat. Add the onion rings and fry for 8 to 10 minutes, or until golden brown. Transfer half the onions to the buttered dish. Cover with the hard-boiled eggs and finish with a layer of the remaining onions. Sprinkle with the salt and cayenne.

Preheat the grill [broiler] to high.

In a small saucepan, melt the remaining butter over moderate heat. Remove the pan from the heat and stir in the flour to make a smooth paste. Gradually add the cream and milk, stirring constantly.

Return the pan to the heat and cook stirring for 2 to 3 minutes or until the sauce is thick and smooth. Add the mustard and 2 tablespoons of the cheese. Continue cooking and stirring for a further 3 minutes.

Pour the sauce over the mixture in the dish. Sprinkle with the remaining cheese.

Cook under the grill [broiler] for about 3 minutes, or until the cheese is bubbling and golden brown.

SCOTCH EGGS

A very old favourite in the British Isles, Scotch Eggs are a delicious and nourishing snack or meal. Served hot with a tomato sauce, or cold with a salad, they are quite quick to prepare. In past centuries, Scotch Eggs were sometimes called birds' nests.

4 servings

Metric/Imperial

500g (1lb) pork sausage meat
2 teaspoons Worcestershire sauce
1 tablespoon flour seasoned with
    ⅛ teaspoon salt and ⅛ teaspoon black pepper
4 hard-boiled eggs

Eggs Baked with Onions may be served with crusty bread and a salad for a delicious light lunch.

1 large egg, well beaten
50g (2oz) dry breadcrumbs
vegetable oil for deep-frying

American

1lb sausage meat
2 teaspoons Worcestershire sauce
1 tablespoon flour seasoned with
  $\frac{1}{8}$ teaspoon salt and $\frac{1}{8}$ teaspoon black
  pepper
4 hard-boiled eggs
1 large egg, well beaten
$\frac{2}{3}$ cup dry breadcrumbs
vegetable oil for deep frying

Place the sausage meat and Worcestershire sauce in a mixing bowl. Add the seasoned flour and blend the mixture with your hands. Divide into 4 equal pieces.

Tasty Glamorgan Sausages are made from a delicious and economical mixture of cheese, onion and herbs, covered with breadcrumbs.

Mould each piece of meat around an egg and roll between your hands to shape.

Place the beaten egg and breadcrumbs in two separate shallow dishes. Dip the eggs first in the beaten egg, and then in the breadcrumbs, coating them thoroughly and shaking off any excess crumbs.

In a large saucepan or deep frying-pan, heat the oil over moderate heat until a small cube of stale bread dropped in turns light brown in 1 minute.

Lower the eggs carefully into the oil. Fry for 5 minutes, or until deep golden brown.

GLAMORGAN SAUSAGES

A marvellous family lunch or supper dish, Glamorgan Sausages are made from a tasty and economical mixture of cheese, onion and herbs. Accompany with chips [French fries] and peas.

2 servings

Metric/Imperial

1 large onion, finely chopped
75g (3oz) Cheddar cheese, grated
50g (2oz) fresh white breadcrumbs
1 tablespoon chopped fresh parsley
$\frac{1}{2}$ teaspoon dried thyme
1 teaspoon salt
$\frac{1}{2}$ teaspoon black pepper
$\frac{1}{4}$ teaspoon dry mustard
1 egg, separated
2 tablespoons flour
75g (3oz) dry white breadcrumbs
50g (2oz) butter
2 tablespoons vegetable oil

American

1 large onion, finely chopped
$\frac{3}{4}$ cup Cheddar cheese, grated
1 cup fresh white breadcrumbs
1 tablespoons chopped fresh parsley
$\frac{1}{2}$ teaspoon dried thyme
1 teaspoon salt
$\frac{1}{2}$ teaspoon black pepper
$\frac{1}{4}$ teaspoon dry mustard

1 egg, separated
2 tablespoons flour
1 cup dry white breadcrumbs
¼ cup butter
2 tablespoons vegetable oil

In a medium-sized mixing bowl, combine the onion, cheese, fresh breadcrumbs, parsley, thyme, salt, pepper, mustard and egg yolk. Lightly beat the egg white in a separate bowl and set aside.

With your hands, shape the mixture into eight sausages. Dip in the flour, then in lightly beaten egg white and then roll in the dry breadcrumbs.

In a large frying-pan, melt the butter and oil over moderate heat. When the foam subsides, add the sausages and fry turning occasionally, for 5 to 8 minutes, or until well browned on all sides.

EGGS ESSEN

A delicious combination of green pepper, onion, tomatoes, frankfurters and eggs, Eggs Essen is a colourful and substantial meal in itself.

4-6 servings

Metric/Imperial

4 tablespoons vegetable oil
1 medium-sized onion, finely chopped
2 medium-sized potatoes, peeled and diced
50g (2oz) ham, diced
1 small green pepper, white pith removed, seeded and finely chopped
250g (8oz) can peeled tomatoes, drained and chopped
8 frankfurters, thinly sliced
¼ teaspoon dried basil

Eggs Essen is a simple, tasty and colourful dish for the family.

6 eggs
1 teaspoon salt
½ teaspoon black pepper

American

4 tablespoons vegetable oil
1 medium-sized onion, finely chopped
2 medium-sized potatoes, peeled and diced
¼ cup ham, diced
1 small green pepper, membrane and seeds removed, finely chopped
1 cup canned tomatoes, drained and chopped
8 frankfurters, thinly sliced
¼ teaspoon dried basil
6 eggs

1 teaspoon salt
½ teaspoon black pepper

Preheat the oven to very hot (230°C/450°F or Gas Mark 9).

In a large frying-pan, heat the oil over moderate heat. Add the onion and potatoes and cook, stirring occasionally, for 5 minutes.

Add the ham, green pepper, tomatoes, frankfurters and basil. Cook, stirring occasionally, for 15 minutes. Turn the mixture into a medium-sized ovenproof dish, smoothing the top.

Break the eggs on top of the mixture and sprinkle with the salt and pepper. Bake in the upper part of the oven for 8 to 10 minutes or until the whites of the eggs are set.

EGG, SAUSAGE AND PEPPER CASSEROLE

This piquant and filling casserole, flavoured with spices and herbs, makes an interesting supper dish.

4 servings

Metric/Imperial

3 tablespoons vegetable oil
2 medium-sized onions, sliced
2 large green peppers, white pith removed, seeded and finely sliced
2 large tomatoes, peeled and sliced
1 teaspoon paprika
½ teaspoon dried thyme
½ teaspoon salt
¼ teaspoon black pepper
8 beef or pork sausages
8 eggs
½ teaspoon prepared mustard
1 tablespoon tomato purée
100ml (4 fl oz) tomato juice
3 tablespoons Parmesan cheese, grated

American

3 tablespoons vegetable oil
2 medium-sized onions, sliced
2 large green peppers, membrane and seeds removed, finely sliced
2 large tomatoes, peeled and sliced
1 teaspoon paprika
½ teaspoon dried thyme
½ teaspoon salt
¼ teaspoon black pepper

8 sausages
8 eggs
½ teaspoon prepared mustard
1 tablespoon tomato paste
½ cup tomato juice
3 tablespoons Parmesan cheese, grated

Preheat the oven to moderate (180°C/350°F or Gas Mark 4). Grease a large baking dish.

In a small frying-pan heat 2 tablespoons of the oil over moderate heat. Add the onions, peppers, tomatoes, paprika, thyme, salt and pepper. Fry, stirring occasionally, for 8 to 10 minutes or until the onions and peppers are soft and the tomatoes pulpy. Turn the mixture into the greased baking dish.

Heat the remaining oil in the frying-pan. Add the sausages and fry for 5 minutes or until browned all over. Arrange the sausages on top of the vegetables, leaving a gap between each one. Break one egg into each gap.

In a small mixing bowl, combine the mustard and tomato purée. Stir in the tomato juice and pour the mixture over the ingredients in the baking dish. Sprinkle the cheese on top.

Bake in the centre of the oven for 20 to 30 minutes or until the eggs are set and the sausages cooked.

EGG AND CHEESE RISSOLES

These delicious savoury rissoles make an inexpensive light main dish. They can be accompanied by cooked vegetables or a green salad.

2-3 servings

Metric/Imperial

250ml (8 fl oz) milk
½ teaspoon salt
¼ teaspoon black pepper
¼ teaspoon dried dill
⅛ teaspoon grated nutmeg
25g (1oz) butter
2 tablespoons flour
100g (4oz) Cheddar cheese, grated
1 tablespoon chopped fresh parsley
5 hard-boiled eggs, chopped
25g (1oz) dry white breadcrumbs
2 tablespoons vegetable oil

American

1 cup milk
½ teaspoon salt
¼ teaspoon black pepper
¼ teaspoon dried dill
⅛ teaspoon grated nutmeg
2 tablespoons butter
2 tablespoons flour
1 cup Cheddar cheese, grated
1 tablespoon chopped fresh parsley
5 hard-boiled eggs, chopped
⅛ cup dry white breadcrumbs
2 tablespoons vegetable oil

Heat the milk, salt, pepper dill and nutmeg gently for 5 minutes. Set aside to cool to lukewarm.

In another pan, melt the butter over moderate heat. Remove from the heat and stir in the flour to make a smooth paste. Gradually add the lukewarm milk, stirring constantly. Return the pan to moderate heat and add the grated cheese and parsley. Cook, stirring constantly, until the sauce becomes very thick and smooth.

Remove from the heat and fold in the hard-boiled eggs. Allow the mixture to cool to room temperature and then place in the refrigerator to chill for 30 minutes.

Shape into 6 patties and flatten them slightly. Coat each patty with breadcrumbs.

In a large frying-pan, heat the oil over moderate heat. Add the rissoles and fry for 4 minutes on each side, or until golden brown.

EGG CUTLETS

A substantial, economical dish, Egg Cutlets may be served with a green vegetable or salad.

2-4 servings

Metric/Imperial

4 hard-boiled eggs, finely chopped
2 tablespoons cooked rice
2 tablespoons fresh white breadcrumbs
2 tablespoons grated Cheddar cheese
1 tablespoon chopped fresh parsley
1 teaspoon Worcestershire sauce

1 teaspoon salt
½ teaspoon black pepper
1 egg, separated
2 tablespoons dry white breadcrumbs
50g (2oz) butter

American

4 hard-boiled eggs, finely chopped
2 tablespoons cooked rice
2 tablespoons fresh white
  breadcrumbs
2 tablespoons grated Cheddar cheese
1 tablespoon chopped fresh parsley
1 teaspoon Worcestershire sauce
1 teaspoon salt
½ teaspoon black pepper
1 egg, separated
2 tablespoons dry white breadcrumbs
¼ cup butter

Combine the hard-boiled eggs, rice, breadcrumbs, cheese, parsley, Worcestershire sauce, salt and pepper.

Stir in the egg yolk and mix well. Form into small cutlet shapes.

Beat the egg white lightly. Brush the cutlets with it and roll them in the breadcrumbs.

In a medium-sized frying-pan, melt the butter over moderate heat. When the foam subsides add the cutlets and fry for 6 to 8 minutes or until golden brown on both sides.

EGG AND CREAM CHEESE TART

This simple Egg and Cream Cheese Tart is excellent for a family weekend lunch.

One 23cm (9in) Tart

Metric/Imperial

250g (9oz) cream cheese
100ml (4 fl oz) double cream
6 eggs
6 spring onions, finely chopped
½ teaspoon salt
¼ teaspoon white pepper
175g (6oz) Shortcrust Pastry I

American

9oz cream cheese
½ cup heavy cream
6 eggs

6 scallions, finely chopped
½ teaspoon salt
¼ teaspoon white pepper
1 recipe Shortcrust Pastry I

Preheat the oven to fairly hot (190°C/375°F or Gas Mark 5).

In a mixing bowl, beat the cream cheese and cream together with a wooden spoon until smooth. Beat in the eggs, onions [scallions], salt and pepper.

On a floured board, roll out the dough into a circle, lay it over a 23cm (9-inch) flan tin. Gently ease the dough into the tin and trim the edges.

Spoon in the cream cheese mixture and bake for 30 minutes or until the pastry is golden brown and the filling is set.

EGG RATATOUILLE

An unusual dish to serve for a light supper, Egg Ratatouille needs no accompaniment other than crusty bread and butter.

4 servings

Metric/Imperial

2 large aubergines, washed and sliced
2½ teaspoons salt

500g (1lb) courgettes, washed and
  sliced
3 tablespoons vegetable oil
1 large onion, sliced and pushed out
  into rings
1 large garlic clove, crushed
1 green pepper, white pith removed,
  seeded and sliced
4 tomatoes, peeled and chopped
100g (4oz) mushrooms, wiped and
  sliced (optional)
¼ teaspoon black pepper
¼ teaspoon dried basil
4 eggs
25g (1oz) butter

American

2 large eggplants, washed and sliced
2½ teaspoons salt
1lb zucchini, washed and sliced
¼ cup vegetable oil
1 large onion, sliced and separated
  into rings
1 large garlic clove, crushed
1 green pepper, membrane and seeds
  removed, sliced
4 tomatoes, peeled and chopped
¼lb mushrooms, wiped and sliced
  (optional)

Egg and Cream Cheese Tart is a creamy, rich dish for a family lunch.

¼ teaspoon black pepper
¼ teaspoons dried basil
4 eggs
2 tablespoons butter

Place the aubergine [eggplant] slices in a colander and place the courgette [zucchini] slices on a plate. Sprinkle with 1 teaspoon of salt and leave for 30 minutes.

Dry the slices with kitchen paper.

In a very large saucepan, heat the oil over moderate heat. Add the onion and garlic and fry for 5 to 7 minutes or until soft and translucent. Add the courgettes [zucchini], aubergines [eggplants] and green pepper to the pan and continue cooking for 10 minutes. Stir in the tomatoes and mushrooms (if using them) and sprinkle over the remaining salt, the pepper and the basil. Half cover the pan, reduce the heat and simmer the ratatouille, stirring occasionally, for 45 minutes.

Five minutes before it is ready, fry the eggs in the butter.

Turn the ratatouille into a warmed serving dish and top with the fried eggs.

CHEESE AND ONION PIE

This economical pie can be served hot or cold as an hors d'oeuvre, or as a light luncheon or supper dish with a tossed, mixed salad.

---

4 servings

Metric/Imperial

---

3 tablespoons butter
3 medium-sized onions, finely
    chopped
2 garlic cloves, crushed
250g (8oz) Cheddar cheese, grated
1 egg, lightly beaten
½ teaspoon white pepper
250g (8oz) Shortcrust Pastry I

American

---

3 tablespoons butter
3 medium-sized onions, finely
    chopped
2 garlic cloves, crushed
2 cups Cheddar cheese, grated
1 egg, lightly beaten
½ teaspoon white pepper

1 recipe Shortcrust Pastry I

Preheat the oven to fairly hot (200°C/400°F or Gas Mark 6). Grease a medium-sized pie dish with 1 tablespoon of the butter.

In a frying-pan, melt the remaining 2 tablespoons of butter over moderate heat. Add the chopped onions and garlic, reduce the heat to low and cook gently for about 10 minutes, stirring occasionally, until soft and translucent but not brown.

In a medium-sized mixing bowl, combine the onion mixture with the grated cheese. Add most of the beaten egg (keep a little to glaze the pie crust), and the pepper and beat to blend well.

Divide the dough ball into two portions, one slightly larger than the other. On a lightly floured surface, roll out the larger portion until it is quite thin and is large enough to overlap the sides of the pie dish. Line the pie dish, and trim off excess dough. Spoon the cheese-and-onion mixture into the dish, spreading it evenly over the bottom.

Roll out the other portion of dough to a circle slightly larger than the pie dish. Place on top of the filling. Fold under the overhanging dough and press the edges together with your fingertips. Brush the surface with the remaining beaten egg.

Bake in the centre of the oven for about 35 minutes, or until the pastry is deep golden.

EGG AND POTATO PIE

Quick and easy to prepare, Egg and Potato Pie is ideal to serve as a main dish for a family lunch or supper.

4-6 servings

Metric/Imperial

---

1 tablespoon butter
5 medium-sized potatoes, peeled,
    boiled and thinly sliced
6 hard-boiled eggs, sliced
100g (4oz) ham, finely chopped
100g (4oz) Cheddar cheese, grated
½ teaspoon salt
½ teaspoon black pepper
300ml (10 fl oz) sour cream

2 tomatoes, sliced
1 tablespoon chopped chives

American

---

1 tablespoon butter
5 medium-sized potatoes, peeled,
    boiled and thinly sliced
6 hard-boiled eggs, sliced
½ cup ham, finely chopped
1 cup Cheddar cheese, grated
½ teaspoon salt
½ teaspoon black pepper
1¼ cups sour cream
2 tomatoes, sliced
1 tablespoon chopped chives

Preheat the oven to moderate (180°C/350°F or Gas Mark 4).

Grease a large ovenproof casserole with the butter and arrange a layer of the potatoes on the bottom. Cover with a layer of hard-boiled egg and chopped ham. Sprinkle a little of the cheese, salt and pepper on top. Continue making layers until all the ingredients have been used, ending with a layer of potatoes. Pour the sour cream over the top. Decorate with the sliced tomatoes and sprinkle over the chopped chives.

Bake for 45 minutes.

RIVERSIDE APPLE FLAN

Appetizing and savoury, Riverside Apple Flan makes an ideal quick, light supper dish. Serve with a tossed green salad or grilled [broiled] tomatoes.

---

4 servings

Metric/Imperial

---

1 x 23cm (1 x 9in) flan case made with
    175g (6oz) Shortcrust Pastry I,
    baked blind and cooled
1 tablespoon butter
6 streaky bacon slices, chopped
2 large cooking apples, peeled, cored
    and chopped
425ml (15 fl oz) White Sauce, hot
175g (6oz) Cheddar cheese, grated
1 teaspoon salt
½ teaspoon white pepper

American

---

1 x 9in pie shell made with Shortcrust
    Pastry I, baked blind and cooled

1 tablespoon butter

6 bacon slices, diced

2 large tart green apples, peeled, cored and chopped

1⅞ cups thick White Sauce, hot

1½ cups Cheddar cheese, grated

1 teaspoon salt

½ teaspoon white pepper

Preheat the grill [broiler] to high. Place the flan case on a large flameproof plate.

In a medium-sized frying-pan, melt the butter over moderate heat. When the foam subsides, add the bacon and fry for 5 to 7 minutes, turning frequently, or until golden brown and crisp. Remove and drain.

Add the apples to the pan and, stirring frequently, cook for 5 minutes or until just tender.

Place the white sauce in a mixing bowl and stir in the bacon, apples and cooking juices, and half the grated cheese. Season with the salt and pepper. Stit until the cheese has melted.

Pour the sauce mixture into the flan case and sprinkle with the remaining cheese. Place the plate on the rack of the grill [broiler] pan and cook for 5 minutes or until the cheese is golden brown and bubbling.

BACON AND EGG PIE

Delicious eaten hot or cold, this is an easily-made pie. It is a good dish for light lunches, suppers, or for a family picnic.

4 servings

Metric/Imperial

175g (6oz) Shortcrust Pastry I

1 teaspoon butter

250g (8oz) streaky bacon, rinds removed

½ teaspoon black pepper

4 eggs

a little milk

Riverside Apple Flan is ideal to serve at a picnic.

American

1 recipe Shortcrust Pastry I

1 teaspoon butter

½lb bacon

½ teaspoon black pepper

4 eggs

a little milk

Preheat the oven to fairly hot (200°C/400°F or Gas Mark 6).

Grease a 20cm (8-inch) diameter sandwich tin or pie plate with 1 teaspoon of butter.

Break off two-thirds of the pastry and set aside the smaller piece. On a floured board, roll out the larger piece into a round 5cm (2 inches) larger than the tin. Line the tin with this and trim the edges.

Chop the bacon into small pieces.

Arrange in the pastry shell, leaving 4 wells for the eggs. Break an egg into each well. Sprinkle with pepper. Brush the edge of the pastry with a little water. Roll out the remaining pastry into a circle and cover the pie. Trim the edges, pinch them together to seal and make a decorative pattern. Brush the top of the pie with milk and decorate with pastry shapes. Make a slit in the centre to allow steam to escape.

Place the pie in the centre of the oven and bake for 40 minutes. When the top becomes sufficiently brown, cover with aluminium foil and continue baking.

CHEESE CHARLOTTE

This savoury charlotte makes a light and tasty supper dish.

This tasty Cheese Charlotte, topped with crisply fried bacon, is a light and tasty dish.

4 servings

Metric/Imperial

1 thick slice white bread cut into cubes
200ml (7 fl oz) milk
8 slices of white bread, crusts removed
40g (1½oz) butter
3 eggs, separated
1½ tablespoons flour
250g (8oz) Cheddar cheese, grated
½ teaspoon salt
¼ teaspoon grated nutmeg
100ml (4 fl oz) single cream

American

1 thick slice white bread, cubed
⅞ cup milk
8 slices of white bread, crusts removed
3 tablespoons butter
3 eggs, separated
1½ tablespoons flour
2 cups Cheddar cheese, grated
½ teaspoon salt
¼ teaspoon grated nutmeg
½ cup light cream

Preheat the oven to moderate (180°C/350°F or Gas Mark 4).

Put the bread cubes in a shallow dish and sprinkle over half of the milk. In another dish, spread out the bread slices and sprinkle with the remaining milk. Leave to soak.

In a large bowl, cream the butter and mix in the egg yolks, one at a time. Stir in the flour. Add the soaked bread cubes, cheese, salt and nutmeg. Blend well and stir in the cream.

Beat the egg whites until stiff; fold into the cheese mixture.

Line a greased, straight-sided, flame-proof dish or casserole with the soaked bread slices. Pour in the cheese mixture. Bake for 35 to 40 minutes.

QUICHE LORRAINE

The classic French quiche, Quiche Lorraine (keesh law-rain) is traditionally served, hot or cold, as a first course. It also makes a beautifully light lunch or

supper dish served with a mixed salad.

4-6 servings

Metric/Imperial

1 x 23cm (1 x 9in) flan case made with
    175g (6oz) Shortcrust Pastry I,
    baked blind and cooled
100g (4oz) Cheddar cheese, thinly
    sliced
175g (6oz) streaky bacon, grilled
    until crisp and crumbled
150ml (5 fl oz) single cream
3 eggs
½ teaspoon salt
½ teaspoon white pepper

American

1 x 9in pie shell, made with Shortcrust
    Pastry I, baked blind and cooled
1 cup Cheddar cheese, thinly sliced
6oz bacon, broiled until crisp and
    crumbled
⅝ cup light cream
3 eggs
½ teaspoon salt
½ teaspoon white pepper

Preheat the oven to fairly hot (200°C/
400°F or Gas Mark 6). Place the flan
case on a baking sheet.

Cover the bottom of the flan case
with the cheese slices, then with the
crumbled bacon.

Combine the cream, eggs, salt and
pepper and beat well to blend. Pour
over the cheese.

Bake in the centre of the oven for 25
to 30 minutes or until the filling is set
and golden brown on top.

CHEESE AND HAM SOUFFLE

This Cheese and Ham Soufflé is a light
but satisfying supper dish.

4 servings

Metric/Imperial

100g (4oz) butter
2 tablespoons fine dry white
    breadcrumbs
75g (3oz) flour
450ml (16 fl oz) milk, scalded
100g (4oz) Cheddar cheese, grated
75g (3oz) ham, finely chopped

6 eggs, separated
½ teaspoon salt
½ teaspoon paprika
⅛ teaspoon cayenne pepper

American

½ cup butter
2 tablespoons fine dry white
    breadcrumbs
¾ cup flour
2 cups milk, scalded
1 cup Cheddar cheese, grated
⅓ cup ham, finely chopped
6 eggs, separated
½ teaspoon salt
½ teaspoon paprika
⅛ teaspoon cayenne pepper

Preheat the oven to fairly hot (190°C/
375°F or Gas Mark 5). Place a double
piece of greaseproof or waxed paper
around the outside of a 1-litre (2-pint)
[5-cup] soufflé dish and tie with string.
The paper should come 5cm (2 inches)
higher than the rim of the dish. Butter
the paper and the dish with one-quarter
of the butter, then dust lightly with the
breadcrumbs, shaking out the excess.

In a large saucepan, melt the remaining butter over moderate heat. Stir in
the flour and cook, stirring constantly,
for 1 minute.

Remove the pan from the heat and
gradually stir in the scalded milk. Add
the cheese and ham to the mixture and
stir until the cheese has melted.

In a small mixing bowl, lightly beat
the egg yolks. Add about one-quarter of
the hot cheese mixture and stir well.

Slowly return the egg yolk mixture to
the saucepan, stirring constantly. Season the mixture with the salt, paprika
and cayenne. Set the pan aside to allow
the mixture to cool slightly.

Beat the egg whites until they form
stiff peaks and gently fold into the
cooled cheese-and-ham mixture.

Pour the mixture into the soufflé dish.
Bake for 35 minutes or until the top is
puffed up and lightly browned.

CORN SOUFFLE

This recipe produces a lovely light
golden soufflé which is sure to be
popular.

4 servings

Metric/Imperial

3 tablespoons butter
3 tablespoons flour
250ml (8 fl oz) milk
250g (8oz) cooked sweetcorn kernels
salt and pepper
¼ teaspoon mustard
100g (4oz) grated cheese
3 eggs, separated

American

3 tablespoons butter
3 tablespoons flour
1 cup milk
1 cup cooked or canned corn kernels
salt and pepper
¼ teaspoon mustard
1 cup grated cheese
3 eggs, separated

Preheat the oven to moderate (180°C/
350°F or Gas Mark 4). Butter a 1½-litre
(2½-pint) [6¼-cup] soufflé or pie dish.

Melt the butter in a saucepan. Remove from the heat and stir in the flour.
Gradually blend in the milk, return to
the heat and bring to the boil, stirring
constantly. Cook until the sauce is
thickened and smooth. Add the cooked
corn, salt, pepper, mustard and most of
the cheese: allow to cool slightly.

Stir the egg yolks into the sauce,
one at a time. Beat the egg whites until
stiff, and gently fold into the corn
mixture. Pour into the prepared dish.
Sprinkle with the remaining cheese and
bake for 20-30 minutes until well risen
and golden brown.

SPINACH SOUFFLE WITH HAM

A tasty mixture of spinach, ham and
cheese combines to make this a satisfying dish to serve for a light lunch.

4 servings

Metric/Imperial

75g (3oz) butter
2 shallots, finely chopped
100g (4oz) ham, finely chopped
50g (2oz) flour
100g (4 fl oz) milk

4 tablespoons spinach purée
½ teaspoon salt
1 teaspoon black pepper
1 teaspoon paprika
50g (2oz) Swiss or Cheddar cheese, grated
2 tablespoons creamy milk
4 egg yolks
5 egg whites

American

⅜ cup butter
2 shallots, finely chopped
½ cup ham, finely chopped
½ cup flour
½ cup milk
4 tablespoons spinach purée
½ teaspoon salt
1 teaspoon black pepper
1 teaspoon paprika
½ cup Swiss or Cheddar cheese, grated
2 tablespoons creamy milk
4 egg yolks
5 egg whites

Preheat the oven to fairly hot (200°C/400°F or Gas Mark 6). Grease a 1½-litre (2½-pint) [6¼-cup] soufflé dish with 1 tablespoon of the butter. Set aside.

In a medium-sized saucepan, melt one third of the remaining butter over moderate heat. When the foam subsides, add the shallots and ham and cook, stirring frequently, for 3 to 4 minutes or until the shallots are soft and translucent but not brown. Remove from the pan and keep warm.

Add the remaining butter to the pan and melt it over moderate heat. Remove from the heat and stir in the flour to make a smooth paste. Gradually add the milk, stirring constantly. Stir in the spinach.

Return the pan to the heat and cook, stirring constantly for 2 to 3 minutes or until the sauce is thick and smooth. Stir in the salt, pepper, paprika and cheese and cook, stirring constantly, for a further 2 minutes or until the cheese has melted. Remove the pan from the heat and stir in the cream. Add the shallot and ham mixture and stir well to mix. Set aside to cool to lukewarm, then beat in the egg yolks, one at a time.

Beat the egg whites until they form stiff peaks. With a metal spoon, carefully fold into the sauce. Pour the mixture into the prepared soufflé dish, place in the centre of the oven and reduce the temperature to fairly hot (190°C/375°F or Gas Mark 5). Bake for 25 to 30 minutes or until the soufflé has risen and is golden brown on top, and a skewer inserted into the centre comes out clean. Serve immediately.

CHEESE SOUFFLE

A perfect soufflé is generally considered to be a tricky, temperamental dish to make, but this recipe for Cheese Soufflé is very easy to prepare.

6-8 servings

Metric/Imperial

50g (2oz) plus 1 tablespoon butter
150g (5oz) cheese, coarsely grated (preferably a mixture of Gruyére and Parmesan)
4 tablespoons flour
300ml (10 fl oz) milk, scalded
1 teaspoon salt
⅛ teaspoon white pepper
⅛ teaspoon ground mace
⅛ teaspoon paprika
5 egg yolks
6 egg whites
¼ teaspoon cream of tartar

American

¼ cup plus 1 tablespoon butter
1¼ cups cheese, coarsely grated (preferably a mixture of Gruyére and Parmesan)
4 tablespoons flour
1¼ cups milk, scalded
1 teaspoon salt
⅛ teaspoon white pepper
⅛ teaspoon ground mace
⅛ teaspoon paprika
5 egg yolks
6 egg whites
¼ teaspoon cream of tartar

Preheat the oven to moderate (180°C/350°F or Gas Mark 4).

With the tablespoon of butter, grease a 1½-litre (2½-pint) [6¼-cup] soufflé dish. Sprinkle 4 tablespoons of the grated cheese around the inside of the dish and, with a table knife, press it on to the bottom and sides.

In a large saucepan, melt the remaining butter over moderate heat. Stir the flour into the butter and cook, stirring constantly, for 1 minute. (Do not let this roux brown.)

Remove the pan from the heat. Gradually add the milk, stirring constantly for 1 minute or until thick and smooth.

Remove the pan from the heat and add ½ teaspoon salt, the pepper, mace and paprika. Beat the egg yolks, a little at a time, into the hot sauce. Set the pan aside to allow the mixture to cool slightly.

Beat the egg whites until foamy. Add the remaining salt and the cream of tartar. Continue beating until the egg whites form stiff peaks.

Stir the remaining cheese into the hot sauce. When thoroughly mixed in spoon the egg whites on top and gently but quickly fold them in with a metal spoon.

Spoon the mixture into the prepared soufflé dish. With a table knife, carefully mark a deep circle in the centre of the soufflé.

Bake in the centre of the oven for 40-45 minutes or until lightly browned on top and well risen. Serve at once.

PIZZA NAPOLETANA

A well-known pizza, which exists in many different versions.

4-6 servings

Metric/Imperial

250g (8oz) Pizza Dough or Scone Dough
250g (8oz) tomatoes, skinned and chopped
12 anchovy fillets
about 12 black olives, stoned
¼ teaspoon dried basil
4-6 slices Bel Paese or Mozzarella cheese
1 tablespoon olive oil
black pepper

American

1 recipe Pizza Dough or Scone Dough
1 cup tomatoes, skinned and chopped
12 anchovy fillets
about 12 ripe olives, pitted

Cheese Souffle is always a perfect dish to serve for a light meal. Accompany with a salad.

¼ teaspoon dried basil
4-6 slices Bel Paese or Mozzarella cheese
1 tablespoon olive oil
black pepper

Shape the dough into a round on a floured baking sheet and cover with the chopped tomatoes. Make a lattice with the anchovy fillets. Decorate with the olives, sprinkle with basil and pepper and cover with slices of cheese. Leave the pizza to stand for about 10 minutes.

Preheat the oven to fairly hot (200°C/400°F or Gas Mark 6).

Sprinkle the pizza with the olive oil and bake near the top of the oven for 25-30 minutes.

PIZZA SICILIANA

For an authentic Pizza Siciliana use a spicy Italian sausage such as pepperoni.

4-6 servings

Metric/Imperial

250g (8oz) Pizza Dough or Scone Dough
150ml (5 fl oz) thick Tomato Sauce
3 cooked sausages, halved lengthwise

12 black olives, stoned and sliced
50g (2oz) Cheddar cheese, grated
¼ teaspoon dried basil
salt and pepper
1 tablespoon olive oil

American

1 recipe Pizza Dough or Scone Dough
⅝ cup thick Tomato Sauce
3 cooked sausages, halved lengthwise
12 ripe olives, pitted and sliced
¼ cup Cheddar cheese, grated
¼ teaspoon dried basil
salt and pepper
1 tablespoon olive oil

Shape the dough into a round on a floured baking sheet. Cover with the

Tomato Sauce, slices of sausage, sliced olives, and grated cheese. Sprinkle with basil and salt and pepper. Leave the pizza to stand for about 10 minutes. Preheat the oven to hot (200°C/400°F or Gas Mark 6). Moisten the pizza with the olive oil and bake at the top of the oven for 25-30 minutes.

PIZZA MARGHERITA

Pizza Margherita is a quick and simple pizza, especially if you use Scone Dough.

4-6 servings

Metric/Imperial

250g (8oz) Pizza Dough or Scone Dough
4-6 tomatoes, thinly sliced
8 slices Bel Paese or Mozzarella
   cheese
salt and pepper
$\frac{1}{4}$ teaspoon dried oregano
1 tablespoon olive oil

American

1 recipe Pizza Dough or Scone Dough
4-6 tomatoes, thinly sliced
8 slices Bel Paese or Mozzarella
   cheese
salt and pepper

$\frac{1}{4}$ teaspoon dried oregano
1 tablespoon olive oil

Shape the dough into a round on a floured baking sheet. Cover with the sliced tomatoes and cheese. Sprinkle with salt and pepper and oregano. Leave the pizza to stand for about 10 minutes. Preheat the oven to fairly hot (200°C/400°F or Gas Mark 6).
Moisten the pizza with the olive oil and bake for 25 to 30 minutes.

Pizza Margherita makes a marvellously tasty light meal.

Rice, pulses and pasta

Rice is the staple food of about two-thirds of the world's population and as the price of our Western staple food items such as bread and potatoes increases, it has come to feature prominently in most people's diets. In cities, and wherever there is a big immigrant population, rice and pasta and associated food products are readily obtainable. Plenty of people now have access to Indian food stores, where they can purchase the spices which go into an authentic Indian curry, and also Italian stores which sell not only the standard spaghetti and noodles, but also lasagne, fettucini, rigatoni, tagliatelle and the many other different types of pasta in all shapes and sizes which are not only fun to cook with but immensely popular with children. Just try a handful of alphabet pasta in a home-made soup, and you have a meal which is not only good to eat but educationally improving!

If you have never tried brown rice or wholewheat pasta (available from health food stores) you should do so. The nutty taste and texture of these products is really nice, and they are not only very wholesome but they don't become sticky when cooked like white rice and pasta.

Less well-known, and very under-used except by health food enthusiasts and vegetarians, are pulses. These are dried mature beans and peas, and can be used in much the same way as pasta, rice or potatoes to bulk out a meal. They include lentils, split peas, kidney beans, haricot beans and black-eyed beans. Their great drawback is that all pulses (except lentils and split peas) have to be pre-soaked, usually overnight, before cooking, and even then they need a lot of cooking to soften them. A pressure cooker can be a great help here. The advantages are that pulses are cheap and extremely nutritious. Bear in mind that 75g (3oz) of dried peas or beans is generally enough for one substantial serving, since the pulses increase in weight and volume during soaking and cooking. Try Baked Beans with Pork as a filling supper dish, guaranteed to be popular with children. You don't have to serve these dried peas and beans as a meal in their own right, of course; they make a nice vegetable accompaniment too, although they do benefit from the addition of herbs, bacon pieces, or plenty of seasoning to give them extra flavour.

EGG NOODLES WITH CREAMY CHEESE SAUCE

Egg Noodles with Creamy Cheese Sauce makes a delicious supper or quick lunch dish, or in smaller portions it makes an ideal hors d'oeuvre.

4 servings

Metric/Imperial

75g (3oz) butter
75ml (3 fl oz) double cream
¾ teaspoon salt
¼ teaspoon white pepper
75g (3oz) Parmesan cheese, grated
25g (1oz) Cheddar cheese, grated
500g (1lb) egg noodles

American

6 tablespoons butter
⅜ cup heavy cream
¾ teaspoon salt
¼ teaspoon white pepper
¾ cup Parmesan cheese, grated
¼ cup Cheddar cheese, grated
1lb egg noodles

In a large bowl cream the butter with a wooden spoon until it is soft and fluffy. Gradually beat in the cream and add ¼ teaspoon salt and the pepper. Stir in 4 tablespoons of the Parmesan and all the Cheddar cheese.

Cook the noodles in plenty of boiling salted water until just tender. Drain thoroughly and transfer to a warmed serving dish. Spoon the cheese mixture on top and toss until the noodles are well coated.

Serve the remaining Parmesan cheese separately.

NOODLES WITH HAM

A quick supper dish, Noodles with Ham may be sprinkled with grated Parmesan cheese just before serving. Serve the noodles with a dish of creamed or chopped spinach.

4 servings

Metric/Imperial

500g (1lb) noodles, cooked, drained and kept hot

50g (2oz) butter
½ teaspoon salt
½ teaspoon black pepper
1 teaspoon dried basil
250g (8oz) ham, cut into thin strips
1 small garlic sausage, cut into thin strips
2 large tomatoes, peeled and cut into strips

American

1lb noodles, cooked, drained and kept hot
¼ cup butter
½ teaspoon salt
½ teaspoon black pepper
1 teaspoon dried basil
1 cup ham, cut into thin strips
1 small garlic sausage, cut into thin strips
2 large tomatoes, peeled and cut into strips

In a large saucepan, heat the noodles and butter gently and toss them until well coated.

Add the remaining ingredients. Increase the heat to moderate and cook, stirring frequently, for 6 to 8 minutes or until very hot.

PASTA WITH VEAL AND MUSHROOMS

This is a rich dish which needs only a lightly tossed green salad to make a delicious and sustaining supper.

4 servings

Metric/Imperial

50g (2oz) plus 1 tablespoon butter
1 small onion, chopped
6 bacon slices, chopped
250g (8oz) veal, finely minced
½ teaspoon salt
¼ teaspoon black pepper
⅛ teaspoon dried oregano
500g (1lb) button mushrooms, wiped clean and sliced
225ml (8 fl oz) single cream
2 tablespoons chopped fresh parsley
175g (6oz) egg noodles, cooked, drained and kept hot
175g (6oz) green egg noodles, cooked, drained and kept hot

50g (2oz) Parmesan cheese, grated

American

5 tablespoons butter
1 small onion, chopped
6 bacon slices, chopped
1 cup ground veal
½ teaspoon salt
¼ teaspoon black pepper
⅛ teaspoon dried oregano
1lb small mushrooms, wiped clean and sliced
1 cup light cream
2 tablespoons chopped fresh parsley
2¼ cups fettucini, cooked, drained and kept hot
2¼ cups spinach noodles, cooked, drained and kept hot
½ cup Parmesan cheese, grated

In a medium-sized frying-pan, melt the main quantity of butter over moderate heat. When the foam subsides add the onion and bacon and cook, stirring occasionally, for 5 to 7 minutes or until soft and translucent but not brown.

Add the veal and cook, stirring constantly, for 5 minutes or until well browned. Stir in the salt, pepper, oregano and mushrooms and cook, stirring occasionally, for a further 5 minutes or until the mushrooms are tender.

Add the cream and parsley and stir well. Reduce the heat to low and cook, stirring occasionally, for a further 3 to 5 minutes or until hot but not boiling.

Place the noodles in a large serving dish and toss in the remaining butter.

Pour over the veal and mushroom mixture. Toss well and serve with the grated Parmesan cheese.

GREEN RIBBON PASTA IN TUNA FISH SAUCE

This simple and colourful pasta dish is a good 'emergency' meal since most of the ingredients can be kept in the store cupboard.

4-6 servings

Easy-to-make Noodles with Ham is simply delicious.

Metric/Imperial

3 tablespoons vegetable oil
350g (12oz) canned tuna fish, drained and flaked
2 tablespoons chopped fresh parsley
425ml (15 fl oz) chicken stock, hot
1½ teaspoons black pepper
500g (1lb) tagliatelle verdi, cooked, drained and kept hot
1 tablespoon butter

American

3 tablespoons vegetable oil
1¼ cups canned tuna fish, drained and flaked
2 tablespoons chopped fresh parsley
1¾ cups chicken stock, hot
1½ teaspoons black pepper
1lb green ribbon-shaped pasta (tagliarini), cooked, drained and kept hot
1 tablespoon butter

In a medium-sized frying-pan, heat the oil over moderate heat. Reduce the heat to low and add the tuna fish and 1½ tablespoons of the parsley.

Cook, stirring constantly, for 5 minutes, then add the stock and black pepper. Continue cooking for a further 5 minutes, stirring frequently.

Place the tagliatelle in a large serving bowl, add the butter and toss until it is thoroughly coated. Pour over the sauce and sprinkle with the remaining parsley.

BOLOGNESE SAUCE

A tasty combination of minced meat and vegetables, this famous Italian Bolognese Sauce is served over pasta, usually spaghetti.

4 servings

Metric/Imperial

25g (1oz) butter
1 tablespoon vegetable oil
100g (4oz) streaky bacon, rind removed, finely chopped
1 medium-sized onion, finely chopped
1 carrot, scraped and finely chopped
1 celery stalk, finely chopped
250g (8oz) minced beef
100g (4oz) chicken livers, finely chopped
396g (14oz) can tomatoes, drained
2 tablespoons tomato purée
425ml (15 fl oz) chicken stock
1 teaspoon dried basil
1 bay leaf
½ teaspoon salt
4 grindings black pepper

American

2 tablespoons butter
1 tablespoon vegetable oil
¼lb bacon, finely chopped
1 medium-sized onion, finely chopped
1 carrot, scraped and finely chopped
1 celery stalk, finely chopped
½lb ground beef
¼lb chicken livers, finely chopped
1 x 14oz can tomatoes, drained
2 tablespoons tomato paste
2 cups chicken stock
1 teaspoon dried basil
1 bay leaf
½ teaspoon salt
4 grindings black pepper

Heat the butter and oil in a medium-sized saucepan over moderate heat. When the foam subsides add the bacon, onion, carrot and celery. Stirring occasionally, cook for 8 to 10 minutes or until the vegetables begin to brown.

Add the minced beef and, stirring, cook for about 10 minutes or until the meat is well browned.

Continue stirring and add all the remaining ingredients. Reduce the heat, cover the pan and simmer for 1 hour.

Pour the sauce over pasta and serve.

MACARONI CHEESE

This popular dish turns up regularly in most households.

4 servings

Metric/Imperial

250g (8oz) macaroni
2 tablespoons butter
4 tablespoons flour
425ml (15 fl oz) milk
½ teaspoon mustard
salt and pepper
175g (6oz) Cheddar cheese, grated

American

2 cups macaroni
2 tablespoons butter
4 tablespoons flour
2 cups milk
½ teaspoon mustard
salt and pepper
1½ cups Cheddar cheese, grated

Boil the macaroni in plenty of salted water for about 7 minutes or according to the instructions on the packet.

Meanwhile make a White Sauce with the butter, flour and milk. Add the mustard, salt and pepper to taste.

Add most of the cheese. Return the pan to the heat and cook, stirring, until the cheese is melted; then add the cooked macaroni, stir well and pour it into a buttered heatproof dish. Sprinkle with the remaining cheese and grill [broil] until golden brown, or brown in a hot oven.

HAM AND MACARONI CASSEROLE

This easy-to-make and economical dish is ideal for a light lunch or supper.

3 servings

Metric/Imperial

75g (3oz) plus 1 teaspoon butter
1 medium-sized onion, chopped
2 celery stalks, trimmed and chopped
175g (6oz) macaroni, cooked and drained
2 eggs, lightly beaten
3 tablespoons sour cream
100g (4oz) ham, diced
½ teaspoon black pepper
½ teaspoon dried mixed herbs
50g (2oz) Cheddar cheese, grated
25g (1oz) fresh white breadcrumbs

American

6 tablespoons butter
1 medium-sized onion, chopped
2 celery stalks, trimmed and chopped
1½ cups macaroni, cooked and drained
2 eggs, lightly beaten
3 tablespoons sour cream
½ cup ham, diced
½ teaspoon black pepper

½ teaspoon dried mixed herbs (basil, oregano, marjoram, thyme)
½ cup Cheddar or American cheese, grated
½ cup fresh white breadcrumbs

Preheat the oven to moderate (180°C/350°F or Gas Mark 4). Lightly grease an ovenproof casserole.

In a medium-sized frying-pan, melt two-thirds of the butter over moderate heat. When the foam subsides add the onion and celery and cook, stirring occasionally, for 5 to 7 minutes or until the onion is soft and translucent but not brown.

Add the macaroni and the remaining butter to the pan and keep warm.

Beat the eggs and sour cream together; stir in the ham, pepper and mixed herbs. Transfer the frying-pan mixture to the egg mixture and stir until thoroughly combined.

Spoon into the prepared casserole and sprinkle over the cheese and breadcrumbs. Bake for 30 to 40 minutes.

PASTA NEAPOLITAN-STYLE

Pasta Neapolitan-style is a warming, filling dish. Serve with a green salad.

4 servings

Metric/Imperial

2 tablespoons vegetable oil
1 large onion, thinly sliced
1 garlic clove, crushed
675g (1½lb) can tomatoes
2 tablespoons tomato purée
½ teaspoon salt
½ teaspoon black pepper
1 teaspoon dried basil
½ teaspoon dried oregano
1 bay leaf
350g (12oz) pasta shapes, spaghetti or macaroni
50g (2oz) butter
50g (2oz) Parmesan cheese, grated

American

2 tablespoons vegetable oil
1 large onion, thinly sliced
1 garlic clove, crushed
2½ cups canned tomatoes
2 tablespoons tomato paste

½ teaspoon salt
½ teaspoon black pepper
1 teaspoon dried basil
½ teaspoon dried oregano
1 bay leaf
¾lb spaghetti, or 3 cups macaroni, noodles or seashells
¼ cup butter
½ cup Parmesan cheese, grated

In a large saucepan, heat the oil over moderate heat. Add the onion and garlic and cook, stirring occasionally, for 5 to 7 minutes, or until soft and translucent but not brown.

Stir in the tomatoes, tomato purée, the salt, pepper, basil, oregano and bay leaf, mashing the tomatoes with a wooden spoon until pulpy.

Reduce the heat, cover and simmer for 40 to 45 minutes or until the sauce is rich and thick. If it becomes too dry add a little cold water.

Cook the pasta in plenty of boiling salted water for 8 to 10 minutes or until just tender. Serve with the sauce poured over, sprinkled with the grated cheese.

MEXICAN CHILLI SPAGHETTI

A popular pasta dish in Mexico, Mexican Chilli Spaghetti makes an excitingly different meal.

4 servings

Metric/Imperial

3 tablespoons vegetable oil
2 medium-sized onions, thinly sliced
1 garlic clove, crushed
350g (12oz) spaghetti, broken into short lengths
396g (14oz) can tomatoes
½ teaspoon salt
¼ teaspoon black pepper
1 teaspoon dried oregano
¼ teaspoon ground cumin
1 green chilli, finely chopped
600ml (1 pint) chicken stock

American

3 tablespoons vegetable oil
2 medium-sized onions, thinly sliced
1 garlic clove, crushed
¾lb spaghetti, broken into short lengths

1 x 14oz can tomatoes
½ teaspoon salt
¼ teaspoon black pepper
1 teaspoon dried oregano
¼ teaspoon ground cumin
1 green chili pepper, finely chopped
2½ cups chicken stock

In a large, deep frying-pan, heat the oil over moderate heat. Add the onions and garlic and cook, stirring occasionally, for 5 to 7 minutes or until soft and translucent but not brown.

Stir in the spaghetti, tomatoes, salt, pepper, oregano, cumin and chilli and cook, stirring occasionally, for a further 5 minutes.

Pour in the chicken stock and bring the mixture to the boil. Reduce the heat and simmer gently, stirring occasionally, for 10 to 15 minutes or until the liquid has been absorbed and the spaghetti is just tender.

KIDNEY BEAN AND HERB CASSEROLE

Kidney Bean and Herb Casserole is an easy-to-do and filling dish which provides a good family supper.

4 servings

Metric/Imperial

250g (8oz) streaky bacon, diced
1 large onion, finely chopped
2 garlic cloves, crushed
1 large red or green pepper, white pith removed, seeded and thinly sliced
4 celery stalks, trimmed and cut into short lengths
250g (8oz) tomatoes, peeled and chopped
1 bay leaf
2 bouquet garni
1 teaspoon salt
½ teaspoon black pepper
350g (12oz) dried red kidney beans, soaked, cooked and drained
2 tablespoons chopped fresh parsley
2 tablespoons chopped fresh chives
50g (2oz) Parmesan cheese, grated

American

½lb bacon, diced
1 large onion, finely chopped

2 garlic cloves, crushed

1 large red or green pepper, membrane
and seeds removed, thinly sliced

4 celery stalks, trimmed and sliced
into short lengths

1 cup tomatoes, peeled and chopped

1 bay leaf

2 bouquet garni

1 teaspoon salt

$\frac{1}{2}$ teaspoon black pepper

$1\frac{1}{2}$ cups dry red kidney beans, soaked,
cooked and drained

2 tablespoons chopped fresh parsley

2 tablespoons chopped fresh chives

$\frac{1}{2}$ cup Parmesan cheese, grated

In a large, flameproof casserole, cook
the bacon over moderate heat for 5 to
7 minutes or until crisp and browned.
Add the onion, garlic, red or green
pepper and celery and cook, stirring
occasionally, for 8 to 10 minutes or
until the onion is golden brown.

Add the tomatoes, bay leaf, bouquet
garni, salt and pepper and stir well to
mix. Reduce the heat, cover and simmer
for 30 minutes.

Stir in the beans, parsley and chives.
Re-cover and simmer for a further 15
minutes or until the beans are heated
through. Sprinkle with the cheese.

PEASE PUDDING

Once a popular dish in England, Pease
Pudding seems recently to have fallen
into some disfavour. A pity, because it
makes a hearty, healthy accompaniment
to the cheaper meat dishes, such as
boiled beef, that it was intended to
stretch out. Traditionally Pease Pudding was cooked in a cheesecloth bag
in the same pot as the meat.

**Kidney Bean and Herb Casserole is
a colourful and tasty dish.**

136

6-8 servings

Metric/Imperial

500g (1lb) green split peas, soaked for
   3 hours and drained
1 medium-sized onion, finely chopped
1 teaspoon salt
25g (1oz) butter
½ teaspoon Worcestershire sauce
1 teaspoon black pepper

American

2 cups split peas, soaked for 3 hours
   and drained
1 medium-sized onion, finely chopped
1 teaspoon salt
2 tablespoons butter
½ teaspoon Worcestershire sauce
1 teaspoon black pepper

Place the peas and onion in a medium-sized saucepan. Pour over enough water just to cover and add ½ teaspoon of the salt. Bring to the boil, reduce the heat, cover and simmer, stirring occasionally, for 2 hours or until the peas are very soft.

Drain off the cooking liquid and rub the pea mixture through a strainer into a mixing bowl. Alternatively, purée in a food mill or electric blender.

Stir in the butter, Worcestershire sauce, ¼ teaspoon salt and the pepper and beat well to blend.

BARLEY AND MUSHROOM CASSEROLE

Cooked in this way, barley makes a delicious alternative to potatoes. It may be served with lamb, beef or poultry. Chopped fresh parsley or thyme may be added. For the best results, use fine or medium-sized pearl barley.

4 servings

Metric/Imperial

50g (2oz) butter
2 medium-sized onions, chopped
250g (8oz) mushrooms, wiped and
   sliced
250g (8oz) pearl barley
¾ teaspoon salt
¾ teaspoon black pepper
300ml (10 fl oz) chicken stock

American

¼ cup butter
2 medium-sized onions, diced
½lb mushrooms, wiped and sliced
1 cup pearl barley
¾ teaspoon salt
¾ teaspoon black pepper
1¼ cups chicken stock

Preheat the oven to warm (170°C 325°F or Gas Mark 3).

Melt the butter in a frying-pan over low heat. Add the onions and cook, stirring occasionally, for about 5 minutes or until golden. Add the mushrooms and cook for 3 minutes.

Transfer the onions and mushrooms to an ovenproof casserole. Add the barley, salt and pepper. Pour in the stock and stir to mix.

Cover the casserole and cook for 40 minutes or until the barley is tender and all the liquid is absorbed.

HOPPIN' JOHN

A traditional West Indian recipe now firmly incorporated into the American Southern 'soul' food repertoire, Hoppin' John is a spicy mixture of black-eye beans, rice, tomatoes and onion. It is particularly tasty when served with the other staples of 'soul', such as ham hocks, smothered pork chops and collard greens.

6 servings

Metric/Imperial

250g (8oz) dried black-eye beans,
   soaked overnight and drained
1 litre (2 pints) water
1½ teaspoons salt
250g (8oz) long-grain rice
1 tablespoon vegetable oil
1 medium-sized onion, finely chopped
396g (14oz) can tomatoes
¼ teaspoon cayenne pepper
½ teaspoon black pepper

American

1⅓ cups dried black-eyed peas, soaked
   overnight and drained
5 cups water
1½ teaspoons salt

1⅓ cup long-grain rice
1 tablespoon vegetable oil
1 medium-sized onion, finely chopped
1 x 14oz can tomatoes
¼ teaspoon cayenne pepper
½ teaspoon black pepper

Place the beans in a large saucepan and pour in the water and 1 teaspoon of salt. Bring to the boil, reduce the heat, partially cover the pan and simmer for 1⅔ hours.

Stir in the rice, cover the pan and simmer for 15 minutes.

Meanwhile, in a small frying-pan, heat the oil over moderate heat. Add the onion and cook, stirring occasionally, for 5 to 7 minutes, or until soft and translucent but not brown. Stir in the tomatoes, cayenne, pepper and remaining salt.

Pour the onion and tomato mixture into the beans and rice and stir to blend. Re-cover the pan and simmer for a further 15 to 20 minutes or until the rice and beans are tender.

RED BEAN CASSEROLE

A hearty and economical dish, Red Bean Casserole may be served as the main course for a vegetarian meal, accompanied by a green salad.

4-6 servings

Metric/Imperial

2 tablespoons vegetable oil
2 large onions, finely chopped
2 garlic cloves, crushed
3 large potatoes, peeled and cubed
4 medium-sized carrots, scraped and
   cut into short lengths
1 medium-sized turnip, peeled and
   cubed
500g (1lb) dried red kidney beans,
   soaked overnight and drained
2 tablespoons golden syrup
300ml (10 fl oz) water
1 teaspoon salt
½ teaspoon black pepper

American

2 tablespoons vegetable oil
2 large onions, finely chopped
2 garlic cloves, crushed

3 large potatoes, peeled and cubed

4 medium-sized carrots, scraped and cut into short lengths

1 medium-sized turnip, peeled and cubed

2 cups dry red kidney beans, soaked overnight and drained

2 tablespoons light corn syrup

1¼ cups water

1 teaspoon salt

½ teaspoon black pepper

Preheat the oven to moderate (180°C/350°F or Gas Mark 4).

In a large flameproof casserole, heat the oil over moderate heat. Add the onions and garlic and fry, stirring occasionally, for 5 to 7 minutes or until soft and translucent but not brown. Stir in the potatoes, carrots, turnip and kidney beans and cook for a further 5 minutes or until the vegetables are golden.

Pour over the syrup and water and add the salt and pepper, stirring well to mix.

Cover the casserole and cook in the centre of the oven for 45 minutes or until the beans are tender.

ITALIAN-STYLE BAKED BEANS

A tasty dish from the Piedmont region of Italy, this is an economical casserole of haricot beans, bacon, garlic and basil. It may be served as a filling lunch dish.

6 servings

Metric/Imperial

500g (1lb) dried white or red haricot beans, soaked overnight and drained

3 garlic cloves, crushed

1½ tablespoons dried basil

½ teaspoon salt

½ teaspoon black pepper

½ teaspoon ground cinnamon

8 streaky bacon slices, coarsely chopped

American

2 cups dry Garbanzos or flageolets, soaked overnight and drained

3 garlic cloves, crushed

1½ tablespoons dried basil

½ teaspoon salt

½ teaspoon black pepper

½ teaspoon ground cinnamon

8 slices bacon, coarsely chopped

Preheat the oven to very cool (140°C/275°F or Gas Mark 1).

Place all the ingredients in a large ovenproof casserole. Stir well and add just enough water to cover.

Cover the casserole and bake for 3 to 3½ hours or until the beans are very tender but still firm.

DARIUS CASSEROLE

A modest but delicious dish, this lamb and bean casserole is perfect for a family supper. Serve with boiled potatoes and a green vegetable for a really special meal.

4 servings

Metric/Imperial

¾ litre (1½ pints) water

250g (8oz) dried beans, soaked overnight and drained

100g (4oz) dried peas, soaked overnight and drained

1kg (2lb) stewing lamb, cubed

2 onions, quartered, plus 1 small onion, finely chopped

2 teaspoons salt

½ teaspoon black pepper

425ml (15 fl oz) chicken stock

396g (14oz) can tomatoes

1½ tablespoons lemon juice

½ teaspoon turmeric

American

3¾ cups water

1 cup lima beans, soaked overnight and drained

½ cup dried peas, soaked overnight and drained

2lb lean boned shoulder of lamb, cubed

2 onions, quartered, plus 1 small onion, finely chopped

2 teaspoons salt

½ teaspoon black pepper

2 cups chicken stock

1 x 14oz can tomatoes

1½ tablespoons lemon juice

½ teaspoon turmeric

In a large saucepan, bring the water to the boil over high heat. Add the beans and peas and boil for 2 minutes.

Remove the pan from the heat and allow the beans and peas to soak for 1 hour. Drain the beans in a colander and set them aside.

Place the lamb in a large flameproof casserole. Scatter the onion quarters on top and cover with the peas and beans. Add the salt and pepper and pour in the chicken stock.

Bring the mixture to the boil and skim any scum off the surface. Reduce the heat, cover and simmer for 1 hour. Stir in the tomatoes, lemon juice, turmeric and chopped onion. Re-cover and simmer for a further 1½ hours or until the peas and beans are tender.

VEGETARIAN LENTIL LOAF

Lentils are packed with protein and consequently this delicious loaf is very nutritious. Serve it with a piquant sauce, baked potatoes and salad.

4-6 servings

Metric/Imperial

25g (1oz) butter

350g (12oz) lentils, cooked until the skins split and drained

250g (8oz) Cheddar cheese, grated

2 medium-sized onions, very finely chopped

50g (2oz) mushrooms, wiped clean and thinly sliced

½ teaspoon salt

½ teaspoon black pepper

½ teaspoon ground cloves

1 tablespoon finely chopped fresh parsley

75g (3oz) dry brown breadcrumbs

1 egg, lightly beaten

3 tablespoons creamy milk

6 parsley sprigs

American

2 tablespoons butter

¾lb lentils, cooked until the skins split and drained

Serve Barley and Mushroom Casserole with lamb, beef or poultry.

2 cups Cheddar cheese, grated
2 medium-sized onions, very finely
    chopped
$\frac{1}{2}$ cup mushrooms, wiped clean and
    thinly sliced
$\frac{1}{2}$ teaspoon salt
$\frac{1}{2}$ teaspoon black pepper
$\frac{1}{2}$ teaspoon ground cloves
1 tablespoon finely chopped fresh
    parsley
1 cup dry wholewheat breadcrumbs
1 egg, lightly beaten
3 tablespoons creamy milk
6 parsley sprigs

Preheat the oven to moderate (180°C/
350°F or Gas Mark 4). Generously
grease a 500g (1lb) loaf tin with half the
butter.

In a large mixing bowl, combine the
lentils, cheese, onions and mushrooms,
mixing until well blended. Stir in the
salt, pepper, cloves and chopped parsley.
Add the breadcrumbs, egg and milk

and beat until all the ingredients are
well blended.

Spoon the mixture into the loaf tin.
Dot with the remaining butter and bake
for 45 to 50 minutes or until a skewer
inserted into the centre of the loaf
comes out clean. Decorate with the
parsley sprigs.

BAKED BEANS WITH PORK

There are many variations to this very
American dish. In colonial New
England, this nourishing combination
of beans, salt pork and molasses was
often baked with the week's bread and
then eaten with slices of brown bread
still hot from the oven. Canned baked
beans are but a pale reflection of the real
thing, and this is predictably a favourite
with children. It is a very rich and filling
dish, so serve with a simple green
vegetable or crusty bread.

4-6 servings

Metric/Imperial

500g (1lb) haricot beans
2 tablespoons black treacle
2 teaspoons Worcestershire sauce
2 teaspoons dry mustard
$\frac{1}{2}$ tablespoon brown sugar
$\frac{1}{2}$ teaspoon black pepper
350g (12oz) streaky pork, diced
1 large onion, chopped
2 sticks celery, chopped
1 teaspoon salt

American

1lb haricot beans
2 tablespoons molasses
2 teaspoons Worcestershire sauce
2 teaspoons dry mustard

Darius Casserole is an economical
dish of lamb, beans, peas, tomatoes
and onions.

½ tablespoon brown sugar
½ teaspoon black pepper
¾lb salt pork, diced
1 large onion, chopped
2 sticks celery, chopped
1 teaspoon salt

Wash the haricot beans and soak them in plenty of cold water overnight. Retain the water they were soaked in.

Preheat the oven to warm (180°C/350°F or Gas Mark 4). In a medium-sized saucepan heat the bean water, which should measure about 600ml (1 pint) [2½ cups]. Stir in the treacle [molasses], Worcestershire sauce, mustard, sugar and pepper.

Mix the beans, pork and vegetables in a deep casserole and pour over the liquid. Add more hot water if necessary

A hearty dish from Belgium, Rice with Chicken and Vegetables.

to come just to the top of the mixture, since the beans will absorb further liquid during cooking.

Cover and place in the preheated oven to cook for three hours. Check the beans occasionally during cooking to make sure they do not dry out. Taste, and add salt and any further seasoning as required.

RISOTTO ALLA BOLOGNESE

A light Italian dish, Risotto alla Bolognese (ree-saw-toh al-lah boh-loh nyay-zeh) is a mixture of Italian or long-grain rice, ham, meat sauce and grated cheese. Serve as a light lunch or supper, with Garlic Bread and a mixed salad.

4-6 servings

Metric/Imperial

100g (4oz) butter

1 medium-sized onion, thinly sliced
100g (4oz) ham, chopped
500g (1lb) Italian or long-grain rice
1 litre (2 pints) beef stock, boiling
225ml (8 fl oz) Bolognese Sauce
25g (1oz) Parmesan cheese, grated

American

½ cup butter
1 medium-sized onion, thinly sliced
¼lb mild-cured ham, chopped
2⅔ cups Italian or long-grain rice
5 cups beef stock, boiling
1 cup Bolognese Sauce
¼ cup Parmesan cheese, grated

In a large, heavy saucepan, melt three-quarters of the butter over moderate heat. When the foam subsides, add the onion and cook, stirring occasionally, for 5 to 7 minutes or until soft and translucent but not brown.

Add the ham and rice, reduce the heat to low and cook, stirring frequently

for 5 minutes. Pour over approximately one-third of the boiling stock. Regulate the heat so that the rice is bubbling all the time. Stir occasionally with a fork. When the rice swells and the liquid is absorbed add another one-third of the stock. Continue cooking the rice in this way until tender and moist but still firm.

Stir in the remaining butter, the Bolognese sauce and the grated cheese and mix well to blend. Simmer for 1 minute, stirring frequently.

RISOTTO ALLA MILANESE

Risotto alla Milanese can be served as a delicious accompaniment to grilled [broiled] fish.

4 servings

Metric/Imperial

1 small onion, peeled and finely chopped
4 tablespoons butter
250g (8oz) long-grain rice
600ml (1 pint) chicken stock
salt and pepper
good pinch of powdered saffron (optional)
2 teaspoons water
4 tablespoons Parmesan cheese, grated

American

1 small onion, peeled and finely chopped
4 tablespoons butter
1¼ cups long-grain rice
2½ cups chicken stock
salt and pepper
good pinch of powdered saffron (optional)
2 teaspoons water
4 tablespoons Parmesan cheese, grated

Melt half the butter in a saucepan and sauté the onion until tender but not browned. Add the rice and cook, stirring until the butter has been absorbed and the rice is translucent.

Add the stock, season, cover and simmer very gently for about 20 minutes without stirring or removing the lid, until all the liquid has been absorbed and the rice is tender.

If liked blend the saffron with the

water and stir in to give a golden colour, mixing thoroughly with a fork. Stir in the remaining butter and the Parmesan cheese.

RICE WITH CHICKEN AND VEGETABLES

A hearty, nourishing rice dish from Belgium, this risotto makes a complete meal in itself.

4-6 servings

Metric/Imperial

6 streaky bacon slices, diced
50g (2oz) butter
2 chicken breasts, skinned and cut into strips
2 medium-sized onions, thinly sliced and pushed out into rings
2 large green peppers, white pith removed, seeded and coarsely chopped
250g (8oz) small button mushrooms, wiped clean and halved
300g (10oz) long-grain rice
5 medium-sized tomatoes, peeled and coarsely chopped
300g (10oz) canned sweetcorn, drained
½ teaspoon dried thyme
1 teaspoon salt
½ teaspoon black pepper
¼ teaspoon celery salt
¼ teaspoon cayenne pepper
2 teaspoons Worcestershire sauce (optional)
375ml (13 fl oz) chicken stock
50g (2oz) Parmesan cheese, grated

American

6 bacon slices, diced
¼ cup butter
2 chicken breasts, skinned and cut into strips
2 medium-sized onions, thinly sliced and separated into rings
2 large green peppers, membranes and seeds removed, coarsely chopped
½lb small mushrooms, wiped clean and halved
1⅔ cups long-grain rice
5 medium-sized tomatoes, peeled and coarsely chopped
1¼ cups corn, drained

½ teaspoon dried thyme
1 teaspoon salt
½ teaspoon black pepper
¼ teaspoon celery salt
¼ teaspoon cayenne pepper
2 teaspoons Worcestershire sauce (optional)
1⅝ cups chicken stock
½ cup Parmesan cheese, grated

In a medium-sized flameproof casserole, fry the bacon over moderate heat for 5 minutes or until it is crisp and golden and has rendered most of its fat. Remove and drain.

Add half the butter. When the foam subsides, add the chicken strips and fry, stirring frequently, for 6 to 8 minutes or until lightly browned. Add to the bacon.

Add the onions and peppers and fry, stirring frequently, for a further 3 minutes. Remove the vegetables and add to the bacon and chicken.

Add the remaining butter and, when the foam subsides, the rice. Fry, stirring constantly, for 3 minutes. Stir in the chicken, bacon and vegetable mixture, the tomatoes, sweetcorn, thyme, salt, pepper, celery salt, cayenne and the Worcestershire sauce. Stir well to mix and pour over the stock.

Bring to the boil, stirring constantly. Reduce the heat, cover and simmer for 20 to 25 minutes or until the rice is cooked and tender and has absorbed all the liquid.

LAMB AND RICE

This is a tasty supper dish that is easy to prepare. Serve with a green salad.

4 servings

Metric/Imperial

50g (2oz) butter
1kg (2lb) shoulder or leg of lamb, trimmed and cubed
250g (8oz) long-grain rice
6 tomatoes, peeled and coarsely chopped
1 teaspoon salt
½ teaspoon black pepper
1 teaspoon dried thyme
75g (3oz) sultanas or seedless raisins
300ml (10 fl oz) chicken stock

American

¼ cup butter
2lb shoulder or leg of lamb, trimmed
   and cubed
1⅓ cups long-grain rice
6 tomatoes, peeled and coarsely
   chopped
1 teaspoon salt
½ teaspoon black pepper
1 teaspoon dried thyme
½ cup golden or seedless raisins
1¼ cups chicken stock

In a medium-sized flameproof casserole, melt the butter over moderate heat. When the foam subsides, add the meat cubes and fry, stirring and turning frequently, for 5 to 8 minutes, or until browned. Reduce the heat, cover the pan and cook for 45 minutes.

Increase the heat slightly and stir in the rice. Fry, stirring constantly, for 3 minutes. Add the tomatoes, salt, pepper, thyme and sultanas or raisins. Fry, stirring constantly for 3 minutes. Pour in the stock and bring to the boil. Reduce the heat, cover and simmer for 30 minutes or until the meat is tender and the rice has absorbed all the liquid.

CHICKEN LIVER RISOTTO

Tasty and inexpensive, Chicken Liver

Risotto is very simple to prepare and ideal to serve as a main dish for lunch or supper with a green salad.

4 servings

Metric/Imperial

50g (2oz) butter
1 medium-sized onion, finely chopped
100g (4oz) mushrooms, wiped clean
   and sliced
300g (10oz) long-grain rice
600ml (1 pint) boiling chicken stock
8 chicken livers, cut into small pieces
2 tablespoons chopped fresh parsley
50g (2oz) Parmesan cheese, grated

American

¼ cup butter
1 medium-sized onion, finely chopped
¼lb mushrooms, wiped clean and
   sliced
1⅔ cups long-grain rice
2½ cups boiling chicken stock
8 chicken livers, diced
2 tablespoons chopped fresh parsley
½ cup Parmesan cheese, grated

In a large, heavy saucepan, melt three-quarters of the butter over moderate heat. Add the onion and cook, stirring occasionally, for 8 minutes or until soft and translucent but not brown. Add the mushrooms and cook for a further 3 minutes.

Add the rice and cook, stirring constantly, for 2 minutes. Pour on the stock and bring back to the boil. Cover, reduce the heat to very low and simmer gently for 20 minutes or until the liquid is absorbed and the rice is tender.

Meanwhile prepare the chicken livers. Melt the remaining butter in a medium-sized frying-pan, add the livers and cook gently for 10 minutes, stirring occasionally.

When the rice is cooked stir in the chicken livers and parsley. Put the mixture into a warmed serving dish and sprinkle on the Parmesan cheese.

PORK FRIED RICE

This is a wonderful way to use up left-over pork. Serve Pork Fried Rice on its own as a light luncheon dish, or for supper accompanied by a salad. Chicken or beef may be substituted for the pork if you prefer.

4 servings

Metric/Imperial

3 tablespoons vegetable oil
1 small onion, finely chopped
2 celery stalks, trimmed and finely
   chopped
2 small carrots, scraped and finely
   chopped
250g (8oz) cooked roast pork, cut into
   strips 2.5cm (1in) long
½ small cabbage, coarse outer leaves
   removed, washed and finely
   shredded
½ teaspoon black pepper
2 tablespoons soy sauce
250g (8oz) cooked long-grain rice
2 eggs, lightly beaten
¼ teaspoon salt

American

3 tablespoons vegetable oil
1 small onion, finely chopped
2 celery stalks, trimmed and finely
   chopped

Chicken Liver Risotto with Mushrooms is a tasty and inexpensive dish. Serve with Parmesan cheese and salad for a light meal.

Give generous servings of Pork Fried Rice as it disappears like magic!

2 small carrots, scraped and finely chopped

1 cup cooked roast pork, cut into strips 1in long

½ small cabbage, coarse outer leaves removed, washed and finely shredded

½ teaspoon black pepper

2 tablespoons soy sauce

3 cups cooked long-grain rice

2 eggs lightly beaten

¼ teaspoon salt

In a large frying-pan, heat 2 tablespoons of the oil over moderate heat. Add the onion, celery and carrots and cook, stirring constantly, for 5 minutes. Stir in the pork, cabbage, pepper, soy sauce and rice and cook, stirring constantly, for a further 2 to 3 minutes or until the mixture is hot. Moisten with a little

water or chicken stock if the mixture is dry. Set aside and keep hot.

In a small frying-pan, heat the remaining oil over moderate heat. When the oil is hot, add the beaten eggs and salt and cook for 2 minutes. When the bottom is set and lightly browned turn the omelette over, using a fish slice. Cook for a further 2 to 3 minutes or until the omelette is completely set. Remove the pan from the heat and, using the fish slice, remove the omelette from the pan. Cut the omelette into narrow strips.

Spoon the rice mixture on to a warmed serving dish. Garnish with the omelette strips and serve at once.

BEEF AND POTATO CURRY

A simple, easy-to-make curry, best served with plain boiled rice, a cucumber and yogurt salad and sweet tomato or mango chutney.

4 servings

Metric/Imperial

50g (2oz) melted butter

2 onions, finely chopped

1 garlic clove, finely chopped

1 tablespoon curry powder (or to taste)

675g (1½lb) lean stewing steak, cut into cubes

425ml (15 fl oz) water

1 teaspoon salt

2 bay leaves

1lb small potatoes, scrubbed

American

¼ cup melted butter

2 onions, finely chopped

1 garlic clove, finely chopped

1 tablespoon curry powder (or to taste)

1½lb lean stewing steak, cut into cubes

1⅞ cups water

1 teaspoon salt

2 bay leaves

1lb small potatoes, scrubbed

In a large saucepan, melt the butter and fry the onions and garlic for 6 to 8 minutes or until lightly browned. Add the curry powder and continue to fry, stirring frequently, for 6 minutes. If the mixture gets too dry, sprinkle with 1 to 2 tablespoons of water.

Add the meat cubes and, turning and tossing, fry for 6 minutes or until the meat is well browned on all sides. Add the water, salt and bay leaves. Increase the heat to high. When the mixture begins to bubble, cover the pan, reduce the heat to low and simmer for 1¼ hours.

Add the potatoes and bring the curry to the boil again. Cover and simmer for a further 45 minutes, or until the meat and potatoes are tender. Taste the curry and add more salt if necessary. Transfer to a warmed serving dish.

FRANKFURTER CURRY

This curry is unusual in that it only takes about 30 minutes to prepare and cook. Serve with plain boiled rice.

4 servings

Metric/Imperial

300ml (½ pint) boiling water

Serve Beef and Potato Curry with rice and chutneys.

3 tablespoons desiccated coconut
1kg (2lb) tomatoes, fresh or canned
2 medium-sized onions, chopped
2 cloves of garlic, crushed
75g (3oz) butter
2 tablespoons curry powder
1 tablespoon flour
½ teaspoon ground ginger
salt and pepper
2 tablespoons mango chutney
4 frankfurter sausages, sliced

American

1¼ cups boiling water
3 tablespoons shredded coconut
2lb tomatoes, fresh or canned
2 medium-sized onions, chopped
2 cloves of garlic, crushed
6 tablespoons butter
2 tablespoons curry powder
1 tablespoon flour
½ teaspoon ground ginger
salt and pepper
2 tablespoons mango chutney
4 frankfurters, sliced

Pour the boiling water on to the coconut and leave to infuse. Skin the tomatoes, if necessary, and quarter.

Melt the butter in a saucepan and sauté the onion and garlic until softened but not browned. Add the curry powder, flour and ginger and cook, stirring, for a few minutes.

Strain the coconut, keeping the

liquid and discarding the coconut.

Add the coconut liquid with the tomatoes to the saucepan. Season with salt and pepper to taste, and simmer uncovered for 15 minutes. Add the chutney and the sliced sausages. Reheat and check the seasoning.

SAG GOSHT

As Indian spices become more generally available, more people are making really authentic Indian dishes at home. This lamb and spinach curry is for the more adventurous. Serve with rice or Chapatti.

4 servings

Metric/Imperial

50g (2oz) butter
1½ teaspoons mustard seeds
2 garlic cloves, crushed
seeds of 3 whole cardamom pods, crushed
1 tablespoon ground coriander
1 piece fresh root ginger, peeled and finely chopped
1kg (2lb) lean boned lamb, cut into cubes
1 medium-sized onion, finely chopped
3 green chillis, finely chopped
1 teaspoon sugar
1 teaspoon turmeric
1kg (2lb) spinach, trimmed, washed and chopped
1½ teaspoons salt
½ teaspoon black pepper
3 tablespoons yogurt

American

¼ cup butter
1½ teaspoons mustard seeds
2 garlic cloves, crushed
seeds of 3 whole cardamom pods, crushed
1 tablespoon ground coriander
1 piece fresh root ginger, peeled and finely chopped
2lb lean boned lamb, cut into cubes
1 medium-sized onion, finely chopped
3 green chilis, finely chopped
1 teaspoon sugar
1 teaspoon turmeric
2lb spinach, trimmed, washed and chopped

Colourful Curried Eggs is an ideal dish for an impromptu meal.

1½ teaspoons salt
½ teaspoon black pepper
3 tablespoons yogurt

In a large flameproof casserole, melt the butter over moderate heat. Add the mustard seeds and, when they begin to pop, stir in the garlic, cardamom, coriander and ginger. Fry, stirring constantly, for 1 minute. Add the lamb cubes and, turning them over frequently, fry for 10 minutes or until they are brown all over.

Add the onion, green chillis and sugar and cook, stirring constantly, for 8 to 10 minutes or until the onion is golden brown. Stir in the turmeric and spinach and cook, stirring frequently, for 3 minutes. Stir in the salt, pepper and yogurt. Cover the pan, reduce the heat to low and cook for 1 hour or until the meat is very tender and the spinach smooth and soft. Uncover the pan and stir well to mix.

Meanwhile, preheat the oven to cool (150°C/300°F or Gas Mark 2). Remove the casserole from the heat and place it in the oven for 20 minutes before serving.

CURRIED EGGS

Curried Eggs are ideal for an impromptu supper since they are quick and easy to prepare and very economical. They should be served with plain boiled rice and a selection of chutneys.

2-4 servings

Metric/Imperial

50g (2oz) raisins
50g (2oz) butter
2 medium-sized onions, finely chopped
1 garlic clove, crushed
1 small tart apple, cored and diced
2 tablespoons flour
2 teaspoons curry powder
250ml (8 fl oz) milk
50ml (2 fl oz) double cream
½ teaspoon salt
¼ teaspoon black pepper
4 hard-boiled eggs, halved
3 tablespoons slivered almonds, toasted

American

⅓ cup raisins
¼ cup butter
2 medium-sized onions, finely chopped
1 garlic clove, crushed
1 small tart apple, cored and diced
2 tablespoons flour

2 teaspoons curry powder
1 cup milk
¼ cup heavy cream
½ teaspoon salt
¼ teaspoon black pepper
4 hard-boiled eggs, halved
3 tablespoons slivered almonds, toasted

Place the raisins in a small mixing bowl and cover them with boiling water. Allow them to soak for 10 minutes, then drain them.

Meanwhile, in a medium-sized saucepan, melt the butter over moderate heat. Add the onions, garlic and apple to the pan. Cook, stirring occasionally, for 8 minutes, or until the onions and apple are soft but not brown.

Stir the flour and curry powder into the pan. Cook, stirring for 3 minutes. Remove the pan from the heat and stir in the milk. Return the pan to the heat. Cook, stirring, for 3 to 4 minutes, or until the sauce has thickened. Stir in the cream, salt and pepper.

With a metal spoon, carefully fold the egg halves into the sauce. Gently simmer the sauce for 4 to 5 minutes, or until the eggs are thoroughly heated.

Remove the pan from the heat. Serve the curry on a bed of rice with the raisins and almonds sprinkled on top.

Vegetable dishes

Although true vegetarians are still in a very small minority in our society, vegetarian cooking is enjoying more popularity today than ever before, and one does not have to look for the reasons. As meat becomes more expensive, people naturally turn to the available alternatives, and these include not only cheese, eggs and dairy products but fresh vegetables, which include protein-rich peas and beans. Dieticians recommend plenty of fresh fruit and vegetables not only for their high vitamin content but also because they help to provide that valuable roughage in the diet which keeps the digestive system working smoothly.

The first recipes in this section are meals in their own right, and the remainder are light meals or vegetable accompaniments. The cook who is preparing a great deal of vegetarian food, particularly for growing children, should be something of a nutritionist too, since it is most important that a main meal should contain protein in some form. This is often provided in these recipes by cheese or eggs; other sources of protein are pulses (dried peas, beans, lentils, soya, etc) and nuts. A balanced non-meat meal will contain one or more of these other protein-rich ingredients, and if it does not, then it should be followed by a dessert made with eggs or milk.

Vegetable accompaniments are a very important aspect of everyday cooking, since they can make or mar a meal. Obviously, you will not want to create elaborate vegetable dishes every day, particularly when you have taken time and trouble over preparing the meat or fish part of the meal, and most of your vegetables will be plainly boiled. Even so, take care over the cooking, particularly the timing, since nothing is worse than overcooked and soggy vegetables. They should be just cooked and no more, retaining a good 'bite' and texture. This applies particularly to green vegetables, which should be cooked in the minimum amount of water possible, or preferably steamed. Spinach should be cooked very quickly, in just the water that remains on the leaves after washing, with the lid tightly on the pan. Quick and minimal cooking not only ensures a much nicer texture and flavour but also means that less of the vitamin content is destroyed.

To get the very best out of vegetables, include plenty of crunchy salads in your family's diet, which can contain not only the standard lettuce, tomato, spring onions (scallions), and cucumber but also cress, young raw spinach leaves, grated carrots, chopped celery, peppers, shredded raw cabbage and freshly chopped herbs. Some exciting salad ideas are given here, as well as plenty of delicious hot vegetable accompaniments, lots of recipes for serving the versatile potato and altogether a host of both new and traditional ways of serving vegetables to brighten up a plain omelette or a grilled (broiled) chop and turn it into something really special.

CAULIFLOWER MEXICANA

This is a spicy version of cauliflower cheese, which will delight those who like really piquant dishes.

2 servings

Metric/Imperial

1 medium-sized cauliflower, in flowerets
1 tablespoon butter
1 medium-sized onion, finely sliced
150g (5oz) tomato purée mixed with 150ml (5 fl oz) water
1 teaspoon chilli seasoning, or ½ teaspoon chilli powder
1 tablespoon capers
2 tablespoons chopped fresh parsley
3 tablespoons breadcrumbs
3 tablespoons Parmesan cheese, grated
1 tablespoon vegetable oil

American

1 medium-sized cauliflower, separated into florets
1 tablespoon butter
1 medium-sized onion, finely sliced
⅝ cup tomato paste mixed with ⅝ cup water
½ teaspoon chilli powder
1 tablespoon capers
2 tablespoons chopped fresh parsley
3 tablespoons breadcrumbs
3 tablespoons Parmesan cheese, grated
1 tablespoon vegetable oil

Preheat the oven to hot (220°C/425°F or Gas Mark 7).

Prepare, boil and drain the cauliflower flowerets.

Melt the butter in a small frying-pan, add the sliced onion and cook gently for 5 minutes, or until transparent but not brown. Place in a flameproof casserole with the tomato purée and water, chilli seasoning, capers and parsley. Stir and bring the mixture to a boil over moderate heat on top of the stove.

Add the cauliflower and stir to coat the flowerets well. Sprinkle the top with the breadcrumbs, cheese and oil and bake for 10 to 15 minutes.

Cauliflower Mexicana is a delicious vegetable dish.

NUT AND CAULIFLOWER FLAN

An inexpensive and easy-to-make dish, Nut and Cauliflower Flan may be eaten either hot or cold.

4-6 servings

Metric/Imperial

1 x 23cm (1 x 9in) flan case made with 175g (6oz) Shortcrust Pastry I, baked blind
1 small cauliflower, trimmed and separated into flowerets
¼ teaspoon salt
2 eggs, lightly beaten
100ml (4 fl oz) single cream
75g (3oz) walnuts, chopped
¼ teaspoon black pepper
100g (4oz) Cheddar cheese, grated
25g (1oz) butter
1 medium-sized onion, finely chopped
2 medium-sized tomatoes, peeled and sliced

American

1 x 9in pie shell made with 6oz Shortcrust Pastry I, baked blind
1 small head of cauliflower, trimmed and separated into florets
¼ teaspoon salt
2 eggs, lightly beaten
½ cup light cream
½ cup walnuts, chopped
¼ teaspoon black pepper
1 cup American cheese, grated
2 tablespoons butter
1 medium-sized onion, finely chopped
2 medium-sized tomatoes, peeled and sliced

Preheat the oven to moderate (180°C/350°F or Gas Mark 4). Place the flan case on a baking sheet.

Cook the cauliflower in a little salted water until barely tender. Drain and cool, then chop finely.

Combine the eggs, cream, walnuts, salt, pepper and grated cheese, beating until well blended.

In a small frying-pan, melt the butter over moderate heat. When the foam subsides add the onion and cook, stirring occasionally, for 5 to 7 minutes or until soft and translucent but not brown. Add to the egg mixture.

Arrange the cauliflower in the bottom of the flan case and cover with the sliced tomatoes. Pour the egg and cream mixture over.

Bake in the centre of the oven for 30 to 35 minutes or until the filling is golden brown and firm.

EGGPLANT FIESTA

A colourful dish, Eggplant Fiesta is an exotic mixture of aubergines [eggplants], tomatoes, onions and rice.

4 servings

Metric/Imperial

3 medium-sized aubergines
3½ teaspoons salt
100ml (4 fl oz) vegetable oil
3 medium-sized onions, thinly sliced and pushed out into rings
6 large tomatoes, peeled and sliced
1 large green pepper, white pith removed, seeded and finely sliced

1 bay leaf
½ teaspoon dried thyme
¼ teaspoon black pepper
⅛ teaspoon dried oregano
½50g (8oz) long-grain rice
250ml (16 fl oz) cold water
45g (1oz) butter, melted
2 teaspoon grated nutmeg

American

3 medium-sized eggplants
3½ teaspoons salt
½ cup vegetable oil
3 medium-sized onions, thinly sliced
   and separated into rings
6 large tomatoes, peeled and sliced
1 large green pepper, membrane and
   seeds removed, finely sliced
1 bay leaf
½ teaspoon dried thyme
¼ teaspoon black pepper
⅛ teaspoon dried oregano
1⅓ cups long-grain rice

Nut and Cauliflower Flan is both
easy to make and to eat!

2 cups cold water
2 tablespoons butter, melted
⅛ teaspoon grated nutmeg

Cut the aubergines [eggplants] into thin
slices. Place in a colander and sprinkle
with 2 teaspoons of the salt. Set aside
for 30 minutes, then dry on kitchen
paper.

In a large frying-pan, heat 2 tablespoons of the oil over moderate heat.
Add one-third of the aubergine [egg-
plant] slices and cook, turning occasionally, for 7 to 8 minutes, or until light
brown. Remove and keep warm while
the remaining slices are cooked, using
3 tablespoons of the remaining oil.

Add the remaining oil to the frying-
pan. Add the onions, tomatoes, green
pepper, bay leaf, thyme, ½ teaspoon salt,
the pepper and oregano and cook,
stirring occasionally, for 5 to 7 minutes
or until the onions are soft and translucent but not brown.

Carefully stir the cooked aubergine
[eggplant] slices into the mixture. Reduce the heat, cover and simmer, stir-

ring occasionally, for 20 minutes.

Meanwhile, put the rice, water and
1 teaspoon salt in a large saucepan.
Bring to the boil, cover, reduce the heat
and simmer for 15 minutes, or until all
the liquid has been absorbed.

Stir in the butter and nutmeg.
Continue stirring until the rice is
thoroughly coated, then arrange in a
ring on a heated serving platter. Spoon
the aubergine [eggplant] mixture into
the centre.

MUSHROOM QUICHE

A marvellously tasty dish, Mushroom
Quiche may be served hot or cold.

4-6 servings

Metric/Imperial

1 x 23cm (1 x 9in) flan case made with
   Shortcrust Pastry I, baked blind
FILLING
50g (2oz) butter
2 shallots, finely chopped

500g (1lb) button mushrooms, wiped clean and thinly sliced
¼ teaspoon salt
¼ teaspoon white pepper
¼ teaspoon grated nutmeg
100ml (4 fl oz) single cream
3 eggs
50g (2oz) Cheddar cheese, grated

American

---

1 x 9in pie shell made with Shortcrust Pastry I, baked blind
FILLING
¼ cup butter
2 shallots, finely chopped
1lb small mushrooms, wiped clean and thinly sliced
¼ teaspoon salt
¼ teaspoon white pepper
¼ teaspoon grated nutmeg
½ cup light cream
3 eggs
½ cup Cheddar or American cheese, grated

Preheat the oven to fairly hot (200°C/400°F or Gas Mark 6). Place the flan case on a baking sheet.

In a large frying-pan, melt the butter over moderate heat. When the foam subsides add the shallots and cook, stirring occasionally, for 3 to 4 minutes or until soft and translucent but not brown. Add the mushrooms and cook, stirring occasionally, for 3 minutes. Stir in the salt, pepper and nutmeg.

Combine the cream, eggs and grated cheese and beat well to blend. Add to the mushrooms, stirring until well blended. Pour into the flan case.

Bake the quiche for 25 to 30 minutes or until the filling is set and golden brown on top.

MUSHROOM PIE

A nourishing and sustaining dish, Mushroom Pie is very simple to make. Serve with green vegetables.

4-6 servings

Metric/Imperial

175g (6oz) Rough Puff Pastry
25g (1oz) butter

A filling and nutritious dish, Mushroom Pie is perfect as a main course for a vegetarian meal.

2 medium-sized onions, finely chopped
750g (1½lb) button mushrooms, wiped clean
1 tablespoon butter, melted
1 teaspoon salt
¼ teaspoon black pepper
150ml (5 fl oz) double cream
¼ teaspoon cayenne pepper
½ teaspoon dried oregano
4 hard-boiled eggs, sliced
a little milk

American

---

1 recipe Rough Puff Pastry
2 tablespoons butter
2 medium-sized onions, finely chopped
1½lb small mushrooms, wiped clean
1 tablespoon butter, melted
1 teaspoon salt
¼ teaspoon black pepper
⅝ cup heavy cream
¼ teaspoon cayenne pepper

½ teaspoon dried oregano
4 hard-boiled eggs, sliced
a little milk

Preheat the oven to fairly hot (200°C/ 400°F or Gas Mark 6).

In a large frying-pan, melt the butter over moderate heat. When the foam subsides add the onions and fry, stirring occasionally, for 5 to 7 minutes or until soft and translucent but not brown. Transfer to a deep pie dish.

Arrange the mushrooms on top of the onions and coat with the melted butter. Season with ½ teaspoon of the salt and ⅛ teaspoon of the pepper. Pour over the cream and sprinkle over the remaining salt and pepper, the cayenne and oregano. Top with slices of hard-boiled egg.

On a floured surface, roll out the dough to 2.5cm (1 inch) larger than the top of the pie dish. Trim the edges and cut out a narrow strip around the dough.

Dampen the rim of the dish and press the dough strip on top. Lightly moisten the strip.

Lift the dough onto the dish, trim and crimp the edges to seal. Cut a fairly large cross in the centre and brush the top with milk. Decorate with the trimmings and brush these with milk.

Bake for 30 minutes or until the pastry is golden brown.

MUSHROOM AND HAM PANCAKES

An easy-to-make and quite delicious dish, Mushroom and Ham Pancakes are a perfect snack lunch. Serve with a tossed green salad.

| 4-6 servings |
| Metric/Imperial |
| 250g (8oz) Pancake Batter |

50g (2oz) butter
2 medium-sized onions, chopped
2 shallots, finely chopped
1 garlic clove, crushed
350g (12oz) button mushrooms, wiped clean and sliced
½ teaspoon dried thyme
½ teaspoon salt
¼ teaspoon freshly ground black pepper
1 bay leaf
100g (4oz) ham, chopped
100ml (4 fl oz) double cream
225g (8 fl oz) White Sauce
50g (2oz) Cheddar cheese, grated

| American |
| 2 cups Pancake Batter |

Mushroom and Ham Pancakes are an economical and filling dish. They are ideal for a summer meal served with salad.

¼ cup butter

2 medium-sized onions, chopped

2 shallots, finely chopped

1 garlic clove, crushed

¾lb small mushrooms, wiped clean and sliced

½ teaspoon dried thyme

½ teaspoon salt

¼ teaspoon freshly ground black pepper

1 bay leaf

½ cup ham, diced

½ cup heavy cream

1 cup White Sauce

½ cup Cheddar cheese, grated

Fry the pancakes according to the instructions in the basic recipe and keep them warm.

In a large frying-pan, melt the butter over moderate heat. When the foam subsides add the onions, shallots and garlic and cook, stirring occasionally, for 5 to 7 minutes, until soft and translucent but not brown.

Add the mushrooms, thyme, salt, pepper and bay leaf and stir well. Cook, stirring occasionally, for 3 minutes. Stir in the ham and cook, stirring occasionally, for 3 minutes. Stir in the cream, mixing well. Remove the bay leaf.

Preheat the oven to moderate (180°C/350°F or Gas Mark 4). Lightly grease a medium-sized baking dish.

Lay one pancake out flat in the prepared dish. Spoon about 2 tablespoons of the filling on to it. Continue making layers of pancake and filling until the ingredients are used up, ending with a pancake.

Pour over the White Sauce and sprinkle with grated cheese. Bake for 30 minutes or until the top is brown.

STUFFED ONIONS

The onions in this recipe are stuffed with a delicious mixture of bacon and ham, flavoured with herbs. Serve Stuffed Onions as a light lunch dish with a crisp green salad.

4 servings

Metric/Imperial

4 large Spanish onions, peeled

1 teaspoon salt

50g (2oz) butter

4 streaky bacon slices, rinds removed, chopped

100g (4oz) ham, finely diced

50g (2oz) fresh white breadcrumbs

1 tablespoon chopped fresh parsley

½ teaspoon dried thyme

1 bay leaf, finely crumbled

½ teaspoon black pepper

American

4 large Bermuda onions, peeled

1 teaspoon salt

¼ cup butter

4 bacon slices, chopped

½ cup ham, finely diced

1 cup fresh white breadcrumbs

1 tablespoon chopped fresh parsley

½ teaspoon dried thyme

1 bay leaf, finely crumbled

½ teaspoon black pepper

Cut off and discard a slice from the top of each onion. Cut off and discard a very thin slice from the bottom to give the onions a flat base. Using a metal teaspoon, carefully remove the centre from each onion, leaving a 1cm (½in) thick shell. Chop the scooped out onion and place in a large mixing bowl.

Place the onion shells in a large saucepan, cover with water and add ½ teaspoon of the salt. Bring to the boil, cover, reduce the heat and simmer for 5 minutes. Transfer the onions to a plate; discard the cooking liquid.

Preheat the oven to fairly hot (190°C/275°F or Gas Mark 5). Grease a large deep baking dish.

Add the bacon, ham, breadcrumbs, herbs, the remaining salt and the pepper to the onion in the mixing bowl. Combine thoroughly.

In a large frying-pan, melt half of the remaining butter over moderate heat. When the foam subsides, add the onion mixture and fry, stirring occasionally, for 5 to 7 minutes or until soft but not brown.

Spoon the stuffing into the onion shells, doming it up in the centre. Place the onions in the prepared baking dish, with any leftover stuffing around the base. Dot with the remaining butter.

Cover the dish and bake for 30 to 35 minutes or until the onions are tender.

ONION, EGG AND POTATO PIE

An inexpensive dish, Onion, Egg and Potato Pie makes a delightful vegetarian meal, or light supper for the family.

4-6 servings

Metric/Imperial

175g (6oz) Rough Puff Pastry

25g (1oz) butter, melted

3 medium-sized onions, thinly sliced and pushed out into rings

4 medium-sized potatoes, cooked and sliced

1 teaspoon salt

½ teaspoon black pepper

1 teaspoon paprika

1 teaspoon dried basil

4 medium-sized tomatoes, peeled and sliced

2 hard-boiled eggs, sliced

150ml (5 fl oz) double cream

a little milk

American

1 recipe Rough Puff Pastry

2 tablespoons butter, melted

3 medium-sized onions, thinly sliced and separated into rings

4 medium-sized potatoes, cooked and sliced

1 teaspoon salt

½ teaspoon black pepper

1 teaspoon paprika

1 teaspoon dried basil

4 medium-sized tomatoes, peeled and sliced

2 hard-boiled eggs, sliced

⅝ cup heavy cream

a little milk

Preheat the oven to fairly hot (200°C/400°F or Gas Mark 6).

In a large frying-pan, melt the butter over moderate heat. When the foam subsides, add the onions and fry, stirring occasionally, for 5 to 7 minutes or until soft and translucent but not brown. Transfer to a medium-sized deep pie dish.

Cover with the potato slices and season with half the salt, pepper, paprika and basil. Top with the tomatoes and the eggs. Sprinkle over the remaining seasonings and pour in

Stuffed Onions are both easy to make and economical. Beer is a perfect accompaniment.

the cream.

On a floured surface, roll out the dough to 2.5cm (1in) larger than the top of the pie dish. Trim the edges and cut out a narrow strip around the dough. Dampen the rim of the dish and press the dough strip onto it. Lightly moisten the strip.

Lift the dough on to the dish, trim and crimp the edges to seal. Cut a fairly large cross in the centre and brush with milk. Decorate with the dough trimmings and brush with milk.

Bake for 30 minutes or until the pastry is golden brown.

ELLA'S TOMATO AND POTATO PIE

This simple and substantial informal supper dish is sure to be popular.

6 servings

Metric/Imperial

1kg (2lb) potatoes, cut into quarters
2 teaspoons salt
6 tablespoons milk
50g (2oz) butter
⅛ teaspoon grated nutmeg
4 eggs, lightly beaten
1 leek, sliced
1kg (2lb) fresh tomatoes, peeled and sliced or 792g (28oz) can tomatoes
¼ teaspoon black pepper
1 teaspoon Worcestershire sauce
1 teaspoon paprika
8 slices streaky bacon, grilled until crisp and crumbled
250g (8oz) canned creamed sweetcorn
50g (2oz) Parmesan cheese, grated

American

2lb potatoes, cut into quarters
2 teaspoons salt
6 tablespoons milk
4 tablespoons butter
⅛ teaspoon grated nutmeg
4 eggs, lightly beaten
1 leek, sliced
2lb fresh tomatoes, peeled and sliced
¼ teaspoon black pepper
1 teaspoon Worcestershire sauce
1 teaspoon paprika
8 slices bacon, broiled until crisp and crumbled

1 x 8oz can cream-style corn
½ cup Parmesan cheese, grated

Drain the potatoes and mash with 1 teaspoon salt, milk, half the butter and the nutmeg. When cool, stir in the eggs, mixing thoroughly.

Preheat the oven to moderate (180°C/350°F or Gas Mark 4). Grease a medium-sized flameproof casserole.

In a medium-sized saucepan, melt the remaining butter over moderate heat. When the foam subsides, add the leek, tomatoes, remaining salt, the pepper, Worcestershire sauce and paprika. Cook, stirring occasionally, for 15 minutes, or until the tomatoes are soft and the sauce is fairly thick.

Line the bottom of the casserole with about half of the potato mixture. Spread the tomato mixture on top, then the bacon. Arrange a layer of sweetcorn on top of the bacon. Top with the remaining potato mixture and sprinkle with the grated cheese.

Bake for 15 minutes.

POTATO CASSEROLE

A hearty and warming meal for the family, Potato Casserole is ideal for cold winter nights.

4 servings

Metric/Imperial

25g (1oz) butter
2 shallots, coarsely chopped
2 celery stalks, trimmed and coarsely chopped
1 garlic clove, crushed
1kg (2lb) potatoes, peeled and thinly sliced
250g (8oz) carrots, scraped and thinly sliced
4 streaky bacon slices, chopped
396g (14oz) can tomatoes
225ml (8 fl oz) beef stock
1 teaspoon salt
½ teaspoon black pepper
2 teaspoons paprika
¼ teaspoon dried basil

Onion, Egg and Potato Pie is substantial and delicious.

American

2 tablespoons butter
2 shallots, coarsely chopped
2 celery stalks, trimmed and coarsely chopped
1 garlic clove, crushed
2lb potatoes, peeled and thinly sliced
1 cup carrots, scraped and thinly sliced
4 bacon slices, chopped
1 x 14oz can tomatoes
1 cup beef stock
1 teaspoon salt
½ teaspoon black pepper
2 teaspoons paprika
¼ teaspoon dried basil

In a large frying-pan, melt the butter over moderate heat. When the foam subsides add the shallots, celery and garlic and cook, stirring occasionally, for 3 to 4 minutes or until soft and translucent but not brown.

Add the potatoes, carrots and bacon and cook, stirring frequently, for 15 minutes or until the potatoes are golden brown.

Pour in the tomatoes, stock, salt, pepper, paprika and basil. Bring to the boil, stirring frequently. Reduce the heat, cover and simmer for 10 minutes or until the potatoes are tender.

SPINACH WITH TOMATOES AND GARLIC

A wonderfully sustaining vegetarian dish from Provence, Spinach with Tomatoes and Garlic makes an excellent luncheon or supper dish.

6 servings

Metric/Imperial

1kg (2lb) spinach, trimmed, washed, drained and chopped
3 tablespoons vegetable oil
1 large onion, coarsely chopped
4 medium-sized potatoes, peeled and diced
2 garlic cloves, crushed
396g (14oz) can tomatoes, chopped
½ teaspoon salt
½ teaspoon black pepper
6 slices of bread, toasted
6 eggs, lightly poached

American

2lb spinach, drained and chopped
3 tablespoons vegetable oil
1 large onion, coarsely chopped
4 medium-sized potatoes, peeled and diced
2 garlic cloves, crushed
1 x 14oz can tomatoes, chopped
½ teaspoon salt
½ teaspoon black pepper
6 slices bread, toasted
6 eggs, lightly poached

Cook the spinach in a minimum of boiling salted water and drain thoroughly.

In a large saucepan, heat the oil over moderate heat. Add the onion and cook for 5 to 7 minutes or until soft and translucent but not brown. Add the potatoes, garlic, tomatoes, salt and pepper and stir to mix.

Cover the pan, reduce the heat and cook for 45 minutes, or until the potatoes are tender. Stir in the spinach and continue to cook for 5 minutes.

Place the slices of toasted bread on serving plates, ladle on the spinach mixture and top with a poached egg.

HERB AND SPINACH FLAN

Herb and Spinach Flan is a perfect light dish to serve during long, warm summer evenings.

4-6 servings

Metric/Imperial

1 x 23cm (1 x 9in) flan case made from 175g (6oz) Shortcrust Pastry I, baked blind and cooled
FILLING
50g (2oz) butter
1 small onion, thinly sliced and pushed out into rings
3 streaky bacon slices, chopped
500g (1lb) spinach, cooked
2 eggs, lightly beaten
150ml (5 fl oz) double cream
½ teaspoon salt
¼ teaspoon black pepper
1 teaspoon dried thyme
½ teaspoon dried basil
2 teaspoons chopped fresh parsley

50g (2oz) Cheddar cheese, grated

American

1 x 9in pie shell made from Shortcrust Pastry I, baked blind and cooled
FILLING
2oz butter
1 small onion, thinly sliced and separated into rings
3 bacon slices, chopped
1lb spinach, cooked
2 eggs, lightly beaten
$\frac{5}{8}$ cup heavy cream
$\frac{1}{2}$ teaspoon salt
$\frac{1}{4}$ teaspoon black pepper
1 teaspoon dried thyme
$\frac{1}{2}$ teaspoon dried basil
2 teaspoons chopped fresh parsley
$\frac{1}{2}$ cup Cheddar cheese, grated

Preheat the oven to fairly hot (200°C/400°F or Gas Mark 6).

In a large frying-pan, melt the butter over moderate heat. When the foam subsides add the onion and cook, stirring occasionally, for 5 to 7 minutes, or until soft and translucent but not brown. Add the bacon and fry, stirring occasionally, for 5 minutes.

Add the spinach and, stirring frequently, cook the mixture for a further 3 to 5 minutes, or until the spinach is heated through and the ingredients are well blended. Spoon the mixture into the flan case.

Combine the eggs, cream, salt, pepper, thyme, basil and parsley, beating with a fork until well blended. Stir in the cheese, mix well and pour over the spinach.

Bake the flan for 30 minutes or until the filling has set and the top is browned.

COURGETTE [ZUCCHINI] AND TOMATO CASSEROLE

This tasty dish can be served as a light vegetarian luncheon accompanied by crusty French bread, or as an accompaniment to chops.

4 servings

Metric/Imperial

6 courgettes, trimmed and washed

2 tablespoons vegetable oil
1 shallot or spring onion, finely chopped
2 garlic cloves, crushed
1 x 792g (1 x 28oz) can tomatoes
100g (4oz) Cheddar cheese, grated
$\frac{1}{2}$ teaspoon salt
$\frac{1}{2}$ teaspoon black pepper

American

6 zucchini, trimmed and washed
2 tablespoons vegetable oil
1 shallot or scallion, finely chopped
2 garlic cloves, crushed
2 x 14oz can tomatoes
1 cup Cheddar cheese, grated
$\frac{1}{2}$ teaspoon salt
$\frac{1}{2}$ teaspoon black pepper

Cut the courgettes [zucchini] into slices crosswise.

In a large, heavy frying-pan, heat the oil over moderate heat. Add the

Herb and Spinach Flan is perfect for a light summer meal.

courgette [zucchini] slices, chopped shallot or spring onion [scallion] and crushed garlic cloves and mix well. Reduce the heat, cover and cook the courgettes [zucchini] for 10 minutes, or until they are tender. Turn them occasionally.

Preheat the oven to moderate (180°C/350°F or Gas Mark 4).

Grease an ovenproof casserole. Spoon in one-third of the tomatoes, arrange half the courgettes [zucchini] on top and sprinkle with half the grated cheese. Add the remaining vegetables, ending with a layer of tomatoes and top with the remaining grated cheese. Sprinkle with salt and pepper and bake for 45 minutes.

COURGETTE [ZUCCHINI] AND TOMATO QUICHE

A delightful combination of courgettes [zucchini] and tomatoes makes this an extra-special dish. Serve hot or cold, either as a first course to a dinner or, with Garlic Bread and a mixed green salad, as a delicious lunch or supper.

4-6 servings

Metric/Imperial

---

1 x 23cm (1 x 9in) flan case made with
   Shortcrust Pastry I, baked blind
FILLING
50g (2oz) butter
2 garlic cloves, crushed

A simple but appetizing dish, Courgette [Zucchini] and Tomato Quiche is delicious.

4 courgettes, trimmed and sliced
1 teaspoon salt
1 teaspoon black pepper
½ teaspoon dried oregano
100ml (4 fl oz) single cream
3 eggs
50g (2oz) Cheddar cheese, grated
5 small tomatoes, peeled and thinly
   sliced

American

---

1 x 9in pie shell, made with Shortcrust
   Pastry I, baked blind

FILLING

¼ cup butter

2 garlic cloves, crushed

4 zucchini, trimmed and sliced

1 teaspoon salt

1 teaspoon black pepper

½ teaspoon dried oregano

½ cup light cream

3 eggs

½ cup Cheddar or American cheese, grated

5 small tomatoes, peeled and thinly sliced

Preheat the oven to fairly hot (200°C/400°F or Gas Mark 6). Place the flan case on a baking sheet.

In a large frying-pan, melt the butter over moderate heat. When the foam subsides, add the garlic and cook, stirring frequently, for 1 minute. Add the courgettes [zucchini] and half the salt and pepper. Cook, stirring and turning occasionally, for 8 to 10 minutes or until browned. Stir in the remaining salt and pepper and the oregano.

Combine the cream, eggs and grated cheese and beat well to blend. Arrange the courgettes [zucchini] and tomato slices in concentric circles in the flan case.

Pour over the cream mixture.

Bake in the centre of the oven for 35 to 40 minutes or until the filling is set and golden bown.

COURGETTES [ZUCCHINI] BAKED WITH AUBERGINES [EGGPLANTS]

This mixture of vegetables cooked in tomato sauce is filling enough to be served on its own with crusty bread as a light luncheon dish, but it also makes an excellent accompaniment to roasted or grilled [broiled] meat.

4-6 servings

Metric/Imperial

2 aubergines, peeled and halved

1 tablespoon plus 1½ teaspoons salt

6 large courgettes, trimmed and washed

3 tablespoons vegetable oil

¼ teaspoon black pepper

6 shallots or spring onions, peeled and finely chopped

1 garlic clove, finely chopped

1 teaspoon sugar

4 tablespoons tomato purée

150ml (5 fl oz) chicken stock

American

2 eggplants, peeled and halved

1 tablespoon plus 1½ teaspoons salt

6 zucchini, trimmed and washed

3 tablespoons vegetable oil

¼ teaspoon black pepper

6 shallots or scallions, peeled and finely chopped

1 garlic clove, finely chopped

1 teaspoon sugar

4 tablespoons tomato paste

⅝ cup chicken stock

Sprinkle the aubergine [eggplant] halves with 1 tablespoon of salt. Place them, cut sides down, on kitchen paper towels to drain for 30 minutes. Cut them into thick slices, lengthways. Cut the courgettes [zucchini] in slices, crosswise.

Preheat the oven to moderate (180°C/ 350°F or Gas Mark 4).

Pour 1 tablespoon of the vegetable oil into a medium-sized ovenproof dish. Put half of the aubergine [eggplant] slices at the bottom and sprinkle with ¾ teaspoon salt and pepper. Cover with half the shallots or spring onions [scallions] and half the garlic. Arrange half the courgettes [zucchini] on top. Repeat the layers, with remaining salt, until all the vegetables are in.

In a large jug, combine the sugar, tomato purée, chicken stock and remaining oil and stir well to blend. Pour over the vegetables in the baking dish, cover with aluminium foil and bake for 1½ hours.

VEGETABLE RISSOLES

Filling and nourishing, Vegetable Rissoles make an ideal vegetarian lunch or supper dish, and the children will love them.

4 servings

Metric/Imperial

100g (4oz) red lentils, soaked overnight, cooked and drained

1 large onion, finely chopped

1 celery stalk, trimmed and finely chopped

2 small carrots, trimmed, scraped and grated

50g (2oz) green beans, cooked and finely chopped

50g (2oz) fresh white breadcrumbs

3 eggs

1½ teaspoons salt

1 teaspoon black pepper

Just the thing for a quick meal – piping hot, crisp Vegetable Rissoles.

1 teaspoon dried mixed herbs

75g (3oz) dry white breadcrumbs

3 tablespoons vegetable oil

American

¼lb red lentils, soaked overnight, cooked and drained

1 large onion, finely chopped

1 celery stalk, trimmed and finely chopped

2 small carrots, trimmed, scraped and grated

¼ cup green beans, cooked and finely chopped

1 cup fresh white breadcrumbs

3 eggs

1½ teaspoons salt

1 teaspoon black pepper

1 teaspoon dried mixed herbs (basil, oregano, marjoram, thyme)

1 cup dry white breadcrumbs

3 tablespoons vegetable oil

Place the lentils, onion, celery, carrots, beans, fresh white breadcrumbs, 2 of the eggs, the salt and pepper and mixed herbs in a mixing bowl. Mix well until thoroughly combined; set aside for 30 minutes.

Using your hands, shape the mixture into 8 equal-sized balls and flatten between the palms of your hands to make small cakes.

Beat the remaining egg in a small shallow dish. Place the dry breadcrumbs on a plate. Dip each rissole first in the egg and then in the breadcrumbs, coating thoroughly and shaking off any excess crumbs.

In a medium-sized frying-pan, heat the oil over moderate heat. Add the rissoles and fry for 10 minutes on each side or until golden brown.

RATATOUILLE

A classic French vegetable casserole, Ratatouille (rah-tah-twee-y'h) is a beautifully simple, yet delicious dish to prepare and serve.

4-6 servings

Metric/Imperial

25g (1oz) butter

3 tablespoons vegetable oil

2 large onions, thinly sliced

2 garlic cloves, crushed

3 medium-sized aubergines, thickly sliced, salted and drained to get rid of excess moisture

2 large green peppers, white pith removed, seeded and chopped

4 medium-sized courgettes, trimmed and sliced

396g (14oz) can tomatoes

1 teaspoon dried basil

1 teaspoon dried rosemary

1½ teaspoons salt

¾ teaspoon black pepper

2 tablespoons fresh chopped parsley

American

2 tablespoons butter

3 tablespoons vegetable oil

2 large onions, thinly sliced

2 garlic cloves, crushed

3 medium-sized eggplants, thickly sliced, salted and drained to get rid of excess moisture

2 large green peppers, membranes and seeds removed, chopped

4 medium-sized zucchini, trimmed and sliced

1 x 14oz can tomatoes

1 teaspoon dried basil

1 teaspoon dried rosemary

1½ teaspoons salt

¾ teaspoon black pepper

2 tablespoons fresh chopped parsley

In a large flameproof casserole, melt the butter with the oil over moderate heat. When the foam subsides, add the onions and garlic and fry, stirring occasionally, for 5 to 7 minutes or until soft and translucent but not brown.

Add the aubergine [eggplant], pepper and courgette [zucchini] slices. Fry for 5 minutes, shaking frequently. Add the tomatoes, basil, rosemary, salt and pepper. Sprinkle over the parsley.

Bring to the boil, reduce the heat, cover and simmer for 40 to 45 minutes or until the vegetables are tender but still firm.

PICNIC SALAD

This fabulous salad makes a filling picnic meal served with either French bread or rolls and butter. Or serve it at home on its own as a first course or a lunch for three or four people. To take the salad on your picnic, place it in a plastic bowl and cover with an airtight lid – it is preferable to chill the salad in the refrigerator for at least one hour.

6 servings

Metric/Imperial

500g (1lb) cooked chicken, diced
175g (6oz) canned sweetcorn, drained
100g (4oz) button mushrooms, wiped clean and thinly sliced
1 large avocado, peeled, stoned and chopped
2 peaches, peeled, stoned and chopped
175g (6oz) cooked long-grain rice,

or diced potatoes, cold
2 shallots, finely chopped
2 tablespoons fresh chives, chopped
1 tablespoon fresh parsley, chopped
DRESSING
150ml (5 fl oz) mayonnaise
3 tablespoons creamy milk
1 tablespoon lemon juice
2 teaspoons curry powder
1 teaspoon salt
½ teaspoon black pepper
⅛ teaspoon cayenne pepper

American

2 cups cooked chicken, diced
¾ cup canned corn, drained
¼lb small mushrooms, wiped clean and thinly sliced

1 large avocado, peeled, pitted and chopped
2 peaches, peeled, pitted and chopped
2 cups cooked long-grain rice, or cold diced cooked potatoes
2 shallots, finely chopped
2 tablespoons fresh chives, chopped
1 tablespoon fresh parsley, chopped
DRESSING
¾ cup mayonnaise
¼ cup half and half or light cream
1 tablespoon lemon juice
2 teaspoons curry powder
1 teaspoon salt
½ teaspoon black pepper
⅛ teaspoon cayenne pepper

First make the dressing. In a large

mixing bowl, beat the mayonnaise, milk and lemon juice together with a wooden spoon. Add the curry powder, salt, pepper and cayenne and stir well to blend.

Add all the salad ingredients and toss thoroughly. Cover the bowl with aluminium foil and chill in the refrigerator for at least 1 hour before serving, tossing occasionally.

AVIYAL

An Indian dish of mixed vegetables cooked with coconut and spices, Aviyal (ah-VEE-yahl) should be served with boiled rice. You may use a combination of any of the following vegetables: carrots, beans, aubergines [eggplants],

Serve Picnic Salad with crusty bread for a sustaining picnic meal.

turnips, cauliflower, green peppers, potatoes, and spring onions [scallions].

4 servings

Metric/Imperial

175ml (6 fl oz) boiling water
3 tablespoons desiccated coconut
4 tablespoons vegetable oil
1 teaspoon mustard seeds
5cm (2in) piece of fresh ginger, peeled and minced
2 garlic cloves, peeled and cut into quarters
1 onion, minced
1 green chilli, minced
1½ teaspoons ground turmeric
1 tablespoon ground coriander
750g (1½lb) mixed vegetables, sliced
1 teaspoon salt

American

¾ cup boiling water
3 tablespoons shredded coconut

Aviyal is a tasty and attractive Indian vegetable curry.

4 tablespoons vegetable oil
1 teaspoon mustard seed
2in piece fresh ginger, peeled and minced
2 garlic cloves, peeled and cut into quarters
1 onion, minced
1 green chilli pepper, minced
1½ teaspoons ground turmeric
1 tablespoon ground coriander
1½lb mixed vegetables, sliced
1 teaspoon salt

Pour the boiling water onto the coconut and leave to infuse.

Heat the oil in a large saucepan over high heat. Add the mustard seeds, ginger and garlic and fry for 30 seconds. Add the onion and green chilli, reduce the heat and, stirring occasionally, fry gently for 10 minutes, or until the onion is golden.

Add the turmeric and ground coriander and cook for 1 minute. Add the vegetables and stir to mix well with the fried spices. Add the salt. Strain the coconut liquid into the pan, discarding the coconut. Stir to mix: if the mixture is too dry add 1 or 2 spoonfuls of water. Cover and simmer for 30 minutes or until the vegetables are tender.

VEGETABLE CURRY

This is a simple curry which can be made with almost any combination of vegetables. Serve on its own, or with rice, chutneys and Poppadums.

4-6 servings

Metric/Imperial

3 tablespoons vegetable oil
2 medium-sized onions, finely
  chopped
3cm (1½in) piece fresh root ginger,
  peeled and finely chopped
2 garlic cloves, crushed
2 green chillis, finely chopped
1 teaspoon turmeric
1 tablespoon ground coriander
1 tablespoon paprika
½ teaspoon cayenne pepper
¼ teaspoon ground fenugreek
¼ teaspoon black pepper
2 tablespoons lemon juice
500g (1lb) potatoes, peeled and cubed
250g (8oz) turnips, peeled and cubed
250g (8oz) carrots, scraped and thinly
  sliced
100g (4oz) French beans, trimmed and
  sliced
100g (4oz) frozen peas
1 teaspoon salt
396g (14oz) can tomatoes

American

3 tablespoons vegetable oil
2 medium-sized onions, finely chopped
1½in piece fresh ginger, peeled and
  finely chopped
2 garlic cloves, crushed
1 teaspoon curry powder (or more to
  taste) mixed to a paste with 2
  tablespoons lemon juice
1lb potatoes, peeled and cubed

½lb turnips, peeled and cubed
½lb carrots, scraped and thinly sliced
½ cup green beans, trimmed and sliced
½ cup frozen peas
1 teaspoon salt
1 x 14oz can tomatoes

In a large saucepan, heat the oil over moderate heat. Add the onions, ginger, garlic and chillis and fry, stirring occasionally, for 6 to 8 minutes or until the onions are golden.

If mixing your own curry powder, in a small bowl, combine the turmeric, coriander, paprika, cayenne pepper, fenugreek and pepper. Add the lemon juice and a little water, if necessary, to make a smooth paste. Add the spice paste to the onion mixture and fry, stirring constantly, for 5 minutes. Add a spoonful of water if it gets too dry.

Add the vegetables to the pan and fry, stirring constantly, for 5 minutes. Stir in the salt and the tomatoes and bring to the boil. Cover, reduce the heat and simmer for 20 to 25 minutes or until the vegetables are cooked. Taste and add more salt if necessary.

VEGETABLE ACCOMPANIMENTS

Vegetables are usually a secondary part of a meal, and as such they are often neglected. Here are some deliciously different ideas to accompany simple cheese, egg or meat dishes, including salads as well as hot vegetable recipes.

FRENCH BEANS WITH TOMATOES

This is a deliciously different way to serve French Beans, and goes particularly well with fish or cheese and egg dishes.

4 servings

Metric/Imperial

4 tomatoes, peeled and chopped
500g (1lb) prepared fresh or frozen
  French beans
3 tablespoons butter
salt and black pepper
chopped parsley

American

4 tomatoes, pelled and chopped
2 cups frozen green beans
3 tablespoons butter
salt and black pepper
chopped parsley

Cook the beans in boiling salted water; drain thoroughly and turn into a warmed serving dish.

Melt the butter in a shallow pan and quickly sauté the diced tomato in it. Add salt, pepper, and parsley and pour over the beans.

BRAISED CELERY

A delicious way to cook celery is to braise it, as the fat and seasonings used in cooking keep the celery moist and flavoursome. The following is a basic recipe for braising celery.

4 servings

Metric/Imperial

2 small heads of celery
100g (4oz) streaky bacon
1 small carrot, scraped and sliced
1 onion, sliced
1 bouquet garni
½ teaspoon salt
¼ teaspoon black pepper
¾ litre (1½ pints) chicken stock
1½ tablespoons flour
2 teaspoons butter

American

2 small heads of celery
¼lb bacon
1 small carrot, scraped and sliced
1 onion, sliced
1 bouquet garni
½ teaspoon salt
¼ teaspoon black pepper
3¾ cups chicken stock
1½ tablespoons flour
2 teaspoons butter

Prepare, trim, wash, boil and drain the celery. Lay the bacon in a large flame-proof casserole. Put in the sliced carrot and onion and place the celery heads on top. Add the bouquet garni, salt, pepper and stock, which should just

Braised Celery is a tasty vegetable dish to serve with roast meat.

cover the celery. Bring to the boil, cover, lower the heat and simmer gently for 1 hour (or bake in a moderate oven for 1½ hours).

Remove the cover for the last 30 minutes of cooking and raise the heat slightly. Remove the celery heads, cut in half lengthways and arrange on a serving dish.

Strain the cooking liquid into a saucepan and bring to the boil. Taste and add seasoning if necessary. Blend the flour and butter in a saucer and form into balls. Add these one at a time to the simmering sauce. When thick and smooth, pour over the celery and serve.

BRAISED RED CABBAGE WITH APPLES

A hearty winter vegetable dish, Braised Red Cabbage with Apples is a traditional Belgian accompaniment for rabbit.

4 servings

Metric/Imperial

2 tablespoons butter
1 small red cabbage
⅛ teaspoon grated nutmeg
½ teaspoon salt
¼ teaspoon black pepper
3 tablespoons vinegar
4 cooking apples, peeled, cored and quartered
1 tablespoon brown sugar

American

2 tablespoons butter
1 small head of red cabbage
⅛ teaspoon grated nutmeg
½ teaspoon salt
¼ teaspoon black pepper
3 tablespoons vinegar

4 tart apples, peeled, cored and
  quartered
1 tablespoon brown sugar

Grease a medium-sized flameproof
casserole with the butter. Quarter the
cabbage. Wash, remove and discard the
core, stem and outer leaves and shred
finely.

Put the shredded cabbage into the
casserole and mix in the nutmeg, salt
and pepper. Sprinkle with the vinegar.
Cover and cook over low heat for 1½
hours, stirring occasionally to prevent
the cabbage from sticking to the bottom
of the pan.

Add the apple quarters and brown
sugar and mix well. Continue cooking
for a further 40 minutes, stirring
occasionally.

COLCANNON

This traditional Irish dish of potatoes
and cabbage used to be served at
Halloween. It makes a tasty supper dish
and is delicious served with fried bacon.

4 servings

Metric/Imperial

500g (1lb) potatoes, peeled and
  quartered
2 small leeks, thoroughly washed and
  chopped
225ml (8 fl oz) single cream
500g (1lb) spring greens or cabbage,
  washed and shredded
1 teaspoon salt
½ teaspoon black pepper
⅛ teaspoon ground mace or nutmeg
100g (4oz) butter

American

1lb potatoes, peeled and quartered
2 small leeks, thoroughly washed and
  chopped
1 cup light cream
1lb greens or cabbage, washed and
  shredded

Peperonata is a colourful Italian
stew, made with peppers, tomatoes
and garlic. Serve it with meat, or on
its own as a light vegetarian meal.

1 teaspoon salt
½ teaspoon black pepper
⅛ teaspoon ground mace or nutmeg
½ cup butter

Boil the potatoes until soft but not
mushy.

Put the leeks in a small saucepan and
pour over one-quarter of the cream.
Simmer for 15 to 20 minutes or until
soft.

Cook the cabbage for 10 to 15
minutes.

Drain the potatoes, sprinkle with the
salt, pepper and mace and beat until
smooth. Add the leeks and their
cooking liquid, the remaining cream
and the butter.

Drain the cabbage and beat it into
the potato mixture.

PEPERONATA

Peperonata is a stew of red peppers and
tomatoes, which may be served as an
accompaniment to roast or grilled
[broiled] meat. Peperonata is equally

Aubergines a la Tunisienne is a marvellous dish which is equally delicious served hot or cold.

good hot or cold and will keep for several days if stored in a screw-top jar with a tablespoon of olive oil on top.

4-6 servings

Metric/Imperial

25g (1oz) butter
2 tablespoons olive oil
1 large onion, thinly sliced
1 garlic clove, crushed
500g (1lb) red or green peppers, pith removed, seeded and cut into strips
500g (1lb) tomatoes, peeled and chopped
½ teaspoon salt
¼ teaspoon black pepper
1 bay leaf

American

2 tablespoons butter
2 tablespoons olive oil
1 large onion, thinly sliced
1 garlic clove, crushed
4 or 5 red or green peppers, membranes and seeds removed, cut into strips
1lb tomatoes, peeled and chopped
½ teaspoon salt
¼ teaspoon black pepper
1 bay leaf

In a large saucepan, heat the butter with the oil over moderate heat. When the foam subsides add the onion and garlic and fry, stirring occasionally, for 5 to 7 minutes or until soft and translucent but not brown.

Add the peppers. Cover, reduce the heat and cook for 15 minutes. Add the tomatoes, salt, pepper and bay leaf and simmer, uncovered, for a further 20 minutes.

If there is too much liquid in the pan, increase the heat and cook until some has evaporated and the stew is thick.

AUBERGINES A LA TUNISIENNE

This dish is equally delicious served either hot or cold. Aubergines à la Tunisienne (oh-bair-jeen ah lah too-NEEZ-yen) goes well with lamb dishes and is especially good with lamb kebabs.

4 servings

Metric/Imperial

3 aubergines
1 tablespoon plus ½ teaspoon salt
4 tablespoons vegetable oil
2 onions, sliced
1 garlic clove, chopped
¼ teaspoon cayenne pepper
¼ teaspoon ground cloves
½ teaspoon ground cumin
500g (1lb) tomatoes, peeled and
   chopped
1 teaspoon ground coriander
1 tablespoon fresh chopped mint
2 tablespoons raisins
½ teaspoon black pepper
2 tablespoons chopped fresh parsley

American

3 eggplants
1 tablespoon plus ½ teaspoon salt
4 tablespoons vegetable oil
2 onions, sliced
1 garlic clove, chopped
¼ teaspoon cayenne pepper
¼ teaspoon ground cloves
½ teaspoon ground cumin
1lb tomatoes, peeled and chopped
1 teaspoon ground coriander
1 tablespoon fresh mint leaves,
   chopped
2 tablespoons raisins
½ teaspoon black pepper
2 tablespoons chopped fresh
   parsley

Cut the aubergines [eggplants] into cubes. Sprinkle with 1 tablespoon salt and put in a colander to drain for 30 minutes. Dry on kitchen paper.
   Heat the oil in a large frying-pan over moderate heat. Add the onions and fry until soft. Add the garlic, the cayenne pepper, cloves and cumin and cook for 2 minutes. Add the aubergine cubes. Stir well and brown the cubes lightly on all sides. Add the tomatoes, coriander, mint, raisins, remaining salt and the pepper. Cook gently, stirring occasionally, until almost all the liquid has evaporated. Stir in the parsley.

AUBERGINE [EGGPLANT] FRITTERS

These fritters are a crisp and tasty accompaniment to serve with chicken, fish and rice dishes.

6 servings

Metric/Imperial

3 aubergines
salt
BATTER
100g (4oz) flour
¼ teaspoon salt
a pinch of turmeric
2 egg yolks
1 tablespoon vegetable oil
150ml (5 fl oz) milk
1 egg white
600ml (1 pint) cooking oil

American

3 eggplants
salt
BATTER
1 cup flour
¼ teaspoon salt
a pinch of turmeric
2 egg yolks
1 tablespoon vegetable oil
⅝ cup milk
1 egg white
2½ cups cooking oil

Cut the aubergines [eggplants] into thin slices, sprinkle with salt and place in a colander to drain for 30 minutes.
   Prepare the batter by sifting the flour, salt and turmeric into a medium-sized bowl. Make a well in the centre and pour in the egg yolks and oil. Beat the egg yolks and oil until they are mixed, slowly incorporating the flour. Add the milk a little at a time and continue beating until the batter is smooth. Cover and set aside in a cool place for 30 minutes.
   Put the egg white in a small bowl and whisk until stiff. Fold into the batter.
   Dry the aubergine slices with kitchen paper. Heat the oil in a deep frying-pan until it is very hot. Dip the aubergine slices in the batter and fry them in oil until crisp and light golden in colour. Drain on kitchen paper.

TURNIPS FRIED IN BUTTER

A simple way of preparing turnips, Turnips Fried in Butter is an attractive dish to serve with lamb cutlets or grilled [broiled] steaks.

4 servings

Metric/Imperial

40g (1½oz) butter
500g (1lb) small turnips, pelled, sliced,
   boiled and drained
½ teaspoon salt
1 teaspoon black pepper
6 parsley sprigs

American

3 tablespoons butter
1lb small turnips, peeled, sliced,
   boiled and drained
½ teaspoon salt
1 teaspoon black pepper
6 parsley sprigs

In a medium-sized frying-pan, melt the butter over moderate heat. When the foam subsides, add the turnips and sprinkle over the salt and pepper. Cook, stirring frequently, for 6 to 8 minutes or until golden brown.
   Transfer the turnips to a warmed serving dish and garnish with the parsley sprigs.

DEEP FRIED ONION RINGS

The perfect vegetable accompaniment for grilled [broiled] steaks or hamburgers, Deep Fried Onion Rings are inexpensive and easy to make.

4 servings

Metric/Imperial

vegetable oil for deep frying
2 large onions, thickly sliced and
   pushed out into rings

225ml (8 fl oz) Fritter Batter II
¼ teaspoon salt

American

vegetable oil for deep frying
2 large onions, thickly sliced and
   separated into rings
1 cup Fritter Batter II
¼ teaspoon salt

Fill a large deep frying-pan one-third
full of vegetable oil. Place over moderate
heat and heat the oil until a small cube
of stale bread dropped in turns light
brown in 40 seconds.

Using tongs, dip the onion rings a
few at a time in the batter, then carefully drop them into the oil. Fry for 3 to
4 minutes or until crisp and golden
brown.

With a slotted spoon, remove the
rings from the pan and drain them on
kitchen paper. Keep hot while you fry
the remaining rings in the same way.

Sprinkle over the salt and serve
immediately.

POTATOES BAKED WITH MILK, CHEESE AND GARLIC

This is a classic French potato dish
which goes magnificently with roast
lamb or veal.

6 servings

Metric/Imperial

1 garlic clove, halved
25g (1oz) butter
1kg (2lb) potatoes, peeled and thinly
   sliced
1 teaspoon salt
1 teaspoon black pepper
175g (6oz) Cheddar cheese, grated
1 egg, lightly beaten
200ml (10 fl oz) milk, scalded
⅛ teaspoon grated nutmeg

American

1 garlic clove, halved
2 tablespoons butter
2lb potatoes, peeled and thinly sliced
1 teaspoon salt
1 teaspoon black pepper
1½ cups American cheese, grated
1 egg, lightly beaten

Potatoes Baked with Milk, Cheese
and Garlic is a classic French dish.

1¼ cups milk, scalded
⅛ teaspoon grated nutmeg

Preheat the oven to fairly hot (190°C/
375°F or Gas Mark 5).

Rub the garlic clove halves over the
insides of a medium-sized baking dish.
Grease with half the butter.

Place about one-third of the potato
slices in the baking dish and sprinkle
over ½ teaspoon of the salt, ½ teaspoon
of the pepper and a little of the grated
cheese. Top with another one-third of
the potatoes. Sprinkle on the remaining
salt and pepper and a little more cheese
and top with the remaining potato
slices.

In a small saucepan, beat the egg,
milk and nutmeg together until they are
well blended. Bring to the boil, then
pour into the baking dish.

Sprinkle the remaining grated cheese
over the top and dot with the remaining
butter.

Bake for 45 to 50 minutes or until the
potatoes are tender but still firm.

POTATO FRITTERS

Potato Fritters, potatoes fried in crispy
batter, taste delicious served as an
accompaniment to meat or fish dishes.

2 servings

Metric/Imperial

500g (1lb) potatoes, peeled, parboiled
   and cut into thick slices
4 tablespoons flour
vegetable oil for deep frying
300ml (10 fl oz) Fritter Batter II

American

1lb potatoes, peeled, parboiled and
   thickly sliced
4 tablespoons flour
vegetable oil for deep frying
1¼ cups Fritter Batter II

Dry the potato slices thoroughly with
kitchen paper. Place the flour on a plate
and pour the batter into a small,
shallow bowl.

Dip the potato slices, a few at a time,
in the flour, coating thoroughly and
shaking off any excess.

Fill a medium-sized deep frying-pan

one-third full with vegetable oil. Heat until a small cube of stale bread dropped in the oil turns golden brown in 50 seconds.

Dip a few of the potato slices into the batter, coating them thoroughly. Carefully lower into the hot oil and fry for 4 to 5 minutes, or until they are cooked and the batter is crisp and golden.

Using a slotted spoon, remove from the oil and drain thoroughly on kitchen paper. Keep hot while you fry and drain the remaining potatoes.

POTATO CROQUETTES

Delicious served with almost any meat, fish or vegetable dish, Potato Croquettes are quick and easy to make.

3-4 servings

Metric/Imperial

750g (1½lb) potatoes, cooked, peeled and mashed
1 egg yolk
50g (2oz) butter
3 tablespoons milk
1 teaspoon salt
½ teaspoon black pepper
1 teaspoon chopped fresh parsley
1 egg, lightly beaten
100g (4oz) dry white breadcrumbs
3 tablespoons vegetable oil

American

1½lb potatoes, cooked, peeled and mashed
1 egg yolk
¼ cup butter
3 tablespoons milk
1 teaspoon salt
½ teaspoon black pepper
1 teaspoon chopped fresh parsley
1 egg, lightly beaten
1⅓ cups dry white breadcrumbs
3 tablespoons vegetable oil

Place the mashed potatoes in a medium-sized mixing bowl and beat in the egg yolk, half the butter and enough milk to make a firm consistency. Add the salt, pepper and parsley and beat until smooth.

With floured hands, break off pieces of the mixture and roll them into sausage shapes or croquettes. Place in one layer on a plate and chill in the refrigerator for 30 minutes, or until firm.

Put the lightly beaten egg on one plate and the breadcrumbs on another.

Dip the croquettes first in the egg, then roll them in the breadcrumbs, coating thoroughly and shaking off any excess.

In a large frying-pan, heat the remaining butter with the oil over moderate heat. When the foam subsides add the croquettes, a few at a time, and fry for 3 to 4 minutes or until crisp and lightly browned all over.

Drain well on kitchen paper and keep hot while you fry the remaining croquettes.

Potato Croquettes and Potato Fritters go well with almost any meat, fish or vegetable dish. They are perfect as a snack meal for children.

IRISH POTATO CAKE

These traditional potato cakes are excellent any time of the day – with bacon and egg for breakfast, with cold meat for lunch or with a light snack for supper.

4 servings

Metric/Imperial

500g (1lb) cooked potatoes
25g (1oz) butter, melted
3 tablespoons flour
1 teaspoon salt
½ teaspoon black pepper
40g (1½oz) butter

American

1lb cooked potatoes
3 tablespoons butter, melted
3 tablespoons flour
1 teaspoon salt
½ teaspoon black pepper
3 tablespoons butter

Mash the potatoes until smooth and stir in the melted butter, flour, salt and pepper.

Turn the mixture out on to a floured surface and press out until it is a circle about 1cm (½-inch) thick. Using a pastry cutter, cut the mixture into rounds.

In a large frying-pan, melt the butter over moderate heat. When the foam subsides add the potato cakes and fry them for about 3 minutes on each side or until golden.

POTATO CAKE

Golden, crisp Potato Cake is excellent served with grilled [broiled] fish or meat.

4 servings

Metric/Imperial

1kg (2lb) potatoes, peeled and cooked
1 small onion, finely chopped
2 teaspoons salt
¼ teaspoon black pepper
1 tablespoon chopped fresh parsley
50g (2oz) butter, softened
2 eggs, lightly beaten
½ teaspoon paprika

American

2lb potatoes, peeled and cooked
1 small onion, finely chopped
2 teaspoons salt
¼ teaspoon black pepper
1 tablespoon chopped fresh parsley
¼ cup butter, softened
2 eggs, lightly beaten
½ teaspoon paprika

Preheat the oven to fairly hot (190°C/375°F or Gas Mark 5).

Mash the potatoes and place them in a mixing bowl. Add the onion, salt, pepper and parsley and mix well.

Beat in nearly all the butter and the eggs, and stir until well blended.

Using the remaining butter, generously grease a medium-sized baking dish.

Spoon the mixture into the dish, flattening the top with a palette knife. Sprinkle over the paprika.

Bake for 20 to 30 minutes or until golden brown and crisp.

LATKES

Latkes (luht-k's) are Jewish potato pancakes which are delicious served with salt beef or hot tongue. They can also be made without the onion and served as a sweet pancake with lemon and sugar or cinnamon.

10 servings

Metric/Imperial

6 medium-sized potatoes, peeled and grated
2 large onions, grated
2 tablespoons flour
½ teaspoon warm water
2 eggs, lightly beaten
1 teaspoon salt
½ teaspoon black pepper
25g (1oz) butter
2 tablespoons vegetable oil

American

6 medium-sized potatoes, peeled and grated
2 large onions, grated
2 tablespoons flour
½ teaspoon warm water
2 eggs, lightly beaten
1 teaspoon salt
½ teaspoon black pepper
2 tablespoons butter
2 tablespoons vegetable oil

Drain off the excess liquid from the grated potatoes and place them in a bowl with the onions, flour, water, eggs, salt and pepper. Beat until blended.

In a large frying-pan heat half the butter and half the oil over moderate heat.

When the foam subsides drop in the potato mixture, a tablespoon at a time, to make small pancakes.

Fry for 3 minutes each side or until the latkes are brown and crisp. Add more oil and butter to the pan if needed.

Transfer to a plate and keep hot while you cook the remaining latkes.

HASH BROWN POTATOES

A popular fried potato dish, Hash Brown Potatoes is particularly good served with chops or other grilled [broiled] meats. Leftover cooked potatoes are ideal for this dish.

4 servings

Metric/Imperial

750g (1½lb) potatoes, peeled and halved
1 tablespoon butter
2 tablespoons bacon dripping or vegetable oil
½ teaspoon black pepper
½ teaspoon salt

American

1½lb potatoes, peeled and halved
1 tablespoon butter
2 tablespoons bacon fat or vegetable oil
½ teaspoon black pepper
½ teaspoon salt

Boil the potatoes until soft but not mushy. Drain and return to the pan. Put on a low heat to dry (do not let them burn). Remove from the heat and mash roughly.

In a large frying-pan, melt the butter with the dripping or oil over moderate heat. When the foam subsides add the potatoes, pepper and salt. Cook, shaking the pan occasionally to prevent sticking, for 20 minutes or until the underside of the potatoes is golden and crisp.

Remove the pan from the heat. Place a warmed serving dish, inverted, over the frying-pan and reverse the two. The potatoes should fall out on to the dish easily.

BASIL BAKED TOMATOES

Tomatoes and onions baked with basil make a fragrant and tasty accompaniment to roast pork, lamb or chicken.

4 servings

Metric/Imperial

75g (3oz) butter
2 large onions, thinly sliced and pushed out into rings
10 large tomatoes, thinly sliced
2 teaspoons dried basil
6 grindings black pepper
1 teaspoon salt
1 teaspoon sugar
75g (3oz) fresh breadcrumbs

American

6 tablespoons butter
2 large onions, thinly sliced and separated into rings
10 large tomatoes, thinly sliced
2 teaspoons dried basil

Basil Baked Tomatoes is an unusual and fragrant dish.

6 grindings black pepper
1 teaspoon salt
1 teaspoon sugar
1 cup fresh breadcrumbs

Preheat the oven to fairly hot (200°C/400°F or Gas Mark 6). Grease an ovenproof dish with a little of the butter.

Melt one-third of the butter in a large frying-pan over low heat. Put in the onion rings and fry for 10 minutes, or until tender but not brown.

Put a layer of onion rings on the bottom of the ovenproof dish, sprinkle with a little basil and cover with a layer of tomato slices. Add a little pepper, salt and a sprinkling of sugar. Dot with butter. Repeat the layers until all the ingredients have been used, ending with a layer of breadcrumbs dotted with butter. Bake for 30 minutes.

TOMATO AND FRENCH BEAN SALAD

The combination of red and green in Tomato and French Bean Salad makes it colourful as well as delicious. This salad is very good with cold meats and has the advantage that it may be prepared well in advance of serving. It is ideal for a picnic.

6-8 servings

Metric/Imperial

500g (1lb) tomatoes, very thinly sliced
500g (1lb) French beans, trimmed, cooked and drained
DRESSING
3 tablespoons wine vinegar
6 tablespoons olive oil
$\frac{1}{4}$ teaspoon salt
$\frac{1}{4}$ teaspoon black pepper
$\frac{1}{2}$ teaspoon prepared mustard
$\frac{1}{2}$ teaspoon sugar
1 garlic clove, crushed

American

1lb tomatoes, very thinly sliced
2 cups cooked green beans
DRESSING
3 tablespoons wine vinegar
6 tablespoons olive oil
¼ teaspoon salt
¼ teaspoon black pepper
½ teaspoon prepared mustard
½ teaspoon sugar
1 garlic clove, crushed

Place all the dressing ingredients in a screw-top jar and shake vigorously until well mixed.

Colourful Tomato and French Bean Salad is delicious served with cold meat and crusty bread. It is ideal for a picnic.

Place the tomatoes and beans in a large serving dish and pour over the dressing. Toss until the vegetables are thoroughly coated.

Chill the salad in the refrigerator before serving.

BEETROOT AND ONION SALAD

This salad makes a refreshing and tasty accompaniment to cold meats, chicken or fish.

4 servings

Metric/Imperial

6 medium-sized beetroots, cooked
2 tablespoons vinegar
5 tablespoons vegetable oil
2 cloves

1 teaspoon sugar
¼ teaspoon salt
¼ teaspoon black pepper
1 large onion, very thinly sliced and pushed out into rings

American

6 medium-sized beets, cooked
2 tablespoons cider vinegar
5 tablespoons vegetable oil
2 cloves
1 teaspoon sugar
¼ teaspoon salt
¼ teaspoon black pepper
1 large onion, very thinly sliced and separated into rings

Trim the beetroots [beets] and slip off the skins. Cut into thin slices and put in a salad bowl.

Mix the vinegar, oil, cloves, sugar, salt and pepper and pour over the

beetroots [beets]. Cover the bowl with aluminium foil or plastic wrap and place in the refrigerator to chill for 1 hour.

Mix in the onion rings, toss the salad and remove the cloves before serving.

RED CABBAGE SALAD

Red Cabbage Salad is crisp and crunchy and makes a good accompaniment to cold meat; or serve it as part of a vegetarian meal.

6 servings

Metric/Imperial

½ medium-sized red cabbage, washed and finely shredded
3 dessert apples, cored and chopped
8 spring onions, trimmed and finely chopped
2 medium-sized carrots, scraped and thinly sliced
50g (2oz) walnuts, chopped
DRESSING
1 tablespoon clear honey
5 tablespoons olive oil
juice of 1 lemon
2 tablespoons wine vinegar
1 teaspoon salt
½ teaspoon black pepper
½ teaspoon caraway seeds

American

½ medium-sized head of red cabbage, washed and finely shredded
3 apples, cored and chopped
8 scallions, trimmed and minced
2 medium-sized carrots, scraped and thinly sliced
⅓ cup walnuts, chopped
DRESSING
1 tablespoon honey
5 tablespoons olive oil
juice of 1 lemon
2 tablespoons wine vinegar
1 teaspoon salt
½ teaspoon black pepper
½ teaspoon caraway seeds

Place the cabbage, apples, spring onions [scallions], carrots and walnuts in a large salad bowl. Set aside.

To make the dressing, put all the ingredients into a screw-topped jar and shake to combine.

Pour the dressing over the salad and toss thoroughly.

Chill in the refrigerator for 30 minutes before serving.

SALADE NICOISE

Salade Niçoise (sah-lahd nee-swahz) is one of the great classic dishes of regional France and its succulent mixture of potatoes, French beans, tomatoes, anchovies and capers in a spicy French Dressing evokes the warmth of its city of origin. Tuna fish is often added to the salad, both in France and outside, although strictly speaking this is not traditional. With the addition of tuna fish, however, and accompanied by crusty bread and lots of well-chilled Provençal white wine, it makes a delightful summer meal. Served without tuna fish, it makes a perfect accompaniment for charcoal grilled [broiled] steaks or roast beef.

3-6 servings

Metric/Imperial

1 small lettuce, separated into leaves, washed and dried
6 medium-sized cold cooked potatoes, diced
300g (10oz) cold cooked French beans, cut into short lengths
6 tomatoes, peeled and quartered
6 tablespoons French Dressing
GARNISH
6 anchovy fillets, halved
10 black olives, stoned
2 tablespoons capers

American

1 small head of lettuce, separated into leaves, washed and dried
6 medium-sized cold cooked potatoes, diced
1¼ cups cold cooked green beans, diced
6 tomatoes, peeled and quartered
½ cup French Dressing
GARNISH
6 fillets of anchovies, halved
10 ripe olives, pitted
2 tablespoons capers

Arrange the lettuce leaves decoratively on a large serving plate.

In a large mixing bowl, combine the potatoes, beans and tomatoes.

Pour over the French dressing and carefully toss the vegetables until thoroughly coated.

Spoon the vegetables on to the lettuce leaves and garnish with the anchovy fillets, olives and capers.

POTATO SALAD

This simple Potato Salad with mayonnaise dressing may be served with cold meat or as one of a selection of salads. Use the green part of the leeks for this recipe and save the white parts for future use.

4 servings

Metric/Imperial

500g (1lb) potatoes, cooked, peeled and sliced
100ml (4 fl oz) mayonnaise
1 tablespoon lemon juice
1 tablespoon vegetable oil
½ teaspoon salt
½ teaspoon black pepper
2 tablespoons chopped fresh chives
4 tablespoons chopped leeks

American

1lb potatoes, cooked, peeled and sliced
½ cup mayonnaise
1 tablespoon lemon juice
1 tablespoon vegetable oil
½ teaspoon salt
½ teaspoon black pepper
2 tablespoons chopped fresh chives
4 tablespoons chopped leeks

Place three-quarters of the potatoes in a mixing bowl. Pour over the mayonnaise and sprinkle with the lemon juice, oil, salt, pepper and 1 tablespoon of chives. Carefully toss until the potatoes are thoroughly coated with the mayonnaise mixture.

Turn into a serving bowl. Arrange the remaining potato slices over the top. Sprinkle with the remaining chives and scatter the leeks around the edge of the bowl.

Cover and place in the refrigerator to chill for 30 minutes before serving.

Desserts

Desserts are an important feature in the menu of every family, especially where there are young children. Many men also appreciate rich, sweet desserts, whereas women tend to prefer lighter desserts (perhaps they are just more figure-conscious), but whatever the preferences of your family it can often tax the imagination to think up new ideas. Of course there are plenty of instant desserts on the market now, many of them excellent, but somehow nothing quite matches up to a home-made apple pie or rounds off a meal like a hot winter pudding.

If you make sweet and savoury pies regularly, it saves time and fuel to make a large batch of pastry and bake several empty shells at a time. Stored in an airtight tin, they will keep in good condition for several days and enable you to produce pastry dishes quickly.

Ice cream is always a favourite quick dessert. Serve with Chocolate Sauce or Fudge Sauce, or use one of the special recipes in this section for turning ice cream into something really special. And when there is no time to prepare a dessert of any kind, serve fresh fruit or cheese and bread. Fresh fruit is in any case one of the best ways of rounding off a meal after a heavy main course.

Because you will want to balance your menus (following a light main course with a substantial dessert and vice versa) the recipes in this section begin with light desserts such as fruit fools and ice cream dishes, followed by heavier desserts such as puddings and pies. The light desserts are particularly good for summer cooking, but on a cold winter's day try Lokshen Pudding, Marmalade Pudding or aromatic Coriander Fruit Crumble.

The best accompaniment to a good dessert is usually custard sauce, ice cream or cream, but for a change try serving sour cream, which complements very sweet dishes admirably with its refreshing tang. To make double [heavy] cream go further, whip it and then fold in a stiffly beaten egg white and a teaspoon of castor [fine] sugar.

MIXED ICE

Mixed Ice consists of home-made raspberry and apricot ice cream piped with whipped cream. Decorate if wished with reserved slices of apricot and whole raspberries.

4-6 servings

Metric/Imperial

300ml (½ pint) double cream
3 tablespoons apricot purée, made from well drained canned apricots
4 tablespoons icing sugar
3 tablespoons raspberry purée, made from frozen or fresh raspberries
100g (4oz) macaroons
75ml (3 fl oz) double cream, stiffly beaten

American

1¼ cups heavy cream
3 tablespoons apricot purée, made from well drained canned apricots
4 tablespoons confectioner's sugar
3 tablespoons raspberry purée, made from frozen or fresh raspberries
macaroons or lady fingers to line the bowls
½ cup whipping cream, stiffly whipped

Whip half the cream until it begins to stiffen. Add the apricot purée and whip together until thick. Stir in half the sugar. Pour into a suitable container and freeze.

Whip the rest of the cream until it begins to stiffen, add the raspberry purée and whip them together until thick. Stir in the rest of the sugar. Pour into a suitable container and freeze.

Line glass bowls with the macaroons. Place spoonfuls of the ice cream into the bowls. Pipe with the cream.

Ice cream is the perfect summer dessert and it can be served in so many different ways. Try Coffee Ice (vanilla ice cream with coffee, cream and chocolate), Almond Ice (a mixture of almond praline and vanilla ice cream), Mixed Ice (home-made raspberry and apricot ice cream with cream), or Vanilla Ice with Hot Sauce.

ALMOND ICE

Almond Ice is an exciting way to turn vanilla ice cream into a really special treat.

4-6 servings

Metric/Imperial

150g (5oz) unpeeled almonds
150g (5oz) castor sugar
1 family-sized block of ice cream

American

1¼ cups unblanched whole almonds
⅝ cup fine sugar
1 quart vanilla ice cream

To make the almond praline, place the nuts and sugar in a heavy-based saucepan. Heat gently, stirring with a metal spoon when the sugar has melted and is beginning to turn to caramel. Continue to stir until the almonds are toasted on all sides. Turn the mixture on to an oiled tin or plate, and leave it to cool.

When the praline has set crush it in to pieces with a rolling pin, and pass it through a coarse mill or a grater.

Place the ice cream in a bowl and gently break it up with a fork. Fold in the praline, reserving a few tablespoons to decorate the top of the ice cream.

Pack the ice cream into a plastic container, cover with waxed or greaseproof paper and return to the frozen food storage compartment of the refrigerator.

To serve, scoop the ice cream into individual glasses and sprinkle with the remainder of the praline.

BANANA ICE CREAM

This is a light-textured banana ice cream which makes a refreshing end to a rich meal. It is extremely quick and easy to make.

6 servings

Metric/Imperial

3 bananas, peeled and sliced
150ml (5 fl oz) sour cream
2 teaspoons lemon juice
1 teaspoon sugar
3 egg whites, stiffly whipped

American

3 bananas, peeled and sliced
⅝ cup sour cream
2 teaspoons lemon juice
1 teaspoon sugar
3 egg whites, stiffly beaten

Place the bananas, sour cream, lemon juice and sugar in a strainer and set over a large bowl and, with the back of a wooden spoon, rub the ingredients through to form a purée. Alternatively, place all the ingredients, except the egg whites, in the jar of an electric blender and blend them until they form a purée.

Using a metal spoon, fold in the egg whites. Spoon the mixture into a freezer tray and place it in the frozen food storage compartment of the refrigerator for 2 hours.

Remove the ice cream from the refrigerator and beat it vigorously with a fork. Return it to the frozen food compartment for 30 minutes or until set.

COFFEE ICE

This ice cream dessert with coffee, cream and flaked chocolate will win you plenty of compliments.

4-6 servings

Metric/Imperial

750ml (1¼ pints) strong black coffee
150ml (5 fl oz) double cream
1 tablespoon castor sugar
1 family block vanilla ice cream
flaked chocolate

American

3 cups strong black coffee
⅝ cup heavy cream
1 tablespoon fine sugar
1 quart vanilla ice cream
flaked semi-sweet chocolate

Make the coffee and chill it well in the refrigerator. Beat the cream until it is stiff and sweeten it with the sugar.

Half fill four tall glasses with the chilled coffee. Add cubes of vanilla ice cream and crown with a whirl of the whipped cream and flakes of chocolate.

VANILLA ICE WITH HOT SAUCE

This is a spectacular way to serve ice cream. It is good enough for a dinner party, and children especially will love it.

4-6 servings

Metric/Imperial

4-6 canned pear halves
175g (6oz) castor sugar
50g (2oz) walnut halves
1 family block of vanilla ice cream
SAUCE
75g (3oz) cocoa powder
75g (3oz) soft brown sugar
75g (3oz) castor sugar
1 teaspoon coffee essence
2 tablespoons butter
300ml ($\frac{1}{2}$ pint) milk

American

4-6 canned pear halves
$\frac{3}{4}$ cup fine sugar
$\frac{1}{2}$ cup halved walnuts
1 quart vanilla ice cream
SAUCE
$\frac{3}{4}$ cup cocoa
$\frac{1}{2}$ cup soft brown sugar
$\frac{3}{8}$ cup fine sugar
1 teaspoon coffee extract
2 tablespoons butter
$1\frac{1}{4}$ cup milk

Drain the pears very well. Put the sugar in a small heavy pan, and melt it, stirring all the time. Do not let it brown. Spear a walnut with a thin skewer and dip it into the melted sugar. Leave it to cool on a plate. Repeat this process with all the walnuts.

Place all the sauce ingredients in a pan. Stir them over a very low heat, until the sugar has dissolved. Bring to the boil slowly. Boil for a few minutes, until it coats the back of the spoon.

Divide the ice cream between individual dishes and place the pear halves on top. Garnish with the nuts and pour over the chocolate sauce.

HOME MADE NATURAL YOGURT

Making yogurt at home is quite simple, but it often has a thin consistency. The addition of dried skimmed milk powder gives a closer curd which is preferable for most desserts. Two methods are given here: Method 1 uses commercial live yogurt and Method 2 uses yogurt culture, which is the most common American method.

Makes 600ml (1 pint) ($2\frac{1}{2}$ cups)

Metric/Imperial

600ml (1 pint) milk
3 tablespoons dried skimmed milk powder (not instant granules)
1 tablespoon commercial live yogurt

American

$2\frac{1}{2}$ cups milk
3 tablespoons dried skim milk powder
1 package yogurt culture

Method 1
Bring the milk to the boil, lower heat and simmer for 5 minutes. Remove to a bowl and cool to blood heat. (If the milk is too warm, the yogurt will separate.) The bowl may be placed in iced water to speed up cooling.

Sprinkle the skimmed milk powder on to the milk and mix it in with a fork. Stir in the live yogurt.

Turn the mixture into a wide-mouthed vacuum jar which has been rinsed out with warm water, close and leave for 12 hours or overnight. Turn out and refrigerate until needed.

Method 2
Heat the milk to 82°C (180°F) and then cool it down to 43°C (110°F).

Sprinkle the skim milk powder onto the milk and stir in with a fork. Stir in the yogurt culture.

Gently pour into the vacuum jar, cover and leave for 7 to 8 hours. Put in the refrigerator when custard-like. It will keep for about 6 days.

YOGURT AND ORANGE WHIP

This refreshing and tangy summer dessert can be made with any fruit. But you do need a blender to make it successfully.

4 servings

Metric/Imperial

8 medium-sized oranges
2 tablespoons honey
600ml (1 pint) yogurt
4 tablespoons chopped walnuts, almonds or hazelnuts

American

8 medium-sized oranges
2 tablespoons honey
$2\frac{1}{2}$ cups natural yogurt
4 tablespoons chopped walnuts, almonds or filberts

Peel the oranges, removing as much of the white pith as possible. Reserve about 2 teaspoons of the orange rind and chop it finely. Set aside.

Chop the orange flesh into small pieces with a serrated-edge knife, and place them in a blender. Add the honey and yogurt and blend at high speed for about 20 seconds, or until the ingredients are well combined. Pour the orange mixture into four individual glass serving dishes. Place them in the refrigerator and chill for at least 2 hours.

Just before serving, sprinkle the tops with the nuts and reserved orange rind.

INSTANT YOGURT PUDDING

This marvellously quick and easy-to-prepare dessert is both delicious and nourishing. It may be served hot or chilled.

4 servings

Metric/Imperial

3 bananas, thinly sliced
3 large oranges, peeled, pith removed, separated into segments
600ml (1 pint) yogurt
4 tablespoons brown sugar

American

3 bananas, thinly sliced
3 large oranges, peeled, membrane and white skin removed, separated into sections
$2\frac{1}{2}$ cups yogurt
4 tablespoons brown sugar

Preheat the grill [broiler] to high.

Place the bananas and oranges in a medium-sized flameproof dish. Pour over the yogurt and mix well.

Sprinkle over the sugar and place the dish under the grill [broiler]. Cook for 3 to 4 minutes or until the sugar caramelizes.

FRUIT SALAD

A salad of fresh fruit is a wonderful dessert and so easy to make. The recipe given below is a basic one and almost any fruit in season may be used or added to those we suggest. A tablespoon or two of liqueur may also be added – brandy or Cointreau are particularly excellent in fruit salad – and the salad may be served with cream.

4 servings

Metric/Imperial

50g (2oz) sugar
175ml (6 fl oz) water
1½ tablespoons lemon juice
1 large apple, peeled, cored and chopped
1 large pear, peeled, cored and chopped
1 large orange, peeled, white pith removed, chopped
1 large peach, peeled, stoned and chopped
1 banana, sliced crosswise
¼ small honeydew melon, peeled, seeded and chopped

American

¼ cup sugar
¾ cup water
1½ tablespoons lemon juice
1 large apple, peeled, cored and sliced
1 large pear, peeled, cored and sliced
1 large orange, peeled, membrane and white skin removed, sliced
1 large peach, peeled, pitted and sliced
1 banana, sliced crosswise
¼ small honeydew melon, peeled, seeded and sliced

Dissolve the sugar in the water and lemon juice over low heat stirring constantly. Increase the heat to moderately high and boil the syrup for 2 to 3

Add Cointreau to Fruit Salad for a particularly delicious dessert.

minutes. Remove from the heat and allow to cool.

Put the syrup in a serving bowl and add the fruit as you cut them. Stir them together with a silver or stainless steel fork. Put in the refrigerator to chill.

FRUIT FOOL

A fruit fool is one of the simplest and most delicious of all summer desserts. The two ingredients are simply fruit and cream. Custard may be substituted for the cream but the result is not nearly so good. Strawberries, gooseberries, raspberries, blackcurrants and apricots make the best fools—and of these, gooseberries, blackcurrants and apricots should be poached in a little water first until they are tender. Drain the fruit as the purée should be thick.

4 servings

Metric/Imperial

1kg (2lb) fresh fruit, washed and prepared
300ml (10 fl oz) double cream, lightly whipped

American

about 7 cups fresh fruit, washed and prepared
1¼ cups whipping cream, lightly whipped

If necessary, poach the fruit first, then drain it. Mash the fruit through a strainer or purée it through a food mill into a large mixing bowl. Allow to cool.

Lightly fold the whipped cream into the purée. Place in the refrigerator and chill for at least 2 hours.

APPLES WITH MERINGUE TOPPING

This is a lovely dessert of apple purée topped with a light meringue mixture. Serve cold with vanilla ice cream.

4-6 servings

Metric/Imperial

25g (1oz) butter
1½kg (3lb) cooking apples, peeled, cored and sliced
finely grated rind of 1 lemon
½ teaspoon ground allspice
3 tablespoons apricot jam
TOPPING
50g (2oz) butter

50g (2oz) sugar
2 eggs, separated
juice and finely grated rind of
    1 small lemon
1 tablespoon flour
50g (2oz) fresh breadcrumbs
50g (2oz) castor sugar

American

2 tablespoons butter
3lb tart apples, peeled, cored and
    sliced
finely grated rind of 1 lemon
½ teaspoon ground allspice
3 tablespoons apricot jam
TOPPING
¼ cup butter
¼ cup sugar
2 eggs, yolks and whites, separated
juice and finely grated rind of
    1 small lemon
1 tablespoon flour
1 cup fresh breadcrumbs
¼ cup fine sugar

In a large saucepan, melt the butter over low heat. When the foam subsides add the apples, lemon rind and allspice. Cover and cook for 15 to 20 minutes or until the apples are very soft.

Remove the pan from the heat and beat in the jam with a wooden spoon, beating until the mixture becomes pulpy. Return the pan to the heat and cook, uncovered, for 3 to 5 minutes or until the mixture has thickened.

Preheat the oven to warm (170°C/ 325°F or Gas Mark 3). Lightly grease a 1½-litre (2½-pint) [1½-quart] baking dish.

Spoon in the apple mixture.

To make the topping, cream the butter and sugar together until light and fluffy. Add the egg yolks, lemon juice and rind, flour and breadcrumbs and mix well.

Beat the egg whites until they form soft peaks. Gradually beat in the castor sugar and continue beating until the egg whites form stiff peaks.

With a metal spoon, fold the egg white mixture into the breadcrumb mixture, then spoon it over the apples. Sprinkle with a little extra castor sugar and bake for 35 to 40 minutes or until the top is golden brown.

Cool, then chill in the refrigerator for at least 2 hours before serving.

DATE AND BANANA DESSERT

A deliciously light and easy-to-prepare dessert, Date and Banana Dessert will please the whole family.

6 servings

Metric/Imperial

8 ripe bananas
500g (1lb) dates, stoned
4 satsumas or 2 oranges, peeled
300ml (10 fl oz) single cream
25g (1oz) plain chocolate, grated

American

8 ripe bananas
1lb dates, pitted
4 satsuma oranges or 2 navel oranges,
    peeled
1¼ cups light cream
1oz semi-sweet chocolate, grated

Thinly slice the bananas, crosswise. Slice the dates in half and separate the satsumas or oranges into sections.

Arrange about one-half of the banana slices on the bottom of a medium-sized serving dish and pour 3 tablespoons of cream on the top. Cover with about one-half of the dates and pour a further 3 tablespoons of cream on top. Arrange a layer of half of the satsuma or orange sections on top, then add 3 tablespoons of cream. Continue alternating layers of fruit and cream until all the ingredients have been added ending with a layer of cream.

Chill the mixture in the refrigerator for at least 1 hour, or until it is quite cold.

Just before serving sprinkle the grated chocolate on top.

ORANGES WITH CINNAMON

An incredibly simple dessert to make, Oranges with Cinnamon requires no cooking and very little preparation. It is one of the very nicest ways to end a meal. Serve well chilled.

4 servings

Metric/Imperial

4 large oranges, peeled and white pith
    removed
2 teaspoons sugar
½ teaspoon ground cinnamon
2 tablespoons orange liqueur

American

4 large oranges, peeled, membrane
    and white skin removed
2 teaspoons sugar
½ teaspoon ground cinnamon
2 tablespoons orange liqueur

Using a very sharp knife, slice the oranges very thinly, crosswise. It is best to do this over a bowl so that you do not lose any juice.

Place the orange slices and any juice in a medium-sized serving dish or in individual dessert dishes. Sprinkle over the sugar, cinnamon and orange-flavoured liqueur. Place the dish or dishes in the refrigerator and chill for 30 minutes before serving.

QUICK PEACH DESSERT

Quick Peach Dessert makes a wonderfully light ending for a summer lunch or dinner.

4 servings

Metric/Imperial

4 fresh peaches, peeled, halved and
    stoned
3 tablespoons double cream
1 tablespoon castor sugar
¼ teaspoon vanilla essence
25g (1oz) dark cooking chocolate,
    finely grated
4 tablespoons slivered almonds

American

4 fresh peaches, peeled, halved and
    pitted
3 tablespoons heavy cream
1 tablespoon fine sugar
¼ teaspoon vanilla
1oz semi-sweet chocolate, finely grated
4 tablespoons slivered almonds

Arrange two peach halves, rounded sides down, in each of 4 individual dessert dishes.

Whisk the cream, sugar and vanilla

Date and Banana Dessert, topped with grated chocolate, makes a mouth-watering end to a meal.

essence together until the mixture forms soft peaks. Gently fold in half the chocolate and half the almonds. Place a little of the mixture in each peach half.

Sprinkle each dish with equal amounts of the remaining grated chocolate and almonds. Chill in the refrigerator for at least 1 hour before serving.

PEACH DESSERT

Peach Dessert is marvellously easy to prepare and delicious to eat.

3 servings

Metric/Imperial
369g (14oz) can peach halves, drained
1 tablespoon soft brown sugar
150ml (5 fl oz) yogurt
1 tablespoon butter
4 tablespoons medium oatmeal
1 tablespoon clear honey

American
1 x 14oz can peach halves, drained
1 tablespoon soft brown sugar
$\frac{5}{8}$ cup yogurt
1 tablespoon butter
4 tablespoons oatmeal
1 tablespoon honey

Put the peach halves into a medium-sized mixing bowl and mash them to a smooth purée. Beat in the brown sugar, then the yogurt, beating until the mixture is well blended.

Place in the refrigerator to chill for 15 minutes.

Meanwhile, in a small saucepan, melt the butter over moderate heat. When the foam subsides add the oatmeal and fry, stirring constantly, for 3 minutes or until lightly toasted. Stir in the honey and remove the pan from the heat. Set the mixture aside until the oatmeal has cooled.

Remove the bowl from the refrigerator and spoon the oatmeal mixture on top.

HONEY-BAKED PEARS

A smooth dessert, Honey-Baked Pears are equally good hot or cold. Serve them with lots of whipped cream.

4 servings

179

Metric/Imperial

25g (1oz) butter

4 large firm pears, peeled, halved and cored

3 tablespoons lemon juice

3 tablespoons brandy (optional)

100ml (4 fl oz) clear honey

½ teaspoon ground cinnamon

¼ teaspoon grated nutmeg

American

2 tablespoons butter

4 large firm pears, peeled, halved and cored

3 tablespoons lemon juice

3 tablespoons brandy (optional)

½ cup honey

½ teaspoon ground cinnamon

¼ teaspoon grated nutmeg

Preheat the oven to moderate (180°C/350°F or Gas Mark 4).

Grease a medium-sized baking dish. Arrange the pear halves in the dish, cut sides down.

Warm the lemon juice, brandy, if using, and honey together over low heat, stirring until it is hot and smooth.

Stir in the cinnamon and nutmeg and pour over the pears. Cut the butter into small pieces and dot them over the mixture. Place the dish in the oven and bake for 30 to 35 minutes or until the pears are tender but still firm.

SUMMER PUDDING

This traditional British pudding must be made the day before it is required. Summer Pudding is also good made with blackberries or blackcurrants.

4-6 servings

Metric/Imperial

1kg (2lb) raspberries, hulled

100g (4oz) castor sugar

100ml (4 fl oz) milk

8 slices stale white bread, crusts removed

American

7 cups raspberries, hulled

½ cup fine sugar

½ cup milk

8 slices stale white bread, crusts removed

Grease a deep pie dish or pudding basin.

Place the raspberries in a large mixing bowl and sprinkle over the sugar. Set aside. Using a teaspoon, sprinkle a little of the milk over each slice of bread to moisten it.

Line the dish or basin with two-thirds of the bread slices, overlapping the edges slightly.

Pour in the raspberries and arrange the remaining bread slices on top to cover them completely.

Soft white bread enclosing fresh juicy raspberries, Summer Pudding is a wonderful dessert.

Compôte of Dried Fruits in red wine makes an attractive dessert.

Place a sheet of greaseproof or waxed paper on top of the dish or basin and put a plate, slightly smaller in diameter than the dish or basin, on top. Place a heavy weight on the plate and put the pudding in the refrigerator to chill for at least 8 hours or overnight.

To unmould, invert a serving plate over the top of the dish or basin and, holding the two firmly together, reverse them giving a sharp shake. The pudding should slide out easily.

COMPOTE OF DRIED FRUITS

This economical and unusual mixture of dried fruits flavoured with cinnamon is a delightful dessert. Serve with custard or cream.

6-8 servings

Metric/Imperial

750g (1½lb) mixed dried fruits (apples, apricots, sultanas, raisins, prunes, etc.)
425ml (15 fl oz) water
150ml (5 fl oz) red wine
225g (8oz) sugar
½ teaspoon ground cinnamon
rind of 1 lemon, cut into thin strips

American

4 cups mixed dried fruits (apples, apricots, raisins, prunes, etc.)
1¾ cups water
⅝ cup red wine
1 cup sugar
½ teaspoon ground cinnamon
rind of 1 lemon, cut into thin strips

Cover the fruit with cold water and soak for at least 12 hours or overnight.

In a large saucepan, bring the water, red wine, sugar, cinnamon and lemon rind to the boil over moderate heat, stirring until the sugar has dissolved. Add the drained fruit, reduce the heat and simmer for 10 to 15 minutes or until the fruit is tender. Remove the fruit and arrange in a deep serving dish. Cover with aluminium foil to keep the fruit warm.

Return the pan to high heat and boil the cooking liquid for about 30 minutes, or until it thickens a little and has reduced somewhat in volume. Pour the syrup over the fruit in the serving dish and either serve immediately or chill in the refrigerator for at least 1 hour.

SYLLABUB

A delightful dish that can be made in a moment, Syllabub is a traditional English dessert. You can reduce the quantities of sherry and brandy for children, but this is the authentic way to make it. Serve either on its own in decorative glasses or with poached fruit – either way it's delicious.

4-6 servings

Metric/Imperial

50g (2oz) sugar
juice of 1 large lemon
rind and juice of ½ orange
6 tablespoons medium-dry sherry

An impressive-looking dessert, Baked Alaska is a sponge cake with ice cream and meringue.

2 tablespoons brandy
300ml (10 fl oz) double cream, beaten until thick but not stiff

American

¼ cup sugar
juice of 1 large lemon
rind and juice of ½ orange
6 tablespoons medium-dry sherry
2 tablespoons brandy
1¼ cups heavy cream, beaten until thick but not stiff

Combine the sugar, lemon juice, orange rind and juice, sherry and brandy. Gradually pour the cream into the bowl, beating constantly with a fork until the ingredients are thoroughly combined.

Cover the bowl and chill in the refrigerator for at least 30 minutes or until ready to serve.

Pour the syllabub into chilled individual serving dishes or glasses.

BAKED ALASKA

An impressive dessert, Baked Alaska is sponge cake topped with ice cream and covered with meringue. It is not difficult to prepare but it does need very speedy, last-minute preparation before serving.

6 servings

Metric/Imperial

2 x 15cm (2 x 6in) Sponge cakes
225g (8oz) apricot jam
1.2 litres (2 pints) vanilla ice cream, softened
MERINGUE
6 egg whites
⅛ teaspoon salt
175g (6oz) castor sugar

American

2 x 6in Sponge cakes

¾ cup apricot jam
5 cups vanilla ice cream, softened
MERINGUE
6 egg whites
⅛ teaspoon salt
¾ cup fine sugar

Spread one cake with the apricot jam. Put the second cake on top. Trim off the corners to make an oval shape.

Put the ice cream on a sheet of aluminium foil and mould it gently to the size of the cake. Cover with foil and place in the frozen food storage compartment of the refrigerator to become hard.

Preheat the oven to very hot (230°C/450°F or Gas Mark 8).

Whip the egg whites and salt until stiff. Beating continuously, add the sugar a little at a time. Continue beating until the whites are stiff and glossy. (Do not overbeat or the whites will begin to collapse.)

Put the cake on a baking sheet. Remove the ice cream from the refrigerator, take off the foil and place the ice cream on top of the cake. Using a spatula, cover the outside of the cake and the ice cream with the meringue mixture, making sure there is no cake or ice cream showing. This must be done very quickly and the meringue must cover the ice cream and cake completely or the ice cream will melt.

Put the baking sheet in the centre of the oven and leave it for 3 to 4 minutes, until the meringue turns a pale golden colour. Serve at once.

BANANAS BAKED WITH CUSTARD

Bananas baked with bread and custard is a simple dessert that children love.

6 servings

Metric/Imperial

4 bananas
6 thin slices buttered bread
50g (2oz) raisins
600ml (1 pint) milk
2 whole eggs plus 2 yolks
2 tablespoons soft brown sugar
½ teaspoon grated nutmeg

American

4 bananas
6 thin slices buttered bread
⅓ cup raisins
2½ cups milk
2 whole eggs plus 2 yolks
2 tablespoons soft brown sugar
½ teaspoon grated nutmeg

Grease a medium-sized baking dish. Peel the bananas and slice into rounds. Halve the bread slices. Put layers of bread, bananas and raisins in the baking dish, ending with a layer of bread.

Heat the milk over moderate heat. Beat the eggs, egg yolks and sugar together. Slowly pour in the milk, stirring continuously. Pour the milk-egg mixture into the baking dish and leave to stand for 30 minutes.

Preheat the oven to fairly hot (190°C/375°F or Gas Mark 5).

Dust the top of the pudding with the nutmeg and bake for 30 minutes.

CREME CARAMEL

Crème Caramel is an exquisitely light dessert. It may be made in advance and chilled in the refrigerator.

6 servings

Metric/Imperial

CARAMEL
100g (4oz) sugar
5 tablespoons water
CRÈME
600ml (1 pint) milk
75g (3oz) sugar
1 teaspoon vanilla essence
2 whole eggs, plus 2 egg yolks

American

CARAMEL
½ cup sugar
5 tablespoons water
CRÈME
2½ cups milk
6 tablespoons sugar
1 teaspoon vanilla
2 whole eggs, plus 2 egg yolks

To make the caramel, in a heavy, medium-sized saucepan, heat the sugar and water over low heat, stirring until the sugar dissolves completely. Increase the heat to moderately high and allow the syrup to come to the boil. Cook for 3 to 4 minutes without stirring, until it turns a light nut-brown colour.

Be careful not to overcook the syrup or it will darken too much and become bitter. Immediately the caramel has reached the right colour, remove the pan from the heat and pour it into 6 individual ramekins or 1 heatproof dish.

Bring the milk and sugar to the boil over moderate heat, stirring occasionally to dissolve the sugar. Set aside to cool.

Beat the eggs and the egg yolks until they thicken and become pale yellow.

Beating continuously, gradually add the milk to the beaten eggs, pouring it through a strainer. Stir in the vanilla essence and pour the mixture into a jug.

Preheat the oven to warm (170°C/325°F or Gas Mark 3).

Pour the milk mixture through a very fine strainer into the 6 ramekins or the dish. Spoon off any froth.

Place the dishes in a deep baking tin and add enough boiling water to reach half way up the sides.

Bake in the lower part of the oven for 40 minutes or until the centre of the crème is firm when pressed.

Remove the dish from the water and allow to cool thoroughly. Chill in the refrigerator for 1 hour. Then run a knife around the edge of the ramekins or dish and place a serving plate on top. Reverse the crème caramel on to it and serve.

LEMON AND LIME CHIFFON

Lemon and Lime Chiffon is an easy to make and very refreshing summer dessert. If you cannot obtain fresh or canned lime juice, use diluted lime juice cordial.

4 servings

Metric/Imperial

4 eggs, separated
100g (4oz) castor sugar
1 teaspoon grated lemon rind
5 tablespoons lemon juice
15g (½oz) gelatine, dissolved in 2

tablespoons warm lime juice
3 tablespoons double cream, stiffly
    whipped

American

4 eggs, yolks and whites separated
½ cup fine sugar
1 teaspoon grated lemon rind
5 tablespoons lemon juice
2 tablespoons gelatin, dissolved in
    2 tablespoons warm lime juice
3 tablespoons whipped cream

Place a heatproof mixing bowl over a pan half filled with hot water, set over low heat. Place the egg yolks and sugar in the bowl and using a wire whisk or rotary beater, beat them until the mixture is frothy and thick enough to hold a ribbon trail on itself when the whisk is lifted from the bowl.

Remove from the heat and beat in the lemon rind and juice and the dissolved gelatine mixture.

When lukewarm beat in the cream.

Beat the egg whites until they form stiff peaks.

With a metal spoon, fold the egg whites into the lemon mixture. Pour into a chilled glass serving bowl or individual sundae glasses. Place in the refrigerator and chill for 3 hours or until set.

CHEESECAKE

Here is a basic recipe which will produce a moist and delicious plain cheesecake. You can use any type of topping or decoration. Try mandarin orange slices, or blueberries or blackcurrants with a jelly glaze, for a really super dessert

6-8 servings

Metric/Imperial

CRUMB CRUST BASE
40g (1½oz) plus 1 teaspoon butter
100g (4oz) digestive biscuits
1 tablespoon brown sugar
FILLING
350g (12oz) curd cheese
150ml (5 fl oz) soured cream
3 eggs, separated
juice and grated rind of 1 lemon

100g (4oz) castor sugar
1 tablespoon plain flour

American

CRUMB CRUST BASE
3 tablespoons plus 1 teaspoon butter
1¼ cup graham cracker crumbs
1 tablespoon brown sugar
FILLING
1½ cups curd or farmer's cheese
⅝ cup sour cream
3 eggs, separated
juice and grated rind of 1 lemon
½ cup fine sugar
1 tablespoon all-purpose flour

Grease a 20cm (8in) diameter flan dish with the teaspoon of butter. Preheat the oven to moderate (170°C/325°F or Gas Mark 3).

In a small saucepan melt the remaining butter over moderate heat and set aside. Crush the biscuits between two layers of paper with a rolling pin, then pour the biscuit crumbs and sugar into the melted butter and combine thoroughly. Press the mixture into the base of the flan dish.

In a large mixing bowl combine all the filling ingredients except the egg whites. Beat the egg whites until they stand in stiff peaks, and fold into the filling mixture with a metal spoon.

Pour the cheesecake filling over the base and place in the centre of the preheated oven. Bake for 45 minutes, or until the cheesecake is slightly risen. Do not overcook, as the cheesecake will become firmer when cooled, and the texture should be moist and slightly crumbly. Chill for at least two hours before serving.

JELLIED CHEESECAKE

This delicious lemon-flavoured cheesecake makes a superbly rich dessert for a dinner party. Decorate with whipped cream and crystallized lemon if liked.

6-8 servings

Metric/Imperial

100g (4oz) crushed digestive biscuits
40g (1½oz) butter, melted
15g (½oz) gelatine

4 tablespoons cold water
1 whole egg
2 egg yolks
100g (4oz) plus 2 tablespoons sugar
¼ teaspoon salt
3 tablespoons milk
juice and grated rind of 1 lemon
350g (12oz) cottage cheese
150ml (5 fl oz) double cream, beaten
    until thick but not stiff
2 egg whites

American

1 cup crushed graham crackers
3 tablespoons butter, melted
2 tablespoons gelatin
4 tablespoons cold water
1 whole egg
2 egg yolks
½ cup plus 2 tablespoons sugar
¼ teaspoon salt
3 tablespoons milk
juice and grated rind of 1 lemon
1½ cups cottage cheese
⅝ cup whipping cream, beaten until
    thick but not stiff
2 egg whites

Combine the crushed biscuits [crackers] and melted butter with a wooden spoon. Lightly press the crumb mixture into a 20cm (8in) spring-form pan, covering the bottom evenly.

In a small saucepan, dissolve the gelatine in the water over low heat. Set aside to cool.

Beat the whole egg, egg yolks, the main quantity of sugar, the salt and milk together with a wire whisk or rotary beater.

Pour into a saucepan, place over low heat and cook, stirring constantly, for 3 to 4 minutes or until the custard thickens. Do not let the custard boil or it will curdle.

Stir in the cooled gelatine and set aside to cool to room temperature.

Mix in the lemon juice and rind, cottage cheese and the remaining sugar. Fold in the cream.

Beat the egg whites until they form stiff peaks and, with a metal spoon, carefully fold into the cheese mixture.

Spoon the mixture into the crumb crust and place in the refrigerator. Leave the cheesecake to chill for at least 2 hours or until set.

Jellied Cheesecake is a delicious, delicately flavoured dessert.

STRAWBERRY CHEESECAKE

Creamy and refreshing, Strawberry Cheesecake may be served as a dessert or with tea or coffee.

---

6 servings

Metric/Imperial

50g (2oz) unsalted butter
500g (1lb) cream cheese
2 eggs, lightly beaten
3 tablespoons castor sugar
⅛ teaspoon vanilla essence
225g (8oz) crushed shortbread biscuits
225ml (8 fl oz) double cream, stiffly whipped
500g (1lb) strawberries, hulled and washed

American

¼ cup sweet butter
1lb cream cheese
2 eggs, lightly beaten

3 tablespoons fine sugar
⅛ teaspoon vanilla
2 cups crushed shortbread cookies
1 cup whipped cream
3⅓ cups strawberries, hulled and washed

Preheat the oven to moderate (180°C/350°F or Gas Mark 4).

Grease a 20cm (8in) loose-bottomed cake tin.

Mash the cream cheese until it is smooth. Mix in the eggs, 2 tablespoons of the castor sugar and the vanilla essence.

Using a wire whisk or rotary beater, beat the mixture together until the eggs are well blended and the mixture is smooth.

In a small saucepan, melt the butter over low heat. Stir in the crushed shortbread crumbs, thoroughly coating them with the butter.

Press the shortbread mixture into the bottom of the prepared cake tin. Spoon the cream cheese mixture on top and smooth it down.

Bake in the centre of the oven for

50 minutes to 1 hour or until the centre of the cake feels firm when pressed. Set the cake aside to cool completely.

To unmould run a sharp knife around the edge of the cake tin. Carefully remove the base of the tin.

Slide the cake off the base on to a flat serving plate. Chill in the refrigerator for 1 hour.

Spread the cream over the surface of the cake. Cover with the strawberries, pressing them lightly into the cream.

Sprinkle over the remaining tablespoon of sugar.

CHERRY FLAN

This delectable German cherry flan makes the ideal dessert for a Sunday or family lunch or dinner.

6-8 servings

Metric/Imperial

500g (1lb) canned stoned Morello cherries, drained, and 150ml (5 fl oz) of the juice reserved

Cherry Flan, a rich German flan flavoured with sour cream and cinnamon, may be served as a dessert or with coffee.

1 tablespoon arrowroot
1 x 23cm (1 x 9in) flan case, made with Shortcrust Pastry II, baked blind and cooled
2 small eggs
75g (3oz) castor sugar
100ml (4 fl oz) sour cream
¼ teaspoon ground cinnamon

American

1lb canned pitted Bing cherries, drained, and ⅝ cup of the juice reserved
1 tablespoon arrowroot
1 x 9in pie shell made with Shortcrust Pastry II, baked and cooled
2 small eggs
⅜ cup fine sugar
½ cup sour cream
¼ teaspoon ground cinnamon

Preheat the oven to fairly hot (190°C/375°F or Gas Mark 5).

Place the reserved can juice and the arrowroot in a small saucepan. Bring to the boil, stirring constantly; cook for 2 minutes or until thick and smooth.

Stir in the cherries and spoon the mixture into the flan case.

Place the eggs and sugar in a heat-proof mixing bowl. Set over a pan half-filled with hot water. Using a wire whisk or rotary beater, whisk the mixture until it is thick and will make a ribbon trail on itself.

Gently stir in the sour cream and cinnamon and pour over the cherries in the flan case.

Bake the flan in the centre of the oven for 30 minutes or until the topping is lightly browned. Allow to cool.

STRAWBERRY FLAN

Strawberry Flan makes a simple and very attractive summer dessert.

4-6 servings

Metric/Imperial

1 x 23cm (1 x 9in) flan case made with sponge

500g (1lb) strawberries, hulled, washed and halved
4 tablespoons redcurrant jelly
1 tablespoon water
1 teaspoon lemon juice
150ml (5 fl oz) double cream

American

1 x 9in single layer sponge cake
3⅓ cups strawberries, hulled, washed and halved
4 tablespoons redcurrant jelly
1 tablespoon water
1 teaspoon lemon juice
⅝ cup whipping cream

Place the flan case on a decorative serving dish and arrange the strawberry halves in circles over the bottom.

In a small saucepan, dissolve the red-currant jelly in the water over low heat. Cook, stirring, for 1 minute. Add the lemon juice, and stir well.

Pour the glaze over the strawberries and place the flan in the refrigerator. Leave for 30 minutes or until the glaze has set.

Beat the cream until it forms stiff peaks.

Spoon into a forcing bag fitted with

Strawberry Flan is a splendid summer dessert.

a star-shaped nozzle and pipe in decorative swirls over the top of the flan.

PEACH FLAN

Sweet and melting Peach Flan is best made when peaches are plentiful. Serve the flan with single [light] cream.

4-6 servings

Metric/Imperial

1 x 23cm (1 x 9in) flan case, made with Shortcrust Pastry I, baked blind
4 large peaches, peeled, stoned and sliced
TOPPING
2 tablespoons ground almonds
1 tablespoon chopped almonds
1 tablespoon chopped walnuts
3 tablespoons soft brown sugar
1 teaspoon grated orange rind
1 tablespoon butter

American

1 x 9in pie shell, made with Shortcrust Pastry I, baked
4 large peaches, peeled, pitted and sliced
TOPPING
2 tablespoons ground almonds
1 tablespoon slivered almonds
1 tablespoon chopped walnuts
3 tablespoons soft brown sugar
1 teaspoon grated orange rind
1 tablespoon butter

Place the cooled flan case on a flame-proof serving dish and arrange the peach slices in it.

Preheat the grill [broiler] to high.

To make the topping, combine the ground and chopped almonds, the walnuts, sugar and orange rind. Sprinkle the topping over the peach slices and dot the top with the butter.

Place the dish under the grill [broiler] and cook for 4 minutes or until the topping is crisp and bubbling.

PRUNE AND APPLE MERINGUE FLAN

A delicious combination of prunes, apples and sweet meringue makes this pie an ideal dessert.

6-8 servings

Metric/Imperial

1 x 23cm (1 x 9in) flan case, made with Shortcrust Pastry I, unbaked
FILLING
175g (6oz) prunes, soaked overnight, drained, stoned and halved
250g (8oz) cooking apples, weighed after peeling, coring and slicing
1 teaspoon lemon juice
50g (2oz) sultanas or seedless raisins
½ teaspoon ground cinnamon
2 tablespoons sugar
MERINGUE
3 egg whites
175g (6oz) castor sugar

American

1 x 9in pie shell, made with Shortcrust Pastry I, unbaked
FILLING
¾ cup prunes, soaked overnight, drained, pitted and halved
½lb tart apples, weighed after paring, coring and slicing
1 teaspoon lemon juice
⅓ cup golden or seedless raisins
½ teaspoon ground cinnamon
2 tablespoons sugar
MERINGUE
3 egg whites
¾ cup fine sugar

Preheat the oven to fairly hot (200°C/400°F or Gas Mark 6). Place the flan case on a baking sheet.

Combine the prunes, apples, lemon juice, sultanas, cinnamon and 1 tablespoon of the sugar. Transfer the mixture to the flan case, smoothing it out evenly. Sprinkle over the remaining sugar. Place in the centre of the oven and bake for 15 minutes.

Meanwhile beat the egg whites until they form stiff peaks. Beat in 1 tablespoon of the castor sugar and continue beating until the meringue is stiff and glossy With a metal spoon, fold in the remaining sugar.

Prune and Apple Meringue Flan makes a satisfying dessert.

Remove the baking sheet from the oven and reduce the temperature to moderate (180°C/350°F or Gas Mark 4).

Spoon the meringue over the filling to cover it completely. Pull the meringue, using the back of the spoon, into decorative peaks.

Return the flan to the oven and continue baking for 20 to 25 minutes or until the meringue has set and is golden brown.

MOLASSES CRUMB PIE

Molasses and soda combine to make this sweet but very light pie. Serve in small slices as a dessert with sour cream or as a snack for children.

6-8 servings

Metric/Imperial

1 x 23cm (1 x 9in) flan case, made from Shortcrust Pastry II, baked blind and cooled
100g (4oz) plain flour
½ teaspoon salt

combined. Pour the mixture into the prepared flan case. Spoon the topping over the top.

Bake in the centre of the oven for 15 to 20 minutes or until the topping is light and golden brown.

LEMON MERINGUE PIE

The secret of a good Lemon Meringue Pie is the contrast between the tangy lemon flavour of the filling and the sweetness of the meringue topping – so don't oversweeten the filling. The amount of sugar given in this recipe is just right for good sized juicy lemons.

4-6 servings

Metric/Imperial

1 x 23cm (1 x 9in) flan case, made from
  Shortcrust Pastry II, baked blind
FILLING
juice and finely grated rind of 2 lemons
300ml (10 fl oz) water
50g (2oz) castor sugar
3 tablespoons arrowroot, dissolved in
  2 tablespoons water
4 egg yolks, lightly beaten
MERINGUE
4 egg whites
175g (6oz) plus 1 tablespoon castor
  sugar

American

1 x 9in pie shell, made from Shortcrust
  Pastry II, baked and cooled
FILLING
juice and finely grated rind of 2 lemons
1¼ cups water
¼ cup fine sugar
3 tablespoons arrowroot, dissolved in
  2 tablespoons water
4 egg yolks, lightly beaten
MERINGUE
4 egg whites
¾ cup plus 1 tablespoon fine sugar

Preheat the oven to moderate (180°C/ 350°F or Gas Mark 4).

To make the filling, combine the lemon juice, rind, water and sugar in a saucepan, set over moderate heat and cook, stirring frequently, until the sugar has dissolved. Stir in the dissolved arrowroot and continue cooking, stirring

---

50g (2oz) butter
25g (1oz) cooking fat
50g (2oz) soft brown sugar
1 teaspoon bicarbonate of soda
3 tablespoons hot water
3 tablespoons black treacle

American

1 x 9in pie shell, made from Shortcrust
  Pastry II, baked and cooled
1 cup all-purpose flour
½ teaspoon salt
¼ cup butter
2 tablespoons lard
⅓ cup soft brown sugar

1 teaspoon baking soda
¼ cup hot water
¼ cup molasses

Preheat the oven to moderate (180°C/ 350°F or Gas Mark 4). Place the flan case on a baking sheet.

Sift the flour and salt into a mixing bowl. Add the butter and fat, cut into small pieces and rub into the flour until the mixture resembles coarse bread-crumbs. Stir in the sugar.

In another mixing bowl, dissolve the soda in the hot water. Add the molasses or black treacle and stir well until

frequently for 5 minutes or until thick.

Allow to cool to lukewarm, then beat in the egg yolks.

Spoon the lemon and egg yolk mixture into the pastry case, smoothing it down. Bake for 5 minutes or until the filling has set.

To make the meringue, beat the egg whites until frothy. Gradually beat in the sugar and continue beating until the mixture forms stiff peaks.

Pile the meringue on top of the lemon filling to cover it completely.

Bake in the centre of the oven for 20 to 25 minutes or until the meringue has set and is golden brown.

BAKEWELL TART

A traditional English dessert and a great favourite with children, Bakewell Tart is both easy to make and inexpensive.

---

4 servings

Metric/Imperial

100g (4oz) Shortcrust Pastry I
2 tablespoons raspberry jam
2 eggs, separated
75g (3oz) fresh breadcrumbs
75g (3oz) sugar
4 tablespoons melted butter
100g (4oz) ground almonds
grated rind and juice of 1 lemon
a pinch of salt

American

½ recipe Shortcrust Pastry I
2 tablespoons raspberry jam
2 eggs, yolks and whites separated
1½ cups fresh breadcrumbs
⅜ cup sugar
4 tablespoons melted butter
⅔ cup ground almonds
grated rind and juice of 1 lemon
a pinch of salt

Preheat the oven to hot (220°C/425°F or Gas Mark 7).

On a lightly floured board, roll out the pastry and line a 20cm (8in) flan tin. Spread a layer of jam on the bottom of the tart. Put the egg yolks in a medium-sized mixing bowl and beat well. Add the breadcrumbs, sugar, melted butter, almonds, grated lemon

rind and lemon juice and mix well.

Beat the egg whites with a pinch of salt until stiff. Fold into the egg-yolk mixture. Spread over the jam. Bake in the centre of the oven for 30 minutes or until the filling is firm and lightly browned.

TREACLE TART

This is another economical and popular favourite – and a good way to use up yesterday's loaf of bread.

---

6 servings

Metric/Imperial

---

1 x 20cm (1 x 8in) flan case, made with
    Shortcrust Pastry I, baked blind
    and cooled
grated rind of a small lemon
2 teaspoons lemon juice
175ml (6 fl oz) golden syrup
50g (2oz) fresh white breadcrumbs

American

---

1 x 8in tart shell, made with Shortcrust
    Pastry I, baked and cooled
grated rind of a small lemon
2 teaspoons lemon juice
¾ cup light corn syrup
¾ cup fresh white breadcrumbs

Heat the oven to moderate (190°C/375°F or Gas Mark 5). Place the flan case on a baking sheet.

Grate the lemon zest into a bowl and place over a saucepan of hot water. Add the lemon juice and golden [light corn] syrup and mix together thoroughly. Stir in the breadcrumbs.

Spoon the mixture into the pastry shell.

Bake in the centre of the oven for 20 minutes or until golden brown.

APPLE AMBER

A delicious and good-looking dessert, Apple Amber can be served hot or cold.

---

4 servings

Metric/Imperial

100g (4oz) Shortcrust Pastry I

500g (1lb) cooking apples
50g (2oz) butter
sugar
grated rind of 1 lemon
juice of 1 lemon
2 egg yolks, lightly beaten
MERINGUE
2 egg whites
75g (3oz) castor sugar

American

½ recipe Shortcrust Pastry I
1lb tart apples
¼ cup butter
sugar
grated rind of 1 lemon
juice of 1 lemon
2 egg yolks, lightly beaten
MERINGUE
2 egg whites
⅜ cup fine sugar

Line a 20cm (8in) pie dish with the pastry. Preheat oven to very hot (230°C/450°F or Gas Mark 8).

For the filling, peel, core and slice the apples. Put 2 tablespoons of cold water into a saucepan, add the apples and the butter and cook until tender. Add sugar to taste.

Rub the mixture through a sieve or beat until smooth. Add the lemon rind, lemon juice and egg yolks, mix together and pour into pastry lining the pie dish. Bake for about 30 minutes or until the pastry is browned and the filling set. Reset the oven temperature to very cool (130°C/250°F or Gas Mark ½).

For the meringue, whisk the egg whites until very stiff. Fold in two-thirds of the sugar. Pile the meringue lightly on top of the apple filling. Dredge with the remaining sugar. Bake for 30 to 40 minutes or until crisp on top.

AMERICAN APPLE PIE

In American Apple Pie the apples are cut in rather thick slices, and the filling is spiced with cinnamon, allspice and nutmeg and thickened with cornflour.

---

6 servings

Metric/Imperial

300g (10oz) Shortcrust Pastry I

An apple-filled pastry shell, Apple Amber is topped with meringue.

175g (6oz) sugar
1 teaspoon cinnamon
¼ teaspoon ground allspice
¼ teaspoon grated nutmeg
1 tablespoon cornflour
1kg (2lb) cooking apples, peeled, cored and thickly sliced
1 tablespoon lemon juice
25g (1oz) butter
a little milk

American

1½ recipes Shortcrust Pastry I
¾ cup sugar
1 teaspoon cinnamon
¼ teaspoon ground allspice
¼ teaspoon grated nutmeg
1 tablespoon cornstarch
2lb tart apples, peeled, cored and thickly sliced
1 tablespoon lemon juice
2 tablespoons butter
a little milk

Grease the bottom and sides of a 23cm

(9in) pie dish.

Divide the pastry in half. On a floured board roll out one half in a circle large enough to line the pie dish. Lay it over the pie dish and gently ease into place without pulling or stretching the pastry. Trim so that it is even with the outer rim.

Preheat oven to fairly hot (190°C/ 375°F or Gas Mark 5).

For the filling, blend the sugar, cinnamon, allspice, nutmeg and cornflour [cornstarch], in a large mixing bowl. Add the sliced apples and lemon juice and toss together thoroughly but gently.

Fill the pie shell with the apple mixture, piling it higher in the centre. Although it may seem quite high it will shrink when it bakes. Dot the top of the filling with butter.

For the top crust, roll out the remaining half of the pastry into a circle about 30cm (12in) across.

Lift it onto the filling. With scissors trim to within 6mm (¼in) of the dish. Tuck the overhang under the edge of the bottom crust all round and press down to seal the two and make a

crimped design.

Brush with milk and cut two small gashes in the top to allow the steam to escape.

Bake in the middle of the oven for 40 minutes or until golden brown.

DATE AND APPLE PIE

Serve this delicious pie with lots of whipped cream.

6 servings

Metric/Imperial

350g (12oz) Shortcrust Pastry I
750g (1½lb) cooking apples, peeled, cored and sliced
175g (6oz) dates, stoned and chopped
1 tablespoon lemon juice
½ teaspoon ground cinnamon
50g (2oz) sugar
2 tablespoons butter
a little milk

American

1½ recipes Shortcrust Pastry I
1½lb Jonathon or Winesap apples,

peeled, cored and sliced
1 cup dates, pitted and finely chopped
1 tablespoon lemon juice
½ teaspoon ground cinnamon
¼ cup sugar
2 tablespoons butter
a little milk

Combine the apples, dates, lemon juice cinnamon and sugar.

Preheat the oven to fairly hot (190°C/ 375°F or Gas Mark 5).

Lightly grease a 23cm (9in) pie dish with the remaining tablespoon of vegetable fat. Remove the dough from the refrigerator and divide it into two pieces – two-thirds and one-third. Return the smaller portion to the refrigerator. On a floured surface, roll out the larger piece into a circle about 35cm (14in) across. Lay it over the pie dish and gently ease into position without pulling or stretching. Trim off the excess dough so that it is even with the outer rim.

Fill the pie shell with the apple mixture, piling it higher in the centre. Dot the top with the butter.

Remove the remaining dough from the refrigerator and roll it out into a circle about 30cm (12in) across.

Gently drape it over the filling and with a pair of scissors, trim so that it is 6mm (¼in) larger all round than the dish. Tuck the overhang under the edge of the bottom crust all round and press down to seal the two crusts and make a crimped design.

Brush the top of the pie with milk and cut two small gashes in the centre to allow the steam to escape. Bake in the centre of the oven for 1 hour or until golden brown.

BANANA CREAM PIE

This American banana pie is made with short crust pastry and topped with meringue. It is inexpensive and easy to make and it looks and tastes good. Serve cold.

6 servings

Metric/Imperial

175g (6oz) Shortcrust Pastry I
2 ripe bananas, peeled and sliced
3 egg yolks
75g (3oz) castor sugar

Banana Cream Pie, made with short-crust pastry and topped with meringue, is a tempting dessert.

¼ teaspoon salt
2 tablespoons cornflour
1 tablespoon butter
450ml (16 fl oz) milk
1 teaspoon vanilla essence or ¼ teaspoon grated nutmeg
MERINGUE
3 egg whites
175g (6oz) castor sugar
2 tablespoons shredded almonds

American

1 recipe Shortcrust Pastry I
2 ripe bananas, peeled and sliced
3 egg yolks
⅜ cup fine sugar
¼ teaspoon salt
2 tablespoons cornstarch
1 tablespoon butter
2 cups milk
1 teaspoon vanilla or ¼ teaspoon grated nutmeg
MERINGUE
3 egg whites
¾ cup fine sugar

2 tablespoons shredded almonds

Preheat the oven to fairly hot (200°C/ 400°F or Gas Mark 6).

On a floured board, roll the pastry out and line a 23cm (9in) pie tin. Put in the refrigerator for 10 minutes.

Prick the bottom and sides of the pastry with a fork, line it with aluminium foil and weigh it down with dried beans or peas. Bake for 10 minutes. Remove the aluminium foil and bake for 5 minutes more or until golden.

Reset the oven to cool (150°C/ 300°F or Gas Mark 2).

To prepare the filling, beat the egg yolks in a mixing bowl. Gradually beat in the sugar, salt, cornflour [cornstarch] and butter.

Put the milk in a small saucepan and bring almost to boiling point. Pour slowly into the egg mixture, stirring continuously. Place the bowl in a pan of boiling water and cook and stir the custard until it thickens. Cool the custard and then add the vanilla essence or nutmeg.

Arrange the banana slices in the baked pie shell. Pour the custard over them.

Beat the egg whites until stiff. Beat in one tablespoon of sugar and then fold in the remainder. Pile the meringue on top of the custard and spread to cover the top completely.

Sprinkle with the shredded almonds and bake for 15 to 20 minutes, or until light browned.

PUMPKIN PIE

Pumpkin Pie is a super dessert with a lovely creamy filling. Although traditionally served at a Thanksgiving Day dinner in the United States after the turkey, it makes a delightful end to any meal.

6 servings

Metric/Imperial

1 x 23cm (1 x 9in) flan case, made with Shortcrust Pastry I, unbaked

FILLING

100g (4oz) brown sugar

$\frac{1}{8}$ teaspoon salt

$1\frac{1}{2}$ teaspoons ground cinnamon

$\frac{1}{2}$ teaspoon ground ginger

$\frac{1}{4}$ teaspoon ground cloves

682g (24oz) can puréed pumpkin

3 eggs, lightly beaten

300ml (10 fl oz) single cream

American

1 x 9in pie shell, made with Shortcrust Pastry I, unbaked

FILLING

$\frac{2}{3}$ cup brown sugar

$\frac{1}{8}$ teaspoon salt

$1\frac{1}{2}$ teaspoons ground cinnamon

$\frac{1}{2}$ teaspoon ground ginger

$\frac{1}{4}$ teaspoon ground cloves

$3\frac{1}{2}$ cups canned pumpkin

3 eggs, lightly beaten

$1\frac{1}{4}$ cups light cream

Place the flan case on a baking sheet. Preheat the oven to fairly hot (190°C/ 375°F or Gas Mark 5).

Combine the sugar, salt, cinnamon, ginger and cloves in a small bowl. Place the pumpkin purée in a large mixing bowl, add the eggs and mix well. Gradually stir in the sugar and spice mixture and the cream and beat well until smooth.

Pour the mixture into the flan case. Bake the pie for 45 to 50 minutes or until a knife inserted in the filling comes out clean.

American Pumpkin Pie is traditionally served on Thanksgiving Day.

ORANGE-FLAVOURED BANANA FRITTERS

Perfect for a warming dessert or snack, Orange-Flavoured Banana Fritters may be served sprinkled with sugar or on their own with whipped cream.

4-6 servings

Metric/Imperial

6 large bananas
225g (8oz) castor sugar
300ml (10 fl oz) Fritter Batter I
vegetable oil for deep frying
225ml (8 fl oz) fresh orange juice
2 tablespoons orange liqueur

American

6 large bananas
1 cup fine sugar
1¼ cups Fritter Batter I
vegetable oil for deep frying
1 cup fresh orange juice
2 tablespoons orange liqueur

Cut the bananas in half, lengthways, and then cut the pieces across in half.

Place one-quarter of the sugar in a saucer. Roll the banana pieces in it to coat them evenly, shaking off any excess.

Place the fritter batter in a small bowl. Fill a medium-sized deep frying-pan one-third full with the vegetable oil. Place the pan over moderate heat and heat the oil until a small cube of stale bread dropped in turns golden in 50 seconds.

Dip a few of the banana pieces in the fritter batter to coat them thoroughly and drop them carefully into the hot oil. Fry for 3 to 4 minutes or until deep golden brown.

Drain well on kitchen paper and transfer to a warmed serving dish to keep hot while you fry the remaining bananas.

Place the remaining sugar, the orange juice and liqueur in a small saucepan. Set over low heat and cook, stirring constantly, until the sugar has dissolved. Increase the heat and boil the syrup, without stirring, for 3 minutes or until it has thickened slightly. Pour over the fritters.

APPLE FRITTERS

Apple fritters make a popular dessert, and are particularly good topped with dollops of whipped cream.

4 servings

Metric/Imperial

100g (4oz) Fritter Batter I
fat for deep frying
3 medium apples, peeled, cored and

An unusual dessert, Orange-Flavoured Banana Fritters are easy to make and are delicious served with sugar and fresh cream.

sliced into rings

American

1 cup Fritter Batter I
fat for deep frying
3 apples, peeled, cored and sliced into
rings

Heat the fat - it is the correct temperature when a drop of batter immediately rises to the surface and begins to brown. Dip each apple piece into the batter and, making sure it is thoroughly coated, drop it into the hot fat and fry until it is puffed up and golden brown. Drain on absorbent paper and keep warm. Continue to fry the apple fritters this way, and serve them sprinkled with castor [fine] sugar.

COFFEE CRUMBLE

This crumble pudding is as delicious as it is economical. It may be eaten hot but tastes especially good cold. Serve it with lightly whipped cream.

4 servings

Metric/Imperial

1 tablespoon flour
2 tablespoons cornflour
1 tablespoon drinking chocolate
225ml (8 fl oz) milk
225ml (8 fl oz) black coffee
6 tablespoons sugar
50g (2oz) margarine
4 tablespoons crumbled sweet
  digestive biscuits
4 tablespoons rolled porridge oats

American

1 tablespoon flour
2 tablespoons cornstarch
1 tablespoon drinking chocolate
1 cup milk
1 cup strong coffee
6 tablespoons sugar
¼ cup margarine
4 tablespoons crumbled graham
  crackers
4 tablespoons rolled oats

Preheat the oven to warm (170°C/ 325°F or Gas Mark 3).
  Blend together the flour, cornflour

An aromatic dessert, Coriander Fruit Crumble is made with blackberries and apples.

[cornstarch] and drinking chocolate. Add a little of the milk and beat the mixture to a thick smooth paste.
  Heat the black coffee with the remaining milk and 4 tablespoons of the sugar over moderate heat. Just before it comes to the boil pour a little into the bowl containing the chocolate paste and stir with a spoon to blend well. Empty the contents of the bowl into the saucepan and, stirring constantly, continue cooking over moderate heat for 2 to 3 minutes or until the mixture becomes thick and smooth.
  Pour the coffee mixture into a shallow baking dish.
  Cream the margarine with the remaining sugar until light and fluffy. Add the biscuit [graham cracker] crumbs and the oats to the bowl and mix well. Spread the crumble topping

evenly over the coffee mixture.
  Bake for 20 minutes.

CORIANDER FRUIT CRUMBLE

This unusual aromatic dessert is inexpensive, simple to make and has a very interesting flavour. Serve it either hot or cold, with cream or vanilla ice cream.

4-6 servings

Metric/Imperial

750g (1½lb) cooking apples, peeled,
  cored and thinly sliced
250g (8oz) fresh blackberries, washed
  and hulled
2 tablespoons brown sugar
1 teaspoon ground cinnamon
TOPPING
100g (4 oz) plain flour
100g (4oz) sugar
100g (4oz) butter
2 teaspoons ground coriander

American

1½lb tart apples, peeled, cored and
    thinly sliced
1 cup blackberries, washed and
    hulled
2 tablespoons brown sugar
1 teaspoon ground cinnamon
TOPPING
1 cup all-purpose flour
½ cup sugar
½ cup butter
2 teaspoons ground coriander seeds

Preheat the oven to moderate (180°C/
350°F or Gas Mark 4).

Put the apples and blackberries in the
baking dish and sprinkle with the brown
sugar and cinnamon.

Put the flour and sugar in a mixing
bowl, add the butter, cut it into pieces
and rub into the flour and sugar until
the mixture resembles breadcrumbs.
Mix in the coriander.

Sprinkle the crumble on top of the
fruit and bake for 45 minutes.

GOOSEBERRY CRUMBLE

Quick and easy to make, Gooseberry
Crumble is a filling, warming dessert
for a family supper. Serve it with cream.

4 servings

Metric/Imperial

750g (1½lb) gooseberries, trimmed
100g (4oz) sugar
2 tablespoons water
TOPPING
100g (4oz) plain flour
75g (3oz) butter
50g (2oz) sugar

American

1½lb gooseberries, trimmed
½ cup sugar
2 tablespoons water
TOPPING
1 cup all-purpose flour
6 tablespoons butter
¼ cup sugar

Rhubarb Brown Betty is delicious
served with cream.

Preheat the oven to moderate (180°C/
350°F or Gas Mark 4). Lightly grease a
medium-sized baking dish.

Arrange the gooseberries in the dish
and sprinkle with the sugar and water.

Sift the flour into a mixing bowl and
rub in the butter until the mixture
resembles fine breadcrumbs. Stir in the
sugar.

Cover the gooseberries with the
crumble mixture and bake for 45
minutes or until the crumble is golden
brown.

RHUBARB BROWN BETTY

A wholesome and scrumptious family
dessert, Rhubarb Brown Betty is even
more delicious when served with
whipped cream. A marvellous end to a
winter's meal.

4-6 servings

Metric/Imperial

175g (6oz) butter, melted
100g (4oz) fresh brown breadcrumbs
175g (6oz) crushed digestive biscuits
100g (4oz) soft brown sugar
1 teaspoon ground cinnamon
¼ teaspoon grated nutmeg
grated rind of 1 lemon
grated rind of 1 orange
750g (1½lb) rhubarb, prepared and
    cooked
100g (4oz) sultanas

American

¾ cup butter, melted
2 cups fresh wholewheat breadcrumbs
1½ cups crushed graham crackers
⅔ cup soft brown sugar
1 teaspoon ground cinnamon
¼ teaspoon grated nutmeg
grated rind of 1 lemon
grated rind of 1 orange
1½lb rhubarb, prepared and cooked
⅔ cup golden or white raisins

Preheat the oven to fairly hot (190°C/
375°F or Gas Mark 5). Generously
grease a medium-sized ovenproof dish.

Combine the breadcrumbs, biscuits
[crackers], sugar, cinnamon, nutmeg,
lemon and orange rind and the melted
butter and mix well.

Place one-third of this mixture on the bottom of the prepared dish, smoothing it down with the back of a spoon. Cover with half of the rhubarb and sprinkle over half of the sultanas. Continue making layers in this way until all the ingredients are used up, ending with a layer of the breadcrumb mixture.

Bake for 30 minutes or until the top is golden brown.

SCANDINAVIAN ALMOND APPLES

A delicious adaptation of a traditional recipe, Scandinavian Almond Apples may be served with lots of whipped cream for a really filling dessert.

7 servings

Metric/Imperial

175g (6oz) sugar
350ml (12 fl oz) water
7 firm cooking apples, peeled and cored
TOPPING
75g (3oz) butter
100g (4oz) sugar
100g (4oz) ground almonds
juice and grated rind of 1 lemon
2 eggs, separated

American

¾ cup sugar
1½ cups water
7 firm tart apples, pared and cored
TOPPING
6 tablespoons butter
½ cup sugar
1 cup ground almonds
juice and grated rind of 1 lemon
2 eggs, yolks and whites separated

In a saucepan large enough to contain the apples in one layer, dissolve the sugar in the water over high heat. When the water boils, reduce the heat to moderate and boil the syrup, without stirring, for 5 minutes. Add the apples, cover and cook for 8 to 10 minutes, or until tender but still firm.

Meanwhile, preheat the oven to warm (170°C/325°F or Gas Mark 3). Grease a baking tin large enough to take the apples in one layer.

To make the topping, beat the butter and sugar together until soft and creamy. Beat in the almonds, lemon juice and rind and egg yolks, beating constantly until thoroughly blended.

Beat the egg whites until they form stiff peaks. With a metal spoon, fold them into the almond mixture.

Transfer the apples to the prepared baking tin. Pour in the syrup and spread the topping over. Bake for 20 minutes or until the topping is golden brown and cooked.

Allow the mixture to cool in the tin for 10 minutes before serving.

ORANGE RICE

A simple pudding for the family, Orange Rice is moulded to give it an attractive appearance, but it will taste just as good if served piled on a shallow serving dish and garnished with orange slices.

4 servings

Metric/Imperial

225g (8oz) round-grain rice
450ml (16 fl oz) water
juice of 1 orange
3 oranges, peeled, white pith removed and segmented
2 tablespoons sugar
225ml (8 fl oz) double cream, stiffly whipped

American

1⅓ cups short-grain rice
2 cups water
juice of 1 orange
3 oranges, pared, membrane and white skin removed and sectioned
2 tablespoons sugar
1 cup whipping cream, stiffly whipped

Brush a 750ml (1½ pint) [1 quart] ring mould with oil.

Put the rice in a large saucepan. Pour over the water and bring to the boil. Cover, reduce the heat and cook for 15 minutes or until the rice is tender and the water has been absorbed.

Transfer to a large mixing bowl and pour over the orange juice. Set aside for 5 minutes.

Stir half the orange segments and the sugar into the rice mixture. Carefully fold in the cream. Spoon the rice mixture into the mould and smooth the top.

Place in the refrigerator to chill for 2 hours or until the rice mixture is firm to the touch.

Run a knife around the edge of the mould. Place a serving plate, inverted, over it and reverse the two; the rice mixture should slide out easily.

Fill the centre of the rice ring with the remaining orange segments and serve.

VANILLA BLANCMANGE

Blancmange can be a really delicious dessert as this recipe proves. It is especially good served with poached fruit and cream.

3-4 servings

Metric/Imperial

40g (1½oz) cornflour
40g (1½oz) sugar
600ml (1 pint) milk
1 vanilla pod

American

6 tablespoons cornstarch
3 tablespoons sugar
2½ cups milk
1 vanilla bean

Combine the cornflour [cornstarch] and sugar. Add 4 tablespoons of the milk and stir until the mixture forms a smooth paste.

In a saucepan, scald (bring to just below boiling) the remaining milk with the vanilla pod over moderate heat. Cover and set aside for 20 minutes. Remove the vanilla pod from the milk, wipe it dry and store for future use.

Return the pan to moderate heat and bring the milk to just under boiling point. Remove the pan from the heat and pour the milk on the cornflour [cornstarch] mixture, stirring constantly. Return the milk mixture to the pan and bring to the boil, stirring constantly. Cook for 3 minutes, stirring.

Meanwhile, rinse a 500ml (1-pint) [2½-cup] decorative mould in cold water. Pour the blancmange mixture into the mould and set aside to cool. Chill in the refrigerator for 2 hours or until the blancmange has set.

Using a fingertip, gently pull the blancmange away from the sides of the mould. Invert a serving dish over the mould and, grasping the two firmly together, reverse them. The blancmange should slide out easily.

SOUFFLE OMELETTE

Soufflé Omelette is cooked in the oven rather than on the top of the stove. Serve the omelette plain or with whipped cream as an elegant dessert.

4-6 servings

Metric/Imperial

1 tablespoon icing sugar
100g (4oz) sugar
6 egg yolks
1 tablespoon finely grated lemon rind
8 egg whites

American

1 tablespoon confectioner's sugar
½ cup sugar
6 egg yolks
1 tablespoon finely grated lemon rind
8 egg whites

Preheat the oven to hot (220°C/425°F or Gas Mark 7). Lightly grease a 23 x 30cm (9 x 12 in) baking dish. Sprinkle over the icing [confectioner's] sugar, shaking out any excess.

In a large mixing bowl, beat the sugar, egg yolks and lemon rind together.

Beat the egg whites until they form stiff peaks. With a metal spoon, carefully fold the egg whites into the egg yolk mixture.

Pour the mixture into the prepared baking dish, shaping it into a dome with a flat-bladed knife. Bake for 8 to 10 minutes or until the omelette is lightly browned. Serve at once.

LEMON SPONGE

A frothy lemon pudding with a delicious flavour and texture, Lemon Sponge is simple to make.

4 servings

Metric/Imperial

3 eggs, separated
grated rind and juice of 1 lemon
225ml (8 fl oz) milk
175g (6oz) sugar
⅛ teaspoon salt
25g (1oz) flour

American

3 eggs, yolks and whites separated
grated rind and juice of 1 lemon
1 cup milk
¾ cup sugar
⅛ teaspoon salt
¼ cup flour

Preheat the oven to warm (170°C/325°F or Gas Mark 3).

Combine the egg yolks, lemon rind and juice and the milk.

Add the sugar, salt and flour, beating with a wooden spoon until the mixture forms a smooth paste.

Beat the egg whites until they form stiff peaks. With a large metal spoon, carefully fold the egg whites in the egg yolk mixture. Spoon into a 1½-litre (2½-pint) [1½-quart] soufflé dish and place in the oven. Bake for 30 minutes or until the pudding is firm and golden brown.

APPLE CHARLOTTE

This delicious hot pudding is said to have been named after the heroine in Goethe's novel *Werther*.

4 to 6 servings

Metric/Imperial

FILLING
1kg (2lb) cooking apples, peeled, cored and cut into quarters
100g (4oz) sugar
rind of 1 lemon
50g (2oz) butter
about half a stale sliced loaf, crusts removed
4 tablespoons melted butter
castor sugar

SAUCE
5 tablespoons apricot jam
3 tablespoons water
2 tablespoons sherry (optional)

American

FILLING
2lb tart apples, peeled, cored and cut into quarters
½ cup sugar
rind of 1 lemon
¼ cup butter
half a loaf stale sliced white bread, crusts removed
4 tablespoons melted butter
fine sugar
SAUCE
5 tablespoons apricot jam
3 tablespoons water
2 tablespoons sherry (optional)

Preheat the oven to moderate (180°C/350°F or Gas Mark 4). Grease a charlotte mould or ovenproof dish.

Put the apples, sugar, lemon rind and butter in a saucepan and, stirring occasionally, simmer gently until the apples are soft. Discard the lemon rind.

Cut the bread slices in halves. Dip in the melted butter and line the bottom and sides of the mould or dish, overlapping slightly. Fill with the apple mixture and cover with a layer of bread slices dipped in melted butter. Sprinkle with castor sugar and bake for 40 minutes or until the top is golden brown.

While the charlotte is baking, put the jam and water in a small saucepan. Stir and bring to the boil. Lower the heat and simmer for 3 minutes. Remove from the heat and stir in the sherry, if using.

Let the charlotte stand for a minute or two before turning it out on to a warmed serving dish. Pour the warm jam sauce over it.

ADAM AND EVE PUDDING

A traditional, inexpensive English pudding, this is an appealing dessert for an informal family lunch or dinner. It should be served hot and can be accompanied by cream or a custard sauce.

4 servings

Metric/Imperial

500g (1lb) cooking apples
150g (5oz) sugar
½ teaspoon cinnamon
2 tablespoons cold water
100g (4oz) soft margarine
100g (4oz) self-raising flour
2 eggs, lightly beaten

American

1lb tart apples
⅝ cup sugar
½ teaspoon cinnamon
2 tablespoons cold water
½ cup soft margarine
1 cup self-raising flour
2 eggs, lightly beaten

Preheat the oven to moderate (180°C/350°F or Gas Mark 4).

Peel and core the apples. Cut into thin slices and put them into a medium-sized, oval pie dish. Sprinkle with the cinnamon, water and 2 tablespoons of the sugar.

To prepare the sponge mixture, put the margarine and the remaining sugar into a mixing bowl and beat until light and creamy. Add the beaten eggs, a little at a time. Sift the flour into the bowl and lightly stir it in.

Pour the sponge mixture over the apples, spreading it evenly. Bake in the middle of the oven for 30 minutes or until risen and pale golden brown. Reduce the oven heat to cool (150°C/300°F or Gas Mark 2) for another 30 minutes.

SPOTTED DICK

Spotted Dick is a traditional British dessert made with suet and dried fruit. It is very filling, so is best served after a light first course, with custard sauce.

6-8 servings

Metric/Imperial

225g (8oz) flour
1 teaspoon salt
2 tablespoons sugar
2 teaspoons baking powder
⅛ teaspoon ground cloves
75g (3oz) shredded suet
100g (4oz) currants
50g (2oz) sultanas
6 to 8 tablespoons water

American

2 cups flour
1 teaspoon salt
2 tablespoons sugar
2 teaspoons baking powder
⅛ teaspoon ground cloves
⅜ cup shredded beef suet
⅔ cup currants
⅓ cup golden raisins
6 to 8 tablespoons water

Sift the flour, salt, sugar, baking powder and cloves into a large mixing bowl. Stir in the suet, currants and sultanas. Gradually add 6 tablespoons of water and knead lightly until the dough is light and pliable. Add more water if necessary, spoonful by spoonful.

On a lightly floured surface, roll out the dough to a rectangle 6mm (¼in) thick.

Roll up the dough Swiss [jelly] roll style, pressing the edges together to

Spotted Dick may be filled with strawberry jam.

seal. Wrap the roll loosely in greased aluminium foil, making a pleat in it to allow for expansion.

Half-fill a large saucepan with water and place it over high heat. When the water comes to the boil, put in the pudding, reduce the heat to moderate and steam for 2½ hours, replenishing the water when necessary.

LEMON TAPIOCA PUDDING

Lemon Tapioca Pudding is easy to make, and makes an ideal family dessert. Though the cream included in this recipe makes a thicker and creamier pudding milk may be substituted.

4 servings

Metric/Imperial

50g (2 oz) tapioca
2 tablespoons castor sugar
finely grated rind of 2 lemons
225ml (8 fl oz) milk
300ml (10 fl oz) single cream
2 tablespoons lemon juice
½ teaspoon ground mixed spice or allspice
1 tablespoon butter
3 eggs, separated
2 tablespoons soft brown sugar

American

⅓ cup tapioca
2 tablespoons fine sugar
finely grated rind of 2 lemons
1 cup milk
1¼ cups light cream
2 tablespoons lemon juice
½ teaspoon ground allspice
1 tablespoon butter
3 eggs, yolks and whites separated
2 tablespoons soft brown sugar

Place the tapioca, sugar, lemon rind, milk and cream in a saucepan.

Set the pan over moderately low heat and cook the mixture, stirring frequently, for 15 minutes, or until fairly thick.

Stir in the lemon juice and the mixed spice or allspice. Set aside to cool to lukewarm.

Preheat the oven to moderate (180°C/350°F or Gas Mark 4). Grease a deep-sided baking dish.

Beat the egg yolks into the cool tapioca mixture.

Beat the egg whites until they form stiff peaks.

With a metal spoon, fold the egg whites into the tapioca mixture. Turn in to the prepared baking dish. Sprinkle over the brown sugar and dot with the butter.

Bake in the centre of the oven for 25 to 30 minutes or until the pudding is thick and creamy and the top has caramelized.

CHERRY TAPIOCA

A filling and nourishing dessert for a winter's meal, Cherry Tapioca is both economical and simple. Decorate with whipped cream or fresh cherries.

4 servings

Metric/Imperial

396g (14 oz) can sweetened, stoned cherries, drained
300ml (10 fl oz) milk
225ml (8 fl oz) single cream
50g (2 oz) tapioca
½ teaspoon vanilla essence
½ teaspoon grated lemon rind
½ teaspoon grated nutmeg

American

1 x 14 oz can Bing or Queen Anne cherries, drained
1¼ cups milk
1 cup light cream
⅓ cup tapioca
½ teaspoon vanilla
½ teaspoon grated lemon rind
½ teaspoon grated nutmeg

Place the cherries in a medium-sized baking dish. Preheat the oven to warm (170°C/325°F or Gas Mark 3).

Heat the milk and cream (bring to just under boiling point) over low heat. Add the tapioca, vanilla essence, lemon rind and nutmeg and, stirring constantly with a wooden spoon, simmer the mixture for 3 to 4 minutes, or until it thickens.

Pour over the cherries. Bake for 45 minutes or until the tapioca is brown on top. Let stand for 5 minutes before serving.

SANCTUARY PUDDING

A delicious pudding, Sanctuary Pudding may be served with lots of warm custard for a winter dessert.

4 servings

Metric/Imperial

40g (1½ oz) butter
25g (1 oz) plain flour
175ml (6 fl oz) milk
1 tablespoon grated orange rind
1 teaspoon grated nutmeg
2 tablespoons soft brown sugar
2 egg yolks, lightly beaten
50g (2 oz) sultanas or seedless raisins
1 large cooking apple, peeled, cored and diced
2 egg whites, stiffly beaten

American

3 tablespoons butter
¼ cup all-purpose flour
¾ cup milk
1 tablespoon grated orange rind
1 teaspoon grated nutmeg
2 tablespoons soft brown sugar
2 egg yolks, lightly beaten
⅓ cup golden or seedless raisins
1 large tart apple, pared, cored and diced
2 egg whites, stiffly beaten

Grease a 1-litre (2-pint) [1½-quart] ovenproof dish and set it aside. Preheat the oven to warm (170°C/325°F or Gas Mark 3).

In a small saucepan melt two-thirds of the butter over moderate heat. Remove the pan from the heat and, with a wooden spoon, stir in the flour to make a smooth paste. Gradually add the milk, stirring constantly to avoid lumps. Return to the heat and stir in the orange rind and nutmeg. Cook, stirring constantly, for 2 to 3 minutes or until very thick.

Remove the pan from the heat and beat in the sugar. Add the beaten egg yolks, a little at a time, and continue beating until the ingredients are thoroughly blended. Stir in the sultanas.

In a small frying-pan, melt the remaining butter over moderate heat. When the foam subsides add the apple and cook, stirring frequently, for 4 to 5 minutes or until golden brown. Drain the apple on kitchen paper and stir into the milk mixture.

With a metal spoon, fold the stiffly beaten egg whites into the mixture. Spoon the batter into the prepared dish.

Place the dish in a baking tin and pour in enough hot water to come half-way up the sides. Bake for 1 hour or until a knife inserted in the centre comes out clean.

To unmould, place a serving dish, inverted, over the top of the dish and, holding the two firmly together, reverse them.

SAGO PUDDING

Sago Pudding makes an excellent family dessert. Serve it either hot or cold accompanied by fresh or stewed fruit and whipped cream. Or stir in lots of strawberry jam.

2-3 servings

Metric/Imperial
450ml (16 fl oz) milk
50g (2oz) sago
½ teaspoon salt
1 tablespoon butter
50g (2oz) sugar
½ teaspoon ground cinnamon
2 teaspoons grated lemon rind
2 egg yolks

American
2 cups milk
⅓ cup sago
½ teaspoon salt
1 tablespoon butter
¼ cup sugar
½ teaspoon ground cinnamon
2 teaspoons grated lemon rind
2 egg yolks

Pour the milk into a saucepan and set

A satisfying milk pudding, Sago Pudding, served hot or cold, is an excellent winter dessert.

over moderate heat. When hot but not boiling, sprinkle over the sago and salt. Bring to the boil and cook, stirring constantly, for 10 minutes or until the mixture thickens and the sago becomes clear.

Meanwhile, preheat the oven to moderate (180°C/350°F or Gas Mark 4). Grease a 2-litre (3-pint) [2-quart] soufflé or straight-sided ovenproof dish with the butter and set aside.

Reduce the heat to low and add the sugar, cinnamon and lemon rind to the sago. Cook, stirring constantly, for 2 to 3 minutes or until the sugar dissolves. Remove the pan from the heat and stir in the egg yolks.

Pour into the prepared dish and bake for 30 to 35 minutes or until the pudding is brown on top and of a thick creamy consistency.

MARMALADE PUDDING

A traditional steamed pudding, Marmalade Pudding is a rich and filling dish made with suet. Served with custard sauce, it makes a delicious winter dessert.

6-8 servings

Metric/Imperial

100g (4oz) shredded suet
100g (4oz) fresh breadcrumbs
50g (2oz) sugar
1 teaspoon grated orange rind
3 eggs, lightly beaten
1 tablespoon orange juice
4 tablespoons orange marmalade

American

½ cup shredded beef suet
2 cups fresh breadcrumbs
¼ cup sugar
1 teaspoon grated orange rind
3 eggs, lightly beaten
1 tablespoon orange juice
4 tablespoons orange marmalade

Lightly grease a 500ml (1-pint) [2½-cup] pudding basin.

Combine the suet, breadcrumbs, sugar and orange rind. Add the eggs and orange juice and beat until the mixture is well blended.

In a small saucepan, melt the marmalade over low heat, stirring constantly. Pour the marmalade into the bottom of the pudding basin. Then pour over the suet mixture.

Cover the basin with a piece of aluminium foil with a pleat in the middle and tie on with string.

Place the basin in a large saucepan and pour in enough boiling water to come about two-thirds of the way up the sides of the basin. (Alternatively, place the basin in the top half of a steamer.) Cover the pan and place it over low heat. Steam the pudding for 2½ hours, adding more boiling water as necessary.

TOFFEE [CARAMEL] PUDDING

A sticky, sweet pudding, Toffee [Cara-mel] Pudding is a children's favourite. Serve either hot or cold on its own or with custard.

4-6 servings

Metric/Imperial

100g (4oz) butter
100g (4oz) soft brown sugar
6 tablespoons golden syrup
225ml (8 fl oz) milk, scalded
½ teaspoon vanilla essence
⅛ teaspoon ground cloves
4 thick slices white bread, each cut into 4 strips

American

½ cup butter
⅔ cup soft brown sugar
6 tablespoons light corn syrup
1 cup milk, scalded
½ teaspoon vanilla
⅛ teaspoon ground cloves
4 thick slices white bread, each cut into 4 strips

Melt the butter over moderate heat. When the foam subsides add the sugar and cook, stirring constantly until dissolved. Add the syrup and stir well until thoroughly combined. Cook the mixture for 5 minutes or until golden brown.

Meanwhile mix together the milk, vanilla essence and cloves. Arrange the strips of bread in a warmed serving dish and pour over the milk.

Remove the pan from the heat and set aside to cool for 3 minutes. Pour the sauce over the bread, coating it completely, and serve immediately.

LOKSHEN PUDDING

This deliciously filling pudding is an ideal dessert to serve on a cold winter's day when the family feels really hungry.

4-6 servings

Metric/Imperial

75g (3oz) butter
250g (8oz) fine egg noodles, cooked and drained
50g (2oz) sugar
3 egg yolks
75ml (3 fl oz) orange juice
175g (6oz) sultanas or seedless raisins
50g (2oz) chopped almonds
75g (3oz) chopped candied peel
½ teaspoon ground ginger
1 teaspoon ground cinnamon
3 egg whites, stiffly beaten

American

6 tablespoons butter
2 cups fine noodles, cooked and drained
¼ cup sugar
3 egg yolks
⅜ cup orange juice
1 cup golden or seedless raisins
½ cup slivered almonds
½ cup chopped candied citrus peel
½ teaspoon ground ginger
1 teaspoon ground cinnamon
3 egg whites, stiffly beaten

Preheat the oven to fairly hot (200°C/400°F or Gas Mark 6). Grease a large baking dish and place the noodles in it.

Cream the butter and sugar together until pale and fluffy. Beat in the egg yolks, one at a time. Carefully stir in the orange juice. Add the sultanas, almonds, candied peel, ginger and cinnamon and stir gently to mix. With a metal spoon, carefully fold in the egg white until just combined.

Spoon the mixture into the baking dish and carefully mix it into the noodles. Bake for 30 minutes or until the pudding has set and is lightly browned.

HONEY GINGER PUDDING

Quick, easy and economical to prepare, Honey Ginger Pudding is an ideal dessert for a family meal.

4 servings

Metric/Imperial

25g (1oz) butter
6 slices white bread, crusts removed and cut into strips
50g (2oz) preserved ginger, thinly sliced
3 tablespoons honey
1 egg, lightly beaten
225ml (8 fl oz) milk

American

2 tablespoons butter

6 slices white bread, crusts removed
    and cut into strips

⅓ cup candied ginger, thinly sliced

3 tablespoons honey

1 egg, lightly beaten

1 cup milk

Preheat the oven to moderate (180°C/ 350°F or Gas Mark 4). Grease a medium-sized pie dish.

Make layers of the bread and ginger in the dish. Gently heat the butter and honey together. Beat in the egg and milk and pour the mixture over the bread and ginger.

Bake for 40 to 45 minutes or until the top is golden brown.

FRUIT PUDDING

This fruit pudding with a suet crust is just the dessert for the family on a chilly summer's night. Apples, blackberries and apples, blackcurrants, gooseberries or plums may be used. Serve the pudding with custard sauce.

6 servings

Metric/Imperial

250g (8oz) Suetcrust Pastry

750g (1½lb) fresh fruit, washed and
    prepared

50 to 100g (2 to 4oz) sugar, depending
    on tartness of the fruit

American

1 recipe Suetcrust Pastry

1½lb fresh fruit, washed and hulled

¼ to ½ cup sugar, depending on the
    tartness of the fruit

Lightly grease a 1-litre (2-pint) pudding basin.

On a lightly floured board, roll out the dough to a large circle about 1cm (½in) thick. Cut a triangle (about one-third of the diameter) out of the circle and reserve it.

Line the greased basin with the large piece of dough. Dampen the edges from where the triangle was cut and bring them together. Press the dough to the shape of the basin and trim the top edges.

Half fill a large saucepan with water and slowly bring to the boil.

Put the fruit in the lined basin and sprinkle the sugar on top. Lightly knead the reserved piece of dough and the trimmings together and roll them out to a circle to cover the basin.

Dampen the edges of the dough and place it on top of the fruit. Press the edges together to seal. Cover with aluminium foil with a plate in the centre and tie on with string.

Put the basin into, or in a steamer over, the saucepan of boiling water. Cover with a lid and steam for 2½ hours, adding more boiling water when necessary.

DATE PUDDING

A warming dessert for a winter lunch, this steamed pudding may be served with custard sauce.

4 servings

Metric/Imperial

100g (4oz) self-raising flour

175g (6oz) dates, stoned and chopped

100g (4oz) fresh white breadcrumbs

50g (2oz) sugar

2½ tablespoons treacle

100g (4oz) shredded suet

½ teaspoon mixed spice

1 egg, lightly beaten

3 to 4 tablespoons cold water

American

1 cup self-raising flour

1 cup dates, pitted and chopped

2 cups fresh white breadcrumbs

¼ cup sugar

2½ tablespoons molasses or corn syrup

½ cup (¼lb) beef suet

½ teaspoon ground allspice

1 egg, lightly beaten

3 to 4 tablespoons cold water

Lightly grease a 1-litre (2-pint) pudding basin.

Sift the flour into a mixing bowl. Mix in the dates, breadcrumbs, sugar, treacle [molasses], suet, mixed spice and beaten egg.

Beat until well mixed. Add just enough water to give a soft, dropping consistency.

Turn the mixture into the greased pudding basin. Cover with a piece of aluminium foil with a pleat in the centre and tie on with string.

Half fill the lower half of a steamer with water and bring to the boil. Place the pudding in the top half, cover, reduce the heat and steam for 2½ hours, adding more water when necessary.

Alternatively, place the basin on a rack or inverted saucer in a large saucepan and add enough water to come up to the rim.

FRENCH CHERRY PUDDING

This is the basic – and traditional – version of clafoutis. It may be served on its own or with cream or a light custard sauce.

6 servings

Metric/Imperial

600g (1¼lb) fresh black cherries,
    washed and stoned, or use canned
    black cherries, stoned and drained

175ml (6 fl oz) milk

2 eggs

2 teaspoons vanilla essence

5 tablespoons icing sugar

7 tablespoons plain flour

⅛ teaspoon salt

American

1¼lb fresh Bing cherries, washed and
    pitted, or substitute canned
    cherries, drained

¾ cup milk

2 eggs

2 teaspoons vanilla

5 tablespoons confectioner's sugar

7 tablespoons all-purpose flour

⅛ teaspoon salt

Preheat the oven to moderate (180°C/ 350°F or Gas Mark 4). Grease a medium-sized baking dish. Dry the cherries thoroughly on kitchen paper.

In a large mixing bowl, blend the milk, eggs and vanilla essence, beating until smooth. Add 4 tablespoons of the sugar, 1 tablespoon at a time, whisking constantly, and make sure that each is absorbed before the next one is added. Add the flour, tablespoonful by tablespoonful in the same way, adding the salt with the last one. The batter should be very smooth and of a very light pancake batter consistency.

Pour into the greased baking dish and add the cherries, spreading them evenly throughout the batter. Bake in the centre of the oven for 50 minutes to 1 hour or until a knife inserted in the middle comes out clean.

FRENCH PLUM PUDDING

This variation on the classic French clafoutis tastes best when made with fresh plums. Canned plums can be used instead.

A traditional French dessert, French Cherry Pudding (Clafoutis), is delicious served with cream.

6 servings

Metric/Imperial

600g (1¼lb) fresh, dark plums
3 tablespoons Grand Marnier or Cognac
50g (2oz) granulated sugar
175ml (6 fl oz) milk
2 eggs
2 teaspoons vanilla essence
5 tablespoons icing sugar
7 tablespoons plain flour
⅛ teaspoon salt

American

1¼lb fresh Italian plums
3 tablespoons Grand Marnier or Cognac
¼ cup sugar
¾ cup milk
2 eggs
2 teaspoons vanilla
5 tablespoons confectioner's sugar
7 tablespoons all-purpose flour
⅛ teaspoon salt

Drop the plums into boiling water and cook them for 10 to 15 seconds only. Remove and slip off the skins. Halve, stone and slice thinly.

Arrange in a medium-sized shallow bowl and pour the Grand Marnier or Cognac and granulated sugar over them, stirring to coat the fruit thoroughly. Set aside for about 45 minutes, basting occasionally with the liquid.

Preheat the oven to moderate (180°C/350°F or Gas Mark 4). Grease a medium-sized baking dish.

In a large mixing bowl, blend the milk, eggs and vanilla essence, beating until smooth. Add 4 tablespoons of the sugar, 1 tablespoon at a time, whisking constantly, and make sure that each tablespoon is absorbed before the next one is added. Add the flour, tablespoonful by tablespoonful in the same way, adding the salt with the last one. The batter should be very smooth and of a very light pancake batter consistency.

Pour into the greased baking dish and add the plum slices with the liquid, spreading them evenly throughout the batter. Bake in the centre of the oven

for 50 minutes to 1 hour or until a knife inserted in the middle comes out clean. Sprinkle with the remaining sugar.

BREAD AND BUTTER PUDDING

A perennial favourite, Bread and Butter Pudding is easy and economical to make and delicious to eat.

3 to 4 servings

Metric/Imperial

6 thin slices of white bread, crusts removed and liberally buttered
75g (3oz) seedless raisins
½ teaspoon grated nutmeg
2 tablespoons sugar
CUSTARD
2 eggs
425ml (15 fl oz) milk
1 tablespoon sugar
½ tablespoon vanilla essence

American

6 thin slices of white bread, crusts removed and liberally buttered
¾ cup seedless raisins
½ teaspoon grated nutmeg
2 tablespoons sugar
CUSTARD
2 eggs
2 cups milk
1 tablespoon sugar
½ teaspoon vanilla

Grease the bottom and sides of a medium-sized, shallow baking dish.

Cut the slices of bread into quarters. Place a layer (buttered side up) on the bottom of the dish and sprinkle with half the raisins, nutmeg and 1 tablespoon sugar.

Add a second layer of bread and sprinkle on the rest of the raisins, nutmeg and sugar. Top with a final layer of bread, butter side up.

To make the custard, beat the eggs in a large mixing bowl. Heat the milk, sugar and vanilla essence. Add the heated milk mixture to the eggs, beating continuously to combine well. Strain the mixture over the bread and let stand for at least 30 minutes or until

the bread has absorbed most of the liquid.

Preheat the oven to fairly hot (190°C/375°F or Gas Mark 5).

Bake the pudding in the centre of the oven for 35 to 45 minutes or until the top is crisp and golden.

SEMOLINA PUDDING WITH FRUIT AND NUTS

A delicious variation on the traditional semolina pudding, Semolina Pudding with Fruit and Nuts makes a filling winter dessert. Or serve cold as an unusual breakfast dish.

4 servings

Metric/Imperial

1 tablespoon unsalted butter
600ml (1 pint) single cream
50g (2oz) semolina
1 teaspoon grated lemon rind
75g (3oz) sugar
½ teaspoon mixed spice
50g (2oz) sultanas
50g (2oz) slivered or chopped blanched almonds
2 eggs, separated

American

1 tablespoon sweet butter
2½ cups light cream
½ cup semolina flour
1 teaspoon grated lemon rind
⅜ cup sugar
½ teaspoon ground allspice
⅓ cup golden raisins
½ cup slivered almonds
2 eggs, yolks and whites separated

Preheat the oven to moderate (180°C/350°F or Gas Mark 4). Lightly grease a medium-sized baking dish.

Heat the cream over moderate heat. When the cream is hot but not boiling, sprinkle over the semolina and, stirring constantly, bring to the boil. Cook, stirring constantly, for 2 to 3 minutes or until thick and smooth.

Remove the pan from the heat and stir in the lemon rind, the butter, one-third of the sugar, the mixed spice, slivered almonds and egg yolks. Beat until thoroughly combined.

Beat the egg whites until they form soft peaks. Fold in the remaining sugar and continue to whisk the mixture until it forms stiff peaks.

Using a metal spoon, fold the egg white mixture into the semolina. Spoon into the prepared dish and bake for 30 minutes.

CHOCOLATE PUDDING

This is a traditional English baked Chocolate Pudding. Quick and easy to prepare, it may be served with chocolate or custard sauce.

6 servings

Metric/Imperial

100g (4oz) butter
175g (6oz) plain flour
½ teaspoon salt
1 teaspoon baking powder
100g (4oz) sugar
50g (2oz) cocoa powder
2 eggs, lightly beaten
5 tablespoons milk
¼ teaspoon vanilla essence

American

½ cup butter
1½ cups all-purpose flour
½ teaspoon salt
1 teaspoon baking powder
½ cup sugar
½ cup cocoa
2 eggs, lightly beaten
5 tablespoons milk
¼ teaspoon vanilla

Preheat the oven to fairly hot (190°C/375°F or Gas Mark 5). Grease a medium-sized pie or soufflé dish.

Sift the flour, salt and baking powder into a mixing bowl. Rub in the remaining butter and stir in the sugar and cocoa.

Beat in the eggs and milk and continue beating until the mixture is smooth and of a dropping consistency. Add the vanilla essence.

Pour the mixture into the greased pie or soufflé dish and place it in the oven just above centre. Bake for 30 to 40 minutes or until a skewer inserted into the pudding comes out clean.

Meals in a hurry

When it is a question of producing a meal in double-quick time, most people rush for the can-opener or raid the refrigerator for so-called convenience foods.

However, convenience foods are, indisputably, expensive. There are certain exceptions to this rule as with most rules. Baked beans are such a part of the staple diet in the Western world today that the price remains low, and it can also be cheaper to buy canned tomatoes, corn, and even canned potatoes when the fresh variety is scarce and expensive. So shop carefully. Take advantage of special offers and keep a stock of the most useful canned foods ready for emergencies. Remember that canned vegetables are already cooked and generally only need to be heated through thoroughly. When using canned meat dishes always follow the manufacturer's instructions.

Foods which are frozen lose very little of their vitamin content and are generally preferable to canned food in this respect. If you have a freezer then there will be little problem when it comes to producing meals in a hurry – you can always have ready-to-cook pies, hamburgers, frozen vegetables and so on available for unexpected guests and unplanned meals. If you don't have a freezer and you buy frozen food, remember to put it in the freezing compartment of your refrigerator without delay: once it is thawed you cannot re-freeze it and it will have to be used the same day. Don't overcook frozen vegetables. Commercially frozen vegetables are blanched before freezing in the same way that the home freezer owner prepares produce for freezing, so they will need correspondingly less cooking time.

Dried foods which you should keep in stock include soups, stock cubes, quick-cooking pasta, quick-dried garden peas, dried onions and of course herbs and spices. Dried breadcrumbs (your own will be better than the commercial variety) are always useful for coating fish, Scotch Eggs, pork or veal escalopes and rissoles, all of which are quick to cook. Keep a couple of sauce mixes handy, and remember that you can use condensed soups to make sauces and fillings for omelettes and pancakes. Pastry mixes and cake mixes save time when baking.

Convenience foods, whether frozen, canned or dried, are an indispensable part of the modern diet and have done much to take the drudgery out of everyday cooking. For working mothers, bachelors - and for people who simply don't like cooking - they offer an almost instant solution to the problem of fast catering. The advantages are obvious, and as instructions for cooking generally appear on the can or packet there is not much that can go wrong.

Most of the recipes in this section use fresh foods, but you can experiment in endless ways with convenience foods. Interesting serving suggestions are often given on the packet or can by the manufacturer, and you can follow these or adapt them to what you have available. Try using a stuffing mix to top a meat or fish pie, or add a stuffing mix to minced [ground] beef and form into patties for frying. Add a can of drained mushrooms and a can of tomatoes, plus seasoning, to any white fish, top with breadcrumbs and grated cheese and bake in the oven until golden brown for a quick and tasty casserole. Use instant mashed potato for Potato Croquettes (page 168), and to top Shepherd's Pie (page 75) and Cottage Pie (page 244).

Remember too that you can always add your own touches to a 'package' meal. Soups particularly lend themselves to a little personal treatment - add a sprinkling of parsley, a dash of cream swirled into each helping, or a topping of sizzling croûtons before serving. Add some chunks of lightly cooked root vegetables to a canned stew, or serve sausages, frozen fish portions and grilled chops with an appropriate sauce, even if it is only from a packet sauce mix. Serve a bowl of fresh salad with an instant meal, or garnish with fresh parsley, tomato or lemon slices as appropriate. These are all little touches which not only add to eye appeal but will improve the meal nutritionally.

The following are some useful quick recipes using convenience foods. Some are simply suppertime snacks, but most can be regarded as a meal in their own right, depending on the quantity you serve, the accompaniments you offer – and of course, the size of the appetites involved. Many use common storecupboard items, so there is no need for shopping beforehand.

TUNA NOODLE BAKE

This recipe makes good use of basic convenience foods and ingredients. Use quick-cooking noodles for extra speed.

4 servings

Metric/Imperial

300ml (10 fl oz) milk
175g (6oz) Cheddar cheese, grated
75g (3oz) butter
1 medium-sized onion, finely chopped
175g (6oz) noodles, cooked and drained
1 teaspoon salt
¼ teaspoon pepper
2 tablespoons breadcrumbs
226g (8oz) canned tuna fish, flaked

American

1¼ cups milk
1½ cups Cheddar cheese, grated
⅜ cup butter
1 medium-sized onion, finely chopped
1½ cups noodles, cooked and drained
1 teaspoon salt
¼ teaspoon pepper
2 tablespoons breadcrumbs
1 x 8oz can tuna fish, flaked

Preheat the oven to moderate (180°C/350°F or Gas Mark 4).

Put the milk, cheese and butter in a large saucepan and heat gently until melted. Remove the saucepan from the heat and stir in the onion, noodles, salt, pepper, breadcrumbs and tuna fish.

Pour this into a buttered casserole and bake uncovered for about 20 minutes or until brown and crisp on top.

JIFFY TUNA SURPRISE

When you're short of time and ideas, this is just the dish for a family supper. It may be prepared in very little time from just a few ingredients in your storecupboard. Serve it with rice or noodles.

2-3 servings

Metric/Imperial

50g (2oz) butter
1 large onion, chopped

1 garlic clove, chopped
½ teaspoon curry powder
226g (8oz) can tomatoes
226g (8oz) can tuna fish, flaked
1 teaspoon dried basil
2 tablespoons sultanas
½ teaspoon salt
¼ teaspoon black pepper

American

¼ cup butter
1 large onion, chopped
1 garlic clove, chopped
½ teaspoon curry powder
1 x 8oz can tomatoes
1 x 8oz can tuna fish, flaked
1 teaspoon dried basil
2 tablespoons golden raisins
½ teaspoon salt
¼ teaspoon black pepper

In a medium-sized saucepan melt the butter over moderate heat. When the foam subsides add the onion and garlic and fry for 5 minutes, or until soft and translucent but not brown. Stir in the curry powder and add all the remaining ingredients.

Bring to the boil, reduce the heat and simmer gently for 10 minutes.

SAUSAGE AND CHUTNEY SPECIAL

Sure to be a hit with children, Sausage and Chutney Special can be served as a substantial snack or supper dish.

4 servings

Metric/Imperial

4 small pork sausages
2 teaspoons vegetable oil
2 eating apples, peeled, cored and diced
1 large pickled gherkin, diced
juice of ½ lemon
3 drops Tabasco sauce
3 tablespoons milk
salt, pepper and paprika
4 slices buttered toast
4 thin slices Cheddar cheese
8 slices tomato

American

4 small sausages

2 teaspoons vegetable oil
2 apples, peeled, cored and diced
1 large gherkin, diced
juice of ½ lemon
3 drops Tabasco sauce
3 tablespoons milk
salt, pepper and paprika
4 slices buttered toast
4 thin slices Cheddar cheese
8 slices tomato

Fry the sausages in oil until cooked and golden. Put the apple and gherkin into a small saucepan with the lemon juice, Tabasco, milk, salt, pepper and paprika. Simmer for 2 to 3 minutes, stirring, until the apple is tender.

Preheat the grill [broiler] to moderate. Divide the mixture on to the 4 slices of toast and spread evenly. Top each with sausage, slice of cheese and 2 slices of tomato. Grill [broil] until the cheese starts to melt.

WINNSBORO BEAN RAREBIT

Winnsboro is a small town in Texas, near Dallas, and this delicious, easy-to-make dish is a typical snack of the area. Serve for lunch or supper.

4 servings

Metric/Imperial

25g (1oz) butter
1 medium-sized onion, finely chopped
1 garlic clove, crushed
1 green pepper, white pith removed, seeded and finely chopped
396g (14oz) can kidney beans, drained
396g (14oz) can baked beans
4 tablespoons tomato ketchup
1 tablespoon Worcestershire sauce
½ teaspoon salt
1 teaspoon black pepper
½ teaspoon chilli powder
175g (6oz) Cheddar cheese, grated
4 large slices hot, buttered toast

American

2 tablespoons butter
1 medium-sized onion, finely chopped
1 garlic clove, crushed
1 green pepper, membrane and seeds removed, finely chopped
1 x 14oz can kidney beans, drained

Spicy Winnsboro Bean Rarebit is easy to make and delicious to eat!

1 x 14oz can baked beans
4 tablespoons tomato ketchup
1 tablespoon Worcestershire sauce
½ teaspoon salt
1 teaspoon black pepper
½ teaspoon chili powder
1½ cups Cheddar or American cheese, grated
4 large slices hot, buttered toast

In a medium-sized frying-pan, melt the butter over moderate heat. When the foam subsides add the onion, garlic and green pepper and fry, stirring occasionally, for 5 to 7 minutes or until the onion is soft and translucent but not brown. Stir in the kidney beans, baked beans, ketchup, Worcestershire sauce, salt, pepper and chilli powder and stir well. Cook, stirring occasionally, for a further 5 minutes.

Stir in the cheese and cook, stirring constantly, for a further 3 minutes or until the cheese has melted and the mixture is hot and thick. Serve on the toast slices.

FRANKFURTER BAKE

Frankfurter Bake is an ideal family dish when you're short of time and money. It is quick, easy and economical to prepare and tastes really delicious.

4 servings

Metric/Imperial

2 x 428g (2 x 15oz) cans baked beans
500g (1lb) frankfurters, thickly sliced
3 tablespoons soft brown sugar
250g (8oz) Cheddar cheese, grated

American

3½ cups canned baked beans
1lb frankfurters, thickly sliced
3 tablespoons soft brown sugar
2 cups Cheddar cheese, grated

Preheat the oven to moderate (180°C/350°F of Gas Mark 4).

Place the beans and frankfurters in a baking dish and sprinkle with the sugar. Cover with grated cheese. Bake for 45 minutes, or until the cheese has melted and is beginning to brown.

PIZZA SANDWICH

These individual pizza sandwiches are ideal for a lunch or supper snack.

1 serving

Metric/Imperial

1 slice of white bread
1 large tomato, sliced
salt and pepper
⅛ teaspoon dried oregano
4-6 canned or fresh sardines
2-3 black olives, stoned
1 slice of Bel Paese or Mozzarella
   cheese

American

1 slice of white bread
1 large tomato, sliced
salt and pepper
⅛ teaspoon dried oregano
4-6 canned or fresh sardines
2-3 ripe black olives, pitted
1 slice of Mozzarella or Parmesan or
   Romano cheese

Preheat the grill [broiler] to moderate. Butter the slice of bread and cover with the sliced tomato. Sprinkle with salt, pepper and a little oregano. Place the sardines on top, garnish with the stoned olives, and lay the slice of cheese over the top.

Place under the grill [broiler] and cook until the cheese is melted and slightly browned.

QUICK NATURAL MEALS
No one who truly cares about food and good eating will want to rely on convenience foods every time a meal has to be prepared in a hurry. There are plenty of superb natural foods which deserve to be classed as convenience foods, notably dairy products, eggs and vegetables. Many nutritious meals require no cooking at all. When the weather is hot and nobody wishes to spend hours working in the kitchen, the simplest and best meals are salads, which can offer endless variety and are unbeatable from the health aspect. Prepare some potato salad, quiches, meat loaf or Scotch Eggs in advance, keep a stock of continental sausage, canned meat and fish, eggs and a variety of cheeses, and you will never be short of ingredients for a nutritious cold platter. Salad vegetables will keep fresh for several days if washed and tied in a polythene bag

and stored in the refrigerator, but keep salad dressings separately and add them just before you serve. Ring the changes on the old salad themes by serving Beetroot and Onion Salad (page 171), Red Cabbage Salad (page 172), Salad Niçoise (page 172), or Tomato and French Bean Salad (page 170).

It is when the weather is cold that something more warming and substantial is needed. The following quick meals are good standard fare for any situation when you only have half an hour or so to prepare and cook a main meal and you will note that omelettes figure prominently. They are great standbys for working mothers and for everyone who occasionally has to prepare a snatched lunch, or a meal for ravenous appetites after a long day out. If you usually have three courses, start with soup or a cold starter and finish off the meal with fresh fruit, yogurt or ice cream, so that you only need to concentrate your energies on producing one course.

CORN BAKE

Corn Bake is a delicious and different dish to serve the family. It only takes 25 minutes to prepare and cook.

4 servings

Metric/Imperial

3 tablespoons butter
½ a green pepper, white pith removed,
   seeded and sliced
1 medium-sized onion, sliced
2 tablespoons flour
1 teaspoon prepared mustard
225ml (8 fl oz) milk
4 tomatoes, peeled and quartered
250g (8oz) cooked sweetcorn
1 teaspoon Worcestershire sauce
2 hard-boiled eggs, sliced
a little melted butter and
   breadcrumbs

American

3 tablespoons butter
½ a green pepper, membrane and
   seeds removed, sliced
1 medium-sized onion, sliced
2 tablespoons flour

1 teaspoon prepared mustard
1 cup milk
4 tomatoes, peeled and quartered
1 cup cooked corn
1 teaspoon Worcestershire sauce
2 hard-boiled eggs, sliced
a little melted butter and
   breadcrumbs

Preheat the oven to moderately hot (200°C/400°F or Gas Mark 6).

Melt the butter and soften the onion and pepper in it. Add the flour and mustard and stir well. Remove from the heat and gradually add the milk. Return to the heat and bring to the boil, stirring constantly.

Add the tomatoes, corn and Worcestershire sauce. Turn into a heatproof dish, top with slices of hard-boiled egg and finally scatter breadcrumbs on the top, spooning a little melted butter over all.

Bake for about 10 to 15 minutes until the Corn Bake is bubbling.

POTATO OMELETTE

This is a very solid and sustaining omelette. It will serve two people as a meal in itself, or three to four if accompanied by a salad or cooked vegetables. Other ingredients such as blanched and chopped pepper and scraps of cooked ham, bacon or continental sausage may be added.

2-4 servings

Metric/Imperial

1 tablespoon vegetable oil
1 large potato, peeled and finely diced
1 medium-sized onion, peeled and
   chopped
2 tomatoes, peeled and chopped
4 eggs
salt and pepper
1 tablespoon chopped fresh parsley
50g (2oz) Cheddar cheese, grated

American

1 tablespoon vegetable oil
1 large potato, peeled and finely diced
1 medium-sized onion, peeled and
   chopped
2 tomatoes, peeled and chopped

A simple but filling dish, Spanish Omelette is made with peas, tomatoes and pimentos, and flavoured with onion and garlic.

4 eggs
salt and pepper
1 tablespoon chopped fresh parsley
½ cup Cheddar or American cheese, grated

In a large frying-pan with a lid, warm the oil and add the finely diced potato and onion. Cook over moderate heat, stirring occasionally, until the potatoes and onion are lightly browned. Lower the heat, cover, and continue to cook for a further 5 to 7 minutes, or until the potatoes are cooked through. Add the chopped tomatoes and any other ingredients, cover and warm through.

Meanwhile, beat the eggs with seasoning to taste. Stir in the parsley and pour the eggs over the contents of the pan, moving the pan to distribute the eggs evenly. Cook for 3 to 4 minutes.

Pre-heat the grill [broiler]. When the omelette is setting underneath but still liquid on top, sprinkle over the grated cheese and place under the hot grill [broiler] until the cheese is melted and the omelette is puffed up and lightly browned. Remove from the heat, cut into halves or wedges, and serve immediately.

SPANISH OMELETTE

Spanish Omelette is a classic dish, with many regional variations – the version given here is a relatively simple one with pimentoes, onion and garlic. It is different from an ordinary omelette in that it is usually cooked on both sides.

2-3 servings

Metric/Imperial

2 tablespoons vegetable oil
1 onion, finely chopped
3 garlic cloves, crushed
2 medium-sized tomatoes, peeled and chopped
6 tablespoons canned pimentoes, chopped (optional)
6 eggs
¼ teaspoon salt
¼ teaspoon black pepper
1 tablespoon milk
50g (2oz) frozen peas

American

2 tablespoons vegetable oil
1 onion, finely chopped
3 garlic cloves, crushed
2 medium-sized tomatoes, peeled and chopped
6 tablespoons canned pimentos, chopped (optional)
6 eggs
¼ teaspoon salt
¼ teaspoon black pepper
1 tablespoon milk
¼ cup frozen peas

In a medium-sized frying-pan, heat the oil over moderate heat. Add the onion and garlic and fry, stirring occasionally, for 5 to 7 minutes or until soft and translucent but not brown. Stir in the tomatoes and pimentoes, if using, and

211

fry for a further 3 minutes. Remove the pan from the heat and keep warm.

Beat the eggs, salt, pepper and milk together with a fork. Stir in the peas.

Preheat the grill [broiler] to high.

Return the pan to the heat and pour the egg mixture over the vegetables. Stir the mixture together, then leave it for a few minutes until the bottom sets. Reduce the heat to low. Lift the bottom edges of the omelette, tilting the pan away from you so that the liquid egg on top runs on to the bottom. Put the pan down and leave until the omelette begins to set again.

Place under the grill [broiler] for 2 minutes to set the top.

OMELETTE PROVENCALE

This is just one version of the traditional French Omelette Provençale. It is delicately herb-flavoured, and is best served with a simple green salad.

4 servings
Metric/Imperial
8 eggs
salt and black pepper
2 tablespoons water
4 tablespoons butter
FILLING
1 medium onion, sliced
2 tablespoons butter
8 large tomatoes, peeled and chopped
½ teaspoon dried oregano
½ teaspoon dried basil
salt and pepper

American
8 eggs
salt and black pepper
2 tablespoons water
4 tablespoons butter
FILLING
1 medium onion, sliced
2 tablespoons butter
8 large tomatoes, peeled and chopped
½ teaspoon dried oregano
½ teaspoon dried basil
salt and pepper

Prepare the filling first. Gently sauté the onion in the melted butter. Add the tomatoes and simmer for about 10 minutes. Season with the herbs, salt and pepper.

Set the pan to one side of the stove to keep hot.

Break four of the eggs at a time into a bowl. Season with salt and pepper and add 1 tablespoon of water. Melt half the butter in an omelette pan and pour the beaten eggs on to it.

Start cooking, at a very high temperature, then reduce the heat a little. To prevent the omelette sticking, shake the pan to and fro and keep the egg mixture moving with a fork. While the omelette is still 'runny' in the centre, add half of the tomato and onion filling.

Cook until the egg mixture is fairly firm and serve immediately.

Repeat the process with the remaining four eggs.

OMELETTE ARNOLD BENNETT

Omelette Arnold Bennett is different from the classic French omelette in that the eggs are separated and the omelette finishes cooking under the grill [broiler]. Serve with puréed spinach.

2-3 servings
Metric/Imperial
40g (1½oz) butter
100g (4oz) cooked, flaked, smoked haddock
150ml (5 fl oz) double cream
6 eggs, separated
3 tablespoons grated Parmesan cheese
½ teaspoon salt
¼ teaspoon black pepper
1 tablespoon finely chopped fresh parsley

American
3 tablespoons butter
¼lb cooked finnan haddie (smoked haddock)
⅝ cup heavy cream
6 eggs, separated
3 tablespoons grated Parmesan cheese
½ teaspoon salt
¼ teaspoon black pepper
1 tablespoon finely chopped fresh parsley

In a small frying-pan, melt two-thirds of the butter over moderate heat. When the foam subsides add the smoked haddock and 2 tablespoons of the cream, stirring well to mix. When the cream is hot set aside to cool.

Beat the egg yolks with half of the cheese and the salt, pepper and parsley. Add the fish mixture.

Beat the egg whites until they form stiff peaks. With a metal spoon, fold them into the haddock mixture.

Preheat the grill [broiler] to high.

In a large omelette pan, melt the remaining butter over moderate heat. When the foam subsides pour in the egg mixture. Leave it for 2 minutes or until the bottom sets and becomes brown.

Sprinkle over the remaining cheese and pour over the remaining cream. Remove the pan from the heat and place under the grill [broiler]. Cook for 30 seconds.

PIPERADE

One of the great classic French regional dishes, Pipérade originated in the Basque country near Bearn, although it is now popular all over France.

2-3 servings
Metric/Imperial
3 tablespoons vegetable oil
1 small onion, finely chopped
2 garlic cloves, crushed
1 green pepper, white pith removed, seeded and chopped
1 red pepper, white pith removed, seeded and chopped
3 tomatoes, peeled and chopped
6 eggs
¼ teaspoon salt
¼ teaspoon black pepper
2 tablespoons water

American
3 tablespoons vegetable oil
1 small onion, finely chopped
2 garlic cloves, crushed
1 green pepper, membrane and seeds removed, chopped
1 red pepper, membrane and seeds removed, chopped

3 tomatoes, peeled and chopped
6 eggs
¼ teaspoon salt
¼ teaspoon black pepper
2 tablespoons water

In a large frying-pan, heat the oil over moderate heat. Add the onion, garlic and peppers and cook, stirring occasionally, for 5 to 7 minutes or until the onion is soft and translucent but not brown. Stir in the tomatoes and cook, stirring occasionally, for 5 minutes.

Meanwhile beat the eggs, salt, pepper and water together until well mixed.

Pour all the egg mixture into the pan with the tomato mixture. Stir, then leave for a few seconds until the bottom sets. Using a palette knife or spatula, lift the edges of the omelette and tilt the pan away from you so that the liquid

A classic French omelette, Pipérade is made with a mixture of green and red peppers and tomatoes.

egg escapes from the top and runs on to the pan.

Put the pan down and leave until the omelette begins to set again.

Slide on to a warmed serving dish, cut into portions and serve at once.

MUSHROOM AND BACON OMELETTE

A sustaining dish, Mushroom and Bacon Omelette may be served with grilled [broiled] tomatoes and a salad.

2 servings
Metric/Imperial

25g (1oz) butter
1 small onion, finely chopped
2 streaky bacon slices, diced
4 mushrooms, wiped clean and thinly sliced
4 eggs
¼ teaspoon salt
¼ teaspoon black pepper

1½ tablespoons cold water

American

2 tablespoons butter
1 small onion, finely chopped
2 slices bacon, diced
4 mushrooms, wiped clean and thinly sliced
4 eggs
¼ teaspoon salt
¼ teaspoon black pepper
1½ tablespoons cold water

In a small frying-pan, melt half the butter over moderate heat. When the foam subsides add the onion and bacon and cook, stirring occasionally, for 5 minutes. Add the mushrooms and cook for a further 3 minutes, or until the mushrooms are lightly cooked and the bacon is crisp. Transfer the mixture to a plate and keep warm.

Beat the eggs, salt, pepper and water together with a fork. Add the onion mixture and beat until well mixed.

In a medium-sized omelette pan,

melt the remaining butter over moderate heat. When the foam subsides, pour in the egg mixture. Stir, then leave for a few seconds until the bottom sets. Reduce the heat to low. Using a palette knife or spatula lift the edges of the omelette and, at the same time, tilt the pan so that the liquid egg escapes from the top and runs on to the pan. Put the pan down and leave until the omelette begins to set again. Tilt the pan again and, with the help of the palette knife, flip one half over to make a semi-circle.

Cut into two and serve at once.

HERB OMELETTE

One of the great classic French omelettes, Herb Omelette makes a delicious and elegant lunch dish.

2-3 servings

Metric/Imperial

6 eggs
¼ teaspoon salt
¼ teaspoon black pepper
2 tablespoons cold water
1½ tablespoons chopped fresh mixed herbs
1 tablespoon butter

American

6 eggs
¼ teaspoon salt
¼ teaspoon black pepper
2 tablespoons cold water
1½ tablespoons chopped fresh mixed herbs (parsley, chervil, chives and tarragon)
1 tablespoon butter

Beat the eggs, salt, pepper, water and herbs together with a fork until well mixed.

In a large omelette pan, melt the butter over moderate heat. When the foam subsides pour in the egg mixture. Stir, then leave for a few seconds until the bottom sets. Reduce the heat to low. Using a palette knife or spatula, lift the edges of the omelette, tilting the pan so that the liquid egg escapes from the top and runs on to the pan. Put

the pan down and leave until the omelette begins to set again. Tilt the pan and, with the help of the palette knife, flip one half over to make a semi-circle.

Cut into portions and serve at once.

ONION OMELETTE

A delicious supper dish, Onion Omelette may be served with fried potatoes and Brussels sprouts.

2-3 servings

Metric/Imperial

25g (1oz) butter
2 small onions, thinly sliced
6 eggs
¼ teaspoon salt
¼ teaspoon black pepper
2 tablespoons cold water
1 tablespoon chopped fresh parsley

Ranchers Eggs are baked with vegetables and cheese.

American

2 tablespoons butter
2 small onions, thinly sliced
6 eggs
¼ teaspoon salt
¼ teaspoon black pepper
2 tablespoons cold water
1 tablespoon chopped fresh parsley

In a small frying-pan, melt half the butter over moderate heat. When the foam subsides add the onions and cook, stirring occasionally, for 5 to 7 minutes or until soft and translucent but not brown. Set aside and keep warm.

Beat the eggs, salt, pepper, water and parsley together with a fork until well mixed.

In a large omelette pan, melt the remaining butter over moderate heat. When the foam subsides, pour in the egg mixture. Stir, then leave for a few seconds until the bottom sets. Reduce the heat to low. Using a palette knife or spatula, lift the edges of the omelette and, at the same time, tilt the pan so that the liquid egg escapes from the top and runs on to the pan. Put the pan down and leave until the omelette begins to set again.

Spoon over the onions. Tilt the pan again, and, with the help of the palette knife, flip one half of the omelette over to make a semi-circle.

Cut into portions and serve at once.

RANCHERS EGGS

A relatively inexpensive supper dish, Ranchers Eggs is delicious served with slices of fresh bread.

6 servings

Metric/Imperial

1 tablespoon vegetable oil
2 garlic cloves, crushed
2 medium-sized onions, finely chopped
6 large tomatoes, peeled and chopped
50g (2oz) canned pimentoes, chopped
1 green chilli, seeded and chopped
1 teaspoon sugar
1 teaspoon salt
½ teaspoon black pepper

Stuffed Aubergines [Eggplants] is a filling, tasty dish.

½ teaspoon ground coriander
12 eggs
175g (6oz) Cheddar cheese, grated
1 tablespoon butter
¼ teaspoon chilli powder

American

1 tablespoon vegetable oil
2 garlic cloves, crushed
2 medium-sized onions, finely chopped
6 large tomatoes, peeled and chopped
1 x 2oz can pimentoes, chopped
1 green chili pepper seeded and chopped
1 teaspoon sugar
1 teaspoon salt
½ teaspoon black pepper
½ teaspoon ground coriander
12 eggs
1½ cups Cheddar cheese, grated
1 tablespoon butter
¼ teaspoon chili powder

Preheat the oven to very hot (230°C/450°F or Gas Mark 8).

In a large frying-pan heat the oil over moderate heat. Add the garlic and onions and fry, stirring occasionally, for 5 to 7 minutes, or until soft and translucent but not brown. Add the tomatoes, pimentoes, chilli, sugar, salt, pepper and coriander.

Reduce the heat and simmer, stirring frequently, for 15 to 20 minutes.

Transfer the mixture to a large oven-proof baking dish. With the back of a tablespoon make 12 hollows in the mixture. Break an egg into each hollow.

Sprinkle the cheese over the eggs. Dot with the butter and sprinkle on the chilli powder.

Bake in the centre of the oven for 6 to 8 minutes or until the cheese is golden brown and the eggs have set.

STUFFED AUBERGINES [EGGPLANTS]

This delicious dish takes only 30 minutes to prepare and cook.

4 servings

Metric/Imperial

2 medium-sized aubergines
4 tablespoons vegetable oil
1 large onion, sliced
1 large clove of garlic, chopped
6 canned tomatoes, chopped
salt and freshly ground black pepper
a large pinch of dried marjoram
1 tablespoon chopped fresh parsley
3 tablespoons fresh breadcrumbs
2 tablespoons butter

American

2 medium-sized eggplants
4 tablespoons vegetable oil
1 large onion, sliced
1 large clove of garlic, chopped
6 canned tomatoes, chopped
salt and freshly ground black pepper
a large pinch of dried marjoram
1 teaspoon chopped fresh parsley
3 tablespoons fresh breadcrumbs
2 tablespoons butter

Preheat the oven to fairly hot (190°C/375°F or Gas Mark 5).

Wipe the aubergines [eggplants]. Cut each in half lengthwise and scoop out the pulp. Sprinkle a little salt inside the cases and turn upside down to drain.

Heat the oil and gently cook the onion and garlic. Chop the pulp from the aubergines [eggplants], add this to the pan, with the chopped tomatoes. Cook a little longer, then season with the salt, pepper and herbs, and add the breadcrumbs.

Drain and wipe the aubergine [eggplant] shells and spoon in the filling. Dot with the butter and bake for about 20 minutes.

Variations:
Prepare the aubergines [eggplants] as above, and try an alternative filling, mixed with the pulp.

250g (8oz) of minced [ground] beef fried with a finely chopped onion, a tablespoon of tomato purée and seasoned well. Bind with a beaten egg.

250g (8oz) of minced [ground] beef fried with a finely chopped onion, and seasoned with ¼ teaspoon chilli powder, a little salt and a tablespoon of chutney or pickle.

STUFFED PEPPERS

Stuffed vegetables make a quick and sustaining meal.

6 servings

Metric/Imperial

6 green peppers, white pith removed and seeded
STUFFING
1 onion, finely chopped
100g (4oz) mushrooms, wiped and chopped
2 tablespoons butter
4 tomatoes, peeled and chopped
175g (6oz) rice, cooked
salt and pepper
½ teaspoon dried thyme
300ml (10 fl oz) beef stock

American

6 green peppers, membranes and seeds removed
STUFFING
1 onion, finely chopped
¼lb mushrooms, wiped and chopped
2 tablespoons butter
4 tomatoes, peeled and chopped
10 cups cooked rice
salt and pepper
½ teaspoon dried thyme
1¼ cups beef stock

Preheat the oven to moderate (180°C/350°F or Gas Mark 4).

Parboil the peppers for 5 minutes, drain and refresh under cold water.

Fry the onion in the melted butter until it is soft but not brown and add the mushrooms to it. Add the tomatoes and cooked rice and season with salt, pepper and herbs.

Stuff the peppers with this mixture and pack them into a well buttered deep heatproof dish. Spoon over the stock. Bake for about 20 minutes basting frequently.

Variations:
In place of the stock spoon a Tomato Sauce or tomato soup over the peppers.

Replace the four tomatoes with 175g (6 oz) [¾ cup] of shredded ham, and add a little finely chopped garlic or garlic salt to the onions in the pan.

Any chopped, leftover meat may be used as the main ingredient.

STUFFED BAKED POTATOES

Baked potatoes will take between 30 minutes and one hour to cook, depending on size. The advantage of this dish is that all the actual preparation is done in the last 15 minutes, leaving you free to attend to other things while the potatoes are cooking.

4 servings

Metric/Imperial

8 potatoes
a little vegetable oil
salt
4 tablespoons butter
50g (2oz) Cheddar cheese, grated
75ml (3 fl oz) sour cream
2 tablespoons chopped spring onions or chives
6 slices streaky bacon, fried until crisp

American

8 Idaho potatoes
a little vegetable oil
salt
4 tablespoons butter
½ cup Cheddar or American cheese, grated
⅜ cup sour cream
2 tablespoons chopped scallions or fresh chives
6 slices bacon, fried until crisp and crumbled

Preheat the oven to fairly hot (220°C/425°F or Gas Mark 7).

Choose firm smooth potatoes: new potatoes are not suitable for baking. Wash, scrub and dry them and prick all over with a fork. Rub a little oil into the skins, roll them in salt, and bake in the oven until cooked.

Cut the potatoes in half, scoop out the insides, and mix with the butter, cheese, sour cream and chopped spring onions or chives. Refill the potato shells and return to the oven to reheat thoroughly.

Chop the bacon into small pieces and sprinkle over the potatoes.

Variations:
A small bunch of watercress, chopped and mixed with a little cream cheese, salt, black pepper.

Coarsely chopped celery mixed with the cooked flesh of the potato, and a little melted butter.

Chopped red pepper with a pinch of marjoram mixed into the flesh of the potato with a little butter.

SPAGHETTI ALLA CARBONARA

This delicious dish of spaghetti tossed with eggs and bacon strips takes only 20 minutes to prepare and cook.

4 servings

Metric/Imperial

500g (1lb) spaghetti or macaroni shapes
75g (3oz) butter
6 slices bacon or ham
4 eggs
2 tablespoons Parmesan cheese, grated
salt and freshly ground black pepper
extra Parmesan

Delicious Spaghetti alla Carbonara is a quickly prepared dish of spaghetti tossed with eggs and bacon.

American

1lb spaghetti or macaroni shapes
6 tablespoons butter
6 slices bacon or ham
4 eggs
2 tablespoons Parmesan cheese, grated
salt and freshly ground black pepper
extra Parmesan

Boil the spaghetti in plenty of salted water until tender (about 12 minutes). Drain well, put into a heated dish with half the butter.

Meanwhile cut the ham or bacon into matchstick-sized strips and fry in the remaining butter until it starts to crisp.

When the spaghetti is cooked, beat the eggs in a bowl and add them to the fried bacon or ham. Stir until the mixture starts to thicken, so that it has a slightly granular appearance, but it is not as thick as scrambled eggs.

Season the eggs and bacon, add the grated Parmesan cheese and pour the mixture over the spaghetti, stirring with a wooden spoon so that the ingredients are evenly distributed in the dish.

Serve with extra grated Parmesan cheese.

CHINESE SWEET AND SOUR PORK

Chinese quick-cooking dishes work on the principle that the ingredients are very thinly sliced or diced and then stir-fried rapidly. Chinese Sweet and Sour Pork is a good example of this method of cooking. Serve with plain, boiled rice or noodles.

4 servings

Metric/Imperial

500g (1lb) raw pork, thinly sliced
2 medium-sized carrots, scraped and thinly sliced
2 small green peppers, white pith removed, seeded and thinly sliced
2 tablespoons vegetable oil
100g (4oz) green peas
SAUCE
2 tablespoons soy sauce
150ml (5 fl oz) stock or water

Liver and Sausage Brochettes is an extremely colourful and tasty dish.

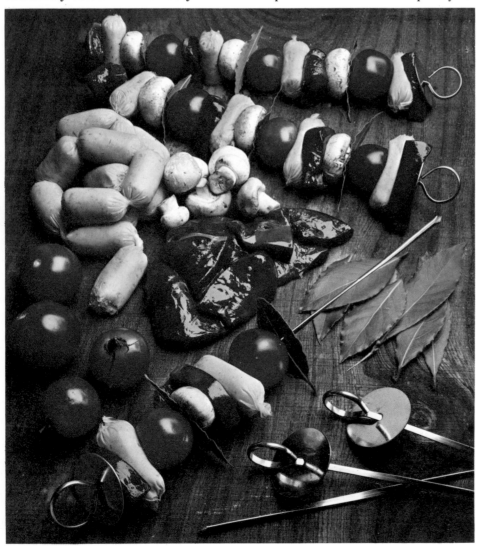

1 tablespoon cornflour
1 tablespoon brown sugar
1 tablespoon vinegar
salt

American

1lb boned loin of pork, thinly sliced
2 medium-sized carrots, scraped and thinly sliced
2 small green peppers, membrane and seeds removed, thinly sliced
2 tablespoons vegetable oil
1 cup green peas
SAUCE
2 tablespoons soy sauce
⅝ cup stock or water
1 tablespoon cornstarch
1 tablespoon brown sugar
1 tablespoon vinegar
salt

Heat the oil in a shallow pan and add the pork slices. Sauté them quickly for

a few minutes. Add the vegetables and sauté for a further 3 minutes.

Mix the ingredients for the sauce together and pour them over the pork and vegetable mixture. Stir the mixture steadily until it comes to the boil. Cover and simmer for a further 10 minutes, stirring frequently. Season with a little more vinegar, salt and sugar if necessary. The pork should be cooked and the vegetables still crisp.

LIVER AND SAUSAGE BROCHETTES

An unusual and exceptionally tasty dish, Liver and Sausage Brochettes consist of bite-sized pieces of liver, chipolata sausages, mushrooms, tomatoes and bay leaves threaded on skewers and quickly grilled [broiled]. Sprays of thyme may be substituted for the bay leaves, and pieces of onion or green pepper may also be added. The brochettes are served on a bed of rice and may be accompanied by a salad.

4 servings

Metric/Imperial

500g (1lb) calf's liver
500g (1lb) small (chipolata) sausages
250g (8oz) button mushrooms, wiped clean
175g (6oz) butter, melted
black pepper
24 bay leaves
6 large tomatoes, quartered or 24 tiny tomatoes

American

1lb calf liver
1lb small sausages
½lb small mushrooms, wiped clean
¾ cup butter, melted
black pepper
24 bay leaves
6 large tomatoes, quartered or 24 cherry tomatoes

Preheat the grill [broiler] to moderate.

Cut the liver into cubes. Leave the sausages and mushrooms whole.

Pour the melted butter into a shallow bowl and roll the liver cubes in it. Season with black pepper.

Squeeze the centre of each sausage, twist and cut to form two smaller sausages.

Thread the liver cubes, sausages, mushrooms, bay leaves and tomatoes on eight long skewers in alternating order.

Brush the brochettes with half the remaining melted butter.

Place the skewers under the grill [broiler] and cook for 6 to 8 minutes on each side, brushing them with the remaining butter when you turn them over.

DIJON KIDNEYS

Dijon Kidneys can be prepared and cooked in just 25 minutes. The mustard sauce makes this delicious dish acceptable even to those who do not usually like the flavour of kidneys.

4 servings

Metric/Imperial

750g (1½lb) lambs' kidneys, prepared and roughly chopped

1 tablespoon margarine
1 tablespoon vegetable oil
2 tablespoons flour
300ml (10 fl oz) milk
2-3 tablespoons French mustard
salt and black pepper
6 tablespoons coarsely chopped fresh parsley
250g (8oz) rice, cooked and drained

American

1½lb lamb kidneys, prepared and roughly chopped
1 tablespoon margarine
1 tablespoon vegetable oil
2 tablespoons flour
1¼ cups milk
2-3 tablespoons French mustard
salt and black pepper
6 tablespoons coarsely chopped fresh parsley
1 cup rice, cooked and drained

Heat the margarine and oil in a large thick-bottomed saucepan. Add the kidneys and cook over medium heat for 4 to 5 minutes, turning constantly to ensure even cooking.

Quickly prepared Dijon Kidneys is made with a delicious mustard sauce. Serve with boiled rice.

Transfer to a serving dish and place in a low oven to keep warm.

Add the flour to the fat remaining in pan. Stir well, then pour on the milk and stir over medium heat until a smooth thick sauce is obtained.

Stir in the mustard, season to taste with salt and pepper and add the chopped parsley. Simmer gently for 5 minutes.

Put the kidneys and their juices back into the pan and stir into the sauce, then turn into the centre of a serving dish. Surround with a ring of rice.

DEVILLED KIDNEYS

Liver and kidneys are useful for many quick meals. Serve Devilled Kidneys sprinkled with chopped parsley, creamy mashed potatoes and a green vegetables or rice, macaroni or noodles.

Metric/Imperial

8 lambs' kidneys, prepared and
chopped
1 tablespoon flour
2 tablespoons butter
2 onions, chopped
225-300ml (8-10 fl oz) water
a few drops of Tabasco sauce
salt

American

8 lamb kidneys, prepared and diced
1 tablespoon flour
2 tablespoons butter
2 onions, diced
1-1¼ cups water
a few drops of Tabasco sauce
salt

Toss the kidneys in the flour. Melt half
the fat and sauté the onions until
cooked but not browned, then remove
them temporarily from frying-pan.
Heat the remaining fat in the pan to
smoking hot and brown the kidneys,
stirring all the time.

Return the onions to the pan, and add
the water, stirring continuously. Add
the salt and Tabasco sauce, taste, and
adjust if necessary. Simmer, covered,
for 15 minutes or until the kidneys are
cooked.

If a thicker sauce is liked blend about
1 teaspoon cornflour [cornstarch] with
some of the gravy and add this to the
pan, stirring until thickened.

KIDNEYS IN BUTTER

This dish is one of the quickest ways to
prepare kidneys. Serve the kidneys with
creamed potatoes and French beans.

4 servings

Metric/Imperial

25g (1oz) butter
12 lambs' kidneys, cleaned, prepared
and thinly sliced
2 tablespoons dry sherry
1 tablespoon lemon juice
½ teaspoon prepared English mustard
¼ teaspoon black pepper
¼ teaspoon sugar

American

2 tablespoons butter
12 lamb kidneys, cleaned, prepared
and thinly sliced
2 tablespoons dry sherry
1 tablespoon lemon juice
½ teaspoon prepared mustard
¼ teaspoon black pepper
¼ teaspoon sugar

In a medium-sized frying-pan, melt the
butter over moderate heat. Add the
kidney slices and cook, stirring frequently, for 5 minutes.

Pour the sherry and lemon juice into
the dish and add the mustard, pepper
and sugar. Cook for a further 2 minutes
stirring constantly.

LIVER WITH ONIONS

This is a classic Italian dish, a simple
and tasty combination of liver and
onions. Traditionally, calf's liver is
used, though any type of liver can be
cooked in this way. It may be accompanied by potatoes or noodles.

4 servings

Metric/Imperial

750g (1½lb) calf's liver, very thinly
sliced
1 teaspoon salt
¼ teaspoon black pepper
25g (1oz) butter
2 tablespoons vegetable oil
3 large onions, thinly sliced and
pushed out into rings
1 tablespoon chopped fresh parsley

American

1½lb calf liver, very thinly sliced
1 teaspoon salt
¼ teaspoon black pepper
2 tablespoons butter
2 tablespoons vegetable oil
3 large onions, thinly sliced and
separated into rings
1 tablespoon chopped fresh parsley

Rub the liver with the salt and pepper.

In a large frying-pan, melt the butter
with the oil over moderate heat. When
the foam subsides, add the onions. Fry,
stirring occasionally, for 5 to 7 minutes,
or until soft and translucent but not
brown.

Add the liver slices to the pan, a few
at a time, and fry for 2 to 3 minutes on
each side. Remove and keep warm
while the remaining slices are fried.

Remove the pan from the heat and
turn the liver and onions into a warmed
serving dish. Sprinkle with the parsley
and serve at once.

CREAMED CHICKEN LIVERS

This savoury mixture is an unusual way
of preparing chicken livers.

4 servings

Metric/Imperial

50g (2oz) butter
2 onions, thinly sliced and pushed out
into rings
12 chicken livers, cut into strips
225ml (8 fl oz) single cream
2 hard-boiled eggs, coarsely chopped
½ teaspoon salt
½ teaspoon white pepper
½ teaspoon paprika

American

¼ cup butter
2 onions, thinly sliced and separated
into rings
12 chicken livers, cut into strips
1 cup light cream
2 hard-boiled eggs, coarsely chopped
½ teaspoon salt
½ teaspoon white pepper
½ teaspoon paprika

In a medium-sized frying-pan melt
half of the butter over moderate heat.
When the foam subsides add the onion
rings and fry for 6 to 8 minutes or until
golden brown. Transfer to a large plate.

Add the chicken liver strips to the
pan and fry for 4 to 5 minutes, adding
more butter if necessary. Mix them
with the onions.

Add the remaining butter to the
frying-pan and melt it over low heat.
Add the cream, livers, onions, eggs,
salt, pepper and paprika.

Cook, stirring briskly, for 4 to 5
minutes but do not boil.

Bread, cakes and biscuits (cookies)

All the recipes in this section are intended to be standards for family baking. You won't find recipes for luxury gateaux, but you will hopefully find plenty of economical and quick cakes and biscuits [cookies], many of which can be made with ingredients generally on hand in a store-cupboard, when you have time to spare and feel creative. Of course, today you can buy a whole assortment of cake mixes, bread mixes and other instant bakes, which are a great help for busy cooks but don't provide quite the satisfaction of doing it all yourself.

Although biscuits [cookies] are obtainable in variety and fairly cheaply, they too can never compare with the ones you bake yourself, and even though you will find that your home-made biscuits [cookies] disappear fast, they are so quick to cook that you can make a double quantity and bake in two batches, or store a batch of dough in a covered container in the refrigerator for a couple of days.

Bread-making at home is enjoying a massive revival, and you will find here recipes for ordinary white Household Bread, delicious Wholewheat Bread and quick Irish Soda Bread. If you want to be really adventurous with yeast cookery, try Chelsea Buns or Crumpets for a special treat.

Many of the cakes are tried-and-tested traditional favourites. Victorian Orange Buns were enjoyed by children a hundred years ago, and you will find them just as popular today with both children and adults. If you have never tried making Parkin, a moist oatmeal ginger-bread from the North of England, real Scottish Shortbread, or those American specialities Devil's Food Cake, Brownies and Banana Walnut Loaf, then follow the recipes given here and you will soon find out why these are established favourites in so many homes.

HOUSEHOLD BREAD

Simple and economical to make, Household Bread is ordinary white bread, the type most often seen in shops. But like anything home-made, it certainly looks and tastes better. This recipe makes enough dough to fill four 500g (1lb) loaf tins, but it is more interesting to bake the bread in different containers, or shape the dough into individual braids, rolls, long French-style loaves or round Italian-style loaves.

Four 500g (1lb) loaves

Metric/Imperial

1 teaspoon sugar
¾ litre (1½ pints) lukewarm water
25g (1oz) dried yeast
1½ kg (3lb) strong plain flour
1 tablespoon salt

American

1 teaspoon sugar
3¾ cups lukewarm water
1 x 1oz cake compressed yeast
12 cups enriched all-purpose flour
1 tablespoon salt

Grease the four tins. Dissolve the sugar in one-third of the lukewarm water. Sprinkle on the dried yeast, whisk and leave in a warm, draught-free place for 15 to 20 minutes or until puffed up and frothy.

Put the flour and the salt into a warmed, large mixing bowl. Make a well in the centre and pour in the yeast and the remaining lukewarm water. Using your hands or a spatula, gradually draw the flour into the liquid. Continue mixing until all the flour is incorporated and the dough comes away from the sides of the bowl.

Turn out on to a floured board and knead for about 10 minutes or until elastic and smooth.

Put in a greased bowl and cover with a damp cloth. Leave in a warm, draught-free place for 1 to 1½ hours or until doubled in bulk.

Knead the dough again on a floured surface for about 8 minutes, cut into 4, shape and place the loaves in the tins. Cover with a damp cloth and return to a warm place for about 45 minutes or until the dough has risen to the top of the tins.

Preheat the oven to very hot (240°C/ 475°F or Gas Mark 9).

Place the tins in the centre of the oven and bake for 15 minutes. Then lower the temperature to hot (220°C/ 425°F or Gas Mark 7), put the bread on a lower shelf and bake for another 25 to 30 minutes.

Remove the bread from the tins and rap the undersides with your knuckles. If it sound hollow, it is cooked. If not, lower the oven temperature to fairly hot, return the loaves, upside-down, to the oven and bake for 5 to 10 minutes.

Cool the loaves on a wire rack.

WHOLEWHEAT BREAD

Home-made wholewheat bread is far superior to any commercial brown bread. Although it is most delicious when freshly baked, stored correctly the bread keeps extremely well and can be served up to a week after baking.

To make cheese bread, add 350g (12 oz) [3 cups] of grated cheese to the flour with the yeast mixture.

Four 500g (1lb) loaves

Metric/Imperial

1 teaspoon sugar
¾ litre (1½ pints) lukewarm water
25g (1oz) dried yeast
1½ kg (3lb) stone-ground wholewheat flour
1 tablespoon salt
2 tablespoons honey
1 tablespoon vegetable oil

American

1 teaspoon brown sugar
3¾ cups lukewarm water
1 x 1oz cake compressed yeast
12 cups coarsely ground wholewheat flour
1 tablespoon salt
2 tablespoons honey
1 tablespoon vegetable oil

Irish Soda Bread is easy to make and delicious to eat

Grease the 4 loaf tins. Dissolve the sugar in one-third of the lukewarm water. Sprinkle on the dried yeast, whisk and leave in a warm, draught-free place for 15 to 20 minutes until puffed up and frothy.

Put the flour and salt into a large warmed mixing bowl. Make a well in the centre and pour in the yeast mixture, the honey, the remaining luke-warm water and the oil. Using your fingers or a spatula, gradually draw the flour into the liquid. Continue mixing until all the flour is incorporated and the dough comes away from the sides of the bowl.

Turn the dough out on to a floured board or marble slab and knead for 10 minutes or until elastic and smooth.

Put in a greased bowl and cover with a damp cloth. Leave in a warm, draught-free place for 1 to 1½ hours or until doubled in bulk.

Knead the dough again on a floured

For unusual-shaped loaves, bake Wholewheat Bread in flower pots.

surface for about 8 minutes. Cut into 4 pieces, and place the loaves in the tins. Cover with a damp cloth and return to a warm place for about 45 minutes or until the dough has risen to the top of the tins.

Bake as for Household Bread.

IRISH SODA BREAD

This traditional Irish bread is surprisingly quick and easy to prepare. It should be served slightly warm with butter and jam for tea.

One 20cm (8in) loaf

Metric/Imperial

500g (1lb) flour
1 teaspoon bicarbonate of soda
1 teaspoon salt
100–225ml (4 to 8 fl oz) buttermilk or
   sour milk

American

4 cups flour
1 teaspoon baking soda

1 teaspoon salt
½ to 1 cup buttermilk

Preheat the oven to hot (220°C/425°F or Gas Mark 7). Grease a large baking sheet.

Sift the flour, soda and salt into a large mixing bowl. Gradually beat in the buttermilk until the dough is smooth but firm.

Transfer the dough to a floured board and shape it into a flat, round loaf about 20cm (8-inches) across.

Place the loaf on the baking sheet and cut a deep cross on top. Bake for 30 to 35 minutes or until the top is golden brown.

SCONES [BISCUITS] WITH DRIED FRUIT

Scones with Dried Fruit are best served piping hot, spread with butter, jam and, if liked, cream.

About 12 scones [biscuits]

Metric/Imperial

225g (8oz) plain flour
2 teaspoons baking powder
1 teaspoon bicarbonate of soda
¼ teaspoon salt
40g (1½oz) cooking fat
50g (2oz) castor sugar
50g (2oz) raisins
2 tablespoons currants
1 egg, beaten with 5 tablespoons milk

American

2 cups enriched all-purpose flour
2 teaspoons baking powder
1 teaspoon baking soda
¼ teaspoon salt
3 tablespoons lard
¼ cup fine sugar
⅓ cup raisins
2 tablespoons currants
1 egg, beaten with 5 tablespoons milk

Preheat the oven to very hot (230°C/450°F or Gas Mark 8). Grease a large baking sheet.

Sift the flour, baking powder, soda and salt into a mixing bowl. Rub in the fat until the mixture resembles fine breadcrumbs. Stir in the sugar, raisins and currants. Mix in enough of the egg and milk to form a soft dough. Knead slightly.

Turn the dough out on to a lightly floured board and roll out to about about 1cm (½-inch) thick circles.

Place the circles, well spaced apart, on the prepared baking sheet. Bake for 10 to 15 minutes or until risen and golden brown.

BUTTERMILK SCONES [BISCUITS]

These American scones [biscuits] are easy to make. The addition of buttermilk to the batter makes them especially light and fluffy.

18 scones [biscuits]

Metric/Imperial

50g (2oz) butter

350g (12oz) plain flour
1 teaspoon salt
1 teaspoon baking powder
½ teaspoon bicarbonate of soda
300ml (10 fl oz) buttermilk or sour
   milk

American

¼ cup butter
3 cups all-purpose flour
1 teaspoon salt
1 teaspoon baking powder
½ teaspoon baking soda
1¼ cups buttermilk

Preheat the oven to hot (220°C/
425°F or Gas Mark 7). Grease a
baking sheet.

Left: Serve Scones with Dried
Fruit hot with butter and jam.

Buttermilk Scones are beautifully
light and fluffy.

Sift the flour, salt, baking powder
and soda into a mixing bowl. Rub the
butter into the flour mixture until the
mixture resembles coarse breadcrumbs.
Stir in enough buttermilk to make a
soft dough.

Turn out on to a lightly floured
board and knead gently for 30 seconds.
Roll out to 1cm (½-inch) thickness. Cut
out the scones and place them on the
prepared baking sheet.

Bake for 15 minutes or until a
skewer inserted comes out clean.

FLAPJACKS

Delicious and moist oatmeal squares,
Flapjacks are easy, quick and inexpensive to make.

9 flapjacks

Metric/Imperial

75g (3oz) butter, softened

2 tablespoons soft brown sugar
⅛ teaspoon salt
¼ teaspoon ground ginger
3 tablespoons golden syrup
1 tablespoon honey
175g (6oz) rolled oats

American

6 tablespoons butter, softened
2 tablespoons soft brown sugar
⅛ teaspoon salt
¼ teaspoon ground ginger
3 tablespoons corn syrup
1 tablespoon honey
1½ cups rolled oats

Preheat the oven to fairly hot (190°C/
375°F or Gas Mark 5). Grease a 20cm
(8-inch) square baking tin.

Cream the butter and the sugar
together with a wooden spoon. Add the
salt, ginger, syrup and honey. Beat
until smooth and creamy. Stir in the
rolled oats.

Press the mixture into the tin, smoothing it down with the back of a knife.

Bake in the centre of the oven for 25
minutes, or until lightly browned and
firm to the touch. Cut the flapjacks into
squares and let them cool in the tin for
1 hour before serving.

CHELSEA BUNS

A traditional British recipe, Chelsea
Buns are delicious eaten slightly warm.

10-12 buns

Metric/Imperial

100g (4oz) sugar
150ml (5 fl oz) lukewarm milk
2 teaspoons dried yeast
150g (5oz) butter
500g (1lb) plain flour, warmed
1 teaspoon salt
2 eggs, lightly beaten
2 tablespoons melted butter
150g (5oz) mixed currants and
   sultanas
1 teaspoon mixed spice or ground
   allspice

American

½ cup sugar
⅝ cup lukewarm milk

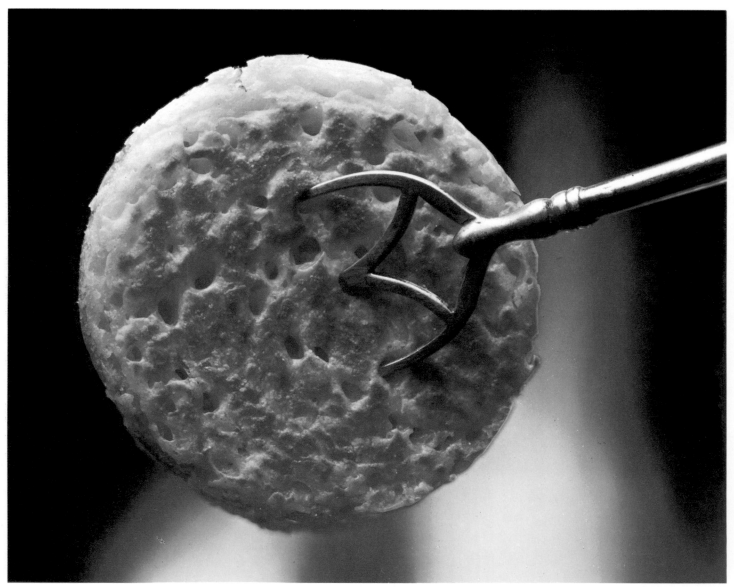

2 teaspoons dried yeast
⅝ cup butter
4 cups all-purpose flour, warmed
1 teaspoon salt
2 eggs, lightly beaten
2 tablespoons melted butter
1 cup currants and raisins, mixed
1 teaspoon ground allspice

Dissolve 1 teaspoon of the sugar in one-third of the lukewarm milk. Sprinkle on the dried yeast, whisk and leave in a warm draught-free place for 15 to 20 minutes or until puffed up and frothy.

Pour the remaining milk into a small saucepan and place it over moderately high heat to scald (bring to just under boiling point). Reduce the heat and add the butter. When melted, set aside to cool to lukewarm.

Sift the flour, salt and half the sugar into a large warmed mixing bowl. Make a well in the centre and pour in the yeast, milk-and-butter mixture and the eggs. Using your fingers or a spoon, gradually draw the flour into the liquid. Continue mixing until all the flour is incorporated and the dough comes away from the sides of the bowl.

Turn out on to a lightly floured surface and knead for about 5 minutes or until elastic and smooth.

Put in a greased bowl, cover with a damp cloth and leave in a warm place for 1 to 1½ hours or until doubled in bulk.

Knead the dough again on a floured surface for about 4 minutes, then roll out into a square. Brush with the melted butter. Sprinkle with the remaining sugar, the currants and sul-

Delicious Crumpets are toasted and eaten hot, spread simply with butter or with honey or jam.

tanas [raisins] and the mixed spice and roll it up like a Swiss [jelly] roll.

Preheat the oven to fairly hot (190°C/ 375°F or Gas Mark 5).

Cut the rolled-up dough into 3cm (1½-inch) thick slices. Place the slices close together, but not touching, on the greased baking sheet and put in a warm place for 20 minutes.

At the end of this time the buns should have risen enough to touch each other. Sprinkle them with a little extra sugar and bake for 30 to 35 minutes or until they are golden brown.

Allow to cool slightly before breaking apart.

226

CRUMPETS

Crumpets are a traditional tea or supper dish, and should ideally be toasted before an open fire, then stacked in a pile with a large knob of butter on top, and the butter allowed to drain slowly through the pile. The crumpets may be eaten simply with butter or with jam or honey. You will need crumpet rings and, if possible, a griddle to cook the crumpets. Otherwise, a baking sheet may be used.

---

24 crumpets

Metric/Imperial

---

1 teaspoon sugar
1 pint lukewarm milk
2 teaspoons dried yeast
500g (1lb) plain flour
½ teaspoon salt
1 egg
75g (3oz) butter, melted

American

---

1 teaspoon sugar
2½ cups lukewarm milk
½ of a 1oz cake compressed yeast
4 cups all-purpose flour
½ teaspoon salt
1 egg
6 tablespoons butter, melted

Dissolve the sugar in one-third of the lukewarm milk. Sprinkle on the dried yeast. Whisk and leave in a warm, draught-free place for 15 to 20 minutes until puffed up and frothy.

Sift the flour and salt into a large warmed mixing bowl. Make a well in the centre and pour in the yeast mixture, the remaining milk, the egg and one-third of the melted butter.

Beat the ingredients with a wooden spoon until they form a smooth thin batter. Cover the bowl with a clean cloth and leave it in a warm, draught-free place for 40 to 45 minutes or until doubled in volume.

Grease a large griddle or baking sheet and the crumpet rings with half

Serve thick slices of Date and Walnut Loaf spread with butter.

of the remaining melted butter. Put the rings on the griddle or baking sheet and place it over moderate heat. When hot, spoon about 2 tablespoons of the batter into each ring to fill it about one-third full. Reduce the heat to moderately low and cook the crumpets for 5 to 6 minutes or until the top surfaces are set and full of holes and the bottoms are golden brown.

Transfer to a wire rack to cool. Grease the griddle and rings again and cook the remaining crumpets.

DATE AND WALNUT LOAF

This easy-to-make teabread is excellent sliced thickly and spread with butter.

One 500g (1lb) loaf

Metric/Imperial

225g (8oz) self-raising flour
½ teaspoon baking powder
1 teaspoon salt
100g (4oz) soft brown sugar

225g (8oz) dates, stoned and chopped
75g (3oz) walnuts, chopped
1 egg
150ml (5 fl oz) milk

American

2 cups self-rising flour
½ teaspoon baking powder
1 teaspoon salt
⅔ cup soft brown sugar
1⅓ cups dates, pitted and chopped
½ cup walnuts, chopped
1 egg
⅝ cup milk

Preheat the oven to moderate (180°C/350°F or Gas Mark 4). Lightly grease a 500g (1 pound) loaf tin.

Sift the flour, baking powder and salt into a mixing bowl. Mix in the sugar, dates and walnuts.

Lightly beat the egg and milk together and stir into the flour mixture.

Mix well until the batter is smooth.

Turn the batter into the prepared loaf tin. Bake for 1 to 1¼ hours, or until a skewer inserted into the centre comes out clean.

Allow to cool in the tin for 5 minutes, then run a knife round the edge and reverse the loaf on to a wire rack. Leave until completely cold before serving.

DATE LOAF

This attractive, honey-glazed loaf will greatly improve if kept in an airtight tin for 1 to 2 weeks.

One 500g (1lb) loaf

Metric/Imperial

225g (8oz) dates, stoned and chopped
150ml (5 fl oz) milk
3½ tablespoons clear honey

1 egg
225g (8oz) self-raising flour
½ teaspoon baking powder
¼ teaspoon grated nutmeg

American

1⅓ cups dates, pitted and chopped
⅝ cup milk
3½ tablespoons honey
1 egg
2 cups self-rising flour
½ teaspoon baking powder
¼ teaspoon grated nutmeg

Lightly grease a 500g (1-pound) loaf tin. Preheat the oven to moderate (180°C/350°F or Gas Mark 4).

In a small saucepan, simmer the dates and the milk over low heat for 10

Banana Walnut Loaf is more a cake than a bread.

228

to 15 minutes or until the dates are soft. Turn into a bowl and beat in 3 tablespoons of the honey and the egg.

Purée the mixture in a blender.

Fold the flour, baking powder and nutmeg into the date purée. Turn the mixture into the greased loaf tin and bake in the centre of the oven for about 1 hour or until the loaf is firm to the touch and lightly browned. Leave to cool in the tin for 10 minutes.

Reverse the loaf on to a wire rack and brush the top with the remaining honey.

BANANA WALNUT LOAF

A moist bread, Banana Walnut Loaf is very easy to make and good to serve at tea-time or with coffee.

One 23cm (9in) loaf

Metric/Imperial

150g (5oz) sugar
50g (2oz) cooking fat
3 eggs
4 bananas, mashed
225g (8oz) plain flour
1 teaspoon baking powder
½ teaspoon salt
¼ teaspoon bicarbonate of soda
175g (6oz) walnuts, chopped

American

⅝ cup sugar
¼ cup lard
3 eggs
4 bananas, mashed
2 cups all-purpose flour
1 teaspoon baking powder
½ teaspoon salt
¼ teaspoon baking soda
1 cup walnuts, chopped

Preheat the oven to moderate (180°C/ 350°F or Gas Mark 4). Grease a 23cm (9-inch) loaf tin.

In a medium-sized mixing bowl, beat the sugar, fat and eggs together with a wooden spoon until light. Beat in the bananas.

Sift the flour, baking powder, salt and soda into the banana mixture and beat well. Stir in the walnuts.

Pour the mixture into the loaf tin

and bake for 1 hour, or until the loaf is done. Test by inserting a skewer in the centre of the loaf. If it comes out clean the loaf is ready. Turn the loaf out of the tin and allow to cool before slicing.

PARKIN

An oatmeal gingerbread which originated in the North of England, Parkin is a moist cake which should be kept for at least a week before serving.

Two 25cm (10in) square cakes

Metric/Imperial

225g (8oz) butter
500g (1lb) plain flour
1 teaspoon bicarbonate of soda
1 teaspoon salt
2 teaspoons ground ginger
500g (1lb) rolled oats
225ml (8 fl oz) dark treacle
225ml (8 fl oz) golden syrup
3 tablespoons honey
2 tablespoons soft brown sugar
350ml (12 fl oz) milk

American

1 cup butter
4 cups all-purpose flour
1 teaspoon baking soda
1 teaspoon salt
2 teaspoons ground ginger
5⅓ cups rolled oats
1 cup molasses
1 cup corn syrup
3 tablespoons honey
2 tablespoons soft brown sugar
1½ cups milk

Grease two 25cm (10-inch) square cake tins and line with non-stick silicone paper. Preheat the oven to warm (170°C/325°F or Gas Mark 3).

Sift the flour, soda, salt and ginger into a large mixing bowl. Add the rolled oats and stir well.

In a medium-sized saucepan, melt the butter with the treacle, syrup, honey and sugar over low heat. Cook, stirring constantly, for 1 minute or until all the ingredients are combined.

Make a well in the centre of the flour mixture and pour in the butter and treacle mixture and the milk. Gradually

draw the flour mixture into the liquid. Continue mixing until all the flour mixture is incorporated. Spoon the batter into the prepared baking tins. Bake for 45 to 50 minutes or until the cakes are firm.

Cool in the tins for 15 minutes before turning out on to a wire rack. When cold store in airtight tins for about 1 week.

RAISIN CAKE

A very rich and satisfying family cake, Raisin Cake should be served in small slices.

One 15cm (6in) cake

Metric/Imperial

1 teaspoon butter
300g (10oz) raisins
50g (2oz) chopped candied peel
150g (5oz) chopped almonds
100g (4oz) sugar
2 teaspoons lemon juice
3 eggs, lightly beaten
75g (3oz) flour
½ teaspoon baking powder
¼ teaspoon ground mace

American

1 teaspoon butter
1⅔ cups raisins
⅓ cup chopped candied peel
1 cup chopped almonds
½ cup sugar
2 teaspoons lemon juice
3 eggs, lightly beaten
¾ cup flour
½ teaspoon baking powder
¼ teaspoon ground mace

Preheat the oven to cool (150°C/300°F or Gas Mark 2).

Using half the butter, grease a 15cm (6-inch) diameter cake tin and line it with greaseproof or waxed paper greased with the remaining butter.

In a medium-sized mixing bowl, combine the raisins, peel, almonds and sugar. Stir in the lemon juice and beaten eggs, beating well with a wooden spoon until the ingredients are thoroughly combined. Sift the flour, baking powder and mace into the bowl and fold the flour mixture in with a metal spoon. Spoon the mixture into the prepared cake tin and place the tin in the oven. Bake for 1 to 1½ hours or until a skewer inserted into the centre of the cake comes out clean.

Remove the tin from the oven and allow it to cool for 20 minutes. Turn the cake out on to a wire rack. Remove and discard the paper.

VICTORIA SANDWICH

Victoria Sandwich is a traditional British cake made with equal quantities of butter, sugar and flour. The high butter content helps the cake remain moist for up to 3 days. Fill the sandwich with jam or Buttercream Icing.

One 18cm (7in) cake

Metric/Imperial

175g (6oz) plus 2 tablespoons butter
175g (6oz) plus 2 tablespoons self-raising flour
¼ teaspoon salt

175g (6oz) castor sugar
3 eggs

American

¾ cup butter
1½ cups self-rising flour
¼ teaspoon salt
¾ cup fine sugar
3 eggs

Preheat the oven to fairly hot (190°C/375°F or Gas Mark 5). Grease two 18cm (7-inch) sandwich tins. Sprinkle flour into each tin, tipping and rotating to coat evenly. Knock out any excess.

Sift the flour and the salt into a mixing bowl.

Cream the butter until soft, add the sugar and continue beating until light and fluffy.

Beat in the eggs, one at a time, adding a tablespoon of the flour mixture with each one. Using a metal spoon, fold the remaining flour mixture into the creamed mixture until the ingredients are thoroughly combined. Spoon the batter into the prepared cake tins, smoothing the surface.

Bake in the centre of the oven for 25 to 30 minutes or until a skewer inserted into the centre comes out clean. Cool on a wire rack.

OIL CHOCOLATE CAKE

This cake, which is mixed in 3 minutes, is really superb. The cake becomes increasingly moist as it is kept, though there is not much chance that you will taste it at its stickiest! Sandwich the cakes together with Buttercream Icing.

One 18cm (7in) cake

Metric/Imperial

175g (6oz) plain flour
2 tablespoons cocoa powder

Right: Serve Victoria Sandwich and Victorian Orange Buns with tea.

Raisin Cake is rich with nuts, raisins and eggs.

1 teaspoon baking powder
1 teaspoon bicarbonate of soda
150g (5oz) sugar
2 tablespoons treacle
2 eggs
150ml (5 fl oz) vegetable oil
150ml (5 fl oz) milk

American

1½ cups all-purpose flour
2 tablespoons cocoa
1 teaspoon baking powder
1 teaspoon baking soda
⅝ cup sugar
2 tablespoons molasses
2 eggs
⅝ cup vegetable oil
⅝ cup milk

Preheat the oven to warm (160°C/ 325°F or Gas Mark 3). Grease two 18cm (7-inch) shallow cake tins. Sprinkle with flour and shake out any excess.

Sift the flour, cocoa powder, baking powder, soda and sugar into a large mixing bowl.

Pour the treacle [molasses], eggs, vegetable oil and milk on to the flour mixture and stir for 2 minutes or until the ingredients are blended.

Pour the cake batter into the two tins. Bake for 40 to 45 minutes or until the cakes spring back when lightly pressed and have shrunk away from the sides of the tins.

Allow to cool for 2 minutes, then run a knife around the edges and turn the cakes out on to a wire rack to cool.

LAZY CHOCOLATE CAKE

A marvellous tea-time treat for the children, Lazy Chocolate Cake is very quick and easy to make.

One 18cm (7in) cake

Metric/Imperial

25g (1oz) butter, melted
100g (4oz) plain flour
¼ teaspoon salt
1 teaspoon baking powder

Oil Chocolate Cake is extremely quick and easy to make.

Right: Delicious Lazy Chocolate Cake is perfect for children's parties.

225g (8oz) sugar
2 eggs
3 tablespoons milk
100g (4oz) dark cooking chocolate, melted
1 teaspoon vanilla essence
1 teaspoon grated orange rind
1 tablespoon orange juice
75g (3oz) chopped hazelnuts
ICING
100g (4oz) dark cooking chocolate
50g (2oz) butter
1 tablespoon cornflour

American

2 tablespoons butter, melted
1 cup all-purpose flour
¼ teaspoon salt
1 teaspoon baking powder

1 cup sugar
2 eggs
3 tablespoons milk
4oz semi-sweet chocolate, melted
1 teaspoon vanilla
1 teaspoon grated orange rind
1 tablespoon orange juice
½ cup chopped filberts
ICING
4oz semi-sweet chocolate
¼ cup butter
1 tablespoon cornstarch

Preheat the oven to fairly hot (190°C/375°F or Gas Mark 5). Lightly grease an 18cm (7-inch) cake tin and set aside.

Sift the flour, salt and baking powder into a large mixing bowl. Stir in the sugar. Make a well in the centre and pour in the butter, eggs and milk. Using a wooden spoon, gradually blend the flour mixture with the liquids, stirring until the mixture forms a smooth batter. Stir in the chocolate, vanilla essence, orange rind and juice, beating until they are well blended. Stir in the nuts.

Spoon the mixture into the prepared cake tin. Bake for 35 to 40 minutes or until a skewer inserted into the centre comes out clean. Leave in the tin for 10 minutes, then place on a wire rack to cool.

To prepare the icing, melt the chocolate in a heatproof mixing bowl placed over a saucepan of boiling water. Add the butter and cornflour [cornstarch] and beat constantly until the mixture forms a smooth paste.

Remove the pan from the heat. With a flat-bladed knife, spread the icing over the cake. Leave to cool for at least 30 minutes.

DEVIL'S FOOD CAKE

Rich and luscious, Devil's Food Cake is a famous American chocolate cake.

One 20cm (8in) cake

Metric/Imperial

100g (4oz) dark cooking chocolate
225ml (8 fl oz) milk
175g (6oz) light brown sugar
3 egg yolks
300g (10oz) plain flour, sifted
1 teaspoon bicarbonate of soda
⅛ teaspoon salt
100g (4oz) butter
175g (6oz) castor sugar
3 tablespoons water
1 teaspoon vanilla essence
2 egg whites
CHOCOLATE FUDGE FROSTING
225ml (8 fl oz) single cream
500g (1lb) castor sugar
⅛ teaspoon salt
50g (2oz) cooking chocolate, grated
3 tablespoons butter
½ teaspoon vanilla essence
50g (2oz) walnuts, chopped

American

4oz semi-sweet chocolate
1 cup milk
1 cup light brown sugar
3 egg yolks
2½ cups all-purpose flour, sifted
1 teaspoon baking soda
⅛ teaspoon salt
½ cup butter
¾ cup fine sugar
¼ cup water
1 teaspoon vanilla
2 egg whites

233

CHOCOLATE FUDGE FROSTING

1 cup light cream
2 cups fine sugar
⅛ teaspoon salt
2oz semi-sweet chocolate, grated
3 tablespoons butter
½ teaspoon vanilla
⅓ cup walnuts, chopped

Preheat the oven to moderate (180°C/350°F or Gas Mark 4).

Put the chocolate, milk, brown sugar and one egg yolk in the top part of a double saucepan or in a bowl placed in a saucepan of hot water. Cook gently, stirring until the chocolate melts and the mixture thickens slightly.

Resift the flour with the soda and salt into a medium-sized bowl.

Cream the butter in a second bowl, and gradually beat in the castor sugar until light and fluffy. Add the remaining egg yolks one at a time, beating well after each addition.

Lightly mix in one-third of the flour, then half the water. Add the remaining flour and water and beat well until smooth. Stir in the vanilla essence. Stirring constantly, add the chocolate mixture.

Beat the egg whites until they form stiff peaks. With a metal spoon, lightly fold into the batter.

Grease three shallow 20cm (8-inch) cake tins. Line the bottoms with greased greaseproof paper. Pour the batter in to the tins, dividing it equally.

Bake for 25 minutes or until a knife plunged into the centre comes out clean.

Loosen the cakes with a knife and turn on to a wire rack to cool.

To make the frosting, bring the cream to the boil over moderate heat. Stir in the sugar, salt and grated chocolate, stir to melt the chocolate. Cover the pan and cook for 3 minutes. Do not stir. Uncover the pan, reduce the heat to low and cook until a teaspoon of the mixture dropped into iced water forms a soft ball.

Plunge the pan into a larger pan filled with cold water.

When the bottom of the pan is cold enough to touch, beat in the butter and vanilla. Continue beating until the frosting thickens and reaches spreading consistency. Stir in the walnuts.

Sandwich the three rounds of cake together with three-quarters of the frosting and spread the remainder over the top and sides. Using a palette knife make swirling patterns on the surface of the cake. Leave the frosting to cool.

CHOCOLATE PEPPERMINT SANDWICH CAKE

This elegant sandwich cake is an interesting combination of chocolate and peppermint.

One 20cm (8in) cake

Metric/Imperial

175g (6oz) soft margarine
175g (6oz) castor sugar
½ teaspoon vanilla essence
3 eggs
100g (4oz) self-raising flour
50g (2oz) cocoa
1 tablespoon warm water
FILLING
75g (3oz) butter
175g (6oz) icing sugar
½ teaspoon peppermint essence
green food colouring

American

¾ cup soft margarine
¾ cup fine sugar
½ teaspoon vanilla
3 eggs
1 cup self-rising flour
½ cup cocoa
1 tablespoon warm water
FILLING
6 tablespoons butter
1½ cup confectioner's sugar
½ teaspoon peppermint oil
green food colouring

Lightly grease two 20cm (8-inch) round sandwich tins. Sprinkle with a little flour, knocking out any excess.

Preheat the oven to fairly hot (190°C/375°F or Gas Mark 5).

Cream the margarine and sugar until light and fluffy. Beat in the vanilla essence.

Add the eggs, one at a time, beating well after each addition until the mixture is thick and creamy.

Sift the flour and cocoa into the bowl

Chocolate Peppermint Sandwich Cake is delicious.

and fold into the mixture with a metal spoon. Stir the water in carefully.

Spoon the mixture into the prepared tins. Bake for 25 to 30 minutes, or until a skewer inserted comes out clean.

Reverse the cakes on to a wire rack

and leave to cool.

To make the icing, cream the butter and icing [confectioner's] sugar until light and creamy. Stir in the peppermint essence and a few drops of green food colouring to make the icing a pale green colour.

Spread the icing over one of the cakes. Place the second cake on top and dust with a little extra sugar.

SHORTBREAD

Shortbread, an invention of the Scots, is now world famous and rightly so. This rich, crisp biscuit [cookie] is traditionally served on New Year's Eve – called Hogmanay in Scotland – with a glass of whisky. But it is equally good served at any time of the year with tea.

Shortbread is often formed into shapes in special moulds. If a mould is not available, shortbread may be shaped on a baking sheet.

Two 15cm (6in) rounds

Metric/Imperial

225g (8oz) butter
225g (8oz) plain flour
100g (4oz) rice flour

100g (4oz) castor sugar

American

1 cup butter
2 cups all-purpose flour
1 cup rice flour
½ cup fine sugar

Grease a large baking sheet.

Sift the flour and rice flour into a mixing bowl and stir in the sugar. Add the butter, cut into small pieces, and rub into the flour mixture until it resembles coarse breadcrumbs.

Knead the mixture gently until it forms a smooth dough. Turn out on to a floured board and divide in half. Form each piece into a circle about 15cm (6 inch) across. Transfer to the baking sheet, crimping the edges with your fingertips. Prick the tops with a fork. Chill in the refrigerator for 20 minutes.

Preheat the oven to moderate (180°C/350°F or Gas Mark 4).

Bake in the centre of the oven for 10 minutes. Reduce the oven temperature to cool (150°C/300°F or Gas Mark 2) and bake for a further 30 to 40 minutes or until crisp and lightly browned.

Cut the circles into triangles. Allow to cool, then sprinkle with sugar.

VICTORIAN ORANGE BUNS

A traditional British recipe, guaranteed to be just as popular with today's children.

12 buns

Metric/Imperial

100g (4oz) plus 1 tablespoon butter
100g (4oz) flour
½ teaspoon baking powder
100g (4oz) sugar
2 eggs
grated rind of 1 orange
75ml (3 fl oz) fresh orange juice
1 tablespoon milk
2 slices candied orange, cut into 12 pieces
1 tablespoon icing sugar

American

½ cup plus 1 tablespoon butter
1 cup flour

½ teaspoon baking powder
½ cup sugar
2 eggs
grated rind of 1 orange
⅜ cup fresh orange juice
1 tablespoon milk
2 slices candied orange, cut into 12 pieces
1 tablespoon confectioner's sugar

Preheat the oven to fairly hot (190°C/375°F or Gas Mark 5). With the tablespoon of butter, grease 12 patty tins.

Sift the flour and baking powder into a mixing bowl and set aside.

In a medium-sized mixing bowl, cream the remaining butter with a wooden spoon until it is soft and creamy. Add the sugar and beat well until the mixture is light and fluffy. Add the eggs, one at a time adding a tablespoon of the flour mixture with each egg, and beat well. Stir in the orange rind and juice. Fold in the remaining flour, and stir in the milk.

Spoon the mixture into the greased patty tins so that each one is two-thirds full. Place one piece of candied orange on top of each bun mixture. Place the patty tins on a baking sheet and bake for 20 to 25 minutes or until the centres of the buns spring back when pressed lightly with a finger. Remove the baking sheet from the oven. Transfer the buns to a wire rack to cool.

Place the buns on a serving dish and sift over the icing [confectioner's] sugar.

SHREDDED COCONUT PYRAMIDS

These little cakes are made with dried coconut, egg whites and sugar. They may be made in different colours by dividing the raw mixture into pieces and adding a few drips of different food colouring to each piece. Serve them with tea or coffee.

12 cakes

Metric/Imperial

2 large egg whites
150g (5oz) desiccated coconut
150g (5oz) castor sugar

American

2 large egg whites
1¼ cups shredded coconut
⅝ cup fine sugar

Preheat the oven to moderate (180°C/350°F or Gas Mark 4).

Grease a large baking sheet.

Beat the egg whites until they form stiff peaks. Sprinkle over the coconut and sugar and fold in with a metal spoon.

Drop tablespoons of the mixture, well spaced, on to the prepared baking sheet. Pinch each one to bring it up into a pyramid shape.

Bake in the centre of the oven for 15 to 20 minutes or until golden brown on the outside and firm to the touch. Cool on a wire rack.

RASPBERRY BUNS

These fruity little buns, made with coconut and raspberry jam, are absolutely delicious. Serve them with tea or coffee.

18 buns

Metric/Imperial

100g (4oz) butter
225g (8oz) plain flour
¼ teaspoon salt
100g (4oz) sugar
50g (2oz) desiccated coconut
1 teaspoon baking powder
2 eggs
100ml (4 fl oz) milk
6 tablespoons raspberry jam

American

½ cup butter
2 cups all-purpose flour
¼ teaspoon salt
½ cup sugar
½ cup shredded coconut
1 teaspoon baking powder
2 eggs
½ cup milk
6 tablespoons raspberry jam

Preheat the oven to hot (220°C/425°F or Gas Mark 7). Grease 18 patty tins.

Sift the flour and salt into a mixing

bowl. Add the butter to the flour, cut it into small pieces and rub into the flour until the mixture resembles fine breadcrumbs.

Stir in nearly all the sugar, the desiccated [shredded] coconut and the baking powder. Fold in the eggs and milk and beat thoroughly until smooth.

Fill the prepared patty tins two-thirds full. Using your thumb, make a depression in the centre of the mixture in each tin and fill each with a teaspoon of the jam. Sprinkle over the remaining sugar.

Bake in the centre of the oven for 20 minutes or until the buns have risen and are golden on top.

LONDON BUNS

These quickly made buns make ideal snacks for children.

8 buns

Metric/Imperial

50g (2oz) butter
225g (8oz) plain flour
2 teaspoons bicarbonate of soda
1 teaspoon cream of tartar
50g (2oz) sugar
100g (4oz) chopped mixed peel
coarsely grated rind of 1 lemon
1 egg yolk
75ml (3 fl oz) milk
2 tablespoons crushed nut brittle
    toffee

American

¼ cup butter
2 cups all-purpose flour
2 teaspoons baking soda
1 teaspoon cream of tartar
½ cup sugar
⅔ cup chopped mixed candied citrus
    peel
coarsely grated rind of 1 lemon
1 egg yolk
⅜ cup milk
2 tablespoons crushed peanut or
    other nut brittle

Preheat the oven to fairly hot (200°C/400°F or Gas Mark 6). Grease two baking sheets.

Sift the flour, soda and cream of

tartar into a mixing bowl. Add the butter and cut it into small pieces. Rub into the flour until the mixture resembles coarse breadcrumbs. Stir in the sugar, chopped peel and lemon rind. Add the egg yolk and milk and stir the mixture until it forms large lumps, adding more milk if too dry.

Using your hands, knead the dough lightly. Form into a large firm ball.

Divide the dough into eight equal pieces. Place the crushed nut brittle in a small bowl. Roll the pieces of dough into balls and dip each one in the crushed nut brittle. Place the buns on the baking sheets and bake for 15 minutes or until golden brown.

DATE CAKES

A delicious combination of dates and honey, these small moist cakes improve with keeping.

12 cakes

Metric/Imperial

75g (3oz) butter
2 tablespoons light brown sugar
3 tablespoons honey
2 eggs, lightly beaten
100g (4oz) plus 2 tablespoons
    self-raising flour
1 teaspoon mixed spice or ground
    allspice
3-4 tablespoons milk
50g (2oz) dates, stoned and finely
    chopped

American

6 tablespoons butter
2 tablespoons light brown sugar
3 tablespoons honey
2 eggs, lightly beaten
1 cup plus 2 tablespoons self-rising
    flour
1 teaspoon ground allspice
3-4 tablespoons milk
⅓ cup dates, pitted and finely chopped

Preheat the oven to fairly hot (200°C/400°F or Gas Mark 6). Lightly grease 12 patty pans.

Cream the butter, sugar and honey together with a wooden spoon. Beat in the eggs.

Sift the main quantity of flour and mixed spice over the butter mixture and, with a metal spoon, lightly fold in. Add sufficient milk to give a dropping consistency.

Sprinkle the remaining flour on to a plate. Roll the dates in it until lightly coated. Add to the batter and fold in. Spoon the batter into the greased patty pans.

Bake for about 15 to 20 minutes or until the cakes have risen and are golden brown. Turn out and cool on a wire rack.

JAM AND COCONUT BARS

Quick and easy to make, Jam and Coconut Bars make a teatime treat.

12 bars

Metric/Imperial

100g (4oz) butter, softened
100g (4oz) sugar
2 eggs, lightly beaten
225g (8oz) plain flour
1 teaspoon baking powder
¼ teaspoon salt
50g (2oz) desiccated coconut
350g (12oz) raspberry or strawberry
    jam

American

½ cup butter, softened
½ cup sugar
2 eggs, lightly beaten
2 cups all-purpose flour
1 teaspoon baking powder
¼ teaspoon salt
½ cup shredded coconut
¾lb raspberry or strawberry jam

Preheat the oven to fairly hot (200°C/400°F or Gas Mark 6). Lightly grease a 20cm (8-inch) square baking tin.

Cream the butter and the sugar together with a wooden spoon until light and fluffy. Beat in the eggs.

Sift the flour, baking powder and salt into another bowl. Gradually add this and coconut to the egg mixture. Mix well.

Spread half of the mixture over the bottom of the prepared baking tin and cover with the jam. Spread the re-

maining mixture on top.

Bake for 25 minutes or until the top is brown and springs back when pressed.

Allow to cool, then cut it into bars.

CHOCOLATE CHIP COOKIES

Great favourites with children, Chocolate Chip Cookies go down well with a glass of ice-cold milk.

About 30 biscuits [cookies]

Metric/Imperial

100g (4oz) butter
100g (4oz) sugar
75g (3oz) brown sugar
1 egg
½ teaspoon vanilla essence
175g (6oz) plain flour
½ teaspoon salt
½ teaspoon bicarbonate of soda
50g (2oz) chopped walnuts
100g (4oz) dark plain chocolate chips

American

½ cup butter
½ cup sugar

Chocolate Chip Cookies and Chocolate Cinnamon Biscuits [Cookies] are scrumptious!

½ cup brown sugar
1 egg
½ teaspoon vanilla
1½ cups all-purpose flour
½ teaspoon salt
½ teaspoon baking soda
¼ cup chopped walnuts
4oz semi-sweet chocolate chips

Preheat the oven to fairly hot (190°C/375°F or Gas Mark 5). Grease a baking sheet.

Cream the butter, mix the sugars together and add them gradually, beating until the mixture is smooth and fluffy. Beat in the egg and vanilla.

Sift the flour with the salt and soda. Stir it into the butter-and-sugar mixture and mix to a smooth batter. Stir in the nuts and chocolate chips.

Drop teaspoonfuls of the mixture on to the baking sheet.

Bake for 10 to 15 minutes or until browned. Transfer to a wire rack.

CHOCOLATE CINNAMON BISCUITS [COOKIES]

These melt-in-the-mouth Chocolate Cinnamon Biscuits [cookies] may be eaten plain or sandwiched together with chocolate, vanilla or almond cream.

25 biscuits [cookies]

Metric/Imperial

225g (8oz) butter
100g (4oz) castor sugar
225g (8oz) self-raising flour
½ teaspoon cinnamon
50g (2oz) cocoa powder
1 teaspoon vanilla essence

American

1 cup butter
½ cup fine sugar
2 cups self-rising flour
½ teaspoon cinnamon
½ cup cocoa
1 teaspoon vanilla

Preheat the oven to moderate (180°C/350°F or Gas Mark 4). Grease a baking dish.

238

Cream the butter with a wooden spoon until pale and fluffy. Gradually add the sugar and beat until smooth. Sift in the flour, cinnamon and cocoa, a little at a time, stirring until the mixture is a smooth paste. Stir in the vanilla essence.

With your hands roll teaspoonfuls of the paste into balls and place them on a baking sheet, leaving a good space

Crisp Coconut Cookies are delicious with tea or coffee.

between each one. Dip a fork in cold water and use to flatten out the balls.

Bake for 12 minutes. Allow the biscuits [cookies] to cool slightly, then lift them off with a spatula.

COCONUT COOKIES

Served with tea or coffee, these delicious crisp Coconut Cookies are sure to be popular with the whole family.

18 biscuits [cookies]

Metric/Imperial

100g (4oz) butter
75g (3oz) soft brown sugar
75g (3oz) desiccated coconut
75g (3oz) rolled oats
6 tablespoons cornflakes
1 tablespoon honey

American

½ cup butter
½ cup soft brown sugar
¾ cup shredded coconut
1 cup rolled oats
6 tablespoons cornflakes
1 tablespoon honey

Preheat the oven to warm (170°C/ 325°F or Gas Mark 3). Grease a medium-sized, shallow, rectangular cake tin.

Mix together the sugar, coconut, rolled oats and cornflakes.

In a small saucepan, heat the butter and honey gently, stirring occasionally. When the butter has melted, stir the mixture into the mixed, dried ingredients.

Spoon into the prepared cake tin and bake for 30 minutes or until the top is golden brown.

Cut the cake into 5cm (2-inch) squares but leave to cool in the tin before serving.

EASTER BUNNIES

These bunny-shaped biscuits [cookies] are ideal for children's parties, especially if you pipe the name of each child on a biscuit [cookie].

10 biscuits [cookies]

Metric/Imperial

75g (3oz) butter
50g (2oz) castor sugar
1 egg, separated
175g (6oz) plain flour
1½ teaspoons baking powder
¼ teaspoon salt
2 tablespoons warm milk

American

6 tablespoons butter
¼ cup fine sugar

1 egg, separated
1½ cups all-purpose flour
1½ teaspoons baking powder
¼ teaspoon salt
2 tablespoons warm milk

In a large mixing bowl, cream the butter and sugar together; add the egg yolk and beat for a further 2 minutes or until light and creamy.

Sift the flour, baking powder and salt into the bowl and stir to mix. Gradually add the milk, stirring until the dough is fairly soft. Cover with a damp cloth and place it in the refrigerator to chill for 1 hour until the dough is fairly firm.

Preheat the oven to fairly hot (200°C/400°F or Gas Mark 6). Grease a large baking sheet.

Turn the dough out on to a lightly floured board and roll it out to ¼-inch thick. Using a 5cm (2-inch) pastry cutter, cut ten rounds for the bodies. Cut another 20 about half that size; ten for the heads and ten to cut in half for the ears. Use a medicine bottle cap or similar to cut ten rounds for the tails.

Assemble the bunnies, pushing the pieces together to form each biscuit and placing the tails half over the bodies. Place on the greased baking sheet and bake in the centre of the oven for 10 minutes.

Brush the biscuits with the egg white and sprinkle with a little extra sugar.

Return to the oven and bake for 10 minutes more or until golden.

Children will love these attractive Easter Bunnies.

PEANUT BUTTER BISCUITS [COOKIES]

These economical biscuits [cookies] will quickly become firm favourites.

24 biscuits [cookies]

Metric/Imperial

75g (3oz) butter
175g (6oz) plain flour
3 tablespoons water
3 tablespoons crunchy peanut butter
2 tablespoons salted peanuts
1 teaspoon sugar

240

Brownies are best when slightly moist and chewy.

American

6 tablespoons butter
1½ cups **all-purpose flour**
3 tablespoons water
3 tablespoons crunchy peanut butter
2 tablespoons salted peanuts
1 teaspoon sugar

Preheat the oven to moderate (180°C/350°F or Gas Mark 4). Grease a very large baking sheet.

Sift the flour into a mixing bowl. Add the butter and cut it into small pieces with a table knife. Rub into the flour until the mixture resembles fine bread-crumbs. Stir in the water and peanut butter. With your hands, mix and knead the dough until it forms a ball. Add a little more water if it is too dry.

On a lightly floured surface, roll out the dough to a rectangle about 15cm by 30cm (6 inches by 12 inches). Trim the edges. Carefully lift the dough on to the prepared baking sheet and cut it into biscuit-sized rectangles. Do not separate the pieces of dough. Sprinkle the top with the salted peanuts and the sugar. Very gently roll the peanuts into the dough.

Bake for 20 minutes. Cool on a wire rack before separating into biscuits.

BROWNIES

A great American favourite, Brownies are nutty chocolate squares. They may be served for tea or with vanilla ice cream for dessert. They are very easy to make and are best when they are slightly moist and chewy.

---

6 brownies

Metric/Imperial

100g (4oz) butter
175g (6oz) plain cooking chocolate
2 tablespoons water
100g (4oz) castor sugar
1 teaspoon vanilla essence
100g (4oz) self-raising flour
⅛ teaspoon salt
2 eggs
50g (2oz) walnuts, chopped

American

½ cup butter
6oz unsweetened chocolate
2 tablespoons water
½ cup fine sugar
1 teaspoon vanilla
1 cup self-rising flour
⅛ teaspoon salt
2 eggs
⅓ cup walnuts, chopped

Preheat the oven to warm (170°C/325°F or Gas Mark 3). Grease a 20cm (8-inch) square baking tin.

Put the chocolate, water and butter in a medium-sized saucepan and melt over very low heat, stirring occasionally. Remove from the heat, stir in the sugar and vanilla and leave to cool.

Sift the flour and salt into a mixing bowl. Gradually stir in the cooled chocolate mixture. Add the eggs and beat well. Fold in the walnuts. Pour the mixture into the greased tin.

Bake for 30 to 35 minutes or until a knife plunged into the centre of the cake comes out clean. When cool, cut into squares.

OATMEAL COOKIES

Golden, crunchy biscuits [cookies] Oatmeal Cookies are delicious with a cup of coffee or a glass of ice-cold milk.

---

25 biscuits [cookies]

Metric/Imperial

75g (3oz) butter
225g (8oz) plus 3 tablespoons soft brown sugar
2 eggs, lightly beaten
1 egg yolk
1 teaspoon vanilla essence
175g (6oz) plain flour
½ teaspoon salt
½ teaspoon baking powder
175g (6oz) oatmeal, soaked in 3 tablespoons milk

241

American

6 tablespoons butter

1⅓ cups plus 3 tablespoons soft brown sugar

2 eggs, lightly beaten

1 egg yolk

1 teaspoon vanilla

1½ cups all-purpose flour

½ teaspoon salt

½ teaspoon baking powder

1½ cups oatmeal, soaked in 3 tablespoons milk

Preheat the oven to moderate (180°C/350°F or Gas Mark 4). Grease two large baking sheets.

Cream the butter and the main quantity of sugar together until thoroughly combined. Beat in the eggs, egg yolk and vanilla essence.

Sift in the flour, salt and baking powder into a mixing bowl. Carefully fold into the butter and sugar mixture, then fold in the oatmeal, stirring until smooth.

Drop teaspoonfuls of the mixture, well spaced apart, on to the prepared baking sheets. Sprinkle over the remaining 3 tablespoons of sugar. Bake for 10 to 12 minutes or until golden brown. Cool on a wire rack.

CHOCOLATE BISCUITS [COOKIES]

These light biscuits [cookies] are ideal to serve for coffee mornings or parties and they make a welcome gift packed in an attractive box.

16 biscuits [cookies]

Metric/Imperial

65g (2½oz) dark cooking chocolate, broken into pieces

1 tablespoon water

3 egg whites

100g (4oz) castor sugar

American

2½oz semi-sweet chocolate, broken into pieces

1 tablespoon water

3 egg whites

½ cup fine sugar

Preheat the oven to moderate (180°C/350°F or Gas Mark 4).

In a double saucepan or small bowl placed over a pan of hot water, melt the chocolate with the water, stirring occasionally.

Beat the egg whites until almost stiff. Add 3 teaspoons of the sugar and beat for 1 more minute. Then with a metal spoon carefully fold in the remaining sugar.

Spoon the egg whites into the saucepan containing the melted chocolate and gently fold together.

Put about 2 tablespoonfuls of the mixture into each of 16 small paper cases placed on a baking sheet. Bake for 20 to 30 minutes.

SHREWSBURY BISCUITS [COOKIES]

These traditional British biscuits [cookies] are very simple to make.

10 biscuits [cookies]

Metric/Imperial

100g (4oz) butter

100g (4oz) sugar

1 egg yolk

225g (8oz) plain flour, sifted

2 teaspoons finely grated lemon rind

American

½ cup butter

½ cup sugar

1 egg yolk

2 cups all-purpose flour, sifted

2 teaspoons finely grated lemon rind

Preheat the oven to moderate (180°C/350°F or Gas Mark 4).

Cream the butter until light and fluffy, stir in the sugar and beat the mixture until smooth and creamy. Beat in the egg yolk until the ingredients are thoroughly combined. Stir in the flour and lemon rind. Using your hands, form the mixture into a ball and knead lightly. Cover and chill in the refrigerator for 10 minutes.

On a lightly floured surface, roll out the dough to 6mm (¼ inch) thick. With a large pastry cutter, cut into circles and place on a baking sheet. Roll and cut the trimmings and place on a second baking sheet.

Bake for 12 to 15 minutes or until golden brown around the edges. Cool on a wire rack.

DERBY BISCUITS [COOKIES]

Originally called Derby Cakes, these hard, crunchy biscuits [cookies] are adapted from an old English recipe.

30 biscuits [cookies]

Metric/Imperial

225g (8oz) butter, cut into small pieces

500g (1lb) flour

225g (8oz) sugar

1 teaspoon ground allspice

225g (8oz) currants

1 egg, lightly beaten

150ml (5 fl oz) milk

American

1 cup butter, cut into small pieces

4 cups flour

1 cup sugar

1 teaspoon ground allspice

1⅓ cups currants

1 egg, lightly beaten

⅝ cup milk

Preheat the oven to fairly hot (190°C/375°F or Gas Mark 5). Lightly grease a large baking sheet.

Sift the flour into a large mixing bowl. Add the butter and rub into the flour until the mixture resembles coarse breadcrumbs. Mix in the sugar, allspice and currants. Make a well in the centre and pour in the beaten egg and milk. Stir the mixture until it forms a stiff dry dough.

Turn out on to a lightly floured board and knead well for about 10 minutes until it becomes smooth. Roll out fairly thinly into a square. Using a plain or fluted pastry cutter, cut into circles.

Place the circles on the baking sheet and bake in the centre of the oven for 12 to 15 minutes, or until the bottoms of the biscuits [cookies] are golden brown.

Allow to cool for 5 minutes before transferring to a wire rack. Store in an airtight tin.

Clever ways with leftovers

Leftover foods need not mean dull meals. With a little skill and originality in the choice and use of well-flavoured colourful vegetables, herbs, spices and sauces it is surprising how many tasty dishes can be prepared. This section is a guide to using up the commonest leftover food items. Leftover cooking is a whole branch of cuisine in its own right, and the skilled cook will not only save on the house-keeping bills but derive a great deal of satisfaction in the process.

Cooked meat and poultry

Cooked meat and poultry should be cooled quickly and stored covered or wrapped in the refrigerator. It will keep well for two to three days. If you want to use the meat in a dish such as Shepherd's Pie, don't mince [grind] or chop it until just before you use it. If you only have a small quantity of leftover meat, don't be afraid to combine it with canned meat or cold bought meat; this applies also of course to small quantities of leftover fish or vegetables.

Many appetizing dishes can be made by chopping the meat and combining it with a well-seasoned white sauce or a sauce mix. Leftover food loses flavour, so it needs plenty of help from well-flavoured sauces, herbs, spices and seasoning. Use the meat, re-heated thoroughly in the sauce, to fill vol-au-vent cases pastry [shells], omelettes or as a filling for stacked savoury pancakes (crêpes), one of the most versatile dishes for hungry families.

SAVOURY PANCAKES

Use the basic pancake recipe given in the Basic Recipes section. Fry pancakes on at a time and keep warm, interleaved with greaseproof [waxed] paper. The following are some suggested fillings. Either stuff each pancake individually and roll them side by side, or layer the pancakes with the filling in a round casserole and serve out into wedges. Pancakes and filling should be heated through together before serving.

Chicken filling. Stir finely-chopped cooked chicken or turkey into half a pint of savoury sauce. Use other flavours such as cheese, capers, chives, sweetcorn, peppers or chutney [relish] to add interest to the sauce.

Mushroom filling. Combine cooked ham, chicken or bacon pieces with lots of lightly fried mushrooms and a little fried onion.

Bacon filling. Mix crispy bacon and a few chunks of pineapple in a white sauce lightly seasoned with prepared mustard.

COTTAGE PIE

This is an excellent way of using left-over cooked beef and boiled potatoes to make a substantial family meal. Served with green vegetables.

6 servings

Metric/Imperial

500g (1lb) cooked beef, minced or finely chopped
300ml (10 fl oz) hot beef stock
1 small onion, chopped
1 tablespoon Worcestershire sauce
1 teaspoon sugar
1 teaspoon salt
1 teaspoon black pepper
½ teaspoon paprika
100g (4oz) Cheddar cheese, grated
750g (1½lb) potatoes, cooked and mashed

American

1lb ground round steak or leftover cooked beef, finely chopped
1¼ cups hot beef stock
1 small onion, chopped
1 tablespoon Worcestershire sauce
1 teaspoon sugar

1 teaspoon salt
1 teaspoon black pepper
½ teaspoon paprika
1 cup Cheddar cheese, grated
1½lb potatoes, cooked and mashed

Preheat the oven to very hot (230°C/450°F or Gas Mark 8).

In a large, heavy saucepan, combine all the ingredients except the cheese and potato and bring to the boil. Pour the mixture into a large pie dish.

In a large mixing bowl, stir three-quarters of the cheese into the mashed potatoes. Spoon the mixture over the meat and sprinkle the rest of the cheese on top.

Bake in the oven for 20 minutes, or until the top is brown.

MEAT PUDDING

This useful recipe for using up leftover cooked meat may be made with lamb, pork, chicken, or a mixture of these. It makes a filling dinner or lunch.

4-6 servings

Metric/Imperial

½ litre (1 pint) White Sauce
4 egg yolks
2 tablespoons vegetable oil
1 large onion, finely chopped
1kg (2lb) cooked lean meat, finely chopped
½ teaspoon salt
¼ teaspoon black pepper
1oz plus 1 teaspoon butter
250g (8oz) button mushrooms, wiped clean and halved
10 slices day-old white bread, crusts removed and thinly buttered
100g (4oz) Gruyere cheese, grated

American

2½ cups White Sauce
4 egg yolks
2 tablespoons vegetable oil
1 large onion, diced
3-4 cups cooked lean meat, finely chopped
½ teaspoon salt
¼ teaspoon black pepper
2 tablespoons plus 1 teaspoon butter
½lb small mushrooms, wiped clean

Savoury Pancakes are delicious filled with sauces made from left-over poultry, meat and vegetables.

and halved
10 slices day-old white bread, crusts removed and thinly buttered
1 cup Gruyère or Swiss cheese, grated

Pour the white sauce into a medium-sized mixing bowl and, using a wooden spoon, beat in the egg yolks. Set aside.

In a large frying-pan, heat the oil over moderate heat, add the onion and fry, stirring occasionally, for 5 to 7 minutes or until it is soft and translucent but not brown. Add the meat, salt

and pepper and fry, stirring occasionally, for 5 minutes. Remove the pan from the heat and set aside.

In a small saucepan, melt 1 ounce (2 tablespoons) of the butter over moderate heat. When the foam subsides, add the mushrooms and cook, stirring frequently, for 3 minutes. Remove the pan from the heat and mix the mushrooms into the white sauce mixture. Set aside.

Preheat the oven to moderate (180°C/ 350°F or Gas Mark 4).

Grease a 3-pint (2-quart) ovenproof mould with the remaining teaspoon of butter. Line the sides and bottom of the mould with the bread, buttered sides facing inwards, overlapping each slice

and reserving enough bread to make a lid.

Spoon a little of the meat and onion mixture into the bottom of the mould and cover with a little of the white sauce and mushroom mixture. Sprinkle over a little grated cheese. Continue making layers in the same way until all the ingredients have been used up. Cover with the remaining bread slices, buttered side down, trimming them to fit the shape of the mould. Cover the top of the mould with aluminium foil.

Place the mould in the centre of the oven and bake for 50 minutes to 1 hour or until the top is golden brown.

Remove the mould from the oven and remove and discard the foil. Run a

sharp-edged knife around the edge of the mould. Hold a warmed serving dish, inverted, over the mould and reverse the two, giving the mould a sharp shake. The pudding should slide out easily.

POTATO AND MEAT CROQUETTES

This is a delicious way of using leftover meat such as chicken, pork, lamb, or beef. Serve with a rich tomato sauce.

4 servings

Metric/Imperial

6 tablespoons olive oil

Serve Meat Pudding with a green vegetable for lunch or dinner.

1 medium-sized onion, finely chopped
1 garlic clove, crushed
1 celery stalk, finely chopped
250g (8oz) cooked meat, finely chopped
3 tomatoes, blanched, peeled and finely chopped
½ teaspoon salt
¼ teaspoon black pepper
½ teaspoon dried thyme
4 medium-sized potatoes, cooked and finely chopped
2 eggs, lightly beaten
100g (4oz) dry breadcrumbs
1 tablespoon chopped fresh parsley
SAUCE
1 tablespoon butter
2 tablespoons flour
300ml (10 fl oz) tomato juice
2 large tomatoes, blanched, peeled and chopped
1 garlic clove, crushed
½ teaspoon salt
¼ teaspoon black pepper
¼ teaspoon cayenne pepper
1 large bay leaf

American

6 tablespoons olive oil
1 medium-sized onion, finely chopped
1 garlic clove, crushed
1 celery stalk, finely chopped
1 cup cooked meat, finely chopped
3 tomatoes, blanched, peeled and finely chopped
½ teaspoon salt
¼ teaspoon black pepper
½ teaspoon dried thyme
4 medium-sized potatoes, cooked and finely chopped
2 eggs, lightly beaten
1⅓ cups dry breadcrumbs
1 tablespoon chopped fresh parsley
SAUCE
1 tablespoon butter
2 tablespoons flour
1¼ cups tomato juice
2 large tomatoes, blanched, peeled and chopped
1 garlic clove, crushed
½ teaspoon salt
¼ teaspoon black pepper
¼ teaspoon cayenne pepper
1 large bay leaf

In a large, heavy saucepan, heat half the olive oil over moderate heat. Add the onion, garlic and celery to the pan and cook for 5 minutes, or until they are soft. Add the meat, tomatoes, salt, pepper, thyme and potatoes. Mix well and cook for 5 to 10 minutes, stirring occasionally, or until the tomatoes are soft.

Remove the pan from the heat and purée the mixture in a food mill or blender, or mash with a fork. Pour the mixture into a medium-sized bowl; allow it to cool. Then place it in the refrigerator to chill for 1 hour, or until it is completely cold.

Meanwhile make the sauce. In a medium-sized saucepan melt the butter over moderate heat. When the foam subsides, add the flour and stir until the mixture forms a thick paste. Gradually add the tomato juice to the pan, stirring constantly until the sauce is thick and smooth.

Add the tomatoes, garlic, salt, pepper, cayenne and bay leaf. Cover the pan, reduce the heat to very low and simmer, stirring occasionally, for 20 to 25 minutes.

Strain the sauce into a bowl and then return it to the saucepan. Set aside.

Removed the puréed meat and potato mixture from the refrigerator. With floured hands, divide the mixture into equal portions. On a floured board, roll and shape the portions into small croquettes.

Put the beaten eggs on one plate and the breadcrumbs on another. Dip the croquettes in the egg and roll them in the breadcrumbs.

In a large frying-pan, heat the remaining oil over moderate heat. When it is hot, add the croquettes. Cook them for 10 minutes, or until they are browned all over. Remove and drain the croquettes well on kitchen paper towels. Arrange them on a warmed serving dish and keep hot.

Quickly reheat the sauce over moderate heat and pour it over the croquettes. Sprinkle the parsley on top and serve immediately.

A tasty way of using up leftover meat, Potato and Meat Croquettes are served with a rich and colourful tomato sauce.

CHICKEN CROQUETTES

These croquettes with a creamy chicken filling are delicious served with peas or asparagus.

4 servings

Metric/Imperial

50g (2oz) butter
1 small onion, finely chopped
4 large mushrooms, wiped and finely chopped
2 tablespoons flour
225ml (8 fl oz) milk or chicken stock
½ teaspoon salt
¼ teaspoon white pepper
1 teaspoon lemon juice
600g (1¼lb) cooked chicken meat, finely chopped
1 tablespoon chopped fresh parsley
1 egg yolk
1 egg, lightly beaten
100g (4oz) dry breadcrumbs
50ml (2 fl oz) vegetable oil

American

¼ cup butter
1 small onion, diced
4 large mushrooms, wiped clean and diced
2 tablespoons flour
1 cup milk or chicken stock
½ teaspoon salt
¼ teaspoon white pepper
1 teaspoon lemon juice
2½ cups cooked chicken meat, finely chopped
1 tablespoon chopped fresh parsley
1 egg yolk
1 egg, lightly beaten
1⅓ cups dry breadcrumbs
¼ cup vegetable oil

In a medium-sized frying-pan, melt half the butter over moderate heat. Add the onion to the pan and cook it for 2 to 3 minutes. Add the chopped mushrooms and continue to cook for 4 to 5 minutes or until tender. Remove the pan from the heat. Set aside.

In a medium-sized saucepan, melt the remaining butter over moderate heat. With a wooden spoon, stir in the flour and cook, stirring, for 2 minutes.

Remove the pan from the heat and gradually add the milk or chicken stock, stirring constantly. When all the liquid has been added and the sauce is smooth, return the pan to the heat. Add

the salt, pepper and lemon juice. Stirring constantly bring the sauce to the boil. Reduce the heat to low and simmer for 3 minutes.

Stir the sautéed mushrooms, onion and chicken into the sauce. Remove the pan from the heat. Add the parsley and leave the mixture to cool, then stir in the egg yolk.

Transfer the mixture to a large mixing bowl and place it in the refrigerator to chill for 30 minutes or until it is completely cold.

With floured hands, divide the mixture into equal portions. On a floured board, roll and shape the portions into croquettes.

Put the lightly beaten egg on one plate and the breadcrumbs on another plate. Dip the croquettes in the egg and roll them in the breadcrumbs.

In a large frying-pan, heat the oil over moderate heat. Add the croquettes to the pan and fry them for 5 to 6 minutes, or until they are browned all over.

Remove and drain the croquettes well on kitchen paper towels. Serve at once.

CREAMED CHICKEN

Creamed Chicken on toast makes a very tasty snack on its own, but for a more substantial meal, serve with peas and grilled [broiled] tomatoes.

4 servings

Metric/Imperial

2 tablespoons butter
2 tablespoons flour
150ml (6 fl oz) chicken stock
75ml (3 fl oz) double cream
½ teaspoon salt
¼ teaspoon black pepper
350g (12oz) cooked chicken, finely shredded
4 slices of toast
4 parsley sprigs

American

2 tablespoons butter
2 tablespoons flour
¾ cup chicken stock
⅜ cup heavy cream
½ teaspoon salt

¼ teaspoon black pepper
1½ cups cooked chicken, finely shredded
4 slices of toast
4 parsley sprigs

In a medium-sized saucepan, melt the butter over moderate heat. Remove the pan from the heat and, with a wooden spoon, stir in the flour. Return the pan to the heat and cook, stirring for 2 minutes.

Remove the pan from the heat and gradually add the chicken stock, stirring constantly until the mixture becomes smooth. Add the cream, salt and pepper, mixing to blend well.

Return the pan to the heat and add the chicken. Cook, stirring occasionally, for 5 to 6 minutes, or until the chicken is heated through.

Remove the pan from the heat and spoon the mixture on to the toast slices. Garnish each with a sprig of parsley.

TURKEY CORONATION

Turkey Coronation is an excellent way of using the remnants of a cooked turkey to make a superb dish for lunch or dinner. The spiciness of the mayonnaise counteracts the tendency of turkey meat to be somewhat dry and bland. Serve the dish with boiled potatoes.

4 servings

Metric/Imperial

600ml (1 pint) mayonnaise
juice of 1 lemon
2 tablespoons curry paste
1 tablespoon apricot jam
½ teaspoon salt
½ teaspoon black pepper
1kg (2lb) cooked turkey, coarsely chopped
250g (8oz) black grapes, halved and seeded

American

2½ cups mayonnaise
juice of 1 lemon
2 tablespoons curry paste
1 tablespoon apricot jam
½ teaspoon salt
½ teaspoon black pepper

4 cups cooked turkey, coarsely chopped
½lb black grapes, halved and seeded

Beat the mayonnaise, lemon juice, curry paste, apricot jam, salt and pepper until thoroughly combined.

Place the turkey and half the grapes in a large serving dish and pour over the mayonnaise mixture. Toss until thoroughly coated. Garnish with the remaining grapes.

TURKEY MEAT MOULD

Turkey Meat Mould is an economical and tasty way to use up leftover turkey.

3-4 servings

Metric/Imperial

1 teaspoon butter
12 slices streaky bacon, rinds removed
250g (8oz) pork sausage meat
250g (8oz) cooked turkey, finely chopped
½ teaspoon salt
¼ teaspoon black pepper
1 teaspoon dried thyme

American

1 teaspoon butter
12 slices bacon
½lb sausage meat
1 cup cooked turkey, finely chopped
½ teaspoon salt
¼ teaspoon black pepper
1 teaspoon dried thyme

Preheat the oven to moderate (180°C/ 350°F or Gas Mark 4). With the teaspoon of butter, grease a 500g (1lb) loaf tin.

Line the tin with the bacon. Spoon in one-third of the sausage meat and smooth the surface. Cover with half the turkey and half the salt, pepper and thyme. Continue making layers in this way, ending with a layer of sausage meat. Cover the tin with foil, place in a baking tin and pour in enough hot water to come halfway up the sides. Bake the mixture for 2 hours or until it has slightly shrunk away from the sides of the tin.

Cut out an oblong of cardboard slightly smaller than the tin. Place in

the tin and put a heavy weight on top, and chill for 8 hours.

COOKED FISH

Cooked fish should not be stored for more than one day, and only in a refrigerator. A can of tuna fish can be combined with a small amount of left-over fish to make up to a usable quantity. Cooked fish in a cheese sauce or combined with other suitable ingredients in a white sauce makes a delicious filling for savoury pancakes. Other ideas are in the Fish section, and these include quick and tasty Kedgeree. Or try this cold Fish Mayonnaise.

FISH MAYONNAISE

A handy way of using up leftover fish, this Fish Mayonnaise makes an attractive summer dish, served with salad.

3 servings
Metric/Imperial
500g (1lb) cooked white fish

2 teaspoons chopped fresh parsley
½ cucumber, peeled and thinly sliced
6 stuffed olives, sliced
1 green pepper, white pith removed, seeded and thinly sliced
2 tomatoes, sliced
225ml (8 fl oz) mayonnaise

American

2 cups cooked white fish
2 teaspoons chopped fresh parsley
½ cucumber, peeled and thinly sliced
6 stuffed olives, sliced
1 green pepper, membrane and seeds removed, thinly sliced
2 tomatoes, sliced
1 cup mayonnaise

Carefully remove all skin and bones from the fish and, using a fork, flake it into small pieces.

Mix the fish into the mayonnaise and pile the mixture in a mound in the centre of a flat serving dish. Sprinkle the parsley over the fish and mayonnaise mixture and surround with the cucumber, olives, green pepper and tomatoes.

Serve immediately.

Attractive to look at and delicious to eat, Turkey Meat Mould may be served with cold bread sauce.

COOKED VEGETABLES

Making cooked vegetables attractive enough to serve up a second time is a much more challenging task than creating a leftover dish from cooked meat or fish. Probably potatoes are the most versatile vegetable in this respect: leftover mashed potato and cabbage can be turned into crispy Bubble and Squeak, always a favourite with children, and many other uses for cooked mashed potato appear in the Vegetable section. Cold boiled potatoes can be sliced and fried up as part of a cooked breakfast.

Other vegetables are not quite so versatile, and one must remember that much of the vitamin content as well as the flavour will have disappeared by the time the vegetables have been cooked and then re-heated. If the vegetables were properly cooked in the first place that is, not overcooked) they can be quickly fried up in butter and served again, or heated through in a suitable

Egg and Vegetable Flan is a tasty way of serving leftover vegetables.

savoury or seasoned white sauce.

You can also use small quantities of leftover vegetables in soups. In fact, inventing your own home-made soup out of a combination of fresh and left-over meat and vegetables can be great fun, but always remember that cooked items can be lacking in flavour and need a well-flavoured home-made stock, or generous seasoning, to taste really good.

BUBBLE AND SQUEAK

This traditional English dish was originally made from leftover boiled beef, mixed with cold mashed potatoes and greens and then fried. Its name comes from the noise it makes when frying. Today, however, the meat is usually omitted and Bubble and Squeak consists only of leftover mashed potatoes and greens. The quantities of each should be approximately equal, but it really depends on how much is left over.

4 servings

Metric/Imperial

250g (8oz) cold mashed potatoes

250g (8oz) cooked, cold greens (cabbage, Brussels sprouts, winter greens)
$\frac{1}{2}$ teaspoon salt
4 grindings black pepper
50g (2oz) butter
1 teaspoon vinegar

American

1 cup cold mashed potatoes
1 cup cold cooked greens (cabbage, Brussels sprouts, kale, collards, etc.)
$\frac{1}{2}$ teaspoon salt
4 grindings black pepper
$\frac{1}{4}$ cup butter
1 teaspoon vinegar

In a large bowl mix the potatoes and greens together. Season with the salt and pepper.

Melt the butter in a large, deep frying-pan over moderately high heat. Add the potato-and-greens mixture. Cook for 5 to 6 minutes, or until thoroughly hot, stirring frequently.

Sprinkle the vinegar on top of the mixture and serve.

EGG AND VEGETABLE FLAN

A quick and nourishing supper dish, Egg and Vegetable Flan is a tasty way to use up leftover vegetables. It may be served either hot or cold.

4 servings

Metric/Imperial

250g (8oz) Shortcrust Pastry I
40g (1$\frac{1}{2}$oz) butter
1 small onion, finely chopped
2 tablespoons flour
300ml (10 fl oz) milk
1 large potato, cooked and sliced
1 large carrot, scraped, cooked and diced
2 tablespoons cooked peas
$\frac{1}{2}$ teaspoon salt
$\frac{1}{4}$ teaspoon white pepper
4 hard-boiled eggs, sliced
50g (2oz) Cheddar cheese, grated

American

1 recipe Shortcrust Pastry I
3 tablespoons butter
1 small onion, finely chopped
2 tablespoons flour
1$\frac{1}{4}$ cups milk
1 large potato, cooked and sliced
1 large carrot, scraped, cooked and diced
2 tablespoons cooked peas
$\frac{1}{2}$ teaspoon salt
$\frac{1}{4}$ teaspoon white pepper
4 hard boiled eggs, sliced
$\frac{1}{2}$ cup Cheddar or American cheese, grated

Preheat the oven to fairly hot (200°C/ 400°F or Gas Mark 6).

Roll out the pastry to $\frac{1}{4}$in thick. Lift the pastry on your rolling pin and lay it over an 8in flan or pie dish. Ease the pastry into the dish and trim the edges with a knife. Bake the pastry blind for 15 minutes. Remove the dish from the oven. Remove the aluminium foil and dried beans. Set the pastry case aside to cool.

Preheat the grill [broiler] to high.

To make the filling, melt the butter in a small saucepan and fry the onion for 5 to 7 minutes, or until it is soft and translucent.

Remove the pan from the heat and stir in the flour to make a smooth paste. Gradually add the milk, stirring constantly.

Return the pan to the heat and, still

stirring, bring the sauce to the boil. Simmer for 2 to 3 minutes, then stir in the potato, carrot, peas, salt and pepper.

Line the bottom of the pastry case with the hard-boiled eggs. Pour the sauce over the eggs. Sprinkle the top with the grated cheese and place the flan under the grill [broiler]. Cook for 3 to 4 minutes, or until the top is lightly brown. Serve at once if you wish to eat the flan hot. Otherwise, allow the flan to cool to room temperature and then chill for 30 minutes in the refrigerator before serving.

RUSSIAN SALAD

A classic dish, Russian Salad is a selection of cooked vegetables coated in mayonnaise. Served with cold cooked chicken, tongue or continental sausage and accompanied by bread or rolls, Russian Salad makes an excellent summer main course.

4-6 servings

Metric/Imperial

---

3 large cooked potatoes, diced
4 medium-sized cooked carrots, diced
100g (4oz) cooked French beans, halved
1 small onion, very finely chopped
100g (4oz) cooked fresh peas, weighed after shelling
225ml (8 fl oz) mayonnaise
¼ teaspoon cayenne pepper
2 hard-boiled eggs, sliced
1 cooked beetroot thinly sliced
2 gherkins, thinly sliced

American

---

3 large cooked potatoes, diced
4 medium-sized cooked carrots, diced
½ cup cooked green beans, sliced
1 small onion, very finely chopped
½ cup cooked peas

1 cup mayonnaise
¼ teaspoon cayenne pepper
2 hard boiled eggs, sliced
1 cooked beet, thinly sliced
2 sweet gherkins, thinly sliced

In a large salad bowl, combine all of the salad ingredients except the mayonnaise and cayenne. Set aside.

In a small bowl, beat the mayonnaise and cayenne together with a fork until they are well blended. Spoon the mayonnaise into the salad bowl and, using two spoons, toss to coat well.

Garnish the salad with the eggs, beetroot [beet] and gherkins and chill in the refrigerator for 15 to 20 minutes before serving.

A colourful mixture of cooked vegetables in mayonnaise, Russian Salad is superb served with lots of crusty bread and chilled white wine.

BREAD

An analysis of wasted food in the average household would almost certainly prove that bread comes at the top of the list. Of course, bread that shows any signs of mould must be discarded immediately, but most of the bread we throw out is just a little stale. We might feed it to the ducks or use it for toast or to make a bread pudding, but beyond that imagination often fails. So here are some more ideas for turning bread which is just a few days old into delicious treats for the family.

Breadcrumbs Fresh breadcrumbs can be used in stuffings and for bread sauce. Dried breadcrumbs can be used for coating fish, Scotch Eggs and rissoles and are simple to make if you make a habit of putting all crusts and slices of leftover bread in a baking tray in the bottom of the oven, where they will dry out and brown slowly if you are using the oven regularly. Two hours in a low oven should be sufficient. Crush them in a food mill or grinder, or with a rolling pin. They will keep for several weeks in a screw-top jar.

Melba toast is marvellous for serving with soups and pâtés. It is crisp and crunchy and easy to make and store. Cut very thin slices of stale bread and put them on a baking tray in a slow oven (150–180°C/300–350°F or Gas Mark 2–4), for about 20 minutes until light brown, curling and crisp. When cold, store in an airtight container.

Croustades are little cases which can be used for serving leftovers like creamed or curried fish, poultry or meat. Reheat them in the oven before serving.

Cut the bread in 2-inch thick slices. Remove the crusts and cut in squares, triangles or rounds. Scoop out the centre of the shapes leaving a hollow and making a case about $\frac{1}{2}$ inch thick. Brush the cases with melted butter and put to brown and crisp in a moderately hot oven (190°C/375°F or Gas Mark 5) for about 15 minutes.

Patty cups can be used in the same way as a pastry case and filled with savoury leftovers. Trim the crusts from thin slices of bread. Spread both sides with soft butter and press each slice in a patty tin so that the bread forms a cup.

Toast in a moderately hot oven (190°C/375°F or Gas Mark 5) for about 15 minutes until crisp and golden.

Garnishes and toppings add a special touch to a simple dish. Cut stale bread into fancy shapes – circles, triangles, cubes, crescents – and then toast or fry them.

Served with leftover dishes as a garnish, or as toppings for soups and stews, they add a crisp texture which is usually missing from these dishes.

FRENCH TOAST

An inexpensive dish popular with children, French Toast is very easy and quick to make. Maple syrup, golden [corn] syrup or a hot or cold fruit sauce may be served with the toast.

4-5 servings

Metric/Imperial

2 egg yolks, lightly beaten
50ml (2 fl oz) milk
120ml (5 fl oz) single cream
$\frac{1}{4}$ teaspoon grated nutmeg
$\frac{1}{4}$ teaspoon vanilla essence
$\frac{1}{8}$ teaspoon ground cinnamon
3 tablespoons castor sugar
8 to 10 small slices white bread, at least 1 day old, crusts removed
25g (1oz) butter

American

2 egg yolks, lightly beaten
$\frac{1}{4}$ cup milk
$\frac{5}{8}$ cup light cream
$\frac{1}{4}$ teaspoon grated nutmeg
$\frac{1}{4}$ teaspoon vanilla extract
$\frac{1}{8}$ teaspoon ground cinnamon
3 tablespoons fine sugar
8 to 10 small slices white bread, at least 1 day old, crusts removed
2 tablespoons butter

In a medium-sized shallow mixing bowl, beat the egg yolks and milk together with a fork. Stir in the cream, nutmeg, vanilla, cinnamon and sugar. Continue stirring until the sugar has dissolved. Place the bread slices in the cream mixture, coating them thoroughly on both sides. Set aside.

In a medium-sized, heavy frying-pan, melt half of the butter over moderate heat. When the foam subsides, place about four of the bread slices in the pan. Fry them for 2 to 3 minutes on each side, or until they are crisp and light brown. With a slotted spoon or spatula, remove the bread slices from the pan and transfer them to a warmed serving dish.

Keep them warm while you fry the remaining slices in the same way, using the rest of the butter. Serve hot.

EGGS

Odd egg yolks and egg whites are another commonly wasted item. They tend to accumulate in the refrigerator and are often forgotten. Egg yolks can be stored for up to two days in a cup, covered with a little water to prevent hardening, and whites will keep for the same length of time in a covered container. Remember to remove egg whites from the refrigerator and allow them to warm to room temperature before beating. The following are a few ideas which will use up leftover egg whites and yolks and add interest and nourishment to your cooking.

Add a beaten egg yolk to thick soups for extra nourishment, flavour and as a thickening agent. But do not let the soup boil after adding the egg or the soup will curdle.

Scrambled eggs can be made from egg yolks alone by adding two tablespoons of milk or water for each yolk when mixing.

Poach an egg yolk hard (in a poacher or in an eggcup standing for 15 minutes in simmering water) and then crumble it or run it through a sieve. Use it as a topping for soups, salads and rice dishes.

Add an egg yolk to a white sauce with half a tablespoon of lemon juice and serve with vegetables or fish. Again do not allow the sauce to boil after adding the egg.

Add stiffly-whisked egg whites to any purée with cream to make a delicious dessert.

Use egg whites to make a meringue top for stewed fruit or a milk pudding. Pop into the oven to set and brown slightly. Serve hot or cold.

Barbecue dishes

Thoughts of summer meals and barbecues naturally go together. Eating outdoors in the shade on a hot summer's day, watching and smelling the food cook and drinking cold wine or beer is a perfect summer activity. Eaten in that setting food always seems to taste better, or perhaps it's just that it does – the flavor of food cooked over charcoal can't be recreated in the kitchen.

Start your barbecue meal with a cold soup – Gazpacho is ideal – or perhaps a plate of Taramasalata (especially if your main course is to be kabobs). Serve lots of salads and if you're cooking steak, chops, chicken or sausages, barbecue vegetables to go with them. Potatoes, sweet potatoes, and pumpkin are all delicious wrapped in foil and cooked in the embers. Corn can be cooked either in foil or on the barbecue grill, but in either case it should be left wrapped in its leaves. The foil-wrapped vegetables will take longer to cook than the meat, so either precook them a little or start cooking them in the barbecue as soon as possible. Cook other vegetables on foil on the grill – onion rings, tomatoes and sweet peppers brushed with oil make a colorful addition to your meal.

We've selected a wide range of barbecue dishes for you to try. When there are so many exciting things to barbecue you won't want to stay every time with traditional steak and sausages. Kabobs are wonderful barbecue fare, as meat and vegetables are combined in the one dish and they're so easy to handle. (A barbecue problem can be finding a good place to rest your plate while cutting steak.) Fish and shellfish cooked out of doors, served with a delicious cold white wine, make a particularly memorable summer meal. You can of course combine a number of dishes for a barbecue buffet party. Give your guests a choice of meat kabobs and barbecued whole fish – both look marvellously decorative.

Finish your meal with fresh fruit salad or barbecued fruit and lots of assorted cheese and fruit. A barbecue is not the time for complicated desserts.

Prepare the barbecue well in advance – at least 20 minutes before you want to start cooking – but wait until the charcoal has stopped flaming or the food will burn. An excellent way to prevent food (particularly meat) sticking is to coat the grill with vegetable oil before use.

Then try tossing herbs and garlic on the fire – they give an extra subtle flavor and smell wonderful. A few bay leaves thrown on the charcoal also add to the flavor of the food and the smoke from pieces of garlic gently cooking in the embers flavors steak and lamb beautifully.

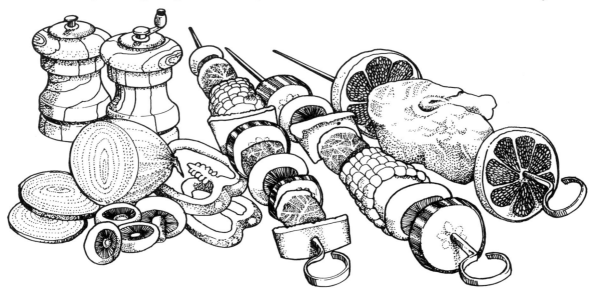

CHICKEN TERIYAKI

This popular Japanese dish will impress family and friends. The cooked golden brown chicken can be served cut into 5cm (2in) pieces.

6 servings

Metric (Cup)

6 chicken breasts, skinned
MARINADE
6 teaspoons clear honey
125ml (½ cup) soy sauce
½ teaspoon salt
½ teaspoon black pepper
2.5cm piece root ginger, peeled and finely chopped
1 garlic clove, crushed
125ml (½ cup) dry white wine

Imperial

6 chicken breasts, skinned
MARINADE
6 teaspoons clear honey
4 fl oz soy sauce
½ teaspoon salt
½ teaspoon black pepper
1in piece root ginger, peeled and finely chopped
1 garlic clove, crushed
4 fl oz dry white wine

Put the honey and soy sauce in a saucepan and heat gently, stirring until well mixed. Remove from the heat and stir in the remaining marinade ingredients.

Arrange the chicken breasts in a shallow dish and pour over the marinade. Turn the chicken to coat with the marinade. Leave to marinate for 2 hours, turning occasionally.

When the coals are ready, place the chicken breasts on the barbecue grid. Cook for 5 to 7 minutes on each side, turning and basting with the marinade from time to time. Serve hot, with any remaining marinade as a sauce.

BARBECUED CHICKEN

This simple dish is one of the most delicious ways to serve chicken. Accompany with French bread and salad.

4 servings

Metric (Cup)

2 small chickens, split in half
oil
SAUCE
6 teaspoons olive oil
6 teaspoons Worcestershire sauce
6 teaspoons tomato purée
1 small onion, finely chopped
9 teaspoons dry red wine
1 garlic clove, crushed
2 teaspoons paprika
½ teaspoon cayenne pepper
1 teaspoon salt
½ teaspoon black pepper
1 teaspoon brown sugar

Imperial

2 small chickens, split in half
oil
SAUCE
6 teaspoons olive oil
6 teaspoons Worcestershire sauce
6 teaspoons tomato purée
1 small onion, finely chopped
9 teaspoons dry red wine
1 garlic clove, crushed
2 teaspoons paprika
½ teaspoon cayenne pepper
1 teaspoon salt
½ teaspoon black pepper
1 teaspoon brown sugar

Mix together the ingredients for the sauce in a saucepan and bring to the boil, stirring. Simmer for 10 minutes.

Brush the chicken halves with oil. When the coals are ready, place the chicken halves on the barbecue grid, skin sides up. Cook for about 6 minutes, then turn and cook the other side for about 6 minutes.

Basting the chicken with the sauce continue cooking for 20 minutes or until cooked through.

SPATCHCOCK

This simple but delicious dish can be garnished with bacon rolls for added interest.

2-4 servings

Metric (Cup)

1 x 1.5kg chicken
9 teaspoons lemon juice
½ teaspoon salt
9 teaspoons butter, melted

Imperial

1 x 3lb chicken
9 teaspoons lemon juice
½ teaspoon salt
1½oz butter, melted

Cut the chicken along the back bone and force open. Lay on a flat surface and press until flat. Insert two long metal skewers through the drumstick on one side, through the breast and out the drumstick on the other side.

Sprinkle with the lemon juice and salt and leave for 1 hour.

When the coals are ready, place the chicken on the barbecue grid. Brush with some of the melted butter and cook for about 15 minutes on each side, brushing with more melted butter from time to time. Use the metal skewers to turn the chicken.

Remove the skewers and carve the chicken.

CHICKEN WITH ORANGE AND FIGS

This decorative skewer dish is ideal for an outdoor party.

8 servings

Metric (Cup)

16 chicken portions
60g (¼ cup) butter, melted
2 large oranges, cut into 8 wedges
16 fresh figs
SAUCE
9 teaspoons cider vinegar
150ml (⅔ cup) water
9 teaspoons sugar
6 teaspoons prepared English mustard
2 garlic cloves, crushed
1 teaspoon salt
½ teaspoon black pepper
1 onion, finely chopped
150ml (⅔ cup) tomato sauce
grated rind and juice of 1 lemon

A dish for a special barbecue, Barbecued Duck is roasted on a spit.

3 teaspoons Worcestershire sauce
60g ($\frac{1}{4}$ cup) butter

Imperial

16 chicken portions
2oz butter, melted
2 large oranges, cut into 8 wedges
16 fresh figs
SAUCE
9 teaspoons cider vinegar
$\frac{1}{4}$ pint water
$1\frac{1}{2}$oz sugar
6 teaspoons prepared English mustard
2 garlic cloves, crushed
1 teaspoon salt
$\frac{1}{2}$ teaspoon black pepper
1 onion, finely chopped
$\frac{1}{4}$ pint tomato sauce
grated rind and juice of 1 lemon
3 teaspoons Worcestershire sauce
2oz butter

First make the sauce. Put all the ingredients in a saucepan and bring to the boil, stirring. Simmer for 20 minutes.

When the coals are ready, place the chicken portions on the barbecue grid. Brush with the melted butter and cook for 5 to 6 minutes or until well browned on all sides. Remove from the heat and thread onto eight skewers, alternating with the orange wedges and figs.

Return to the heat and cook for a further 30 minutes, turning and basting with the sauce from time to time. Serve with any remaining sauce.

CHICKEN TIKKA

Here the chicken pieces must marinate for at least 8 hours to reach their full rich flavour.

4-6 servings

Metric (Cup)

6 chicken breasts, skinned, boned and cut into 2.5cm pieces
MARINADE
150ml ($\frac{2}{3}$ cup) plain yogurt
2 garlic cloves, crushed
2.5cm piece root ginger, peeled and grated
1 small onion, grated
$1\frac{1}{2}$ teaspoons hot chilli powder

3 teaspoons ground coriander
1 teaspoon salt
GARNISH
1 onion, thinly sliced into rings
2 large tomatoes, sliced
6 teaspoons chopped fresh coriander leaves

Imperial

6 chicken breasts, skinned, boned and cut into 1in pieces
MARINADE
$\frac{1}{4}$ pint plain yogurt
2 garlic cloves, crushed
1in piece root ginger, peeled and grated
1 small onion, grated
$1\frac{1}{2}$ teaspoons hot chilli powder
3 teaspoons ground coriander
1 teaspoon salt
GARNISH
1 onion, thinly sliced into rings
2 large tomatoes, sliced
6 teaspoons chopped fresh coriander leaves

Mix together the ingredients for the marinade in a shallow dish. Add the chicken pieces and turn to coat with the marinade. Leave to marinate for 8 hours or overnight, turning occasionally.

Thread the chicken pieces onto skewers.

When the coals are ready, place the skewers on the barbecue grid. Cook for 5 to 6 minutes, turning.

Slide the chicken off the skewers and serve garnished with the onion rings, tomato slices and chopped coriander leaves.

BARBECUED DUCK

Prepare this dish for a very festive barbecue and serve with sweet potatoes (kumaras) and broccoli.

4 servings

Metric (Cup)

1 x 2.25kg duck
1 teaspoon dry mustard
$\frac{1}{4}$ teaspoon cayenne pepper
$\frac{1}{2}$ teaspoon black pepper
SAUCE
1 garlic clove, crushed

$\frac{1}{4}$ teaspoon Tabasco sauce
6 teaspoons Worcestershire sauce
6 teaspoons tomato purée
60ml ($\frac{1}{4}$ cup) dry red wine
2 teaspoons paprika
grated rind and juice of 1 orange
6 teaspoons brown sugar
$\frac{1}{4}$ teaspoon black pepper
$\frac{1}{2}$ teaspoon salt
1 teaspoon arrowroot dissolved in 1 teaspoon water (optional)

Imperial

1 x 5lb duck
1 teaspoon dry mustard
$\frac{1}{4}$ teaspoon cayenne pepper
$\frac{1}{2}$ teaspoon black pepper
SAUCE
1 garlic clove, crushed
$\frac{1}{4}$ teaspoon Tabasco sauce
6 teaspoons Worcestershire sauce
6 teaspoons tomato purée
2 fl oz dry red wine
2 teaspoons paprika
grated rind and juice of 1 orange
6 teaspoons brown sugar
$\frac{1}{4}$ teaspoon black pepper
$\frac{1}{2}$ teaspoon salt
1 teaspoon arrowroot dissolved in 1 teaspoon water (optional)

Prick the skin of the duck all over, then rub in the mustard, cayenne and black pepper. Place the duck on the rôtisserie spit.

Mix together the ingredients for the sauce, except the arrowroot.

When the coals are ready, put the duck over the heat and turn on the rôtisserie motor. Place a shallow foil pan under the duck to catch the dripping fat. This pan will have to be emptied frequently.

Cook the duck for 20 minutes, then baste with the sauce. Continue cooking for $1\frac{1}{2}$ to 2 hours, basting with the sauce from time to time. To test if the duck is cooked, pierce the thigh with a skewer: the juices that run out should be clear.

If you like, thicken the remaining sauce with the arrowroot. Carve the duck and serve with the sauce.

Scallop Kebabs make a perfect barbecue meal.

SCALLOP KEBABS

Skewered scallops wrapped in bacon and served with rice and salad make a very elegant light meal.

4 servings

Metric (Cup)

16 scallops
8 lean bacon rashers, halved crossways and again lengthways
16 button mushrooms, halved
16 small onions, boiled for 8 minutes, drained and halved
2 lemons, quartered
MARINADE
2 garlic cloves, crushed
60ml ($\frac{1}{4}$ cup) olive oil
6 teaspoons lemon juice
6 teaspoons dry sherry
1 teaspoon dried marjoram
1 teaspoon salt
$\frac{1}{2}$ teaspoon black pepper

Imperial

16 scallops
8 lean bacon rashers, halved crossways and again lengthways
16 button mushrooms, halved
16 small onions, boiled for 8 minutes, drained and halved
2 lemons, quartered
MARINADE
2 garlic cloves, crushed
2 fl oz olive oil
6 teaspoons lemon juice
6 teaspoons dry sherry
1 teaspoon dried marjoram
1 teaspoon salt
$\frac{1}{2}$ teaspoon black pepper

Mix together the ingredients for the marinade in a shallow dish.

Wrap each scallop in a piece of bacon and thread onto skewers alternating with the mushroom and onion halves. Place in the dish and turn to coat with the marinade.

Leave to marinate for 30 minutes, turning occasionally.

When the coals are ready, place the kebabs on the barbecue grid. Cook for 10 to 12 minutes, turning and basting with the marinade.

Garnish with the lemon quarters and serve immediately.

257

NEPTUNE KEBABS

For an outdoor dinner party serve Neptune Kebabs followed by barbecued trout and salad.

4 servings

Metric (Cup)

16 green prawns
2 small green capsicums, membrane and seeds removed and cut into squares
16 large button mushrooms
16 sage leaves
2 lemons, cut into 8 wedges
MARINADE
60ml ($\frac{1}{4}$ cup) olive oil
6 teaspoons lemon juice
2 garlic cloves, crushed
1 teaspoon salt
$\frac{1}{2}$ teaspoon black pepper

Imperial

16 green prawns
2 small green capsicums, membrane and seeds removed and cut into squares
16 large button mushrooms
16 sage leaves
2 lemons, cut into 8 wedges
MARINADE
2 fl oz olive oil
6 teaspoons lemon juice
2 garlic cloves, crushed
1 teaspoon salt
$\frac{1}{2}$ teaspoon black pepper

Mix together the marinade ingredients in a shallow dish. Add the prawns and leave to marinate for 1 hour, turning occasionally.

Thread the prawns onto skewers alternating with the capsicum squares, mushrooms, sage leaves and lemon wedges.

When the coals are ready, place the kebabs on the barbecue grid. Cook for 10 minutes, turning and basting with the marinade.

JAPANESE SARDINES

Decorative and delicious, Japanese Sardines are a perfect starter for a barbecued meal.

4 servings

Metric (Cup)

500g fresh sardines (pilchards)
MARINADE
125ml ($\frac{1}{2}$ cup) soy sauce
60ml ($\frac{1}{4}$ cup) vinegar
6 teaspoons lemon juice
30g root ginger, peeled and chopped
2 garlic cloves, crushed
6 teaspoons oil

Imperial

1lb fresh sardines (pilchards)

Delicious Japanese Sardines are cooked with garlic, ginger, soy sauce and lemon juice.

MARINADE

4 fl oz soy sauce
2 fl oz vinegar
6 teaspoons lemon juice
1oz root ginger, peeled and chopped
2 garlic cloves, crushed
6 teaspoons oil

Mix together the ingredients for the marinade in a shallow dish. Put the sardines (pilchards) in the dish, in one layer if possible, and turn to coat with the marinade. Leave to marinate for 2 hours, turning occasionally.

When the coals are ready, arrange the sardines on the barbecue grid. Cook for 2 to 3 minutes on each side.

FISH STEAKS IN FOIL PARCELS

Fish steaks are delicious served with garlic bread and a selection of salads.

4 servings

Metric (Cup)

4 x 250g white fish steaks
1 teaspoon salt
6 teaspoons butter, cut into small
  pieces
SAUCE
6 teaspoons butter
250ml (1 cup) dry red wine
pinch of cayenne pepper
1 teaspoon prepared mustard
2 teaspoons mild chilli sauce
6 teaspoons lemon juice
1 teaspoon brown sugar
3 teaspoons capers
½ teaspoon salt

Imperial

4 x 8oz white fish steaks
1 teaspoon salt
1oz butter, cut into small pieces
SAUCE
1oz butter
8 fl oz dry red wine
pinch of cayenne pepper
1 teaspoon prepared mustard
2 teaspoons mild chilli sauce
6 teaspoons lemon juice
1 teaspoon brown sugar
3 teaspoons capers
½ teaspoon salt

First make the sauce. Melt the butter in a saucepan. Stir in the remaining sauce ingredients and bring to the boil. Simmer for 10 minutes. Remove from the heat.

Cut out four double-thickness pieces of foil large enough to hold a fish steak. Place a steak on each and sprinkle with salt. Dot with butter and wrap the foil around the fish to make neat secure parcels.

When the coals are ready, place the fish parcels on the barbecue grid. Cook for about 10 minutes, turning once. Just before the fish is ready, place the saucepan on the barbecue grid and reheat the sauce.

Turn the fish steaks out of the foil and pour over the sauce.

TROUT IN FOIL PARCELS

Serve barbecued trout for a marvellously festive outdoor meal.

6 servings

Metric (Cup)

6 trout, cleaned
6 fresh thyme sprigs
90g (⅓ cup) butter, cut into 6 pieces
3 lemons, halved
salt
pepper

Imperial

6 trout, cleaned
6 fresh thyme sprigs
3oz butter, cut into 6 pieces
3 lemons, halved
salt
pepper

Cut six double-thickness pieces of foil large enough to hold a fish. Place the trout on the foil. Put a thyme sprig and a piece of butter inside each fish and sprinkle each with the juice of ½ lemon and salt and pepper. Wrap the foil around the fish to make neat secure parcels.

When the coals are ready, put the parcels on the barbecue grid. Cook for about 30 minutes, turning once.

Carefully unwrap the trout and serve immediately.

HAM STEAKS WITH BARBECUE SAUCE

Barbecued pineapple pieces, rice and salad are perfect accompaniments for this dish.

4 servings

Metric (Cup)

4 ham steaks, about 3.5cm thick
3 teaspoons butter, melted
SAUCE
6 teaspoons butter
1 onion, finely chopped
1 garlic clove, crushed
1cm piece root ginger, peeled and
  grated
150ml (⅔ cup) water
470g canned tomatoes
1 celery stalk, finely chopped
6 teaspoons lemon juice
6 teaspoons vinegar
6 teaspoons tomato purée
4 teaspoons Worcestershire sauce
2 teaspoons brown sugar
½ teaspoon dried oregano
1 bay leaf
1 teaspoon salt
¼ teaspoon grated nutmeg

Imperial

4 ham steaks, about 1½in thick
3 teaspoons butter, melted
SAUCE
1oz butter
1 onion, finely chopped
1 garlic clove, crushed
½in piece root ginger, peeled and
  grated
¼ pint water
15oz canned tomatoes
1 celery stalk, finely chopped
6 teaspoons lemon juice
6 teaspoons vinegar
6 teaspoons tomato purée
4 teaspoons Worcestershire sauce
2 teaspoons brown sugar
½ teaspoon dried oregano
1 bay leaf
1 teaspoon salt
¼ teaspoon grated nutmeg

First make the sauce. Melt the butter in a saucepan. Add the onion and fry until it is soft but not brown. Stir in the remaining sauce ingredients and bring to the boil. Simmer for 40 minutes. Strain the sauce and keep hot.

Brush the ham steaks with the melted butter. When the coals are ready, put the steaks on the barbecue grid and cook for 3 to 5 minutes on each side. Serve with the barbecue sauce.

SPARERIBS WITH SWEET AND SOUR SAUCE

Spareribs are a decorative and tasty barbecue favourite. Serve with boiled rice and salad.

4 servings

Metric (Cup)

1.5kg pork spareribs, cut into 2-rib pieces
SAUCE
6 teaspoons vegetable oil
1 large onion, finely chopped
1 garlic clove, crushed
150ml ($\frac{2}{3}$ cup) tomato purée
9 teaspoons lemon juice
$\frac{1}{2}$ teaspoon salt
$\frac{1}{4}$ teaspoon black pepper
$\frac{1}{2}$ teaspoon dried sage
60g ($\frac{1}{4}$ cup) brown sugar
125ml ($\frac{1}{2}$ cup) beef stock
60ml ($\frac{1}{4}$ cup) Worcestershire sauce
2 teaspoons dry mustard

Imperial

3lb pork spareribs, cut into 2-rib pieces
SAUCE
6 teaspoons vegetable oil
1 large onion, finely chopped
1 garlic clove, crushed
$\frac{1}{4}$ pint tomato purée
9 teaspoons lemon juice
$\frac{1}{2}$ teaspoon salt
$\frac{1}{4}$ teaspoon black pepper
$\frac{1}{2}$ teaspoon dried sage
2 oz brown sugar
4 fl oz beef stock
2 fl oz Worcestershire sauce
2 teaspoons dry mustard

First make the sauce. Heat the oil in a saucepan. Add the onion and garlic and fry until the onion is soft but not brown. Stir in the remaining sauce ingredients and bring to the boil. Simmer for 10 minutes.

Meanwhile, arrange the ribs in one layer on the rack in the grilling pan. Grill until browned on both sides. Lift away the rack and pour the fat from the pan. Put the ribs in the pan and pour over the sauce. Turn the ribs to coat well.

When the coals are ready, place the ribs on the barbecue grid. Cook for 20 to 25 minutes, basting occasionally with the sauce. Serve hot, with any remaining sauce.

BARBECUED SPARERIBS

Barbecued Spareribs require fewer ingredients than the previous recipe but a longer preparation time.

4 servings

Metric (Cup)

1 large onion, grated
9 teaspoons sesame oil
90ml ($\frac{1}{3}$ cup) soy sauce
1.5kg pork spareribs, cut into 2-rib pieces

Imperial

1 large onion, grated
9 teaspoons sesame oil
3 fl oz soy sauce
3lb pork spareribs, cut into 2-rib pieces

Mix together the onion, oil and soy sauce in a shallow dish. Add the spareribs and turn to coat with the mixture. Leave to marinate for at least 1 hour.

When the coals are ready, arrange the spareribs on the barbecue grid. Cook for 20 to 25 minutes, turning and basting with the soy sauce mixture.

BARBECUED PORK CHOPS

An interesting variation to normal barbecue fare, Barbecued Pork Chops will soon become a family favourite.

6 servings

Metric (Cup)

6 loin pork chops, about 2.5cm thick
salt
pepper
SAUCE
60ml ($\frac{1}{4}$ cup) red wine vinegar
125ml ($\frac{1}{2}$ cup) tomato sauce
2 teaspoons sugar
$\frac{1}{2}$ teaspoon ground cloves
1 teaspoon celery seeds
$\frac{1}{2}$ teaspoon dry mustard
1 bay leaf

Imperial

6 loin pork chops, about 1in thick
salt
pepper
SAUCE
2 fl oz red wine vinegar
4 fl oz tomato sauce

2 teaspoons sugar
½ teaspoon ground cloves
1 teaspoon celery seeds
½ teaspoon dry mustard
1 bay leaf

Put the ingredients for the sauce in a saucepan and bring to the boil, stirring. Simmer very gently for 30 minutes.

Rub the chops with salt and pepper. When the coals are ready, place the chops on the barbecue grid. Cook for 2 to 3 minutes on each side to brown well,

Baked in a sweet and sour sauce, Barbecued Spareribs is an easy to make, tasty dish.

then brush lightly with the sauce. Cook for a further 7 minutes on each side.

Serve hot, with the remaining sauce.

LAMB PATTIES

These patties are a delicious and different addition to your barbecue recipes.

---

4 servings

Metric (Cup)

1kg minced lamb
1 small onion, finely chopped
1 teaspoon salt
½ teaspoon black pepper
½ teaspoon grated nutmeg

150g (1¼ cups) chopped blanched almonds

Imperial

2lb minced lamb
1 small onion, finely chopped
1 teaspoon salt
½ teaspoon black pepper
½ teaspoon grated nutmeg
5oz chopped blanched almonds

Mix together all the ingredients, using your fingers to combine thoroughly. Divide into 12 portions and shape each into a patty.

When the coals are ready, place the patties on the barbecue grid. Cook for about 8 minutes on each side. Serve hot.

MARINATED LAMB CHOPS

Simply serve potatoes and a salad with Marinated Lamb Chops for a marvellous summer meal.

4 servings

Metric (Cup)

8 small lamb chops
MARINADE
90ml (⅓ cup) olive oil
2 teaspoons prepared French mustard
juice of 1 lemon
6 teaspoons soy sauce
2 garlic cloves, crushed
salt
pepper

Imperial

8 small lamb chops
MARINADE
3 fl oz olive oil
2 teaspoons prepared French mustard
juice of 1 lemon
6 teaspoons soy sauce
2 garlic cloves, crushed
salt
pepper

Mix together the ingredients for the marinade with salt and pepper to taste in a shallow dish. Add the lamb chops, arranging them in one layer, and turn to coat with the marinade. Leave to marinate for about 6 hours, turning occasionally.

When the coals are ready, put the chops on the barbecue grid. Cook for 8 to 10 minutes on each side, basting occasionally with any remaining marinade.

Serve hot.

LAMB CHOPS WITH ROSEMARY OR TARRAGON

Try marinating lamb chops next time you plan them for an indoor meal—not just for the barbecue.

4 servings

Metric (Cup)

8 small lamb chops
4 tomatoes, halved

MARINADE
60ml (¼ cup) olive oil
6 teaspoons lemon juice
½ teaspoon salt
¼ teaspoon black pepper
4 fresh rosemary or tarragon sprigs
1 garlic clove, crushed

Imperial

8 small lamb chops
4 tomatoes, halved
MARINADE
2 fl oz olive oil
6 teaspoons lemon juice
½ teaspoon salt
¼ teaspoon black pepper
4 fresh rosemary or tarragon sprigs

Serve Lamb Chops with Rosemary or Tarragon with crusty rolls.

1 garlic clove, crushed

Mix together the marinade ingredients in a shallow dish. Put the chops in the dish and turn to coat with the marinade. Leave to marinate for 2 hours, turning occasionally.

When the coals are ready, arrange the chops on the barbecue grid. Cook for 8 to 10 minutes on each side. Just before the chops are ready, put the tomato halves on the grid, cut sides up. Cook until just soft.

LEG OF LAMB WITH CORIANDER AND GARLIC

This is a perfect way to cook a leg of lamb. Serve with barbecued root vegetables (wrapped in foil and cooked in the coals) and salad.

6-8 servings

Metric (Cup)

1 x 2.75kg leg of lamb, boned, rolled and tied into shape
6 garlic cloves, halved lengthways
3 teaspoons crushed coriander seeds
1 teaspoon salt
½ teaspoon black pepper
60ml (¼ cup) oil

Imperial

1 x 6lb leg of lamb, boned, rolled and tied into shape
6 garlic cloves, halved lengthways
3 teaspoons crushed coriander seeds
1 teaspoon salt
½ teaspoon black pepper
2 fl oz oil

Make 12 incisions in the lamb and insert a garlic clove half and a few coriander seeds in each. Rub the lamb with salt and pepper. Place the lamb on the rôtisserie spit.

When the coals are ready, put the lamb over the heat and turn on the rôtisserie motor. Brush with a little of the oil and cook for 2½ to 3 hours, brushing with more oil from time to time. To test if the lamb is cooked, pierce it with a skewer: the juices that run out should be only faintly rosy. If you are using a meat thermometer, it should register 67°C/155°F.

SPICY LEG OF LAMB

Spicy Leg of Lamb looks impressive and tastes as good.

4-6 servings

Metric (Cup)

1 x 2kg leg of lamb, boned, rolled and tied into shape
1 large garlic clove, cut into slivers
2 teaspoons dry mustard

½ teaspoon ground ginger
1 teaspoon salt
½ teaspoon black pepper
SAUCE
45g (¼ cup) chutney
9 teaspoons Worcestershire sauce
6 teaspoons soy sauce
6 teaspoons tomato purée
6 teaspoons dry red wine
9 teaspoons butter, melted
¼ teaspoon cayenne pepper
1 onion, finely chopped
1 teaspoon brown sugar

Imperial

1 x 4lb leg of lamb, boned, rolled and tied into shape
1 large garlic clove, cut into slivers
2 teaspoons dry mustard
½ teaspoon ground ginger
1 teaspoon salt
½ teaspoon black pepper
SAUCE
1½oz chutney
9 teaspoons Worcestershire sauce
6 teaspoons soy sauce
6 teaspoons tomato purée
6 teaspoons dry red wine
1½oz butter, melted
¼ teaspoon cayenne pepper
1 onion, finely chopped
1 teaspoon brown sugar

Make several incisions in the meat and insert the garlic slivers. Mix together the mustard, ginger and salt and pepper and rub all over the meat. Place the lamb on the rôtisserie spit.

Mix together the ingredients for the sauce.

When the coals are ready, put the lamb over the heat and turn on the rôtisserie motor. Cook for 2 to 2½ hours, basting with the sauce from time to time. To test if the lamb is cooked, pierce it with a skewer: the juices that run out should be only faintly rosy. If you are using a meat thermometer it should register 67°C/155°F. Serve carved into slices, with the remaining sauce.

LAMB KEBABS IN HERB MARINADE

Kebabs can be served on their own with

rice and salad or combined with other meat dishes.

6-8 servings

Metric (Cup)

1.5kg boned leg of lamb, cut into 2.5cm cubes
375g button mushrooms
18 small tomatoes
8 small onions, boiled for 8 minutes and drained
60g (¼ cup) butter, melted
MARINADE
250ml (1 cup) olive oil
125ml (½ cup) dry white wine
1 onion, finely chopped
1 celery stalk, finely chopped
1 garlic clove, crushed
1 teaspoon dried basil
1 teaspoon dried thyme
3 teaspoons chopped fresh chives
6 black peppercorns, crushed
1 bay leaf
1 teaspoon salt

Imperial

3lb boned leg of lamb, cut into 1in cubes
12oz button mushrooms
18 small tomatoes
8 small onions, boiled for 8 minutes and drained
2oz butter, melted
MARINADE
8 fl oz olive oil
4 fl oz dry white wine
1 onion, finely chopped
1 celery stalk, finely chopped
1 garlic clove, crushed
1 teaspoon dried basil
1 teaspoon dried thyme
3 teaspoons chopped fresh chives
6 black peppercorns, crushed
1 bay leaf
1 teaspoon salt

Mix together the ingredients for the marinade in a shallow dish. Add the lamb cubes and marinate for 6 hours, turning occasionally.

Thread the lamb cubes onto skewers, alternating with the mushrooms, tomatoes and onions. Strain the marinade and reserve.

When the coals are ready, brush the kebabs with melted butter and place on the barbecue grid. Cook for 8 to 10 minutes, turning and basting with the strained marinade.

PORTUGUESE KEBABS

Skewer cooking is great fun at barbecues and very practical—guests don't need to balance a knife and fork as the food is already in bite-size pieces.

4-6 servings

Metric (Cup)

500g pork fillet, cut into 2.5cm cubes
500g boned leg of lamb, cut into
   2.5cm cubes
MARINADE
2 garlic cloves, crushed
3 teaspoons paprika
1 teaspoon dried oregano
2 teaspoons grated orange rind
1 teaspoon salt
½ teaspoon black pepper
1 teaspoon sugar
3 teaspoons chopped fresh mint
3 teaspoons olive oil
6 teaspoons dry sherry

Imperial

1lb pork fillet, cut into 1in cubes
1lb boned leg of lamb, cut into 1in
   cubes
MARINADE
2 garlic cloves, crushed
3 teaspoons paprika
1 teaspoon dried oregano
2 teaspoons grated orange rind
1 teaspoon salt
½ teaspoon black pepper
1 teaspoon sugar
3 teaspoons chopped fresh mint
3 teaspoons olive oil
6 teaspoons dry sherry

Mix together the ingredients for the marinade in a shallow dish. Add the pork and lamb cubes and turn to coat with the marinade. Leave to marinate for 2 hours, turning occasionally.

Thread the pork and lamb cubes onto skewers, alternating them.

When the coals are ready, place the kebabs on the barbecue grid. Cook for 10 to 15 minutes, turning and basting with the marinade.

SOSATIES

Curry powder and chutney give the skewered lamb in this dish an unusual flavour.

4 servings

Metric (Cup)

1kg boned shoulder of lamb, cut into
   2.5cm cubes
MARINADE
9 teaspoons butter
1 large onion, finely chopped
3 teaspoons curry powder
2 teaspoons brown sugar
1 teaspoon salt
½ teaspoon black pepper
3 teaspoons chutney
375ml (1½ cups) white wine vinegar

185ml (¾ cup) water
finely grated rind of ½ lemon

Imperial

2lb boned shoulder of lamb, cut into
   1in cubes
MARINADE
1½oz butter
1 large onion, finely chopped
3 teaspoons curry powder
2 teaspoons brown sugar
1 teaspoon salt
½ teaspoon black pepper
3 teaspoons chutney
12 fl oz white wine vinegar
6 fl oz water
finely grated rind of ½ lemon

Melt the butter in a saucepan. Add the onion and fry until it is soft but not brown. Stir in the remaining marinade ingredients and bring to the boil.

Put the lamb cubes in a shallow dish, in one layer if possible. Pour over the marinade. Allow to cool, then cover and chill for 24 hours.

Thread the lamb cubes onto skewers.

When the coals are ready, place the skewers on the barbecue grid. Cook for 8 to 10 minutes, turning occasionally.

Meanwhile, pour the marinade into a saucepan and bring to the boil. Boil for 10 minutes or until reduced by about one-third. Strain into a sauceboat and serve with the kebabs.

An unusual dish from South Africa, Sosaties are marinated lamb kebabs served with a spicy sauce.

GREEK LAMB KEBABS

Serve with a Greek salad made of onion rings, tomato slices, black olives, pieces of feta and a good salad dressing made with olive oil.

6 servings

Metric (Cup)

1kg boned shoulder of lamb, cut into
    2.5cm cubes
4 onions, quartered
MARINADE
juice of 2 lemons
250ml (1 cup) olive oil
½ teaspoon salt
1 teaspoon black pepper
½ teaspoon dried marjoram

Imperial

2lb boned shoulder of lamb, cut into
    1in cubes
4 onions, quartered
MARINADE
juice of 2 lemons
8 fl oz olive oil
½ teaspoon salt
1 teaspoon black pepper
½ teaspoon dried marjoram

Mix together the ingredients for the marinade in a shallow dish. Add the lamb cubes and turn to coat with the marinade. Leave to marinate for 1 hour, turning occasionally.

Separate the onion quarters into layers.

Thread the lamb cubes onto skewers alternating with the onion pieces.

When the coals are ready, put the kebabs on the barbecue grid. Cook for 10 to 15 minutes, turning and basting with the marinade.

TIKKA KEBAB

Ginger and coriander give this dish its distinct delicious flavour.

4 servings

Metric (Cup)

1kg boned leg of lamb, cut into 2.5cm
    cubes
6 teaspoons oil

MARINADE
10cm piece root ginger, peeled and
    chopped
3 onions, chopped
1 small bunch of fresh coriander
    leaves
3 teaspoons coriander seeds
juice of 1 lemon
2 green chillis, seeded
½ teaspoon black peppercorns

Imperial

2lb boned leg of lamb, cut into 1in
    cubes
6 teaspoons oil
MARINADE
4in piece root ginger, peeled and
    chopped
3 onions, chopped
1 small bunch of fresh coriander
    leaves
3 teaspoons coriander seeds
juice of 1 lemon
2 green chillis, seeded
½ teaspoon black peppercorns

Put the ingredients for the marinade in an electric blender and blend until smooth. Pour into a mixing bowl and add the lamb cubes. Turn to coat with the marinade. Leave to marinate for at least 4 hours, turning occasionally.

Thread the lamb cubes onto skewers.

When the coals are ready, place the kebabs on the barbecue grid. Brush with oil and cook for 8 to 10 minutes, brushing with oil and turning.

SHASHLIK

Colourful Shashlik is always a popular barbecue dish.

4 servings

Metric (Cup)

1kg boned loin of lamb, cut into 2.5cm
    cubes
8 tomatoes, quartered
2 green capsicums, membrane and
    seeds removed and cut into squares
1 lemon, cut into wedges
MARINADE
90ml (⅓ cup) oil
juice of 1 large lemon
2 onions, thinly sliced

Shashlik is a Russian dish of succulent lamb, tomato and capsicum kebabs flavoured with lemon.

½ teaspoon salt
½ teaspoon black pepper

Imperial

2lb boned loin of lamb, cut into 1in cubes
8 tomatoes, quartered
2 green capsicums, membrane and seeds removed and cut into squares
1 lemon, cut into wedges
MARINADE
3 fl oz oil
juice of 1 large lemon
2 onions, thinly sliced
½ teaspoon salt
½ teaspoon black pepper

Mix together the ingredients for the marinade in a shallow dish. Add the lamb cubes and turn to coat with the marinade. Marinate for 8 hours or overnight, turning occasionally.

Thread the lamb cubes onto skewers, alternating with tomato quarters and pieces of green capsicum. Strain the marinade and reserve.

When the coals are ready, place the kebabs on the barbecue grid. Cook for 8 to 10 minutes, turning and basting with the strained marinade.

Serve with the lemon wedges.

HAMBURGERS

Hamburgers offer great scope for innovation—the range of accompaniments is vast. Serve with a selection of pickles and relishes, tomato sauce, mayonnaise, mustard, or French-fried potatoes. Or try spreading a layer of avocado on the hamburger patty.

4 servings

Metric (Cup)

1kg lean minced steak
salt
pepper
dried thyme
1 egg
TO SERVE
4 hamburger buns, halved
sliced tomatoes
lettuce leaves
sliced onion
mustard, tomato sauce and relishes

Imperial

2lb lean minced steak
salt
pepper
dried thyme
1 egg
TO SERVE
4 hamburger buns, halved
sliced tomatoes
lettuce leaves
sliced onion
mustard, tomoto sauce and relishes

Mix together the minced steak, salt, pepper and thyme to taste and the egg, using your fingers to mix the ingredients thoroughly. Divide into four and shape each portion into a patty.

When the coals are ready, put the hamburgers on the barbecue grid. Cook for 5 to 7 minutes on each side or until the hamburgers are cooked to your liking. Just before the hamburgers are ready, put the buns, cut sides down, on the grid to heat through.

Serve the hamburgers on the buns with the accompaniments.

MARINATED STEAK

Steak is inseparable from barbecues, but try serving it marinated for a tasty change. Accompany with a selection of salads.

4 servings

Metric (Cup)

750g rump steak
pepper
MARINADE
¾ teaspoon dry mustard
1½ teaspoons vinegar
1½ teaspoons soy sauce
1 teaspoon lemon juice

Imperial

1½lb rump steak
pepper
MARINADE
¾ teaspoon dry mustard
1½ teaspoons vinegar
1½ teaspoons soy sauce
1 teaspoon lemon juice

Mix together the ingredients for the marinade in a shallow dish. Put the steak in the dish and turn to coat with the marinade. Sprinkle with plenty of pepper and leave to marinate for at least 30 minutes, turning occasionally.

When the coals are ready, put the steak on the barbecue grid. Cook for 4 to 5 minutes on each side or until cooked to your taste. Baste occasionally with any remaining marinade.

Cut into four portions and serve hot.

MARINATED SKIRT OR FLANK STEAK

Another version of marinated steak, this dish should be prepared the day before it is required.

4 servings

Metric (Cup)

1kg skirt or flank steak, well beaten
MARINADE
90ml (⅓ cup) soy sauce
90ml (⅓ cup) medium sherry
90ml (⅓ cup) olive oil
1 garlic clove, crushed

1 teaspoon salt
½ teaspoon black pepper

Imperial

2lb skirt or flank steak, well beaten
MARINADE
3 fl oz soy sauce
3 fl oz medium sherry
3 fl oz olive oil
1 garlic clove, crushed
1 teaspoon salt
½ teaspoon black pepper

Mix together the ingredients for the marinade in a shallow dish. Put the steak in the dish and turn to coat with the marinade. Leave to marinate for at least 8 hours or overnight, turning occasionally.

When the coals are ready, put the steak on the barbecue grid. Cook for 4 to 7 minutes on each side, or until cooked to your taste. Baste with the marinade from time to time. Serve hot, cut in diagonal slices.

STEAK TERIYAKI

Serve this elegant dish for a special barbecue.

4 servings

Metric (Cup)

1kg fillet steak, cut into 5mm thick
   slices
MARINADE
2.5cm piece root ginger, peeled and
   finely chopped
2 garlic cloves, crushed
4 spring onions, finely chopped
6 teaspoons brown sugar
250ml (1 cup) soy sauce
125ml (½ cup) sake or dry sherry
1 teaspoon salt
½ teaspoon black pepper

Imperial

2lb fillet steak, cut into ¼in thick slices
MARINADE
1in piece root ginger, peeled and
   finely chopped
2 garlic cloves, crushed
4 spring onions, finely chopped
6 teaspoons brown sugar
8 fl oz soy sauce

4 fl oz sake or dry sherry
1 teaspoon salt
½ teaspoon black pepper

Mix together the ingredients for the marinade in a shallow dish. Add the steak slices and turn to coat with the marinade. Leave to marinate for 2 hours, turning occasionally.

When the coals are ready, arrange the steak slices on the barbecue grid. Cook for 2 to 3 minutes on each side, basting with the marinade. Serve hot.

SEEKH KEBABS

Kebabs with a difference—made with minced meat these look and taste marvellous.

4 servings

Metric (Cup)

750g minced lamb or steak
60g (1 cup) fresh breadcrumbs
2.5cm piece root ginger, peeled and
   grated
1 green chilli, seeded and finely
   chopped
2 garlic cloves, crushed
1 teaspoon ground cumin
½ teaspoon salt
1 teaspoon finely grated lemon rind
1 teaspoon lemon juice

Imperial

1½lb minced lamb or steak
2oz fresh breadcrumbs
1in piece root ginger, peeled and
   grated
1 green chilli, seeded and finely
   chopped
2 garlic cloves, crushed
1 teaspoon ground cumin
½ teaspoon salt
1 teaspoon finely grated lemon rind
1 teaspoon lemon juice

Mix together all the ingredients, using your fingers to combine them thoroughly. Divide into 16 portions. Press two portions, well spaced, around each of eight greased skewers. The meat portions should be about 10cm (4in) in length.

When the coals are ready, place the

skewers on the barbecue grid. Cook for 6 minutes, turning occasionally.

KIDNEY AND CHICKEN LIVER KEBABS

Kebabs can be made from almost any meat. Serve this combination of kidneys and chicken livers with rice and salad.

4-6 servings

Metric (Cup)

750g chicken livers
500g lambs' kidneys, trimmed and halved
500g cooked ham, cut into 2.5cm cubes
4 large onions, quartered
2 green capsicums, membrane and seeds removed and cut into squares
125g (½ cup) butter, melted

Imperial

1½lb chicken livers
1lb lambs' kidneys, trimmed and halved
1lb cooked ham, cut into 1in cubes
4 large onions, quartered
2 green capsicums, membrane and seeds removed and cut into squares
4oz butter, melted

Thread the chicken livers, kidney halves, ham cubes, onion quarters and green capsicum squares onto skewers. Brush all over with melted butter.

When the coals are ready, place the kebabs on the barbecue grid. Cook for 8 to 10 minutes, turning and brushing with melted butter from time to time.

HOT DOG KEBABS

Hot Dog Kebabs are a great favourite with children.

4 servings

Metric (Cup)

8 frankfurters, cut into 4 pieces
750g canned pineapple chunks, drained
8 bacon rashers, rolled
8 small onions, boiled for 8 minutes and drained

2 green capsicums, membrane and seeds removed and cut into squares
60g (¼ cup) butter, melted

Imperial

8 frankfurters, cut into 4 pieces
1½lb canned pineapple chunks, drained
8 bacon rashers, rolled
8 small onions, boiled for 8 minutes and drained
2 green capsicums, membrane and seeds removed and cut into squares
2oz butter, melted

Thread the frankfurter pieces, pineapple chunks, bacon rolls, onions and green capsicum squares onto skewers. Brush all over with melted butter.

When the coals are ready, put the kebabs on the barbecue grid. Cook for about 15 minutes, turning and brushing with melted butter.

SKEWERED APPLES

You need something sweet to finish your barbecue meal. But it's much more fun to continue barbecue cooking than to bring out a prepared dessert.

8 servings

Metric (Cup)

8 dessert apples
SAUCE
60g (¼ cup) butter
60ml (¼ cup) gin
90ml (⅓ cup) grapefruit juice
9 teaspoons sugar

Imperial

8 dessert apples
SAUCE
2oz butter
2 fl oz gin
3 fl oz grapefruit juice
1½oz sugar

Thread the apples onto skewers. When the coals are ready, put the apples on the barbecue grid and cook for 15 to 30 minutes (depending on size), turning frequently.

Meanwhile, melt the butter in a saucepan on the barbecue grid. Stir in

the remaining sauce ingredients.

Keep the sauce hot and serve with the apples for dipping.

FRUIT KEBABS

Another delicious dessert to cook on your barbecue.

6 servings

Metric (Cup)

6 apricots, halved and stoned
6 large bananas, thickly sliced
2 pears, peeled, cored and thickly sliced
12 pineapple chunks
6 teaspoons butter, melted
3 teaspoons brown sugar
MARINADE
125ml (½ cup) orange juice
125ml (½ cup) lemon juice
6 teaspoons orange-flavoured liqueur
1 teaspoon chopped fresh mint
6 teaspoons clear honey

Imperial

6 apricots, halved and stoned
6 large bananas, thickly sliced
2 pears, peeled, cored and thickly sliced
12 pineapple chunks
1oz butter, melted
3 teaspoons brown sugar
MARINADE
4 fl oz orange juice
4 fl oz lemon juice
6 teaspoons orange-flavoured liqueur
1 teaspoon chopped fresh mint
6 teaspoons clear honey

Mix together the ingredients for the marinade in a shallow dish. Add the fruit and turn to coat with the marinade. Leave to marinate for 1 hour, turning occasionally.

Thread the fruit onto skewers. Brush with the melted butter and sprinkle with the brown sugar.

When the coals are ready, place the kebabs on the barbecue grid and cook for 6 to 8 minutes, turning. Meanwhile, put the marinade in a saucepan and heat on the barbecue grid.

Serve the kebabs with the hot marinade.

Dinner party dishes

All your family meals are special but in your daily role of chef you have to consider budget, nutrition, waistlines, time and ease of preparation when planning and cooking a dinner. Having a dinner party is your opportunity to ignore all these factors and concentrate solely on producing something marvellous to eat.

Length of preparation of the meal now becomes a minor issue. If you love to cook you will enjoy the time spent creating a superb dish for your guests. Read the recipe through carefully before you begin and don't take short cuts – leave them for everyday cooking. If a recipe requires ingredients to be cooked in separate stages, do so – the instruction is there because that is the only way to arrive at the true flavor of the dish.

Only attempt one complicated dish for a dinner party, and do as much as you can well in advance so that you're not too tired to enjoy the evening. One of the secrets of success of any good dinner party is a relaxed atmosphere – which won't be achieved if you're always in the kitchen. And anyhow after doing all that work you owe it to yourself to have fun.

You'll probably be preparing three courses, the appetizer, main course and dessert. Traditionally, formal dinners open with a clear soup, followed by fish, a main course and dessert, but that has little relevance to your dinner party. You may want to begin with appetizers served with drinks, and if you do they must be very small and not too filling. Don't resort to nuts or potato chips, these are filling and far too unimaginative – it's better to serve nothing and let guests sit down to dinner a little hungry. Remember that all the food you serve is equally important. Vegetables, more than any other part of the meal, often tend to be over cooked and badly presented. Strange, as they can be the most visually attractive part of the meal.

Presentation of the food is very important. Everything –

even the very simple components of the meal – must be arranged as attractively as you can. When you're finishing the meal with fruit and cheese make sure the fruit is washed and well polished before bringing it to the table. If you make your own bread, bake a beautiful loaf which can be one of the focal points of the table.

But the taste of the food is of course what the meal is all about. As we have said, take time over cooking, taste as you go to see that the flavor is just right and always use good ingredients. A dinner party is not the time to try to save a few cents. For instance if olive oil is specified in a recipe don't use vegetable oil. Take time over shopping. If you buy tired ingredients, no matter how well you cook them you won't get perfect results.

And don't skimp on wine. You must use a reasonable wine when cooking. The alcohol content evaporates but the taste remains, so you want a wine with a good flavor. Certainly don't try to save on the wine you drink with the meal. The beautiful food you have created deserves a very good wine to complement it. Budget wines can be left for budget meals.

There are no rigid rules to follow in serving wine, though unless you're drinking champagne throughout the meal it is more interesting to serve a different wine with each course in appropriate glasses, ending with a sweet white wine or champagne (semi-sweet or sweet but never dry) with dessert. The only rule to remember is that the wine and food should complement each other. A light dish needs a light wine, a highly flavored dish a robust wine. According to the wine experts some food goes badly with wine, artichokes for instance alter the taste of the wine, but a strong dry white wine served with them will still be delicious.

Do keep a note of the dishes you have served and whom you have invited. It *is* possible to forget and serve the same dish to the same guests at a future dinner. Finally, have fun cooking and have a wonderful evening.

DOLMADAKIA

Served chilled, Dolmadakia are also a perfect accompaniment to an outdoor meal.

8 servings

Metric (Cup)

185g (1 cup) long-grain rice
6 teaspoons olive oil
2 large onions, finely chopped
2 garlic cloves, crushed
250g (1 cup) minced steak
½ teaspoon salt
½ teaspoon black pepper
6 teaspoons chopped fresh parsley
6 teaspoons chopped fresh dill
6 teaspoons pine nuts
250ml (1 cup) lemon juice
250ml (1 cup) beef stock
500g vine leaves in brine, rinsed in hot water and dried with kitchen paper towels
1 lemon, cut into wedges

Imperial

6oz long-grain rice
6 teaspoons olive oil
2 large onions, finely chopped
2 garlic cloves, crushed
8oz minced steak
½ teaspoon salt
½ teaspoon black pepper
6 teaspoons chopped fresh parsley
6 teaspoons chopped fresh dill
6 teaspoons pine nuts
8 fl oz lemon juice
8 fl oz beef stock
1lb vine leaves in brine, rinsed in hot water and dried with kitchen paper towels
1 lemon, cut into wedges

Cook the rice in boiling salted water until it is tender. Drain well.

Heat the oil in a saucepan. Add the onions and garlic and fry until the onions are soft but not brown. Add the minced steak and fry until it is browned. Stir in the salt, pepper, parsley, dill, pine nuts, half the lemon juice and half

Although Duck Terrine is an extravagant pâté to make, it is well worth the time and expense for a special dinner party.

the stock and bring to the boil. Simmer for 10 minutes. Stir in the cooked rice.

Place the vine leaves, shiny sides down, on a flat surface. Place a spoonful of the meat mixture in the centre of each leaf and roll up, tucking in the sides to make a neat parcel. Arrange the rolls in a flameproof casserole. Pour over the remaining lemon juice and stock and place a plate with a weight on it on top of the rolls to keep them in place.

Simmer for 25 minutes. Transfer the vine rolls to a warmed serving dish and pour over the liquid from the casserole. Garnish with the lemon wedges. The dolmadakia may also be served chilled.

MARINATED MUSHROOMS

Serve this delicious salad at any time.

6 servings

Metric (Cup)

500g button mushrooms, stalks trimmed level with the caps
1 teaspoon salt

3 black peppercorns, slightly crushed
2 teaspoons chopped fresh dill
60ml (¼ cup) tarragon vinegar
3 teaspoons lemon juice
60ml (¼ cup) olive oil

Imperial

1lb button mushrooms, stalks trimmed level with the caps
1 teaspoon salt
3 black peppercorns, slightly crushed
2 teaspoons chopped fresh dill
2 fl oz tarragon vinegar
3 teaspoons lemon juice
2 fl oz olive oil

Put the mushrooms in a shallow dish. Mix together the remaining ingredients and pour over the mushrooms. Turn to coat well. Leave to marinate for 2 hours, turning occasionally.

Drain off the marinade before serving.

Marinated Mushrooms may be served as a deliciously different appetizer, or as part of a summer buffet salad.

GLOBE ARTICHOKES PROVENCALE

This elegant dish is very simple to pre-pare. Serve artichokes often to your family when they are in season.

4 servings

Metric (Cup)

4 globe artichokes
6 teaspoons olive oil
4 bacon rashers, diced
2 onions, finely chopped
1 garlic clove, crushed
470g canned tomatoes, drained
3 teaspoons tomato purée
½ teaspoon dried basil
salt
black pepper
6 teaspoons brandy
125ml (½ cup) dry white wine
125ml (½ cup) chicken stock
1 bouquet garni

Imperial

4 globe artichokes
6 teaspoons olive oil
4 bacon rashers, diced
2 onions, finely chopped
1 garlic clove, crushed
15oz canned tomatoes, drained
3 teaspoons tomato purée
½ teaspoon dried basil
salt
black pepper
6 teaspoons brandy
4 fl oz dry white wine
4 fl oz chicken stock
1 bouquet garni

Cut the stalks off the artichokes, level with the bases. Trim the leaves. Cut each artichoke into quarters and scrape out the hairy chokes. Cook in boiling salted water for 5 minutes. Drain well.

Heat the oil in a saucepan. Add the bacon and fry until it is crisp. Add the onions and garlic and fry until the onions are soft but not brown. Stir in the remaining ingredients with salt and pepper to taste.

Add the artichoke quarters to the pan and spoon the sauce over them. Bring to the boil, then cover and simmer gently for 45 minutes.

Remove the bouquet garni and serve.

PALM HEART COCKTAIL

Palm Heart Cocktail is a light, wonderful starter that also has a hint of extrava-gance. Serve with lemon wedges.

4 servings

Metric (Cup)

8 lettuce leaves, shredded
440g canned palm hearts, drained and cut into 1cm slices
3 teaspoons lemon juice
DRESSING
150ml (⅔ cup) mayonnaise

A first course with a difference, Palm Heart Cocktail has a mildly spiced dressing containing Wor-cestershire and Tabasco sauces.

½ teaspoon salt
¼ teaspoon black pepper
¼ teaspoon mild curry powder
6 teaspoons whipped cream
1 teaspoon Worcestershire sauce
¼ teaspoon Tabasco sauce
2 teaspoons tomato sauce
pinch of cayenne pepper

Imperial

8 lettuce leaves, shredded
14oz canned palm hearts, drained and cut into ½in slices
3 teaspoons lemon juice
DRESSING
¼ pint mayonnaise
½ teaspoon salt
¼ teaspoon black pepper
¼ teaspoon mild curry powder
6 teaspoons whipped cream
1 teaspoon Worcestershire sauce

¼ teaspoon Tabasco sauce
2 teaspoons tomato sauce
pinch of cayenne pepper

Divide the shredded lettuce between four serving dishes. Pile the palm hearts on top and sprinkle with lemon juice.

Mix together the ingredients for the dressing, except the cayenne pepper. Pour the dressing over the palm hearts and sprinkle the cayenne on top.

GUACAMOLE RING

This Mexican dish looks colourful and extravagant and tastes marvellous—just right for a special dinner party.

8 to 10 servings

Metric (Cup)

3 large ripe avocados, halved and
   stoned
9 teaspoons mayonnaise
juice of 1 lemon
1 teaspoon prepared French mustard
2 teaspoons Worcestershire sauce
6 teaspoons tomato purée
¼ teaspoon cayenne pepper
½ teaspoon salt
¼ teaspoon black pepper
300ml (1¼ cups) cream
30g gelatine, dissolved in 60ml (¼ cup)
   warm water
GARNISH
500g prawns, shelled
1 green capsicum, membrane and
   seeds removed and cut into rings
2 red capsicums, membrane and seeds
   removed and cut into rings
6 teaspoons lemon juice

A beautiful dish for a summer party, Guacamole Ring is filled with prawns and capsicums.

6 teaspoons chopped chives

Imperial

3 large ripe avocados, halved and
   stoned
9 teaspoons mayonnaise
juice of 1 lemon
1 teaspoon prepared French mustard
2 teaspoons Worcestershire sauce
6 teaspoons tomato purée
¼ teaspoon cayenne pepper
½ teaspoon salt
¼ teaspoon black pepper
½ pint cream
1oz gelatine, dissolved in 2 fl oz warm
   water

1lb prawns, shelled
1 green capsicum, membrane and
   seeds removed and cut into rings
2 red capsicums, membrane and seeds
   removed and cut into rings
6 teaspoons lemon juice
6 teaspoons chopped chives

Scoop the avocado flesh from the skins and put in a mixing bowl. Mash in the mayonnaise, lemon juice, mustard, Worcestershire sauce and tomato purée. Stir in the cayenne, salt and pepper. Whip the cream until thick and fold into the avocado mixture. Stir in the dissolved gelatine.

Pour into a greased 23cm (9in) ring mould. Chill until set.

To make the garnish, combine all the ingredients in a mixing bowl.

Turn out the avocado ring onto a serving plate. Fill the centre with some of the garnish and arrange the remainder around the edge.

TOMATOES PROVENCALE

Combined anchovies and garlic make these stuffed tomatoes a very tasty dish.

6 servings

Metric (Cup)

6 teaspoons olive oil
4 tomatoes, peeled, seeded and
   chopped
2 teaspoons chopped parsley
2 garlic cloves, crushed
60g (1 cup) fresh breadcrumbs, soaked
   in 60ml (¼ cup) beef stock for 10
   minutes
4 anchovy fillets, finely chopped
6 large tomatoes, halved and seeded
30g (¼ cup) dry breadcrumbs
6 teaspoons grated Parmesan cheese

Imperial

6 teaspoons olive oil
4 tomatoes, peeled, seeded and
   chopped
2 teaspoons chopped parsley
2 garlic cloves, crushed
2oz fresh breadcrumbs, soaked in
   2 fl oz beef stock for 10 minutes
4 anchovy fillets, finely chopped

6 large tomatoes, halved and seeded
1oz dry breadcrumbs
6 teaspoons grated Parmesan cheese

Preheat the oven to moderate (180°C/350°F).

Heat half the oil in a frying-pan. Add the chopped tomatoes, parsley and garlic and cook gently for 5 minutes. Stir in the soaked breadcrumbs and anchovies and cook for 2 minutes. Remove from the heat.

Divide the stuffing between the tomato halves and arrange in a baking dish. Mix together the dry breadcrumbs and cheese and sprinkle over the tops. Drizzle over the remaining oil. Bake for 20 minutes and serve hot.

TARAMASALATA

Taramasalata is also a wonderful barbecue starter, especially if followed by Kebabs.

6 servings

Metric (Cup)

500g smoked cod's roe, skinned

4 slices white bread, crusts removed
   and soaked in milk for 15 minutes
4 garlic cloves, crushed
300ml (1¼ cups) olive oil
60ml (¼ cup) lemon juice
½ teaspoon black pepper

Imperial

1lb smoked cod's roe, skinned
4 slices white bread, crusts removed
   and soaked in milk for 15 minutes
4 garlic cloves, crushed
½ pint olive oil
2 fl oz lemon juice
½ teaspoon black pepper

Pound the cod's roe until it is smooth. Squeeze the bread to remove excess milk and add to the roe. Pound together, then beat in the garlic. Gradually beat in the oil, a few drops at a time, and add a few drops of lemon juice from time to time. Continue beating until the mixture is a smooth soft paste.

Taramasalata is one of the specialities of Greek cuisine. Serve as an exciting hors d'oeuvre.

Alternatively, blend all the ingredients together in an electric blender.

Stir in the pepper. Serve with tomato and cucumber slices, black olives and unleavened Greek bread (Pita).

DEEP-FRIED PRAWNS

Deep-fried prawns can also be served as a light main course with salad.

6 servings

Metric (Cup)

750g green prawns
1 large egg
9 teaspoons flour
2 teaspoons cornflour
1 slice root ginger, finely diced
½ teaspoon salt
90ml (⅓ cup) water
vegetable oil
SAUCE
9 teaspoons tomato purée
6 teaspoons soy sauce
1 teaspoon chilli sauce
1 teaspoon sugar

Imperial

1½lb green prawns
1 large egg
¾oz flour
2 teaspoons cornflour
1 slice root ginger, finely diced
½ teaspoon salt
3 fl oz water
vegetable oil
SAUCE
9 teaspoons tomato purée
6 teaspoons soy sauce
1 teaspoon chilli sauce
1 teaspoon sugar

Mix together the sauce ingredients in a small serving bowl.

Remove the shells from the bodies of the prawns, leaving the tails on. Remove the intestinal veins.

Put the egg in a mixing bowl and beat lightly. Sift in the flour and cornflour and mix well. Add the ginger, salt and water and beat until the batter is smooth.

Heat the oil in a deep frying-pan until it is 180°C/350°F. Dip the prawns in the batter, holding them by the tails, then lower into the oil. Fry for 2 to 3 minutes or until golden brown. Drain on paper towels and serve with the sauce.

OYSTERS KILPATRICK

Oysters are always favourite dinner party fare. Serve with very thin slices of bread.

4 servings

Metric (Cup)

60g (¼ cup) butter, softened
32 oysters, on the half shell
2 teaspoons Worcestershire sauce
12 lean bacon rashers, grilled until crisp and crumbled
6 teaspoons chopped parsley
lemon wedges

Imperial

2oz butter, softened
32 oysters, on the half shell
2 teaspoons Worcestershire sauce
12 lean bacon rashers, grilled until crisp and crumbled
6 teaspoons chopped parsley
lemon wedges

Colourful Oysters Kilpatrick are cooked with Worcestershire sauce and bacon.

Preheat the griller to moderate.

Spread a thin layer of butter over each oyster, then sprinkle with the Worcestershire sauce and bacon. Arrange the oysters in one layer in the grilling pan and grill for 2 minutes. (You may have to do this in several batches, so keep the cooked oysters hot while you cook the next batch.)

Sprinkle over the parsley and serve with lemon wedges.

OYSTERS ROCKEFELLER

Oysters Rockefeller is an adaptation of a well-known American recipe from New Orleans, traditionally cooked in a bed of rock salt.

4 servings

Metric (Cup)

rock salt to cover the bottom of 2 large baking dishes in a 1cm thick layer

4 spring onions, finely chopped
2 celery stalks, finely chopped
250g cooked spinach
3 parsley sprigs
1 teaspoon salt
¼ teaspoon black pepper
¼ teaspoon cayenne pepper
60ml (¼ cup) cream
3 teaspoons Pernod
36 oysters, on the half shell

Imperial

rock salt to cover the bottom of 2 large
    baking dishes in a ½in thick layer
4 spring onions, finely chopped
2 celery stalks, finely chopped
8oz cooked spinach
3 parsley sprigs
1 teaspoon salt
¼ teaspoon black pepper

¼ teaspoon cayenne pepper
2 fl oz cream
3 teaspoons Pernod
36 oysters, on the half shell

A rich veal and pork pâté enveloped in golden pastry, Pâté en Croute can be served as a starter or for an elegant summer lunch.

Preheat the oven to very hot (230°C/450°F).

Cover the bottom of the baking dishes with the rock salt. Set aside.

Place the spring onions, celery, spinach, parsley, salt, pepper, cayenne and cream in an electric blender and blend for 2 minutes or until all the ingredients are puréed. Transfer the purée to a medium-sized mixing bowl. Add the Pernod and stir well. Divide the oysters equally between the baking dishes. Cover each one with a teaspoonful of the vegetable purée. Place in the oven and bake for 4 minutes.

Remove the baking dishes from the oven and transfer the oysters to a warmed serving dish.

PATE EN CROUTE

Guests will feel very special when you serve this beautiful pâté.

6-8 servings

Metric (Cup)

250g (1 cup) lean minced veal
125g ($\frac{1}{2}$ cup) minced calf's liver
250g (1 cup) minced belly of pork
60g ($\frac{1}{2}$ cup) dry breadcrumbs
1 garlic clove, crushed
$\frac{1}{2}$ teaspoon dried thyme
$\frac{1}{4}$ teaspoon grated nutmeg
1 teaspoon salt
$\frac{1}{2}$ teaspoon black pepper
3 teaspoons chopped parsley
2 eggs, lightly beaten
6 teaspoons brandy
6 teaspoons butter
125g (1 cup) sliced mushrooms
375g (3 cups) rich shortcrust pastry
90g lean cooked ham, cut into strips
185g veal steak, cut into strips
2 streaky bacon rashers

Imperial

8oz lean veal, minced
4oz calf's liver, minced
8oz belly of pork, minced
2oz dry breadcrumbs
1 garlic clove, crushed
$\frac{1}{2}$ teaspoon dried thyme
$\frac{1}{4}$ teaspoon grated nutmeg
1 teaspoon salt
$\frac{1}{2}$ teaspoon black pepper
3 teaspoons chopped parsley
2 eggs, lightly beaten
6 teaspoons brandy
1oz butter
4oz mushrooms, sliced
12oz rich shortcrust pastry
3oz lean cooked ham, cut into strips
6oz veal steak, cut into strips
2 streaky bacon rashers

Preheat the oven to moderate (180°C/350°F).

Mix together the minced veal, calf's liver, belly of pork, breadcrumbs, garlic, thyme, nutmeg, salt, pepper, parsley, eggs and brandy.

Melt the butter in a frying-pan. Add the mushrooms and fry for 3 minutes. Remove from the heat.

Roll out three-quarters of the dough to about 5mm ($\frac{1}{4}$in) thick and use to line a 1kg (2lb) loaf tin or terrine. Put half the veal mixture in the tin or terrine and cover with a layer of ham strips, a layer of veal strips and a layer of mushrooms. Add the remaining veal mixture, then the rest of the ham and veal strips and mushrooms. Lay the bacon rashers on top.

Roll out the remaining dough and use to cover the tin or dish. Press the edges of the dough together to seal and decorate the top with the dough trimmings.

Bake for 1$\frac{1}{2}$ hours. Cover with foil if the pastry seems to be browning too quickly.

Allow to cool, then remove from the tin.

DUCK TERRINE

Duck, truffles, brandy—a luxurious combination for a marvellous meal starter.

8-10 servings

Metric (Cup)

1 x 3kg duck, skinned, boned and fat removed
125ml ($\frac{1}{2}$ cup) brandy
2 canned truffles, thinly sliced and can juice reserved
250g (1 cup) minced lean veal
500g (2 cups) minced lean pork
2 hard-boiled eggs, finely chopped
1 teaspoon salt
$\frac{1}{2}$ teaspoon black pepper
1 garlic clove, crushed
60g ($\frac{1}{4}$ cup) butter
125g duck or chicken livers, finely chopped
375g unsalted pork fat, cut into very thin slices

Imperial

1 x 6lb duck, skinned, boned and fat removed
4 fl oz brandy
2 canned truffles, thinly sliced and can juice reserved
8oz lean veal, minced
1lb lean pork, minced
2 hard-boiled eggs, finely chopped
1 teaspoon salt
$\frac{1}{2}$ teaspoon black pepper
1 garlic clove, crushed
2oz butter
4oz duck or chicken livers, finely chopped
12oz unsalted pork fat, cut into very thin slices

Cut the duck meat into thin strips and place in a mixing bowl. Pour over half the brandy and stir in the truffles and can juice. Marinate for 1 hour.

Preheat the oven to moderate (180°C/350°F).

Mix together the veal, pork, eggs, salt, pepper, garlic and the remaining brandy. Melt the butter in a frying-pan. Add the livers and fry for 3 minutes. Add the livers to the veal mixture.

Line a large terrine with half the pork fat. Spread one-third of the veal mixture in the bottom of the terrine, then cover with half the duck and truffle mixture. Add another layer of the veal mixture, then the remaining duck and truffle mixture, and finally the remaining veal mixture. Smooth the top and cover with the remaining pork fat.

Cover the terrine and place in a roasting tin. Add enough boiling water to the tin to come halfway up the sides of the terrine. Bake for 1$\frac{1}{2}$ hours.

Pour off any excess liquid from the terrine and leave to cool. Cover with foil and weigh down the meat mixture. Chill for at least 8 hours. Serve at room temperature.

Main dishes

BOEUF BOURGUIGNONNE

This excellent dish can be prepared a day in advance, giving you more time to concentrate on other last minute cooking.

6 servings

Metric (Cup)

185g streaky bacon rashers, rind removed and quartered
3 teaspoons olive oil
1.5kg lean topside, round or blade steak, cut into 2.5cm cubes
1 onion, thinly sliced
1 carrot, sliced
1 teaspoon salt
½ teaspoon black pepper
30g (¼ cup) flour
750ml (3 cups) dry red wine
500ml (2 cups) beef stock
3 teaspoons tomato purée
2 garlic cloves, crushed
½ teaspoon dried thyme
1 bay leaf
60g (¼ cup) butter
18 small onions
500g mushrooms, quartered
6 teaspoons chopped parsley

Imperial

6oz streaky bacon rashers, rind removed and quartered
3 teaspoons olive oil
3lb lean topside, round or blade steak, cut into 1in cubes
1 onion, thinly sliced
1 carrot, sliced
1 teaspoon salt
½ teaspoon black pepper
1oz flour
1¼ pints dry red wine
¾ pint beef stock
3 teaspoons tomato purée
2 garlic cloves, crushed
½ teaspoon dried thyme
1 bay leaf

One of the most famous of all French dishes, Boeuf Bourguignonne is a beef stew with red wine, bacon, onions and mushrooms.

2oz butter
18 small onions
1lb mushrooms, quartered
6 teaspoons chopped parsley

Preheat the oven to warm (160°C/325°F).

Blanch the bacon in boiling water for 10 minutes. Drain well and pat dry with kitchen paper towels.

Heat the oil in a flameproof casserole. Add the bacon and fry until it has rendered most of its fat. Remove the bacon from the pot.

Add the steak cubes to the pot, in batches, and brown on all sides. Remove the cubes from the pot as they are browned.

Add the onion and carrot to the pot and fry until the onion is soft but not brown. Pour the fat from the pot and sprinkle over the salt, pepper and flour. Gradually stir in the wine, stock, tomato purée, garlic, thyme and bay leaf. Bring to the boil. Return the bacon and steak cubes to the casserole and stir well. Cover and transfer to the oven. Cook for 2 hours.

Melt half the butter in a frying-pan. Add the onions and fry until they are golden brown on all sides. Add to the casserole and continue cooking for 45 minutes to 1 hour or until the meat is tender.

Just before the casserole is ready, melt the remaining butter in the frying-pan. Add the mushrooms and fry for 4 to 5 minutes or until just tender.

Remove the bay leaf from the casserole. Stir in the mushrooms and sprinkle over the parsley.

CARPETBAG STEAK

Carpetbag Steak is always popular and surprisingly easy to prepare.

4 servings

Metric (Cup)

1 x 1kg fillet steak, about 5cm thick
12 oysters, shucked
salt
black pepper
¼ teaspoon cayenne pepper
3 teaspoons butter, melted

1 bunch of watercress to garnish

Imperial

1 x 2lb fillet steak, about 2in thick
12 oysters, shucked
salt
black pepper
¼ teaspoon cayenne pepper
½oz butter, melted
1 bunch of watercress to garnish

Preheat the griller to moderately high.

Make a slit in the steak to form a deep pocket. Fill the pocket with the oysters and sprinkle with salt and pepper and the cayenne. Sew up the opening with a trussing needle and string or secure with a skewer.

Place the steak on the rack of the griller and brush with half the melted butter. Put under the griller and cook for 5 to 6 minutes. Turn over and brush with the remaining melted butter. Grill for a further 5 to 6 minutes or until cooked to your taste.

Remove the string or skewer and carve into thick slices. Serve garnished with watercress.

BRAISED BEEF PRINCE ALBERT

If unobtainable you can substitute mushrooms for truffles—but truffles do give the right flavour and a marvellous sense of extravagance.

8 servings

Metric (Cup)

6 truffles, quartered
150ml (⅔ cup) Madeira
90g (⅓ cup) butter
2 carrots, finely diced
1 celery stalk, diced
1 onion, grated
1 slice of cooked ham, diced
salt
black pepper
1 bouquet garni
4 shallots, finely chopped
125g pâté de foie gras
3 teaspoons brandy
pinch of ground allspice
pinch of dried thyme
1 x 1.5kg beef fillet

3 lean bacon rashers, rinds removed
3 teaspoons oil
625ml (2½ cups) beef stock
3 teaspoons arrowroot

Imperial

6 truffles, quartered
¼ pint Madeira
3oz butter
2 carrots, finely diced
1 celery stalk, diced
1 onion, grated
1 slice of cooked ham, diced
salt
black pepper
1 bouquet garni
4 shallots, finely chopped
4oz pâté de foie gras
3 teaspoons brandy
pinch of ground allspice
pinch of dried thyme
1 x 3lb beef fillet
3 lean bacon rashers, rinds removed
3 teaspoons oil
1 pint beef stock
3 teaspoons arrowroot

Put the truffles in a bowl and sprinkle over 6 teaspoons of the Madeira. Leave to marinate for 15 minutes.

Meanwhile, melt 9 teaspoons (1½oz) of the butter in a saucepan. Add the carrots, celery, onion, ham and salt and pepper to taste and cook gently for 15 minutes or until the vegetables are tender but not brown. Stir in 90ml (⅓ cup) [3 fl oz] of the remaining Madeira and the bouquet garni and bring to the boil. Simmer until the liquid has almost evaporated. Remove from the heat.

Preheat the oven to moderate (180°C/350°F).

Melt 3 teaspoons (½oz) of the remaining butter in another saucepan. Add the shallots and fry until they are soft but not brown. Remove from the heat and stir in the pâté, brandy, allspice, thyme, salt and pepper to taste and 3 teaspoons of the remaining Madeira. Mix well.

Make a deep slit down one side of the beef fillet, to within 5mm (¼in) of the other side and of the two ends. Season the inside with salt and pepper and fill with the pâté mixture. Place the truffles on top of the pâté mixture,

reserving their marinade. Press the beef closed.

Place a bacon rasher on top of the fillet and one on each side. Tie the fillet securely with string at 2.5cm (1in) intervals.

Melt the remaining butter with the oil in a flameproof casserole that is large enough to hold the fillet comfortably. Place the fillet in the pot and brown on all sides. Pour off the fat from the pot.

Spoon the vegetable mixture over the fillet and pour enough stock into the pot to come halfway up the sides of the meat. Bring to the boil, then cover tightly and transfer to the oven. Braise for 45 minutes (for rare beef), basting every 15 minutes.

Remove the beef from the casserole and discard the trussing string and bacon. Place on a warmed serving platter and keep hot.

Skim any fat from the liquid in the casserole. Bring to the boil on top of the stove and simmer until reduced to 500ml (2 cups) [¾ pint]. Strain and return to the casserole.

Dissolve the arrowroot in the remaining 3 teaspoons of Madeira and stir into the casserole liquid with the reserved truffle marinating Madeira. Simmer, stirring, until thickened.

Spoon a little of the Madeira sauce over the fillet and surround with freshly cooked vegetables. Serve the remaining sauce in a sauceboat.

FONDUE BOURGUIGNONNE

Use your imagination and taste to choose the accompanying sauces for this dish—but always have a good variety.

4 servings

Metric (Cup)

1kg fillet or rump steak, cut into
  2.5cm cubes

Braised Beef Prince Albert is an elegant dinner party dish of beef fillet stuffed with pâté de fois gras and truffles and covered with bacon strips.

vegetable oil
ACCOMPANIMENTS
1 medium onion, finely chopped
1 large crisp eating apple, cored, finely chopped and sprinkled with 2 teaspoons tarragon vinegar
2 large pickled gherkins, finely chopped
3 teaspoons capers, finely chopped
9 teaspoons chopped fresh herbs (basil, chives, marjoram, etc.)
12 teaspoons prepared mustard
12 teaspoons prepared horseradish sauce
125ml (½ cup) mayonnaise or aioli (garlic mayonnaise)
TOMATO SAUCE

6 teaspoons butter
250g tomatoes, halved
1 teaspoon dried basil
½ teaspoon black pepper
2 teaspoons tomato purée

Imperial

2lb fillet or rump steak, cut into 1in
   cubes
vegetable oil
ACCOMPANIMENTS
1 medium onion, finely chopped
1 large crisp eating apple, cored, finely
   chopped and sprinkled with 2
   teaspoons tarragon vinegar
2 large pickled gherkins, finely chopped

3 teaspoons capers, finely chopped
9 teaspoons chopped fresh herbs
   (basil, chives, marjoram, etc.)
12 teaspoons prepared mustard
12 teaspoons prepared horseradish
   sauce
4 fl oz mayonnaise or aioli (garlic
   mayonnaise)
TOMATO SAUCE
1oz butter
8oz tomatoes, halved
1 teaspoon dried basil
½ teaspoon black pepper
2 teaspoons tomato purée ·

Pile the meat on a serving plate (or four

individual plates). Put the accompaniments in individual bowls.

To make the tomato sauce, melt the butter in a saucepan. Add the tomatoes, basil and pepper and cook gently for 10 minutes or until the tomatoes have pulped. Rub the tomato mixture through a sieve into a mixing bowl. Stir in the tomato purée. Allow to cool, then pour the sauce into a serving bowl.

Heat enough oil to half-fill your fondue pot in a saucepan on top of the stove. The oil should be about 190°C/375°F. Pour it carefully into the fondue pot and place over the lighted spirit burner.

Each guest spears a cube of steak on a fondue fork and fries it in the oil until it is cooked to his taste. The meat is then transferred to the diner's plate, speared on a table fork and dipped into one of the sauces or accompaniments. Other sauces to serve include Béarnaise, Hollandaise, curry mayonnaise and hot pepper or chilli sauce.

TOURNEDOS VERT-PRE

Steak and chips cooked with style—a simple but delicious dinner party dish.

6 servings

Metric (Cup)

6 tournedos, about 2.5cm thick
1 teaspoon salt
½ teaspoon black pepper
90g (⅓ cup) butter
2 teaspoons lemon juice
9 teaspoons chopped parsley
GARNISH
750g potatoes, cut into rectangles
    about 6cm long
vegetable oil
1 teaspoon salt
watercress

Imperial

6 tournedos, about 1in thick
1 teaspoon salt
½ teaspoon black pepper
3oz butter
2 teaspoons lemon juice
9 teaspoons chopped parsley
GARNISH
1½lb potatoes, cut into rectangles
    about 2½in long
vegetable oil
1 teaspoon salt
watercress

Cut the potato rectangles into 'straws' about 3mm (⅛in) wide. Put the straws in a large bowl of cold water and leave for 30 minutes, then drain and pat dry with kitchen paper towels.

Rub the tournedos with half the salt and pepper.

Cream the butter with the remaining salt and pepper and the lemon juice. Beat in the parsley. Form the butter into a roll and freeze until firm.

Preheat the griller to high.

Heat the oil in a deep frying-pan until it is 185°C/360°F. Fry the potato straws in batches until they are crisp and lightly golden brown. Drain on kitchen paper towels and keep hot.

Meanwhile, grill the tournedos for 4 to 8 minutes on each side (depending on how well cooked you like your steaks).

Tournedos Vert-Pre – small beef fillets with chips and watercress – is a speciality of French cuisine.

Arrange the steaks on a warmed serving platter. Top each with a pat of the parsley butter and surround with the potato straws, sprinkled with salt. Garnish with watercress.

STEAK DIANE

Serve this favourite dish with new or sautéed potatoes and a green vegetable.

4 servings

Metric (Cup)

4 fillet steaks
1 teaspoon salt
1 teaspoon black pepper
60g (¼ cup) butter
½ teaspoon finely grated lemon rind
6 teaspoons Worcestershire sauce
6 teaspoons chopped chives
60ml (¼ cup) brandy
60ml (¼ cup) cream

Imperial

4 fillet steaks
1 teaspoon salt
1 teaspoon black pepper
2oz butter
½ teaspoon finely grated lemon rind
6 teaspoons Worcestershire sauce
6 teaspoons chopped chives
2 fl oz brandy
2 fl oz cream

Rub the steaks with salt and pepper. Melt the butter in a frying-pan. Add the steaks and brown quickly on both sides. Stir in the lemon rind, Worcestershire sauce and chives and cook for 1 minute.

Turn the steaks over and pour over the brandy. Cook for 1 minute to warm the brandy, then set alight. Shake the pan gently until the flames have died away.

Continue cooking until the steaks are done to your taste.

Transfer the steaks to a warmed serving platter. Stir the cream into the juices in the pan, then pour over the steaks.

Serve immediately.

SUKIYAKI

You can cook this dish on the stove—but it's so much more decorative and festive to cook in the traditional Japanese way at the table.

4 servings

Metric (Cup)

1kg fillet steak, cut across the grain into very thin slices
250g canned shirataki noodles, drained
125g small spinach leaves
500g flat mushrooms, peeled, stalks removed and halved
1 large carrot, cut into 5cm strips
12 spring onions, cut into 5cm pieces
1 canned bamboo shoot, drained, halved and thinly sliced
250ml (1 cup) dashi or chicken stock
125ml (½ cup) sake or dry sherry
4 eggs
6 teaspoons beef suet
185ml (¾ cup) soy sauce
60g (⅓ cup) brown sugar

Imperial

2lb fillet steak, cut across the grain into very thin slices
8oz canned shirataki noodles, drained
4oz small spinach leaves
1lb flat mushrooms, peeled, stalks removed and halved
1 large carrot, cut into 2in strips
12 spring onions, cut into 2in pieces
1 canned bamboo shoot, drained, halved and thinly sliced
8 fl oz dashi or chicken stock
4 fl oz sake or dry sherry
4 eggs
1oz beef suet
6 fl oz soy sauce
2oz brown sugar

Arrange the steak, noodles, spinach, mushrooms, carrot, spring onions and bamboo shoot on a large serving platter. Pour the stock and sake or sherry into a small bowl. Break an egg into each of four individual serving bowls and lightly beat each with a fork to break up.

Rub the inside of a shallow flame-proof casserole with the suet. Heat on top of the stove (or over a burner at the table). Put about one-quarter of the meat and vegetables in the casserole and pour over about one-quarter of the sake mixture and soy sauce. Add about one-quarter of the sugar.

Cook for 5 to 6 minutes, stirring frequently, or until the meat and vegetables are tender. Transfer the meat and vegetables to individual warmed serving plates and serve with the beaten egg. This portion should be eaten while the next is being cooked. The liquid should always be simmering. As more liquid and sugar are added, the sauce becomes stronger, so it may be necessary to reduce the amounts of these at the end.

VEAL ORLOFF

Serve delicious Veal Orloff with boiled new potatoes and a green vegetable.

8-10 servings

Metric (Cup)

1 x 3kg loin of veal, boned
1 teaspoon salt
½ teaspoon black pepper
1 garlic clove, crushed
16 streaky bacon rashers, rinds removed
625ml (2½ cups) veal or chicken stock
STUFFING
6 teaspoons butter
2 onions, finely chopped
60g (⅓ cup) long-grain rice
185ml (¾ cup) chicken stock
375g (3 cups) chopped mushrooms
SAUCE
6 teaspoons butter
30g (¼ cup) flour
250g (2 cups) grated Gruyère cheese

Imperial

1 x 6lb loin of veal, boned
1 teaspoon salt
½ teaspoon black pepper
1 garlic clove, crushed
16 streaky bacon rashers, rinds removed
1 pint veal or chicken stock
STUFFING
1oz butter
2 onions, finely chopped
2oz long-grain rice
6 fl oz chicken stock
12oz mushrooms, chopped
SAUCE
1oz butter
1oz flour
8oz Gruyère cheese, grated

First make the stuffing. Melt the butter in a saucepan. Add the onions and fry until they are soft but not brown. Stir in the rice and cook for 5 minutes. Stir in the stock and bring to the boil. Cover and simmer for 15 to 20 minutes or until the rice is tender and all the liquid has been absorbed. Remove from the heat and push the rice mixture through a sieve until smooth. Stir in the mushrooms.

Preheat the oven to moderate (180°C/350°F).

Lay the veal flat and rub with the salt, pepper and garlic. Spread with the stuffing and roll up. Cover with the bacon slices and tie with string at 2.5cm (1in) intervals.

Put the veal in a roasting tin and pour over the stock. Cover loosely and roast for 3 hours, basting frequently.

Remove the veal from the tin. Strain the cooking juices and reserve 300ml (1¼ cups) [½ pint]. Remove the string from the veal and replace in the roasting tin. Return to the oven.

To make the sauce, melt the butter in a saucepan. Add the flour and cook, stirring, for 1 minute. Remove from the heat and gradually stir in the reserved stock. Return to the heat and bring to the boil, stirring. Simmer until smooth and thickened. Add the cheese and stir until it has melted.

Pour the cheese sauce over the veal and bake for a further 20 minutes or until the sauce topping is lightly browned.

BLANQUETTE DE VEAU

This popular French dish should be served principally with noodles or rice or boiled or mashed potatoes. Include a light green vegetable if you like or just serve a tossed salad.

4 servings

Metric (Cup)

750g lean veal, cut into 3.5cm cubes
2 onions, each studded with 2 cloves
2 carrots, quartered
90ml (⅓ cup) dry white wine
1 bouquet garni
salt
white pepper
9 teaspoons butter
45g (⅓ cup) flour

150ml (⅔ cup) cream
2 egg yolks
4 slices of toast, cut into triangles
2 lemon slices
parsley sprigs

Imperial

1½lb lean veal, cut into 1½in cubes
2 onions, each studded with 2 cloves
2 carrots, quartered
3 fl oz dry white wine
1 bouquet garni
salt
white pepper
1½oz butter
1½oz flour
¼ pint cream
2 egg yolks
4 slices of toast, cut into triangles
2 lemon slices
parsley sprigs

Put the veal in a saucepan and cover with water. Bring to the boil and simmer for 2 minutes, skimming off any scum that rises to the surface. Add the onions, carrots, wine, bouquet garni and salt and pepper to taste. Cover and simmer for 1½ hours or until the veal is tender.

Transfer the veal to a warmed serving dish and keep hot.

Strain the cooking liquid and reserve 750ml (3 cups) [1¼ pints].

Melt the butter in a saucepan. Add the flour and cook, stirring, for 1 minute. Gradually stir in the reserved cooking liquid and bring to the boil, stirring. Simmer until smooth and thickened.

Beat the cream and egg yolks together. Stir in a little of the hot sauce, then return the mixture to the saucepan. Heat gently, stirring.

Pour the sauce over the veal. Surround with the toast triangles and garnish with the lemon slices and parsley sprigs.

INVOLTINI ALLA CONTADINO

A superb dish, Involtini alla Contadino is one of the delights of Italian cuisine.

4 servings

Metric (Cup)

500g thin veal steaks, pounded and cut into 10cm squares
30g (¼ cup) flour
9 teaspoons butter
6 teaspoons oil
250ml (1 cup) Marsala
250ml (1 cup) chicken stock
STUFFING
6 teaspoons butter
125g chicken livers, finely chopped
60g proscuitto, chopped
1 small onion, finely chopped
1 teaspoon chopped chives
1 teaspoon chopped parsley
¼ teaspoon dried basil
¼ teaspoon dried marjoram
¼ teaspoon salt
pinch of black pepper

Imperial

1lb thin veal steaks, pounded and cut into 4in squares
1oz flour
1½oz butter
6 teaspoons oil
8 fl oz Marsala
8 fl oz chicken stock
STUFFING
1oz butter
4oz chicken livers, finely chopped
2oz proscuitto, chopped
1 small onion, finely chopped
1 teaspoon chopped chives
1 teaspoon chopped parsley
¼ teaspoon dried basil
¼ teaspoon dried marjoram
¼ teaspoon salt
pinch of black pepper

First make the stuffing. Melt the butter in a frying-pan. Add the chicken livers and fry until they are lightly browned. Remove from the heat and stir in the remaining stuffing ingredients.

Divide the stuffing between the veal squares and roll up, tucking in the sides to make neat parcels. Tie with string. Coat the veal rolls with the flour.

Melt the butter with the oil in the frying-pan. Add the veal rolls, in batches, and brown on all sides. Pour off all but 3 teaspoons of the fat from the pan and return all the veal rolls with the Marsala and stock. Bring to the boil, then simmer for 15 minutes or so until the meat is tender.

Serve Involtine alla Contadino with saffron rice for a delightful meal.

Transfer the veal rolls to a warmed serving dish and keep hot. Boil the cooking liquid until it is reduced to about 125ml ($\frac{1}{2}$ cup) [4 fl oz]. Pour over the veal and serve.

NOISETTES D'AGNEAU MONEGASQUE

This decorative dish is simple and quick to make. Serve with mashed potatoes and a green vegetable.

4 servings

Metric (Cup)

6 teaspoons olive oil
1 onion, finely chopped
1 garlic clove, crushed
500g (2 cups) peeled and chopped tomatoes
2 teaspoons chopped fresh basil
1 bay leaf
$\frac{1}{2}$ teaspoon salt
$\frac{1}{2}$ teaspoon black pepper
6 teaspoons tomato purée
60g ($\frac{1}{4}$ cup) butter
8 large mushroom caps
8 short loin lamb chops, cut 2.5cm thick, trimmed and boned
8 circles of bread (7.5cm in diameter), toasted and kept warm
125ml ($\frac{1}{2}$ cup) dry white wine

Imperial

6 teaspoons olive oil
1 onion, finely chopped
1 garlic clove, crushed
1lb tomatoes, peeled and chopped
2 teaspoons chopped fresh basil
1 bay leaf
$\frac{1}{2}$ teaspoon salt
$\frac{1}{2}$ teaspoon black pepper
6 teaspoons tomato purée
2oz butter
8 large mushroom caps
8 short loin lamb chops, cut 1in thick, trimmed and boned
8 circles of bread (3in in diameter), toasted and kept warm
4 fl oz dry white wine

Push each chop into a round shape.

Heat the oil in a saucepan. Add the onion and garlic and fry until soft but not brown. Stir in the tomatoes, basil, bay leaf, salt, pepper and tomato purée and simmer for 30 minutes.

Melt the butter in a frying-pan. Add the mushrooms and fry for 3 to 4 minutes or until tender. Remove from the pan and keep warm.

Add the noisettes to the pan and fry for 4 to 6 minutes on each side or until cooked.

Arrange the toast circles on a warmed serving platter. Place a noisette on each circle and top each with a mushroom cap. Keep hot.

Pour the wine into the frying-pan and bring to the boil. Boil until reduced to half. Stir in the tomato sauce and simmer for 5 minutes. Discard the bay leaf and pour the sauce over the noisettes.

LAMB CHOPS PARMESAN

You can prepare this dish beforehand—and cooking takes only 10 minutes. Simple but delicious.

4 servings

Metric (Cup)

8 chump lamb chops
1 teaspoon salt
1 teaspoon black pepper
60g ($\frac{1}{2}$ cup) dry breadcrumbs
60g ($\frac{1}{2}$ cup) grated Parmesan cheese
1 teaspoon dried basil
30g ($\frac{1}{4}$ cup) flour
1 egg, lightly beaten
60g ($\frac{1}{4}$ cup) butter
6 teaspoons olive oil
GARNISH
lemon slices
parsley sprigs

Imperial

8 chump lamb chops
1 teaspoon salt
1 teaspoon black pepper
2oz dry breadcrumbs
2oz Parmesan cheese, grated
1 teaspoon dried basil
1oz flour
1 egg, lightly beaten
2oz butter
6 teaspoons olive oil
GARNISH
lemon slices
parsley sprigs

Rub the chops with salt and pepper. Mix together the breadcrumbs, cheese and basil. Coat each chop with flour,

then egg and then thickly with the cheese mixture. Chill for 20 minutes.

Melt the butter with the oil in a frying-pan. Add the chops, in batches, and fry for 7 to 10 minutes on each side or until well browned and cooked through.

Serve hot, garnished with lemon slices and parsley sprigs.

LEG OF LAMB WITH PROVENCALE SAUCE

A rich tangy sauce of capsicum and eggplant accompanies the lamb, so you need only serve potatoes or rice and perhaps a tossed salad.

6 servings

Metric (Cup)

6 teaspoons butter
6 lean bacon rashers, rinds removed and chopped
125g (1 cup) cooked rice
6 teaspoons chopped parsley
2 garlic cloves, crushed
$\frac{1}{2}$ teaspoon salt
$\frac{1}{2}$ teaspoon black pepper
1 x 2.5kg boned leg of lamb
1 bouquet garni
185ml ($\frac{3}{4}$ cup) dry red wine
125ml ($\frac{1}{2}$ cup) beef stock
SAUCE
2 large eggplants, cubed
185ml ($\frac{3}{4}$ cup) olive oil
1 large green capsicum, membrane and seeds removed and chopped
2 garlic cloves, crushed
470g canned tomatoes
$\frac{1}{2}$ teaspoon salt
$\frac{1}{2}$ teaspoon black pepper

Imperial

1oz butter
6 lean bacon rashers, rinds removed and chopped
4oz cooked rice
6 teaspoons chopped parsley
2 garlic cloves, crushed
$\frac{1}{2}$ teaspoon salt
$\frac{1}{2}$ teaspoon black pepper
1 x 5lb boned leg of lamb
1 bouquet garni
6 fl oz dry red wine
4 fl oz beef stock

SAUCE
2 large eggplants, cubed
6 fl oz olive oil
1 large green capsicum, membrane and seeds removed and chopped
2 garlic cloves, crushed
15oz canned tomatoes
$\frac{1}{2}$ teaspoon salt
$\frac{1}{2}$ teaspoon black pepper

Preheat the oven to moderate (180°C/350°F).

Melt the butter in a frying-pan. Add the bacon and fry until it is crisp and brown. Add the rice, parsley, garlic and

salt and pepper and cook for 3 minutes. Remove from the heat.

Lay the lamb flat and spread with the rice stuffing. Roll up and secure with string. Put the bouquet garni on the bottom of a roasting tin and put the meat on top.

Bring the wine and stock to the boil and pour over the lamb. Roast for $1\frac{3}{4}$ hours, basting occasionally with the juices in the tin.

Leg of Lamb with Provençale Sauce is substantial and decorative.

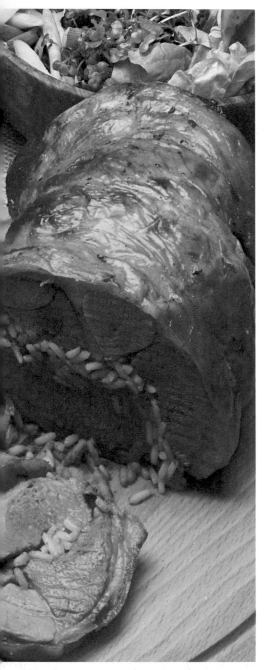

Meanwhile, sprinkle the eggplants with salt and leave for 20 minutes. Rinse and pat dry with kitchen paper towels.

Heat the oil in a saucepan. Add the eggplant cubes and fry until they are lightly browned and tender. Stir in the green capsicum, garlic, tomatoes with the can juice and salt and pepper. Bring to the boil and simmer for 10 minutes or until the sauce is thick and somewhat pulpy.

Transfer the lamb to a warmed serving platter and serve with the sauce.

SADDLE OF LAMB WITH MINT

Here is an unusual way to flavour lamb with mint.

6-8 servings

Metric (Cup)

1 x 3kg saddle of lamb
2 teaspoons salt
2 teaspoons black pepper
8 lemon thyme sprigs
60g (1 cup) fresh breadcrumbs
6 teaspoons chopped fresh mint
1 small onion, grated
3 teaspoons melted butter
185ml ($\frac{3}{4}$ cup) chicken stock
2 teaspoons butter
2 teaspoons flour

Imperial

1 x 6lb saddle of lamb
2 teaspoons salt
2 teaspoons black pepper
8 lemon thyme sprigs
2oz fresh breadcrumbs
6 teaspoons chopped fresh mint
1 small onion, grated
$\frac{1}{2}$oz butter, melted
6 fl oz chicken stock
2 teaspoons butter
2 teaspoons flour

Preheat the oven to moderate (180°C/350°F). Rub the meat with half the salt and pepper. Insert the thyme sprigs between the flesh and fat. Put the saddle, fat side up, on a rack in a roasting tin.

Mix together the breadcrumbs, mint,

onion and the remaining salt and pepper. Stir in the melted butter. Spread this mixture over the fat on the saddle.

Roast for 1 hour, then reduce the temperature to cool (150°C/300°F). Roast for a further 1 to $1\frac{1}{4}$ hours or until the meat is cooked.

Transfer the lamb to a serving platter and keep hot.

Skim the fat from the surface of the cooking juices in the tin. Strain the juices into a saucepan and stir in the stock. Bring to the boil. Combine the butter and flour to make a paste (beurre manié) and add in small pieces to the stock mixture. Simmer, stirring, until thickened. Pour this sauce into a sauceboat and serve with the lamb.

CROWN ROAST OF PORK WITH SAUSAGE AND PRUNE STUFFING

A crown roast of pork is one of the more decorative meat dishes to bring to the dinner table. Carve by cutting between each chop.

8 servings

Metric (Cup)

1 crown roast of pork, consisting of 16 chops, with a 6cm cavity in the centre
1 teaspooon salt
1 teaspoon black pepper
2 teaspoons dried thyme
STUFFING
60g (1 cup) fresh breadcrumbs
60ml ($\frac{1}{4}$ cup) milk
6 teaspoons butter
1 onion, finely chopped
250g sausage mince
2 celery stalks, finely chopped
90g canned stoned prunes, drained and quartered
2 eating apples, peeled, cored and finely chopped
$\frac{1}{2}$ teaspoon salt
$\frac{1}{4}$ teaspoon black pepper
$\frac{1}{2}$ teaspoon dried thyme
$\frac{1}{2}$ teaspoon dried sage
GARNISH
500ml (2 cups) water
185g ($\frac{3}{4}$ cup) castor sugar

75ml (¼ cup plus 3 teaspoons) lemon juice

8 eating apples, peeled, cored and halved

185g canned stoned prunes, drained (can juice reserved) and finely chopped

6 teaspoons icing sugar

SAUCE

6 teaspoons flour

300ml (1¼ cups) dry white wine

300ml (1¼ cups) chicken stock

250ml (1 cup) cream

3 teaspoons prepared mustard

½ teaspoon salt

¼ teaspoon black pepper

Imperial

1 crown roast of pork, consisting of 16 chops, with a 2½in cavity in the centre

1 teaspoon salt

1 teaspoon black pepper

2 teaspoons dried thyme

STUFFING

2oz fresh breadcrumbs

2 fl oz milk

1oz butter

1 onion, finely chopped

8oz sausage mince

2 celery stalks, finely chopped

3oz canned stoned prunes, drained and quartered

2 eating apples, peeled, cored and finely chopped

½ teaspoon salt

¼ teaspoon black pepper

½ teaspoon dried thyme

½ teaspoon dried sage

GARNISH

¾ pint water

6oz castor sugar

2½ fl oz lemon juice

8 eating apples, peeled, cored and halved

6oz canned stoned prunes, drained (can juice reserved) and finely chopped

6 teaspoons icing sugar

SAUCE

½oz flour

½ pint dry white wine

Rich and elegant, Crown Roast of Pork with sausage and prune stuffing is an impressive dinner dish.

½ pint chicken stock

8 fl oz cream

3 teaspoons prepared mustard

½ teaspoon salt

¼ teaspoon black pepper

Preheat the oven to moderately hot (200°C/400°F). Rub the crown roast all over with the salt, pepper and thyme. Place in a roasting tin and fill the cavity with crumpled foil. Cover the ends of the chop bones with foil to prevent them burning. Roast for 20 minutes, then reduce the temperature to warm (170°C/325°F). Continue roasting for 40 minutes.

Meanwhile, make the stuffing. Soak the breadcrumbs in the milk. Melt the butter in the frying-pan. Add the onion and fry until it is soft but not brown. Add the sausage mince and fry until it loses its pinkness. Stir in the celery, prunes and apples and cook for 5 minutes.

Transfer the sausage mince mixture to a mixing bowl and stir in the salt, pepper, thyme, sage and soaked breadcrumbs. Mix well. Remove the foil from the cavity in the crown roast and fill with the stuffing. Pack tightly and dome the top. Return to the oven and continue roasting for 1 hour and 10 minutes or until the pork is cooked.

Thirty minutes before the pork is ready, prepare the garnish. Put the water, sugar and 9 teaspoons of the lemon juice in a saucepan. Heat gently, stirring to dissolve the sugar, then bring to the boil and simmer for 5 minutes. Put the apple halves in the pan and baste with the syrup. Poach gently for 10 to 15 minutes or until tender. Transfer the apples to the grilling pan and allow to cool.

Put the prunes in a saucepan with 90ml (⅓ cup) [3 fl oz] of the can juice and the remaining lemon juice. Cook for 5 minutes, then divide the prunes between the apple halves. Sprinkle over the icing sugar and grill until the sugar has melted and is beginning to caramelize. Remove from the heat.

Transfer the crown roast to a warmed serving dish. Surround with the apple halves. Keep hot while you make the sauce.

Pour off all but 6 teaspoons of the fat

from the roasting tin. Sprinkle over the flour and cook on top of the stove, stirring, for 2 minutes. Gradually stir in the wine and stock and bring to the boil. Simmer for 10 minutes, stirring frequently.

Stir in the cream, mustard, salt and pepper and heat through gently without boiling. Pour the sauce into a warmed sauceboat.

Remove the foil from the ends of the chop bones and replace with paper frills. Serve the crown roast with the sauce.

CANTONESE ROAST PORK

Honey gives a wonderful glaze and flavour to this delicious Chinese dish.

4 servings

Metric (Cup)

1kg pork fillet

6 teaspoons oil

7½ teaspoons clear honey

MARINADE

60ml (¼ cup) soy sauce

3 teaspoons sugar

9 teaspoons dry sherry

½ teaspoon salt

¼ teaspoon black pepper

½ teaspoon ground cinnamon

1 garlic clove, crushed

¼ teaspoon dried rosemary

¼ teaspoon dried marjoram

Imperial

2lb pork fillet

6 teaspoons oil

7½ teaspoons clear honey

MARINADE

2 fl oz soy sauce

3 teaspoons sugar

9 teaspoons dry sherry

½ teaspoon salt

¼ teaspoon black pepper

½ teaspoon ground cinnamon

1 garlic clove, crushed

¼ teaspoon dried rosemary

¼ teaspoon dried marjoram

Cut the pork along the grain into strips about 15cm (6in) long and 2.5cm (1in) wide.

Mix together the ingredients for the

marinade in a shallow dish. Add the pork strips and leave to marinate for 3 hours, turning occasionally.

Preheat the oven to hot (220°C/ 425°F). Put enough water in a roasting tin to make a 2.5cm (1in) layer. Put a rack in the tin. Arrange the pork strips on the rack. Reserve the marinade.

Roast for 12 minutes.

Stir the oil into the reserved marinade and brush over the pork strips. Return to the oven and reduce the temperature to moderate (180°C/350°F). Roast for a further 10 minutes.

Brush the pork strips with the honey and roast for a further 5 minutes. Serve hot.

ROAST LEG OF PORK WITH CREAM AND WINE SAUCE

Serve this superb roast pork with new potatoes and lots of colourful vegetables.

6 servings

Metric (Cup)

9 teaspoons olive oil
6 teaspoons lemon juice
1 teaspoon salt
½ teaspoon black pepper
1 teaspoon dried sage
3 teaspoons chopped parsley
1 x 2.5kg leg of pork
2 garlic cloves, halved
SAUCE
250ml (1 cup) dry white wine
1 teaspoon cornflour dissolved in
   3 teaspoons wine
1 teaspoon dried sage
125ml (½ cup) cream

Imperial

9 teaspoons olive oil
6 teaspoons lemon juice
1 teaspoon salt
½ teaspoon black pepper
1 teaspoon dried sage
3 teaspoons chopped parsley
1 x 5lb leg of pork
2 garlic cloves, halved
SAUCE
8 fl oz dry white wine
1 teaspoon cornflour dissolved in

3 teaspoons wine
1 teaspoon dried sage
4 fl oz cream

Preheat the oven to moderate (180°C/ 350°F). Mix together the oil, lemon juice, salt, pepper, sage and parsley. Make four incisions in the pork and insert the garlic halves. Rub the meat with the oil mixture and leave for 10 minutes.

Place the meat on a rack in a roasting tin and roast for 3 hours.

To make the sauce, put the wine, dissolved cornflour and sage in a saucepan and bring to the boil. Simmer, stirring, for 3 minutes or until thickened. Stir in the cream and heat through gently without boiling.

Serve the pork with the sauce.

PORK FILLETS WITH RED WINE

This delicious pork casserole can be prepared in advance.

6 servings

Metric (Cup)

125g (½ cup) butter
6 teaspoons olive oil
1.5kg pork fillets, cut into thick slices
2 large onions, chopped
1 teaspoon salt
½ teaspoon black pepper
375ml (1½ cups) dry red wine
250g (2 cups) sliced mushrooms
6 teaspoons flour
375ml (1½ cups) cream

Imperial

4oz butter
6 teaspoons olive oil
3lb pork fillets, cut into thick slices
2 large onions, chopped
1 teaspoon salt
½ teaspoon black pepper
12 fl oz dry red wine
8oz mushrooms, sliced
½oz flour
12 fl oz cream

Preheat the oven to moderate (180°C/ 350°F). Melt half the butter with the oil in a flameproof casserole. Add the pork slices, in batches, and brown on all sides. Add the onions and cook until softened. Return the pork slices to the pot and sprinkle over the salt and pepper. Add the wine and bring to the boil.

Cover and transfer to the oven. Cook for 1½ hours or until the pork is tender.

Melt the remaining butter in a saucepan. Add the mushrooms and fry for 3 to 4 minutes or until tender. Add the mushrooms to the casserole and stir well.

Dissolve the flour in the cream and stir into the casserole. Cook gently on top of the stove until the liquid thickens. Serve in the casserole.

ROAST SUCKING PIG STUFFED WITH FETA CHEESE

For a large dinner party nothing could be more decorative and delicious than this dish.

12 servings

Metric (Cup)

1 teaspoon salt
½ teaspoon black pepper
¼ teaspoon dried oregano
60ml (¼ cup) olive oil
125ml (½ cup) lemon juice
1 x 7kg sucking pig
1kg feta cheese, crumbled
3 teaspoons chopped parsley
½ teaspoon paprika

Imperial

1 teaspoon salt
½ teaspoon black pepper
¼ teaspoon dried oregano
2 fl oz olive oil
4 fl oz lemon juice
1 x 14lb sucking pig
2lb feta cheese, crumbled
3 teaspoons chopped parsley
½ teaspoon paprika

Mix together the salt, pepper, oregano, oil and lemon juice. Rub half the mixture into the skin of the pig, inside and out. Leave for 1 hour, then rub with the remaining oil mixture.

Preheat the oven to hot (220°C/ 425°F). Combine the cheese, parsley and paprika and use to stuff the pig. Secure the opening with a skewer or trussing needle and string. Pull the front legs of the pig forward and secure with string. Place a small piece of wood in the pig's mouth to wedge it open. Curl the tail and secure with a toothpick.

Place the pig on its stomach in a deep roasting tin and roast for 30 minutes. Reduce the temperature to warm (170°C/325°F) and roast for a further 2 hours, basting frequently with the juices in the tin.

Increase the temperature to hot (220°C/425°F) and roast for 20 minutes or until the skin is crisp.

Untie the legs, remove the wedge of wood from the mouth and the toothpick from the tail, and remove the skewer or string. Place an apple or orange in the pig's mouth and serve.

JAPANESE CHICKEN AND OYSTER FONDUE

Set the table with chopsticks for this delightful Japanese fondue, but have fondue forks on hand for less adventurous guests.

4-6 servings

Metric (Cup)

---

1 l (4 cups) chicken stock
2 chicken breasts, skinned, boned and
    cut into 3 pieces
60ml (¼ cup) soy sauce
125ml (½ cup) sake or dry sherry
2 large carrots, thinly sliced
12 radishes, thinly sliced
250g canned shirataki noodles, drained
8 spring onions, cut into 2.5cm pieces
12 green prawns
18 oysters, shucked
250g white fish fillets, skinned and cut
    into 5cm squares
18 button mushrooms, halved

Imperial

1¾ pints chicken stock
2 chicken breasts, skinned, boned and
    cut into 3 pieces
2 fl oz soy sauce
4 fl oz sake or dry sherry
2 large carrots, thinly sliced

12 radishes, thinly sliced
8oz canned shirataki noodles, drained
8 spring onions, cut into 1in pieces
12 green prawns
18 oysters, shucked
8oz white fish fillets, skinned and cut
    into 2in squares
18 button mushrooms, halved

Bring the stock to the boil in a saucepan. Add the chicken breasts and simmer for 10 minutes. Strain the stock into a fondue pot or flameproof casserole and set over a burner on the table. Stir in the soy sauce and sake or sherry.

Arrange the chicken breast pieces and remaining ingredients on a large serving platter. Each diner dips an ingredient in the stock, which should always be simmering, and cooks it to his taste.

COQ AU VIN

The preparation of Coq au Vin like many popular dishes tends often to be oversimplified, resulting in a lessening of the flavour. Follow this recipe and you will have a superb dish to serve guests.

---

4 servings

Metric (Cup)

125g lean bacon, rind removed and cut
    into strips 5mm thick and 2.5cm
    long
125g (½ cup) butter
1.5kg chicken pieces

A famous French dish of chicken casseroled in red wine, Coq au Vin is an ideal party dish since it may be prepared well in advance.

½ teaspoon salt
pinch of black pepper
90ml (⅓ cup) brandy
750ml (3 cups) dry red wine
300 to 500ml (1¼ to 2 cups) chicken
 stock
3 teaspoons tomato purée
2 garlic cloves, crushed
1 bouquet garni
3 teaspoons oil
18 small onions
30g (¼ cup) flour
250g (2 cups) sliced mushrooms
4 teaspoons chopped parsley

Imperial

4oz lean bacon, rind removed and cut
 into strips ¼in thick and 1 in long
4oz butter
3lb chicken pieces
½ teaspoon salt
pinch of black pepper
3 fl oz brandy
1¼ pints dry red wine
½ to ¾ pint chicken stock
3 teaspoons tomato purée
2 garlic cloves, crushed
1 bouquet garni
3 teaspoons oil
18 small onions
1oz flour
8oz mushrooms, sliced
4 teaspoons chopped parsley

Blanch the bacon in boiling water for
10 minutes. Drain well and pat dry
with kitchen paper towels. Preheat the
oven to moderate (180°C/350°F).

Melt 6 teaspoons (1oz) of the butter
in a flameproof casserole. Add the
bacon and fry until it is lightly browned.
Remove from the casserole. Add the
chicken pieces, in batches, and brown
on all sides. Sprinkle over the salt and
pepper and return the bacon to the
casserole. Cover and cook for 10
minutes.

Pour over the brandy and set alight.
Shake the casserole gently until the
flame has died away. Stir in the wine
and enough stock to cover the chicken.
Add the tomato purée, garlic and
bouquet garni and bring to the boil.
Cover the casserole and transfer to the
oven. Cook for 30 minutes.

Meanwhile, melt another 6 teaspoons
(1oz) of the butter with the oil in a

frying-pan. Add the onions and brown
on all sides. Transfer the onions to a
baking dish, arranging them in one
layer. Pour over the fat from the frying-
pan and bake the onions for 20 minutes
or until just tender.

Add the onions to the casserole with
the chicken and continue cooking for
10 to 15 minutes or until the chicken is
cooked. Remove the chicken and
onions from the casserole and set aside.
Keep hot.

Bring the liquid in the casserole to
the boil on top of the stove. Boil until
reduced to about 625ml (2½cups) [1
pint]. Discard the bouquet garni.

Mix together 6 teaspoons (1oz) of
the remaining butter and the flour to
make a smooth paste (beurre manié).
Add in small pieces to the liquid in the
casserole and simmer, stirring, until
thickened. Return the chicken pieces
and onions to the casserole and heat
through gently.

Meanwhile, melt the remaining
butter in the frying-pan. Add the mushrooms and fry for 2 to 3 minutes or
until just tender. Stir into the casserole
and simmer for a further 5 minutes.

Serve hot in the casserole, sprinkled
with the parsley.

MANGO CHICKEN

*Try this unusual combination of mango
and spices with chicken when mangoes are
next in season.*

4 servings

Metric (Cup)

2kg chicken pieces
1 teaspoon salt
½ teaspoon black pepper
6 teaspoons butter
6 teaspoons oil
1 large onion, thinly sliced
2 mangoes, peeled, stoned and sliced
1 teaspoon grated lemon rind
¼ teaspoon ground coriander
¼ teaspoon ground cinnamon
250ml (1 cup) chicken stock
250ml (1 cup) cream
2 teaspoons flour dissolved in 3
 teaspoons lemon juice and 3
 teaspoons water

Imperial

4lb chicken pieces
1 teaspoon salt
½ teaspoon black pepper
1oz butter
6 teaspoons oil
1 large onion, thinly sliced
2 mangoes, peeled, stoned and sliced
1 teaspoon grated lemon rind
¼ teaspoon ground coriander
¼ teaspoon ground cinnamon
8 fl oz chicken stock
8 fl oz cream
2 teaspoons flour dissolved in 3
 teaspoons lemon juice and 3
 teaspoons water

Preheat the oven to moderately hot
(190°C/375°F). Rub the chicken pieces
with the salt and pepper. Melt the
butter with the oil in a frying-pan. Add
the chicken pieces and brown on all
sides. Remove from the pan and
arrange in a flameproof casserole.

Add the onion to the frying-pan and
fry until it is soft but not brown. Stir in
the mango slices and fry, turning, for
4 minutes. Add the lemon rind, coriander, cinnamon and stock and bring to
the boil. Pour over the chicken in the
casserole.

Cover the casserole and cook for 1¼
hours or until the chicken is tender.

Transfer the chicken pieces to a
warmed serving dish and keep hot.
Bring the mixture in the casserole to the
boil on top of the stove. Stir in the
cream and dissolved flour and cook
gently, stirring, until thickened. Pour
the sauce over the chicken.

CHAMPAGNE CHICKEN

*Chicken and Champagne—a perfect com-
bination for any dinner party.*

4 servings

Metric (Cup)

1 x 2kg chicken, cut into serving pieces
½ teaspoon salt
½ teaspoon black pepper
6 teaspoons butter
2 onions, thinly sliced
6 teaspoons brandy

Luscious mangoes are cooked with chicken, cream and spices, in Mango Chicken.

250ml (1 cup) chicken stock
150ml (⅔ cup) Champagne
½ teaspoon dried thyme
¼ teaspoon ground mace
1 bay leaf
9 teaspoons flour
185ml (¾ cup) cream
185g (1½ cups) sliced mushrooms
1 teaspoon cornflour dissolved in
   1 teaspoon water

Imperial

1 x 4lb chicken, cut into serving pieces

½ teaspoon salt
½ teaspoon black pepper
1oz butter
2 onions, thinly sliced
6 teaspoons brandy
8 fl oz chicken stock
¼ pint Champagne
½ teaspoon dried thyme
¼ teaspoon ground mace
1 bay leaf
¾oz flour
6 fl oz cream
6oz mushrooms, sliced
1 teaspoon cornflour dissolved in
   1 teaspoon water

Preheat the oven to hot (220°C/425°F). Rub the chicken pieces with the salt and pepper. Melt the butter in a flameproof casserole. Add the onions and fry until they are soft but not brown. Add the chicken pieces and brown on all sides. Transfer the casserole to the oven and bake for 35 minutes.

Add the brandy, stock, Champagne, thyme, mace and bay leaf. Sprinkle over the flour and stir well.

Put the cream and mushrooms in a saucepan and heat gently without boiling. Add to the casserole and bring to the boil on top of the stove. Cover and return to the oven. Cook for a further 40 minutes.

Transfer the chicken pieces to a warmed serving dish and keep hot.

Boil the liquid in the casserole on top of the stove until it has reduced to about two-thirds the original quantity. Taste and adjust the seasoning. Simmer for 10 minutes.

Add the dissolved cornflour and simmer, stirring, until thickened. Pour the sauce over the chicken and serve.

CHICKEN KIEV

Much of the preparation for Chicken Kiev can be done in advance—but the chicken must be fried just before serving.

4 servings

Metric (Cup)

125g (½ cup) butter
3 teaspoons chopped fresh parsley
3 teaspoons chopped fresh chives
1 garlic clove, crushed
½ teaspoon salt
½ teaspoon black pepper
8 chicken breasts, skinned and boned
60g (½ cup) flour
2 eggs, lightly beaten
185g (1½ cups) dry breadcrumbs
vegetable oil

Imperial

4oz butter
3 teaspoons chopped fresh parsley
3 teaspoons chopped fresh chives
1 garlic clove, crushed
½ teaspoon salt
½ teaspoon black pepper
8 chicken breasts, skinned and boned
2oz flour
2 eggs, lightly beaten
6oz dry breadcrumbs
vegetable oil

Beat together the butter, parsley, chives, garlic, salt and pepper. Divide the butter mixture into eight pieces and shape into ovals. Freeze until very firm.

Beat the chicken breasts to flatten them. Place a butter oval on each chicken breast and wrap up, envelope fashion, to make small tube shapes. Coat in the flour, then in the egg and finally in the breadcrumbs. Chill for 1 hour.

Heat the oil in a deep frying-pan until

Chicken with Prawns and Asparagus is a superb Danish chicken casserole which will delight your guests.

it is 185°C/360°F. Fry the chicken breasts, in batches, for 5 to 6 minutes or until they are golden brown. Drain on kitchen paper towels and serve hot.

CHICKEN WITH PRAWNS AND ASPARAGUS

Serve this elegant but substantial dish with noodles or rice and salad.

4 servings

Metric (Cup)

6 teaspoons butter
2.5kg chicken pieces
2 small onions, finely chopped
9 teaspoons flour
500ml (2 cups) chicken stock
1 teaspoon salt
½ teaspoon black pepper
½ teaspoon paprika
¼ teaspoon cayenne pepper
1 teaspoon dried dill
1 bay leaf
6 teaspoons Madeira
500g asparagus, cooked and drained
250g green prawns
150ml (⅔ cup) cream

Imperial

1oz butter
5lb chicken pieces
2 small onions, finely chopped
¾oz flour
¾ pint chicken stock
1 teaspoon salt
½ teaspoon black pepper
½ teaspoon paprika
¼ teaspoon cayenne pepper
1 teaspoon dried dill
1 bay leaf
6 teaspoons Madeira
1lb asparagus, cooked and drained
8oz green prawns
¼ pint cream

Melt the butter in a flameproof casserole. Add the chicken pieces, in batches, and brown on all sides.

Remove the chicken from the pan as it is browned.

Add the onions to the casserole and fry until they are soft but not brown. Stir in the flour and cook, stirring, for 1 minute. Remove from the heat and gradually stir in the stock. Return to the heat and bring to the boil, stirring. Simmer until thickened. Stir in the salt, pepper, paprika, cayenne pepper, dill, bay leaf and Madeira.

Return the chicken pieces to the casserole, cover and simmer for 30 minutes.

Duck à l'Orange is a classic French way to serve roast duck.

Add the asparagus and prawns and cook for a further 30 minutes or until the chicken is tender.

Transfer the chicken, asparagus and prawns to a warmed serving dish. Keep hot.

Stir the cream into the juices in the casserole and heat through without boiling. Discard the bay leaf and pour the sauce over the chicken.

DUCK A L'ORANGE

One of the most popular duck dishes, Duck à l'Orange, with its rich orange liqueur sauce, is decorative enough to serve for any occasion.

4 servings

Metric (Cup)

1 x 2kg duck
½ teaspoon salt
½ teaspoon black pepper
6 teaspoons butter, cut into small pieces
watercress to garnish
SAUCE
3 large oranges
6 teaspoons sugar
6 teaspoons white wine vinegar
250ml (1 cup) brown sauce
6 teaspoons orange-flavoured liqueur
½ teaspoon salt
½ teaspoon black pepper
1 teaspoon redcurrant jelly

Imperial

1 x 4lb duck
½ teaspoon salt
½ teaspoon black pepper
10z butter, cut into small pieces
watercress to garnish
SAUCE
3 large oranges
6 teaspoons sugar
6 teaspoons white wine vinegar
8 fl oz brown sauce
6 teaspoons orange-flavoured liqueur
½ teaspoon salt
½ teaspoon black pepper
1 teaspoon redcurrant jelly

Preheat the oven to hot (220°C/425°F). Prick the duck all over and rub with the salt and pepper. Place the duck on a rack in a roasting tin and dot with the butter. Roast for 20 minutes, then reduce the temperature to moderate (180°C/350°F). Roast for a further 1 hour or until the juices that run out when the thigh is pierced are only faintly rosy.

Meanwhile, remove the rind from one of the oranges and cut into fine strips. Blanch in boiling water for 10 minutes, then drain. Squeeze the juice from the orange and set aside. Peel one of the remaining oranges and slice thinly. Thinly slice the unpeeled third orange. Reserve the orange slices for the garnish.

Put the sugar and vinegar in a saucepan and heat gently, stirring to dissolve the sugar. Bring to the boil and boil until the syrup turns amber in colour. Remove from the heat.

When the duck is cooked, transfer it to a warmed serving platter. Keep hot.

Skim the fat from the juices in the roasting tin. Strain the juices into a saucepan and bring to the boil on top of the stove. Stir in the brown sauce and simmer for 5 minutes. Add the orange rind strips, orange juice, liqueur, salt, pepper and vinegar syrup. Simmer for a further 3 to 4 minutes, then stir in the jelly. Pour the sauce into a warmed sauceboat.

Garnish the duck with the orange slices and watercress. Place some orange slices in a line over the length of the duck.

RED SNAPPER WITH OYSTER STUFFING

A large whole snapper elegantly arranged on a serving platter is perfect dinner party fare. Serve with salad.

6 servings

Metric (Cup)

1 x 2.5kg red snapper, cleaned
1 teaspoon salt
½ teaspoon black pepper
3 thyme sprigs
250ml (1 cup) fish stock or court bouillon
STUFFING
60g (¼ cup) butter
1 small onion, finely chopped
1 small green capsicum, membrane and seeds removed and finely chopped
1 small red capsicum, membrane and seeds removed and finely chopped
75g (½ cup) cooked rice
125g shucked oysters, chopped
1½ teaspoons dried thyme
3 teaspoons Worcestershire sauce
2 teaspoons sugar
1 teaspoon salt
½ teaspoon black pepper
¼ teaspoon cayenne pepper

Imperial

1 x 5lb red snapper, cleaned
1 teaspoon salt
½ teaspoon black pepper
3 thyme sprigs
8 fl oz fish stock or court bouillon
STUFFING
2oz butter
1 small onion, finely chopped
1 small green capsicum, membrane and seeds removed and finely chopped
1 small red capsicum, membrane and seeds removed and finely chopped
2½oz cooked rice
4oz shucked oysters, chopped
1½ teaspoons dried thyme
3 teaspoons Worcestershire sauce
2 teaspoons sugar
1 teaspoon salt
½ teaspoon black pepper
¼ teaspoon cayenne pepper

Rub the fish with the salt and pepper.

Preheat the oven to moderate (180°C/350°F).

To make the stuffing, melt half the butter in a frying-pan. Add the onion and fry until it is soft but not brown. Add the green and red capsicums and cook for 5 minutes. Stir in the remaining stuffing ingredients and cook for 5 minutes. Remove from the heat and allow to cool slightly.

Spoon the stuffing into the fish and secure the opening with a wooden cocktail stick. Place the fish in a greased

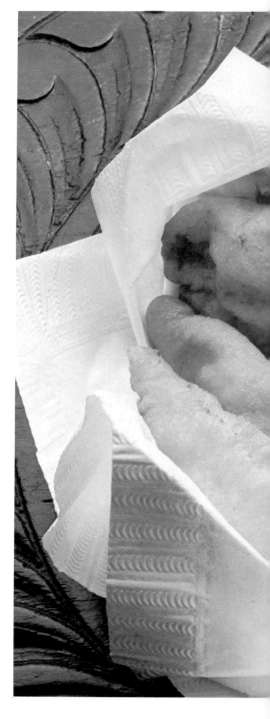

roasting tin and lay the thyme sprigs on top. Pour in the stock or court bouillon. Cover with foil and bake for 45 to 50 minutes or until the fish is cooked.

SEA BREAM (TARAKIHI) BAKED IN LEMON AND MUSHROOM SAUCE

This easy-to-prepare dish is always popular. Serve with new potatoes, a green vegetable and salad.

4 servings
Metric (Cup)

8 sea bream (tarakihi) fillets
60g ($\frac{1}{4}$ cup) butter
30g ($\frac{1}{4}$ cup) flour
925ml ($3\frac{3}{4}$ cups) lukewarm milk
1 teaspoon salt
$\frac{1}{4}$ teaspoon white pepper
1 bouquet garni
60ml ($\frac{1}{4}$ cup) lemon juice
250g (2 cups) sliced mushrooms
1 lemon, quartered

Imperial

8 sea bream (tarakihi) fillets
2oz butter
1oz flour
1$\frac{1}{2}$ pints lukewarm milk
1 teaspoon salt
$\frac{1}{4}$ teaspoon white pepper
1 bouquet garni
2 fl oz lemon juice
8oz mushrooms, sliced
1 lemon, quartered

Place the fish fillets in a shallow oven-proof dish. Preheat the oven to moderate (180°C/350°F).

Melt the butter in a saucepan. Add the flour and cook, stirring, for 1 minute. Remove from the heat and gradually stir in the milk. Return to the heat and bring to the boil, stirring. Simmer until smooth and thickened. Add the salt, pepper, bouquet garni, lemon juice and mushrooms and simmer for 5 minutes.

Pour the sauce over the fish. Cover and bake for 30 minutes.

Remove the bouquet garni and serve garnished with lemon quarters.

FRITTO MISTO DI MARE

Add whatever seafood you like to this marvellous Italian dish, but have a good variety. Squid is a delicious addition.

4 to 6 servings
Metric (Cup)

vegetable oil
2 flounder fillets, skinned and cut into 2.5cm strips
2 whiting (hake) fillets, skinned and cut into 2.5cm strips
250g prawns
250g scallops
8 parsley sprigs
1 lemon, quartered
BATTER
125g (1 cup) flour

Fritto Misto di Mare is a delicious dish of deep-fried fish and shellfish, including prawns, scallops, fish fillets – in fact whatever seafood takes your fancy.

$\frac{1}{4}$ teaspoon salt
1 egg yolk
3 teaspoons oil
250ml (1 cup) milk
2 egg whites

Imperial

---

vegetable oil
2 flounder fillets, skinned and cut into
    1in strips
2 whiting (hake) fillets, skinned and
    cut into 1in strips
8oz prawns
8oz scallops
8 parsley sprigs
1 lemon, quartered
BATTER
4oz flour
$\frac{1}{4}$ teaspoon salt
1 egg yolk
3 teaspoons oil
8 fl oz milk
2 egg whites

Heat the oil in a deep frying-pan until
it is 190°C/375°F.

Meanwhile, make the batter. Sift the
flour and salt into a mixing bowl. Stir in
the egg yolk and oil, then gradually
beat in the milk. Beat the egg whites
until stiff and, with a metal spoon, fold
into the batter.

Remove the shells from the prawns,
leaving the tails intact. Remove the
intestinal veins. Dip the fish and shellfish into the batter, then lower into the
oil. Fry for 3 to 4 minutes or until
crisp and golden brown.

Drain on kitchen paper towels and
serve hot, garnished with parsley sprigs
and lemon quarters.

BARRAMUNDI STEAKS WITH ALMONDS

*Another quick and delicious dish—but as
it can't be prepared in advance choose a
starter, vegetables and dessert that can.*

---

4 servings

Metric (Cup)

---

4 x 250g barramundi steaks
$\frac{1}{2}$ teaspoon salt
pinch of cayenne pepper
60g ($\frac{1}{4}$ cup) butter

60g ($\frac{1}{2}$ cup) slivered almonds
juice of 2 lemons

Imperial

---

4 x 8oz barramundi steaks
$\frac{1}{2}$ teaspoon salt
pinch of cayenne pepper
2oz butter
2oz slivered almonds
juice of 2 lemons

Rub the fish steaks with the salt and
cayenne.

Melt the butter in a frying-pan. Add
the almonds and fry until they are
lightly browned. Remove the almonds
from the pan.

Add the fish steaks to the pan and fry
until they are lightly browned on both
sides. Sprinkle over the almonds and
lemon juice and bring to a simmer.
Cover and cook gently for 10 minutes or
until the fish is cooked.

LOBSTER THERMIDOR

*Popular and delicious, Lobster Thermi-
dor looks marvellous and is extravagantly
right for a dinner party. Serve as the
main course or as a first course for 6 to 8
people.*

---

4 servings

Metric (Cup)

---

4 x 750g lobsters, shells split and grey
    sacs removed
150ml ($\frac{2}{3}$ cup) dry white wine
$\frac{1}{4}$ teaspoon dried chervil
3 teaspoons chopped fresh tarragon
2 small shallots, finely chopped
3 teaspoons chopped parsley
6 teaspoons butter
2 teaspoons olive oil
185ml ($\frac{3}{4}$ cup) bechamel or white sauce
150ml ($\frac{2}{3}$ cup) cream
$\frac{1}{2}$ teaspoon salt
$\frac{1}{4}$ teaspoon black pepper
1 teaspoon prepared French mustard
60g ($\frac{1}{2}$ cup) grated Parmesan cheese

Imperial

---

4 x 1$\frac{1}{2}$lb lobsters, shells split and grey
    sacs removed
$\frac{1}{4}$ pint dry white wine
$\frac{1}{4}$ teaspoon dried chervil

3 teaspoons chopped fresh tarragon
2 small shallots, finely chopped
3 teaspoons chopped parsley
1oz butter
2 teaspoons olive oil
6 fl oz bechamel or white sauce
$\frac{1}{4}$ pint cream
$\frac{1}{2}$ teaspoon salt
$\frac{1}{4}$ teaspoon black pepper
1 teaspoon prepared French mustard
2oz Parmesan cheese, grated

Remove the lobster meat from the
shells and cut into small pieces. Arrange
the empty shells on a large flameproof
serving dish.

Put the wine, chervil, tarragon,
shallots and parsley in a saucepan and
bring to the boil. Boil until reduced to
about half the original quantity. Remove from the heat and strain the wine.
Preheat the griller to high.

Melt the butter with the oil in a
frying-pan. Add the lobster meat and
cook for 3 minutes. Stir in the strained
wine, sauce, cream, salt, pepper and
mustard and cook gently for 3 to 4
minutes or until heated through. Spoon
the lobster mixture into the shells and
sprinkle over the cheese. Grill for 5 to
6 minutes or until the tops are lightly
browned and bubbling.

LOBSTER WITH WHISKY

*This superb lobster dish with a difference
is surprisingly simple to prepare.*

---

4 servings

Metric (Cup)

---

2 x 1kg lobsters, shells split and grey
    sacs removed
60g ($\frac{1}{4}$ cup) butter
1 small onion, finely chopped
$\frac{1}{2}$ teaspoon salt
$\frac{1}{4}$ teaspoon black pepper
60ml ($\frac{1}{4}$ cup) whisky
125ml ($\frac{1}{2}$ cup) cream
3 teaspoons chopped parsley
lemon wedges

Lobster flamed with Scotch whisky,
Lobster with Whisky, is an impressive and simply delicious dish.

Imperial

2 x 2lb lobsters, shells split and grey
    sacs removed
2oz butter
1 small onion, finely chopped
½ teaspoon salt
¼ teaspoon black pepper
2 fl oz whisky
4 fl oz cream
3 teaspoons chopped parsley
lemon wedges

Remove the lobster meat from the shells and cut into small pieces. Reserve the shells.

Melt the butter in a frying-pan. Add the onion and fry until it is soft but not brown. Stir in the lobster meat, salt and pepper. Warm the whisky in a small saucepan, then pour over the lobster mixture. Set alight and shake the pan gently until the flames have died away.

Stir in the cream and heat through gently without boiling.

Arrange the lobster shells on a serving dish and spoon the lobster mixture into them. Sprinkle over the parsley and garnish with lemon wedges.

Prawn Soufflé with Wine Sauce is a superb light dish.

PRAWN SOUFFLE WITH WINE SAUCE

Serve Prawn Soufflé with Wine Sauce for a special summer dinner.

4 servings

Metric (Cup)

375g green prawns
60ml (¼ cup) cream
6 teaspoons butter
30g (¼ cup) flour
250ml (1 cup) milk
1 teaspoon salt
½ teaspoon black pepper
¼ teaspoon grated nutmeg
4 egg yolks
5 egg whites
WINE SAUCE
3 teaspoons butter
3 teaspoons flour
125ml (½ cup) dry white wine
60ml (¼ cup) chicken stock
9 teaspoons cream
½ teaspoon salt
¼ teaspoon black pepper
125g green prawns

Imperial

12oz green prawns
2 fl oz cream

1oz butter
1oz flour
8 fl oz milk
1 teaspoon salt
½ teaspoon black pepper
¼ teaspoon grated nutmeg
4 egg yolks
5 egg whites
WINE SAUCE
½oz butter
3 teaspoons flour
4 fl oz dry white wine
2 fl oz chicken stock
9 teaspoons cream
½ teaspoon salt
¼ teaspoon black pepper
4oz green prawns

Preheat the oven to moderate (180°C/350°F).

Put the prawns and cream in an electric blender and blend to a smooth mixture.

Melt the butter in a saucepan. Add the flour and cook, stirring, for 1 minute. Remove from the heat and gradually stir in the milk. Return to the heat and bring to the boil, stirring. Simmer until smooth and thickened. Stir in the prawn mixture, salt, pepper and nutmeg. Remove from the heat and allow to cool slightly, then stir in the egg yolks.

Beat the egg whites until stiff and fold into the prawn mixture. Spoon into a greased 1.25l (2 pint) soufflé dish. Bake for 30 to 40 minutes or until well risen and golden brown.

Meanwhile, make the sauce. Melt the butter in a saucepan. Add the flour and cook, stirring, for 1 minute. Remove from the heat and gradually stir in the wine and stock. Return to the heat and bring to the boil, stirring. Simmer until smooth and thickened.

Stir in the cream, salt, pepper and prawns and heat through gently. Serve the hot sauce with the soufflé.

SCALLOPS WITH VERMOUTH SAUCE

Scallops are always a special-occasion favourite. Combined with artichokes in this dish they will delight your guests even more. Serve with boiled rice and

sautéed zucchini.

4 servings

Metric (Cup)

16 scallops, removed from the shells and halved
juice of 1 lemon
90g ($\frac{3}{4}$ cup) flour
1$\frac{1}{2}$ teaspoons salt
1 teaspoon black pepper
60g ($\frac{1}{4}$ cup) butter
4 shallots, finely chopped
1 garlic clove, crushed
500g Jerusalem artichokes, peeled, cooked, drained and sliced
125g (1 cup) sliced mushrooms
1 teaspoon dried tarragon
3 teaspoons chopped parsley
90ml ($\frac{1}{3}$ cup) dry vermouth
250ml (1 cup) cream

Imperial

16 scallops, removed from the shells and halved
juice of 1 lemon
3oz flour
1$\frac{1}{2}$ teaspoons salt
1 teaspoon black pepper
2oz butter
4 shallots, finely chopped
1 garlic clove, crushed
1lb Jerusalem artichokes, peeled, cooked, drained and sliced
4oz mushrooms, sliced
1 teaspoon dried tarragon
3 teaspoons chopped parsley
3 fl oz dry vermouth
8 fl oz cream

Put the scallops in a dish and sprinkle over the lemon juice. Leave for 5 minutes.

Mix the flour with $\frac{1}{2}$ teaspoon salt and $\frac{1}{2}$ teaspoon black pepper and use to coat the scallops. Melt the butter in a frying-pan. Add the scallops and cook until they are lightly browned all over. Add the shallots, garlic, artichokes, mushrooms, tarragon, parsley and the remaining salt and pepper and stir well. Cook for 5 minutes.

Warm the vermouth and set alight. Pour flaming over the scallop mixture. Shake the pan gently until the flames have died away, then stir in the cream. Heat through gently and serve hot.

Desserts
GATEAU ST. HONORE

A wonderful elaborate dessert to serve for a very special occasion.

8-10 servings

Metric (Cup)

125g (1 cup) choux pastry dough
1 egg yolk lightly beaten with 1 teaspoon water
125ml ($\frac{1}{2}$ cup) cream
6 teaspoons orange-flavoured liqueur
$\frac{1}{4}$ teaspoon vanilla essence
6 teaspoons castor sugar
PÂTÉ SUCRÉE
125g (1 cup) flour
60g ($\frac{1}{4}$ cup) unsalted butter
6 teaspoons sugar
2 egg yolks
$\frac{1}{4}$ teaspoon vanilla essence
CRÈME ST. HONORÉ
300ml (1$\frac{1}{4}$ cups) milk
1 vanilla pod
4 eggs, separated
125g ($\frac{1}{2}$ cup) sugar
6 teaspoons flour
7g gelatine softened in 9 teaspoons warm water
CARAMEL SYRUP
125g ($\frac{1}{2}$ cup) sugar
60ml ($\frac{1}{4}$ cup) water

Imperial

4oz choux pastry dough
1 egg yolk lightly beaten with 1 teaspoon water
4 fl oz cream
6 teaspoons orange-flavoured liqueur
$\frac{1}{4}$ teaspoon vanilla essence
6 teaspoons castor sugar
PÂTÉ SUCRÉE
4oz flour
2oz unsalted butter
6 teaspoons sugar
2 egg yolks
$\frac{1}{4}$ teaspoon vanilla essence
CRÈME ST. HONORÉ
$\frac{1}{2}$ pint milk
1 vanilla pod
4 eggs, separated
4oz sugar
6 teaspoons flour
$\frac{1}{4}$oz gelatine softened in 9 teaspoons warm water

CARAMEL SYRUP
4oz sugar
2 fl oz water

First make the pâté sucrée. Sift the flour onto a board or marble slab. Make a well in the centre and add the butter, sugar, egg yolks' and vanilla. Work together with your fingertips to make a smooth dough. Chill for 20 minutes.

Preheat the oven to hot (220°C/ 425°F).

Roll out the pâté sucrée to a 20cm (8in) circle about 5mm ($\frac{1}{4}$in) thick. Transfer to a baking sheet. Fill a forcing bag with the warm choux pastry dough and pipe in a ring, 1cm ($\frac{1}{2}$in) wide, around the edge of the dough circle. Pipe the remaining choux pastry into eight small puffs onto another baking sheet. Brush the choux puffs with the egg yolk mixture.

Put the dough circle and choux puffs into the oven and bake for 10 minutes. Prick any bubbles that have formed in the pastry circle and pierce each choux puff. Return to the oven. Reduce the heat to moderately hot (190°C/375°F) and bake for a further 10 minutes. Remove the choux puffs from the oven and transfer to a wire rack to cool. Continue baking the pastry circle for 5 minutes or until it is firm and dry to the touch. Allow to cool.

To make the crème St. Honoré, put the milk and vanilla pod in a saucepan and scald the milk. Remove from the heat. Put the egg yolks and sugar in a heatproof bowl over a pan of hot water and beat until the mixture is thick and pale and will make a ribbon trail on itself when the beater is lifted. (If using an electric mixer, no heat is needed.) Remove from the heat.

Discard the vanilla pod and gradually stir the milk into the egg yolk mixture. Stir in the flour. Strain into the cleaned-out saucepan and cook, stirring, until the custard is thick enough to coat the back of the spoon. Remove from the heat and stir in the gelatine. Allow to cool.

Beat the egg whites until stiff and fold into the custard mixture. Fill the choux puffs with about one-quarter of the crème St. Honoré.

To make the caramel syrup, put the sugar and water in a saucepan and heat gently, stirring to dissolve the sugar. Bring to the boil and boil until the syrup turns a pale golden colour. Remove from the heat.

Dip the choux puffs in the caramel syrup, then arrange them on the choux pastry ring. Fill the centre with the remaining crème St. Honoré. Chill until the crème is set.

Put the cream, liqueur, vanilla and sugar in a bowl and whip until thick. Pipe the cream in stars between the choux puffs.

DOBOZ TORTE

Doboz Torte is a marvellously rich cake made in six thin layers, sandwiched together with chocolate buttercream and covered with buttercream and caramel.

8 servings

Metric (Cup)

6 eggs, separated
125g ($\frac{1}{2}$ cup) castor sugar
1 teaspoon vanilla essence
125g (1 cup) flour
BUTTERCREAM
250g (1 cup) butter
1 teaspoon vanilla essence
250g (1 cup) sugar
60ml ($\frac{1}{4}$ cup) water
6 egg yolks
125g plain cooking chocolate
CARAMEL
125g ($1\frac{1}{2}$ cups) icing sugar

Imperial

6 eggs, separated
4oz castor sugar
1 teaspoon vanilla essence
4oz flour
BUTTERCREAM
8oz butter
1 teaspoon vanilla essence
8oz sugar
2 fl oz water
6 egg yolks
4oz plain cooking chocolate
CARAMEL
4oz icing sugar

First make the buttercream. Cream the

butter and vanilla essence together until light and fluffy. Put the sugar and water in a saucepan and heat gently, stirring to dissolve the sugar. Bring to the boil and boil until the syrup reaches 110°C/230°F. Remove from the heat and allow to cool slightly.

Beat the egg yolks until they are pale and thick. Gradually pour on the syrup, beating constantly. Continue beating until the mixture is cool. Beat in the butter.

Melt the chocolate and stir into the buttercream. Chill while making the cake. Preheat the oven to moderate (180°C/350°F).

Put the egg yolks, half the sugar and the vanilla in a heatproof bowl over a pan of hot water. Beat until the mixture is thick and pale and will make a ribbon trail on itself when the beater is lifted. (If using an electric mixer, no heat is needed.) Remove from the heat.

Beat the egg whites until stiff. Gradually beat in the remaining sugar until the mixture is stiff and glossy. Fold into the egg yolk mixture. Sift over the flour and fold in gently.

Spoon one-sixth of the batter into a greased and floured shallow 20cm (8in) diameter cake tin. (If you have more than one tin of this size, more than one layer may be baked at a time.) Bake for 15 minutes. Turn out onto a wire rack to cool while you make the remaining cake layers.

When all six cake layers have been baked, select the best for the top. Place it on a sheet of foil and lightly oil the foil around the cake so the caramel will not stick. Mark the layer into eight wedges with the blunt side of a knife.

Melt the icing sugar gently in a saucepan, stirring. Cook until the syrup is smooth and golden brown, then remove from the heat and immediately pour over the top cake layer. Smooth the caramel evenly over the surface with an oiled knife. Mark the indentations of the eight wedges through the caramel. Leave to set.

To assemble the cake, sandwich together the remaining five cake layers, using about half the buttercream. Spread a layer of buttercream on top and place the caramel coated cake layer on it. Cover the sides of the cake with

the remaining buttercream, piping a decorative border around the top and bottom edges. Cut the cake with a hot knife.

POUSSE CAFE GATEAU

This splendid rainbow-coloured cake containing lots of liqueur is ideal for a birthday — or any other — celebration.

8 servings

Metric (Cup)

185g ($\frac{3}{4}$ cup) butter
250g (1 cup) sugar
315g ($2\frac{1}{2}$ cups) flour
$2\frac{1}{2}$ teaspoons baking powder
$\frac{1}{4}$ teaspoon salt
3 eggs
125ml ($\frac{1}{2}$ cup) brandy
6 teaspoons milk
90ml ($\frac{1}{3}$ cup) cream
ICING
125g ($\frac{1}{2}$ cup) unsalted butter
500g (3 cups) icing sugar, sifted
2 teaspoons green Chartreuse
2 drops green food colouring
2 teaspoons orange-flavoured liqueur
3 drops orange food colouring
2 teaspoons brandy
2 drops yellow food colouring
2 teaspoons cherry brandy
3 drops red food colouring
2 teaspoons Parfait Amour
2 drops purple food colouring

Imperial

6oz butter
8oz sugar
10oz flour
$2\frac{1}{2}$ teaspoons baking powder
$\frac{1}{4}$ teaspoon salt
3 eggs
4 fl oz brandy
6 teaspoons milk
3 fl oz cream
ICING
4oz unsalted butter
1lb icing sugar, sifted
2 teaspoons green Chartreuse

A very decorative cake, Pousse Cafe Gateau is made with five different liqueurs and food colours.

2 drops green food colouring
2 teaspoons orange-flavoured liqueur
3 drops orange food colouring
2 teaspoons brandy
2 drops yellow food colouring
2 teaspoons cherry brandy
3 drops red food colouring
2 teaspoons Parfait Amour
2 drops purple food colouring

Preheat the oven to moderate (180°C/350°F). Cream the butter with the sugar until the mixture is pale and fluffy. Sift the flour, baking powder and salt into another bowl. Beat the eggs into the creamed mixture one at a time, adding a spoonful of the flour mixture with each egg. Fold in the remaining flour.

Add the brandy, milk and cream and mix well. Pour the batter into a greased 20cm (8in) diameter deep cake tin.

Bake for $1\frac{3}{4}$ to 2 hours or until a skewer inserted into the centre of the cake comes out clean.

Allow to cool slightly in the tin, then turn out onto a wire rack to cool.

To make the icing, cream the butter with a little of the sugar. Gradually cream in the remaining sugar. Divide the mixture into five parts and place each in a small bowl.

Add the Chartreuse and green food colouring to one portion, the orange-flavoured liqueur and orange food colouring to the next, the brandy and yellow food colouring to the third, the cherry brandy and red food colouring to the fourth, and the Parfait Amour and purple food colouring to the last.

Cut the cake into three layers. Place one layer on a serving plate and cover with swirls of the five icings. Put another cake layer on top and cover with swirls of the five icings. Put on the remaining cake layer and cover the top and sides with swirls of the five icings.

A luscious meringue and pineapple soufflé, Faux Soufflé Meringué aux Ananas makes a decorative dessert.

FAUX SOUFFLE MERINGUE AUX ANANAS

This pineapple meringue soufflé is a delightful dessert for a winter dinner.

4 servings

Metric (Cup)
4 egg yolks
125g ($\frac{1}{2}$ cup) castor sugar
$\frac{1}{4}$ teaspoon vanilla essence
2 teaspoons finely grated lemon rind
6 teaspoons cherry-flavoured liqueur
625ml ($2\frac{1}{2}$ cups) milk, scalded
150g canned pineapple rings, drained and chopped
3 egg whites
3 teaspoons icing sugar

Imperial
4 egg yolks
4oz castor sugar
$\frac{1}{4}$ teaspoon vanilla essence
2 teaspoons finely grated lemon rind
6 teaspoons cherry-flavoured liqueur
1 pint milk, scalded

5oz canned pineapple rings, drained and chopped
3 egg whites
3 teaspoons icing sugar

Preheat the oven to warm (170°C/325°F). Beat the egg yolks until pale and thick. Beat in the sugar, vanilla essence, lemon rind and liqueur. Gradually stir in the milk.

Put the pineapple in a 1.25l (2 pint) baking dish and strain in the custard mixture. Cover the dish and place in a roasting tin. Add enough water to the tin to make a 2.5cm (1in) layer. Bake for 1 hour or until the custard is set.

Ten minutes before the custard is ready, beat the egg whites until they will form soft peaks. Add the icing sugar and continue beating until the mixture is stiff and glossy. Spoon the meringue on top of the custard, bringing it up into peaks. Return to the oven and bake for a further 15 to 20 minutes or until the meringue is set and golden brown. Serve hot.

SOUFFLE GRAND MARNIER

Soufflé Grand Marnier is always popular and always special.

4-6 servings

Metric (Cup)

125g (½ cup) castor sugar
5 egg yolks
60ml (¼ cup) Grand Marnier
3 teaspoons finely grated orange rind
7 egg whites
3 teaspoons icing sugar, sifted

Imperial

4oz castor sugar
5 egg yolks
2 fl oz Grand Marnier
3 teaspoons finely grated orange rind
7 egg whites
3 teaspoons icing sugar, sifted

Sprinkle 6 teaspoons of the castor sugar inside a greased 1.8l (2½ pint) soufflé dish to coat the sides. Preheat the oven to moderately hot (190°C/375°F).

Put the remaining castor sugar and the egg yolks in a heatproof bowl over a pan of hot water. Beat until the mixture is thick and pale and will make a ribbon trail on itself when the beater is lifted. (If using an electric mixer, no heat is needed.) Remove from the heat and stir in the liqueur and orange rind. Continue beating until the mixture has cooled.

Beat the egg whites until stiff and fold into the liqueur mixture. Spoon into the soufflé dish. Bake for 25 to 30 minutes or until well risen and golden.

Sprinkle over the icing sugar and serve immediately.

ZABAGLIONE

Light and fluffy, this marvellous Italian custard looks particularly good served in clear glass dishes or large stemmed glasses.

4-6 servings

Metric (Cup)
---
4 egg yolks
60g (¼ cup) castor sugar
60ml (¼ cup) Marsala

Imperial
---
4 egg yolks
2oz castor sugar
2 fl oz Marsala

Put the egg yolks, sugar and Marsala in a heatproof bowl over a pan of hot water. Beat until the mixture is pale and thick. Do not allow to become too hot or the egg yolks will scramble. Serve immediately.

CREPES SUZETTES

Crêpes Suzettes are one of the most popular and famous French desserts.

---
4 – 6 servings

Metric (Cup)

BATTER
155g (1¼ cups) flour
3 teaspoons sugar
3 egg yolks
75g (¼ cup plus 3 teaspoons) butter, melted
125ml (½ cup) milk
125ml (½ cup) cold water
9 teaspoons cherry-flavoured liqueur (optional)
vegetable oil
SAUCE
4 sugar lumps
2 oranges
60g (¼ cup) castor sugar
185g (¾ cup) unsalted butter
90ml (⅓ cup) orange juice
75ml (¼ cup plus 3 teaspoons) orange-flavoured liqueur
9 teaspoons brandy

Imperial

BATTER
5oz flour
3 teaspoons sugar
3 egg yolks
2½oz butter, melted
4 fl oz milk
4 fl oz cold water
9 teaspoons cherry-flavoured liqueur (optional)
vegetable oil
SAUCE
4 sugar lumps
2 oranges
2oz castor sugar
6oz unsalted butter
3 fl oz orange juice
2½ fl oz orange-flavoured liqueur
9 teaspoons brandy

First make the batter. Sift the flour into a mixing bowl and stir in the sugar. Beat in the egg yolks, butter and milk, then gradually beat in the water and liqueur if using. Continue beating until the batter is smooth.

Lightly grease a crêpe pan with a little of the oil. Pour a little of the batter into the centre of the pan and tilt and rotate so the bottom of the pan is covered with a thin layer of batter. Cook for about 1 minute or until the bottom of the crêpe is lightly browned. Turn or flip over and cook the other side for about 30 seconds. Slide the crêpe out of the pan.

Cook the remaining crêpes in the same way and stack them up, interleaving with greaseproof paper. Keep the crêpes warm.

To make the sauce, rub the sugar lumps over the oranges to extract the zest (oil) from the rind. Put the sugar lumps in a mixing bowl and crush with a wooden spoon. Pare the oranges finely, being careful not to take any of the white pith with the rind. Cut the rind into thin strips and add to the bowl. Add half the castor sugar and the butter and cream the mixture together well. Gradually beat in the orange juice and 9 teaspoons of the liqueur.

Turn the orange butter into a frying-pan and melt it. Dip the crêpes in the butter, one at a time, then fold into quarters and arrange in a warmed serving dish. Sprinkle the remaining sugar over the crêpes and pour over any remaining orange butter.

Warm the remaining liqueur and the brandy in a small saucepan. Pour over the crêpes and set alight. Shake the dish gently until the flames have died away, then serve.

BANANAS BEAUHARNAIS

An attractive tasty dessert that is very simple to make.

4 servings
Metric (Cup)
6 bananas
3 teaspoons castor sugar
90ml (⅓ cup) light rum
125g (1 cup) crushed macaroons
3 teaspoons butter, melted
300ml (1¼ cups) cream
Imperial
6 bananas

This classic dessert, **Crêpes Suzettes** with orange liqueur, makes an impressive finish to a dinner party.

3 teaspoons castor sugar
3 fl oz light rum
4 oz macaroons, crushed
½oz butter, melted
½ pint cream

Preheat the oven to moderate (180°C/350°F). Put the bananas in a baking dish and sprinkle over the sugar and rum. Bake for 15 minutes.

Mix together the macaroons and melted butter. Pour the cream over the bananas and cover with the macaroon mixture. Return to a warm oven (170°C/325°F) and bake for a further 20 minutes. Serve hot.

FIGS IN CREME DE CACAO

An unusual dessert, Figs in Crème de Cacao is made quickly and in advance.

A luxurious dish of figs flavoured with rum, crème de cacao, chocolate and cream, Figs in Crème de Cacao is a sumptuously rich dessert.

4 servings

Metric (Cup)

6 teaspoons rum
6 teaspoons crème de cacao
6 teaspoons soft brown sugar
15g gelatine, softened in 3 teaspoons water
250ml (1 cup) cream
10 ripe figs, peeled and chopped
30g plain cooking chocolate
3 egg whites
¼ teaspoon ground ginger
6 teaspoons chopped walnuts

Imperial

6 teaspoons rum
6 teaspoons crème de cacao
6 teaspoons soft brown sugar
½oz gelatine, softened in 3 teaspoons water
8 fl oz cream
10 ripe figs, peeled and chopped

1oz plain cooking chocolate
3 egg whites
¼ teaspoon ground ginger
6 teaspoons chopped walnuts

Put the rum, crème de cacao and sugar in a saucepan and heat gently, stirring to dissolve the sugar. Remove from the heat and stir in the softened gelatine.

Whip the cream until thick. Stir in the figs and gelatine mixture. Melt the chocolate and stir into the fig mixture.

Beat the egg whites with the ginger until stiff. Fold into the fig mixture. Pour into a serving dish and chill until set.

Just before serving, sprinkle with the walnuts.

CREME BRULEE

A wonderful light French dessert of custard cream topped with caramel.

4 servings

Metric (Cup)

5 egg yolks

60g (¼ cup) castor sugar
500ml (2 cups) cream, scalded
1 teaspoon vanilla essence
60g (⅓ cup) light brown sugar

Imperial

5 egg yolks
2oz castor sugar
16 fl oz cream, scalded
1 teaspoon vanilla essence
2oz light brown sugar

Beat the egg yolks and sugar together until the mixture is pale and thick. Gradually stir in the scalded cream. Pour into a saucepan and cook gently, stirring, until the custard is thick enough to coat the back of the spoon. Do not allow to boil.

Remove from the heat and stir in the vanilla.

Strain into a flameproof serving dish, or four individual dishes. Allow to cool, then chill until set.

Preheat the griller to high.

Sprinkle over the brown sugar. Grill until the sugar has melted and caramelized, taking care to remove it before it burns. Serve hot or cold.

BOMBE COPPELIA

Bombe Coppelia is an exquisite concoction of coffee ice cream with a praline cream filling.

10 to 12 servings

Metric (Cup)

1.8l coffee-flavoured ice cream, softened
8 egg yolks
125g ($\frac{1}{2}$ cup) sugar
9 teaspoons dark rum
3 teaspoons water
300ml (1$\frac{1}{4}$ cups) cream
PRALINE
90g ($\frac{1}{3}$ cup) castor sugar
90g ($\frac{1}{2}$ cup) blanched almonds

Imperial

3 pints coffee-flavoured ice cream, softened
8 egg yolks
4oz sugar
9 teaspoons dark rum
3 teaspoons water
$\frac{1}{2}$ pint cream
PRALINE
3oz castor sugar
3oz blanched almonds

Use about three-quarters of the ice cream to line the inside of a chilled 1.8l (3 pint) bombe mould, pressing it firmly against the sides. Place a chilled glass bowl, 2.5cm (1in) smaller than the mould, inside to keep the ice cream in position. Freeze for 1 hour or until firm. Freeze the remaining ice cream.

While the ice cream is freezing, make the praline. Put the sugar in a saucepan and melt gently, stirring. Add the almonds and cook until the nuts are browned. Remove from the heat and pour the mixture onto a greased baking sheet. Cool until firm, then crush.

Beat the egg yolks until pale and thick. Put the sugar, rum and water in a saucepan and heat gently, stirring to dissolve the sugar. Bring to the boil and boil until the syrup is 110°C/230°F. Remove from the heat and slowly pour the syrup onto the egg yolks, beating constantly. Continue to beat as the mixture cools. Stir in the praline.

Whip the cream until thick and fold into the praline mixture. Remove the bowl from the centre of the bombe mould and spoon in the praline mixture. Freeze for 3 hours, or until the praline mixture is firm. Cover with the remaining coffee ice cream. Cover with foil and freeze for 8 hours.

To serve, dip the mould quickly in hot water and turn the bombe out onto a chilled serving dish.

WATERMELON FRUIT BOWL

Perfect for a hot summer evening, this fruit salad looks and tastes superb.

8-10 servings

Metric (Cup)

300ml (1$\frac{1}{4}$ cups) water
60g ($\frac{1}{4}$ cup) sugar
juice of 1 lemon
250ml (1 cup) sweet white wine
1 large watermelon
4 medium peaches, peeled, stoned and sliced
6 large apricots, peeled, stoned and sliced
3 medium pears, peeled, cored and sliced

Imperial

$\frac{1}{2}$ pint water
2oz sugar
juice of 1 lemon
8 fl oz sweet white wine
1 large watermelon
4 medium peaches, peeled, stoned and sliced
6 large apricots, peeled, stoned and sliced
3 medium pears, peeled, cored and sliced

Put the water and sugar in a saucepan and heat gently, stirring to dissolve the sugar. Bring to the boil and boil for 5 minutes. Do not allow to colour. Remove from the heat and stir in the lemon juice and wine. Allow to cool.

Slice the top off the watermelon lengthways and scoop out the flesh. Discard the seeds and cut the flesh into cubes or balls. If you like, make a decorative scalloped edge on the bottom part of the watermelon shell.

Mix together the watermelon flesh, peaches, apricots and pears. Stir in the wine mixture. Pile into the watermelon shell and chill for 30 minutes. (If more convenient, chill the fruit mixture before putting into the watermelon shell.)

Alternatively, serve the fruit mixture in a glass serving bowl.

GUAVA PIE

If fresh guavas are available, stew them in a little water and sugar before adding to the pie.

6 servings

Metric (Cup)

PASTRY
125g (1 cup) self-raising flour
pinch of salt
1$\frac{1}{2}$ teaspoons castor sugar
75g ($\frac{1}{4}$ cup plus 3 teaspoons) butter
$\frac{1}{2}$ egg, beaten with 1$\frac{1}{2}$ teaspoons water
FILLING
6 teaspoons apricot jam
1 egg
1 egg yolk
3 teaspoons sugar
150ml ($\frac{2}{3}$ cup) milk, scalded
150ml ($\frac{2}{3}$ cup) cream, scalded
440g canned guavas, drained
2 teaspoons grated lemon rind
$\frac{1}{2}$ teaspoon grated nutmeg

Imperial

PASTRY
4oz self-raising flour
pinch of salt
1$\frac{1}{2}$ teaspoons castor sugar
2$\frac{1}{2}$oz butter
$\frac{1}{2}$ egg, beaten with 1$\frac{1}{2}$ teaspoons water
FILLING
6 teaspoons apricot jam
1 egg
1 egg yolk
3 teaspoons sugar
$\frac{1}{4}$ pint milk, scalded
$\frac{1}{4}$ pint cream, scalded

A rich dessert, Bombe Coppelia is a mouth-watering combination of coffee ice cream, rum and praline.

Delicious Pavlova was named after the Russian ballerina Anna Pavlova — the built up meringue sides suggest a dancer's 'tutu'.

14oz canned guavas, drained
2 teaspoons grated lemon rind
½ teaspoon grated nutmeg

First make the pastry. Sift the flour, salt and sugar into a mixing bowl. Add the butter and rub into the flour until the mixture resembles breadcrumbs. Stir in the egg mixture and bind to a dough. Chill for 20 minutes.

Preheat the oven to moderate (180°C/350°F).

Roll out the dough and use to line a 20cm (8in) pie dish. Spread the jam over the bottom.

Beat together the egg, egg yolk and sugar. Gradually beat in the milk and cream.

Arrange the guavas in the pastry case and sprinkle with the lemon rind. Strain over the egg mixture and sprinkle the top with the nutmeg. Bake for 45 minutes or until the filling is set and the pastry golden. Serve hot or cold.

PAVLOVA

Our famous meringue is traditionally filled with whipped cream and fruit — try a combination of Kiwi fruit, passionfruit and strawberries for a very decorative effect.

8 servings

Metric (Cup)

5 egg whites
315g (1½ cups) castor sugar
2 teaspoons cornflour
½ teaspoon vanilla essence
1 teaspoon malt vinegar
FILLING
300ml (1¼ cups) cream
3 teaspoons castor sugar
1 teaspoon orange-flavoured liqueur
500g prepared fruit (e.g. strawberries, passionfruit, pineapple, Kiwi fruit)

Imperial

5 egg whites
10oz castor sugar
2 teaspoons cornflour
½ teaspoon vanilla essence
1 teaspoon malt vinegar
FILLING
½ pint cream
3 teaspoons castor sugar
1 teaspoon orange-flavoured liqueur
1lb prepared fruit (e.g. strawberries, passionfruit, pineapple, Kiwi fruit)

Line a baking sheet with non-stick silicone paper and draw a 23cm (9in) circle on the paper. Preheat the oven to cool (150°C/300°F).

Beat the egg whites until stiff. Add 125g (½ cup) [4oz] of the sugar and continue beating for 1 minute or until the mixture is very stiff and glossy Fold in the remaining sugar, the cornflour, vanilla and vinegar.

Spoon one-third of the meringue mixture onto the baking sheet and spread out in the circle to make a round. Put the remaining mixture in a piping bag and pipe around the edge of the circle.

Bake for 1½ hours or until firm and very lightly browned. Allow to cool.

Whip the cream until thick and fold in the sugar and liqueur. Fill the meringue case with the cream and pile the fruit in the centre.

PROFITEROLES WITH CHOCOLATE SAUCE

Profiteroles look and taste impressive but are very easy to make. Try also with a caramel sauce.

---

4 servings

Metric (Cup)

315g (2½ cups) choux pastry dough
300ml (1¼ cups) cream
125g plain cooking chocolate

Imperial

10oz choux pastry dough
½ pint cream
4oz plain cooking chocolate

Preheat the oven to hot (220°C/425°F).

Fill a pastry bag with the warm dough and pipe in circular mounds on a greased baking sheet. Bake for 10 minutes, then reduce the temperature to moderately hot (190°C/375°F). Bake for a further 15 to 20 minutes or until the profiteroles are puffed up and golden brown.

Remove from the oven and make a slit in the side of each puff to allow the steam to escape. Allow to cool.

Set aside 6 teaspoons of the cream and whip the remainder until thick. Divide the whipped cream between the profiteroles, filling them generously. Pile the profiteroles on a serving dish.

Melt the chocolate gently and stir in the reserved cream. Pour over the profiteroles and serve.

It's absolutely impossible to limit yourself to just one of these succulent Profiteroles with Chocolate Sauce. Pile high on a serving dish for a truly impressive dessert.

MACADAMIA NUT PIE

Macadamia Nut Pie has a deliciously light filling flavoured with rum and macadamia nuts.

6 servings

Metric (Cup)

2 eggs, separated
60g (¼ cup) sugar
300ml (1¼ cups) milk, scalded
125g (1 cup) chopped, lightly toasted macadamia nuts
15g gelatine, dissolved in 60ml (¼ cup) warm water
pinch of salt
60ml (¼ cup) dark rum
250ml (1 cup) whipped cream
1 x 23cm flan case, made from Shortcrust Pastry 11, baked blind and cooled

Imperial

2 eggs, separated
2oz sugar
½ pint milk, scalded
4oz macadamia nuts, lightly toasted and chopped
½oz gelatine, dissolved in 2 fl oz warm water
pinch of salt
2 fl oz dark rum
8 fl oz whipped cream
1 x 9in flan case, made from Shortcrust Pastry 11, baked blind and cooled

Put the egg yolks and sugar in a heat-proof bowl over a pan of hot water. Beat well together, then stir in the milk. Cook the custard until it is thick enough to coat the back of the spoon. Do not let it boil or it will curdle.

Remove from the heat and stir in the nuts and dissolved gelatine. Allow to cool, then chill until beginning to set. Stir in the salt and rum.

Beat the egg whites until stiff and fold into the nut mixture. Spoon into the pastry case and chill until set.

Spread the cream over the top.

NEIGE DE PECHES AU CHAMPAGNE

Orange shells filled with a delicious peach and Champagne ice make a beautiful summer dessert.

4 servings

Metric (Cup)

250ml (1 cup) fresh or bottled peach juice
250ml (1 cup) dry Champagne
60g (¼ cup) castor sugar
juice and finely grated rind of 1 small orange
pinch of ground allspice
15g gelatine dissolved in 9 teaspoons warm peach juice
1 egg white
2 very large oranges

Imperial

8 fl oz fresh or bottled peach juice
8 fl oz dry Champagne
2oz castor sugar
juice and finely grated rind of 1 small orange
pinch of ground allspice
½oz gelatine dissolved in 9 teaspoons warm peach juice
1 egg white
2 very large oranges

Put the peach juice, Champagne, sugar, orange rind and juice and allspice in a saucepan and bring to the boil, stirring. Boil for 4 minutes. Remove from the heat and stir in the dissolved gelatine.

Strain the mixture into a freezer-proof dish or freezer tray and allow to cool. Freeze for 30 minutes.

Beat the egg white until stiff. Beat the peach mixture into the egg white, then spoon back into the dish or tray and return to the freezer. Freeze for 1 hour.

Whisk the peach mixture thoroughly once every hour for 4 hours.

Halve the oranges and scoop out the flesh. Spoon the peach mixture into the orange shells and freeze overnight. Soften at room temperature for 15 minutes before serving.

COLD LEMON SOUFFLE

Strawberries or any colourful fruit look good served separately with this cold soufflé.

6 servings

Metric (Cup)

5 eggs, separated
125g (½ cup) castor sugar
finely grated rind and juice of 3 lemons
15g gelatine, dissolved in 60ml (¼ cup) warm water
300ml (1¼ cups) cream

Imperial

5 eggs, separated
4oz castor sugar
finely grated rind and juice of 3 lemons
½oz gelatine, dissolved in 2 fl oz warm water
½ pint cream

Put the egg yolks and sugar in a heat-proof bowl over a pan of hot water. Beat until the mixture is thick and pale and will make a ribbon trail on itself when the beater is lifted. Remove from the heat and beat in the lemon rind and juice. Continue beating until cool.

Stir in the dissolved gelatine.

Whip the cream until thick and fold

Cold Lemon Soufflé looks impressive although it is easy to make.

into the lemon mixture. Beat the egg whites until stiff and fold into the lemon mixture.

Spoon into a soufflé dish and chill until set.

GREEN MELON MOUSSE

This delicate melon mousse is a superb light dessert.

8 servings

Metric (Cup)

1 medium very ripe honeydew melon, halved and seeded
300ml (1¼ cups) cream
60ml (¼ cup) Grand Marnier
finely grated rind of 1 lemon
pinch of ground ginger
4 eggs, separated
125g (¾ cup) soft brown sugar

30g gelatine, dissolved in 60ml (¼ cup) warm water

Imperial

1 medium very ripe honeydew melon, halved and seeded
½ pint cream
2 fl oz Grand Marnier
finely grated rind of 1 lemon
pinch of ground ginger
4 eggs, separated
4oz soft brown sugar
1oz gelatine, dissolved in 2 fl oz warm water

Scoop the flesh from the melon halves and rub through a sieve into a mixing bowl. Stir in the cream, Grand Marnier, lemon rind and ginger.

Beat the egg yolks and sugar together in a heatproof bowl placed over a pan of hot water. Continue beating until the mixture is pale and thick and will make a ribbon trail on itself when the beater is lifted. (If using an electric mixer, no heat is needed.) Remove from the heat and stir into the melon mix-

ture. Strain in the dissolved gelatine and stir well.

Beat the egg whites until they are stiff. Fold into the melon mixture. Spoon into a serving dish and chill until set.

ORANGE AND CHOCOLATE MOUSSE

Orange and chocolate are a perfect combination in this mousse. Serve with whipped cream.

4 servings

Metric (Cup)

2 oranges
4 large sugar cubes
300ml (1¼ cups) cream
1 small vanilla pod
4 eggs, separated
185g plain cooking chocolate, melted
6 teaspoons orange-flavoured liqueur

Imperial

2 oranges
4 large sugar cubes
½ pint cream
1 small vanilla pod
4 eggs, separated
6 oz plain cooking chocolate, melted
6 teaspoons orange-flavoured liqueur

Rub the oranges with the sugar cubes to extract the zest (oil) from the skins. Put the sugar in a heatproof mixing bowl and crush with a spoon.

Scald the cream with the vanilla pod, then remove from the heat and discard the vanilla pod. Gradually stir the cream into the crushed sugar cubes. Beat the egg yolks until pale and thick and beat into the cream mixture.

Place the bowl over a pan of hot water and cook, stirring, until the mixture is thick enough to coat the back of the spoon. Do not boil or the mixture will curdle.

Remove from the heat and stir in the chocolate and liqueur. Allow to cool.

Beat the egg whites until stiff and fold into the chocolate mixture. Spoon into a serving dish and chill for at least 2 hours.

GLOSSARY

To bake blind
To bake a flan or pie case without filling. To prevent the sides from falling, line pastry case with greaseproof [waxed] paper and fill with dried beans or uncooked rice.

To baste
To spoon fat or liquid over food (usually meat or fish) during cooking, to keep it moist.

Beurre manié
A blend of butter and flour added a little at a time to sauces or stews or casseroles for thickening. It may be stored in the refrigerator.

To blanch
To whiten some meats, such as sweetbreads and tripe, by putting into cold water and bringing to the boil. To remove the skins of almonds or tomatoes, by putting into boiling water.
To partly cook some vegetables or fruit, for example, peppers or oranges, to reduce the sharp taste.

To blend
To mix two or more ingredients thoroughly.

Bouquet garni
4 sprigs of parsley, 1 sprig of thyme and a small bay leaf tied in a piece of muslin. Made-up sachets of bouquet garnis are now easily obtained.

To coat
To cover food completely before cooking: i.e. with egg and breadcrumbs, batter, etc.
Food may be coated after cooking, with a sauce or icing.

To curdle
The ingredients separate instead of combining—often through overheating, or through adding one ingredient too fast.

To deep fry
To fry in deep hot fat or oil which completely covers the food.

To dice
To cut into even pieces. Slice the food, cut the slices into strips, and then into cubes.

To dredge
To coat lightly with flour or sugar.

To flake
A term generally used with fish; meaning to divide into small pieces, with a fork.

To fold in
To cut ingredients gently together so that as much air as possible is trapped within the mixture.

To glaze
To give a shine.
Pastry is brushed with beaten egg before baking, or fruit with strained apricot jam.

To knead
To work dough with hands until it is of the required consistency.

To marinate
To steep meat, fish or vegetables in a liquid containing acid, usually in the form of wine and lemon juice, which gives flavour and helps to tenderize meat. The liquid is known as a marinade.

To pare
To remove skin or zest.

To poach
To cook slowly in liquid, which is just simmering, *not* boiling.

To purée
To put through a strainer or into a blender, to achieve a smooth mixture.

Roux
A mixture of melted butter and flour used as the base for many sauces.

To rub in
To rub fat into flour with the fingertips until it looks like fine breadcrumbs.

To sauté
To cook in hot fat, tossing frequently.

To simmer
To cook, *below* boiling point.

Zest
The thin coloured part of the skin of an orange or lemon. Remove it with a very fine grater or gently rub a sugar cube over the surface to absorb the oil.